The breakup of India and Palestine

Manchester University Press

STUDIES IN IMPERIALISM

When the 'Studies in Imperialism' series was founded by Professor John M. MacKenzie more than thirty years ago, emphasis was laid upon the conviction that 'imperialism as a cultural phenomenon had as significant an effect on the dominant as on the subordinate societies'. With well over a hundred titles now published, this remains the prime concern of the series. Cross-disciplinary work has indeed appeared covering the full spectrum of cultural phenomena, as well as examining aspects of gender and sex, frontiers and law, science and the environment, language and literature, migration and patriotic societies, and much else. Moreover, the series has always wished to present comparative work on European and American imperialism, and particularly welcomes the submission of books in these areas. The fascination with imperialism, in all its aspects, shows no sign of abating, and this series will continue to lead the way in encouraging the widest possible range of studies in the field. 'Studies in Imperialism' is fully organic in its development, always seeking to be at the cutting edge, responding to the latest interests of scholars and the needs of this ever-expanding area of scholarship.

General editors:
Andrew Thompson, Professor of Global and Imperial History at Nuffield College, Oxford
Alan Lester, Professor of Historical Geography at University of Sussex and LaTrobe University

Founding editor:
Emeritus Professor John MacKenzie

Robert Bickers, University of Bristol
Christopher L. Brown, Columbia University
Pratik Chakrabarti, University of Houston
Elizabeth Elbourne, McGill University
Bronwen Everill, University of Cambridge
Kate Fullagar, Australian Catholic University
Chandrika Kaul, University of St Andrews
Dane Kennedy, George Washington University
Shino Konishi, Australian Catholic University
Philippa Levine, University of Texas at Austin
Kirsten McKenzie, University of Sydney
Tinashe Nyamunda, University of Pretoria
Dexnell Peters, University of the West Indies
Sujit Sivasundaram, University of Cambridge
Angela Wanhalla, University of Otago
Stuart Ward, University of Copenhagen

To buy or to find out more about the books currently available in this series, please go to: https://manchesteruniversitypress.co.uk/series/studies-in-imperialism/

The breakup of India and Palestine

The causes and legacies of partition

Edited by Victor Kattan and Amit Ranjan

MANCHESTER UNIVERSITY PRESS

Copyright © Manchester University Press 2023

While copyright in the volume as a whole is vested in Manchester University Press, copyright in individual chapters belongs to their respective authors, and no chapter may be reproduced wholly or in part without the express permission in writing of both author and publisher.

Published by Manchester University Press
Oxford Road, Manchester M13 9PL
www.manchesteruniversitypress.co.uk

British Library Cataloguing-in-Publication Data
A catalogue record for this book is available from the British Library

ISBN   978 1 5261 7030 9   hardback
ISBN   978 1 5261 9110 6   paperback

First published 2023
Paperback published 2025

The publisher has no responsibility for the persistence or accuracy of URLs for any external or third-party internet websites referred to in this book, and does not guarantee that any content on such websites is, or will remain, accurate or appropriate.

EU authorised representative for GPSR:
Easy Access System Europe – Mustamäe tee 50,
10621 Tallinn, Estonia
gpsr.requests@easproject.com

Typeset
by New Best-set Typesetters Ltd

*For our wives Amrita and Jyoti
and our children Zachariah and Shanaya*

Contents

List of contributors	ix
Foreword by Lucy Chester	xiii
Acknowledgements	xvi

Introduction: Connecting the partitions of India and Palestine: institutions, policies, laws and people – Victor Kattan and Amit Ranjan ... 1

Part I The partition of British India

1 The Mountbatten Viceroyalty reconsidered: personality, prestige and strategic vision in the partition of India – Ian Talbot ... 35

2 The paradigmatic partition? The Pakistan demand revisited – Ayesha Jalal ... 57

Part II The partition of Palestine

3 Partition and the question of international governance: the 1947 United Nations Special Committee on Palestine – Laura Robson ... 75

4 Fighting for Palestine as a holy duty? The Syrian Muslim Brotherhood and the partition of Palestine in 1947 – Mohamed-Ali Adraoui ... 91

Part III The partitions of India and Palestine compared

5 The communal question and partition in British India and mandate Palestine – Amrita Shodhan ... 113

6 India's dilemmas of pragmatism v. principles: Nehru's preference for a partitioned India but a federal Palestine – P. R. Kumaraswamy — 138

Part IV The consequences of partition for South Asia, the Middle East and beyond

7 The partitions of India and Palestine and the dawn of majority rule in Africa and Asia – Victor Kattan — 159
8 'Unfinished' partition: territorial disputes, unequal citizens and the rise of majoritarian nationalism in India, Pakistan and Bangladesh – Amit Ranjan — 193
9 Civil war, total war or a war of partition? Reassessing the 1948 War in Palestine from a global perspective – Arie M. Dubnov — 222
10 Partitioned identities? Regional, caste and national identity in Pakistan – Iqbal Singh Sevea — 259

Afterword: Partition as imperial inheritance – Penny Sinanoglou — 278
Index — 289

List of contributors

Mohamed-Ali Adraoui is an assistant professor in Middle East History, Politics and International Relations at Radboud University. Trained as a political scientist and a historian working on the international relations of the Middle East with a focus on political and radical Islam, he holds a PhD from Sciences Po Paris and has held several positions at the European University Institute, the National University of Singapore, Georgetown University, Oxford University, the London School of Economics and Political Science and the Scuola Superiore Meridionale. His ongoing research deals with United States' foreign policy towards Islamism. Mohamed-Ali's articles have been published in *International Affairs*, *International Politics*, *Mediterranean Politics* and the *Georgetown Journal of International Affairs*. His monograph *Salafism Goes Global: From the Gulf to the French Banlieues* was published by Oxford University Press in 2020.

Lucy Chester is an associate professor at the University of Colorado at Boulder. She received both her BA summa cum laude and PhD from Yale University. Her first book, *Borders and Conflict in South Asia* (Manchester University Press, 2009), explores the drawing of the boundary between India and Pakistan in 1947. Her current book manuscript (under contract with Oxford University Press) examines connections between India and the Palestine mandate in the 1920s–1940s. Lucy is in the early stages of a project on the geographical imagination of Pakistan. Her work has been supported by the American Institute for Pakistan Studies, the American Institute for Indian Studies and the Smith Richardson Foundation.

Arie M. Dubnov is an associate professor and the Max Ticktin Chair of Israel Studies at George Washington University. Trained in Israel and the US, he is a historian of twentieth-century Jewish and Israeli history, with emphasis on the history of political thought, the study of nationalism, decolonisation and partition politics, with a subsidiary interest in the history of Israeli popular culture. Previously, Arie taught at Stanford University and the University of Haifa. His publications include the intellectual biography

Isaiah Berlin: The Journey of a Jewish Liberal (Palgrave, 2012), and two edited volumes, *Zionism – A View from the Outside* (2010 [in Hebrew]), seeking to put Zionist history in a larger comparative trajectory, and *Partitions: A Transnational History of Twentieth-century Territorial Separatism* (Stanford University Press, 2019, co-edited with Laura Robson).

Ayesha Jalal is the Mary Richardson Professor of History at Tufts University where she teaches at both the History Department and the Fletcher School of Law and Diplomacy. Her publications include *The Sole Spokesman: Jinnah, the Muslim League and the Demand for Pakistan* (Cambridge University Press, 1985 and 1994); *The State of Martial Rule: the Origins of Pakistan's Political Economy of Defence* (Cambridge University Press, 1990), *Democracy and Authoritarianism in South Asia: a Comparative and Historical Perspective* (Cambridge University Press, 1995), *Partisans of Allah: Jihad in South Asia* (Harvard University Press, 2008), *The Pity of Partition: Manto's Life, Times, and Work across the India–Pakistan Divide* (Princeton University Press, 2013) and *The Struggle for Pakistan: A Muslim Homeland and Global Politics* (Harvard University Press, 2014).

Victor Kattan is an assistant professor in the School of Law at the University of Nottingham. He was formerly a senior research fellow at the Middle East Institute at the National University of Singapore (2015–20). Victor is the author of more than thirty articles in peer-reviewed academic journals and the author or editor of four books, including *Making Endless War: The Vietnam and Arab–Israeli Conflicts in the History of International Law* (with Brian Cuddy, Michigan University Press, 2023), *Violent Radical Movements in the Arab World: The Ideology and Politics of Non-State Actors* (with Peter Sluglett, Bloomsbury, 2019), *From Coexistence to Conquest: International Law and the Origins of the Arab–Israeli Conflict* (Pluto Press, 2009) and *The Palestine Question in International Law* (British Institute of International and Comparative Law, 2008).

P. R. Kumaraswamy is a professor at the School of International Studies, Jawaharlal Nehru University, New Delhi. He was a research fellow at the Harry S. Truman Research Institute for the Advancement of Peace, the Hebrew University of Jerusalem (1991–99). He has been researching, teaching and writing on various aspects of the contemporary Middle East since 1999. His works include *India's Israel Policy* (Columbia University Press, 2010) and *The A to Z of the Arab–Israeli Conflict* (Scarecrow, 2009).

Amit Ranjan is a research fellow at the Institute of South Asian Studies, National University of Singapore. Amit is the author of numerous articles and the author or editor of four books: *India–Bangladesh Boundary Disputes: History and Post-LBA Dynamics* (Springer 2018), *Partition of India: Postcolonial Legacies* (edited, Routledge, 2019), *Water Issues in Himalayan South Asia: Internal Challenges, Disputes and Transboundary Tensions* (edited, Palgrave, 2020) and *Contested Waters: India's Transboundary River Water Disputes in South Asia* (Routledge, 2021).

Laura Robson is the Oliver-McCourtney Professor of History at Penn State University. She has written or edited five books, most recently *The Politics of Mass Violence in the Middle East* (Oxford University Press, 2020), a history of the relationship between violence and the state in the twentieth-century Eastern Mediterranean, and *Partitions: A Transnational History of 20th Century Territorial Separatism* (with Arie Dubnov; Stanford University Press, 2019).

Amrita Shodhan is a senior teaching fellow at the University of London's School of Oriental and African Studies (SOAS) where she teaches a course called Histories of Partition: India/Pakistan 1947. She works broadly in the field of community formations and the intersections with the state. Her publications include a *Question of Community: Religious Groups and Colonial Law* (Bhatkal & Sen, 2001). She was a visiting scholar at the Research Institute of the Humanities at the Chinese University of Hong Kong from 2018–2012.

Penny Sinanoglou is an associate professor of history at Pomona College. She is the author of *Partitioning Palestine: British Policymaking at the End of the Empire* (University of Chicago Press, 2019), which won the 2020 Phi Alpha Theta Best First Book award, and related articles and chapters in *The Historical Journal* and in edited volumes on twentieth-century partitions and the history of the British Empire in Palestine. Penny is broadly interested in the intersections between British imperial power and international systems of oversight and governance, the role of ethnicity, religion, gender and nationality in imperial politics, and the changing legal status of imperial subjects in the colonial and postcolonial eras. She is currently writing a legal history of marriage in the nineteenth- and twentieth-century British Empire.

Iqbal Singh Sevea is Director of the Institute of South Asian Studies at the National University of Singapore (NUS) and concurrently a visiting associate professor with the Department of History at NUS. Previously, he was an associate professor with the Department of History at the University of North Carolina at Chapel Hill. His research focuses on modern and contemporary South Asia and modern Islam. Iqbal is the author of *The Political Philosophy of Muhammad Iqbal: Islam and Nationalism in Late Colonial India* (Cambridge University Press, 2012). He is currently completing a book entitled *Islamic Political Thought in Modern South Asia* (Cambridge University Press, forthcoming).

Ian Talbot is Professor Emeritus of Modern South Asian History at the University of Southampton where he was also formerly Head of History, Director of the Centre for Imperial and Post-Colonial Studies and Director of the Humanities Graduate School. His works on partition include *Divided Cities: Partition and Its aftermath in Lahore and Amritsar 1947–1957* (Oxford University Press, 2006) and *The Partition of India* (with Gurharpal Singh, Cambridge University Press, 2009). His most recent publications include: *The History of British Diplomacy in Pakistan* (Routledge, 2021), *A History of Modern South Asia: Politics, States, Diasporas* (Yale University Press, 2016) and (with Tahir Kamran) *Lahore in the Time of the Raj* (Penguin, 2016).

Foreword by Lucy Chester

Resisting imperial modes of telling history and pushing back against empire today, this volume highlights the ways in which imperial power continues to shape our world. It moves away from the imperial 'centre', focusing on ground-level arguments about the future of India and Palestine and on the still unfolding repercussions of those debates. The rich and exciting transnational work on display here demonstrates the larger significance of these cases and of their connections. Moving far beyond comparative history, these chapters provide deeply researched narratives of the links between regions, drawing on a range of different and overlapping source bases. This is not your parents' imperial history. It draws on a wider range of methodologies and sources and asks a broader set of questions, focusing on shared dynamics that shaped both regions, including violence, the role of religion in politics, majoritarian politics, and the persistence of imperial modes of power. Together, these chapters shed light on anticolonial methods, imperial techniques, and the development of nationalism in ways that studying individual cases alone cannot achieve.

This collection stands out for its coherence. The authors, who include emerging scholars as well as a range of established names and whose work spans cultural, political and legal history in addition to political science and sociology, contribute to a sophisticated conversation in which key arguments are reinforced by multiple chapters. This approach lends power to the book's central arguments, which relate to continuity, identity and methodology.

One of this book's primary contributions is the way it lays bare startling continuities, both across the 1947/1948 dividing line and across the territorial and historiographical divisions that conventionally separate India/Pakistan from Israel/Palestine. Ian Talbot argues that the so-called 'transfer of power' from Britain to India and Pakistan was part of the British strategy to maintain empire in new forms, not to end it. He shows that partition was far from inevitable. British leaders could have chosen to pursue other paths, but saw partition as best suited to protect their interests. Penny Sinanoglou's afterword reinforces this view, arguing convincingly that partitions 'had their roots in practices of imperial control'. The continuities between colonisation and decolonisation are crucial to understanding empire's legacies.

Multiple authors demonstrate that the events of 1947 and 1948 had far-reaching and long-lasting effects that shaped the postwar world. Laura Robson's chapter on the 1947 United Nations Special Committee on Palestine (UNSCOP) argues that the UN used this case to show that only ethnonational models of sovereignty would receive a hearing in the remaking of the global order. UNSCOP not only was shaped by but also contributed to an emerging consensus that the UN must play a muscular role, intervening to enforce its ethnonational vision. Arie Dubnov similarly focuses on ongoing processes, writing that partition and decolonisation were part of 'an enduring political operation' that, never quite completed, continues to inflict pain. Iqbal Singh Sevea brings the story into the post-1947 period, which is important given that 1947 is so often seen as a cut-off point. Using the lens of popular culture, Sevea examines state efforts to construct national identity in post-1947 Pakistan and counter-histories that resist these efforts. He shows how regional and national histories coexist, sometimes uneasily.

A second major theme here is identity. Amrita Shodhan uncovers the mechanisms by which colonialism emphasised particular identities as most 'legitimate', eliding groups that did not necessarily identify with each other. She usefully highlights differences between British approaches to partition in India and in Palestine, where it was seen less as an identity issue and more as an existential question about state viability. Both Mohamed-Ali Adraoui and Ayesha Jalal are very good on the difference between religion as theology and religion as nationalist symbol and rallying point. Adraoui focuses on the Syrian Muslim Brotherhood's opposition to the partition of Palestine, showing that its involvement helped change global understandings of the conflict there. Jalal distinguishes between religion as social identity and religion as faith, arguing that the former played a much larger role in the Muslim League's vision of Pakistan. P. R. Kumaraswamy examines the influence of India's Muslim minority on the thinking of Indian leaders, arguing that concern for Muslim opinion shaped a foreign policy that was pragmatic at home and naive abroad. Sevea emphasises that regional, caste, linguistic and gender identities in Pakistan are dynamic, responding to (among other things) official national narratives and shifts in political power. He insists on examining caste identity despite the canard that caste does not exist in Pakistan.

Ranjan and Kattan's chapters turn to the dangers that identity can pose. Ranjan argues that majoritarian nationalism threatens to turn into de facto ethnic democracy. As he writes, 'in India, the state is secular, but society is not'. In keeping with the emphasis on continuities woven throughout the book, he presents key failures of Indian secularism, such as the razing of the Babri Masjid in 1992, as an extension of the 'hostage theory' developed in the 1930s. This theory argued that keeping non-Muslim minorities in Pakistan would safeguard Muslim minorities left in India. Kattan too deals with the basic nature of democracy. He argues that nationalist demands for majority rule in Palestine and India foreshadowed the emergence of new states in Africa and Asia. Notably, he connects these demands to the eventual discrediting, decades later, of apartheid rule in South Africa.

The third argument presented here is a methodological one. The volume not only demonstrates the need to look at connected history but also provides models for how to do so. As Dubnov argues, transnational historians must treat geographical units not as separate and distinct but as part of a whole, searching for their shared context. This volume shows that connected histories are not just a methodological innovation but also a way of getting closer to how these historical actors conceived of themselves and their activities. These actors worked within a wider context that was not limited by colonial or national boundaries. This approach is crucial to moving beyond nationalist narratives that not only fragment historical research but also continue to divide people today. These authors' analyses of democracy and majoritarian nationalism resonate with ongoing world problems, revealing how crucial this history is to present-day events.

Acknowledgements

This book would not have seen the light of day without the support of the Middle East Institute (MEI) and the Institute of South Asian Studies (ISAS) at the National University of Singapore that worked together to co-organise the workshop 'Reflections on the Partitions of India and Palestine after 70 years' held at the Asia–Europe Foundation in Singapore on 15 August 2018. This book is the product of that workshop. We especially want to thank Engseng Ho, then director of the MEI, along with his deputy director Michelle Teo, and Bilahari Kausikan, the chairman of the institute, for their support in organising and providing funding for the workshop. An expression of thanks is especially due to Subrata Kumar Mitra, formerly director of ISAS, and now Emeritus Professor of Political Science at the South Asia Institute, Heidelberg University, who provided invaluable intellectual support and helped set the stage for the organisation of the workshop before he left Singapore. We also extend our gratitude to Professor C. Raja Mohan and his deputy Hernaikh Singh for their help and assistance in organising the workshop after Professor Mitra's departure from Singapore. Finally, we would like to thank Chandrika Mago and Punam Mathur for giving their consent to use Professor P. N. Mago's painting *The Mourners* for the cover of our book, and Sharad Srivastava for taking the image of the painting at the National Gallery of Modern Art in New Delhi.

It would not be an understatement to say that producing this book was a major challenge, having coincided with a once-in-a-century global pandemic, an international move in the midst of a lockdown for one of our editors who was moving to take up a new academic post, and the arrival of our first children. But we are both happy and relieved to see the end product. We thank all the authors for their patience.

Victor Kattan and Amit Ranjan

Introduction
Connecting the partitions of India and Palestine: institutions, policies, laws and people

Victor Kattan and Amit Ranjan

This is not another book about the partition of India, of which there are many.[1] Nor is this a book about the partition of Palestine.[2] Rather, this work takes the form of an edited collection of chapters about partition in both places. It draws attention to the pathways of peoples, geographic spaces, colonial institutions, policies and laws that connect them. This is not to suggest that there were not differences between the two partitions: there were, and these are addressed in some of the contributions to this book. It is merely to suggest that a comparative, transnational and international historical approach to partition might help us answer some of the bigger questions that emerged after these two formative moments, such as the emergence of majoritarian politics and religiously motivated violence, as well as the uneven distribution of political power in many parts of the Middle East and the Indian subcontinent.

Previous works on the partitions of India and Palestine include T. G. Fraser's pioneering study, which looked at these partitions along with that of Ireland, albeit in isolation from each other.[3] Then there was the book edited by Arie Dubnov and Laura Robson (also contributors to this volume) which included three chapters that drew comparisons between the partitions of Ireland, India and Palestine.[4] Where this volume differs from previous studies is in its exclusive focus on the partitions of India and Palestine, the comparisons between them, and their consequences for the Middle East, South Asia and beyond (addressed in Part IV of this volume) which were not covered in the study by Dubnov and Robson. We do not include the partition of Ireland in our study,[5] for the reasons explored below, although we do address earlier imperial divisions, including Ireland, when exploring partition's etymology. While the British Empire is the obvious link to both places, it is not the only one. Just as significant was their timing: the partitions of British India (August 1947) and mandate Palestine (November 1947) occurred within months of each other and were passionately debated by policymakers from all sides.

We believe the timing – August to November 1947 – justifies an exclusive focus on the partitions of India and Palestine. This is not to suggest that the Irish case was not important, but that an in-depth study of these two partitions is justifiable on account of the fact that partition was being advocated, contested and debated in both places at the same time. Moreover, a new global discourse emerged after 1945 that was captured in the Preamble to the United Nations Charter, 'to reaffirm faith in fundamental human rights, in the dignity and worth of the human person, in the equal rights of men and women and of nations large and small'. It was at the UN where the language of self-determination was invoked in respect of India and Palestine, which emerged as early examples of decolonisation beyond the Western world.

While scholars have pointed to continuities between the United Nations and the League of Nations that preceded it in terms of ideas, institutional memory and policy,[6] an important difference was the gradual emergence of anticolonial rhetoric and normative claims that were made by the new nations of the Third World,[7] which distinguished the post-1945 period from the period that preceded it.[8] Although there was non-Western representation at the 1919 Paris Peace Conference, and while anticolonial ideas were articulated at the Comintern in the interwar years,[9] these movements were not in a position to formulate government policy until they had captured the institutions of the state during decolonisation (1945–89) when more than a hundred European colonies became independent states. A major difference between the ideology of the League of Nations and that of the United Nations was that the Soviet Union was a founding member of the latter organisation, and used its influence on the Security Council to hasten the decolonisation process in Africa and Asia.[10] Following the admission of many African and Asian states to the United Nations in the 1960s, where they advocated ideas that were inimical to the interests of the colonial powers, the West lost control over the development of international law. In many ways, postwar human rights – particularly the right to self-determination – were shaped by the antiracist ideas of the socialist bloc and their allies in the Third World that were articulated in the political organs of the United Nations for whom the partitions of India and Palestine were touchstones. This was a very different historical moment to that faced by Irish nationalists who couched their claims to statehood after the First World War as that of an ancient European nation in line with the civilisational language that was in vogue at the turn of the twentieth century.[11] Unlike Irish nationalists, neither Indian, Pakistani or Palestinian nationalists could claim to be representing white Christian nations, when a community's 'degree of civilisation' was associated with the culture of Europe.¹² By the 1960s, self-determination had become a right of *all* peoples, not just civilised or European peoples.¹³ The partitions of India and Palestine led to a complete overhaul of the way in which colonised subjects articulated their right to independence, insisting on a complete and immediate break with the colonial power, irrespective of whether they were 'ready' to assume the burdens of government, while preserving the integrity of the colonial unit that was not to be divided prior to independence.¹⁴ We can trace the emergence of this early 'rights rhetoric' beyond the Western world to the debates on the partitions of India and Palestine in 1947.

Accordingly, this collection attempts to shift the gaze from Whitehall to the people that were responsible for advancing arguments in favour of, or against, partition, and dealing with the consequences. In so doing, it moves the debate from the imperial centre to the colonial periphery. We are just as interested in what the policymakers were doing in London as we are in learning how those policies were interpreted by the political actors on the ground. So, from British officials like Lord Mountbatten, Stafford Cripps, Cyril Radcliffe and Reginald Coupland, we move to Mohammad Ali Jinnah, Jawaharlal Nehru, Mahatma Gandhi, Muhammed Zafrulla Khan, Abdur Rahman, the Khilafat movement, the Muslim League and the Hindu right-wing movement known as Rashtriya Swayamsevak Sangh, or simply RSS. And in Palestine we move from Ernest Bevin, William Ormsby-Gore, Arthur Wauchope and Douglas Harris, to Vladimir Jabotinsky, David Ben Gurion, Chaim Weizmann, the Irgun and the Haganah, to King Abdullah I of Transjordan, the Mufti Al-Hajj Amin al-Husayni of Jerusalem, the Arab Higher Committee and the Muslim Brothers of Syria.

An appreciation of how these partitions were understood by those directly impacted is important, as the movement of peoples caused by their violent aftermath significantly altered the formation of national identity in what became known respectively as India, Pakistan and Bangladesh, and Israel, (occupied) Palestine and Jordan.¹⁵ The issue of identity and its relationship to territory is still fiercely debated to this day, especially among diasporic groups, many of whom left their homes fleeing partition violence. For some, partition was a constitutive moment to be celebrated; for others, it was a tragedy. For those that emerged victorious from the throes of battle, partition marked the birth pangs of statehood. For the vanquished, it was a trauma and moment of despair. This was especially so for those who lost loved ones, livelihoods and memories of places that disappeared as their former homes were transformed into foreign neighbourhoods settled by new people with alien habits, languages and modes of living. Whole cities, towns and villages were renamed: thus, Lyallpur in West Punjab was renamed Faisalabad in honour of King Faisal of Saudi Arabia, and in Palestine, the city of al-Majdal was renamed Ashkelon by the State of Israel, after its inhabitants had either been expelled or had fled the fighting in 1948 for what became known as the Gaza Strip.

The etymology of partition

Partition was not a new idea when it was applied to India and Palestine in 1947, although its origins remain contested. Fraser traced partition's modern genesis to the partitions of the Polish-Lithuanian Commonwealth in the eighteenth century,[16] while Kattan traced the idea of partition to the seventeenth-century 'partition treaties' that purported to divide the Hapsburg Empire.[17] Dubnov and Robson, on the other hand, downplay the Polish partitions in their study, and do not consider the Anglo-Dutch attempt to partition the Habsburg Empire at all. Instead, they associate partition with the 'new conversations surrounding ethnicity, nationhood, and citizenship during and immediately after the First World War'.[18] In their reading, partition was first attempted in Ireland, which was partitioned in May 1921, under the Government of Ireland Act, 1920, amid the Irish War of Independence.[19]

The claim that partition is a twentieth-century phenomenon is contestable. Antoine Mioche, for example, traces the roots of the partition of Ireland to the debates on the Quebec Bill in the British Parliament in the eighteenth century,[20] which was explicitly referenced by Prime Minister Lloyd George in the debates on Ireland in 1919.[21] With regard to British India, Lucy Chester refers to the 1905 partition of Bengal as a prelude to the 1947 partition.[22] While the debates on the partitions of the Habsburg Empire, Quebec, Bengal, Ireland, India and Palestine all appear to implicate the British Empire, other scholars have argued that partition was not a peculiarly British practice at all, especially when considered in the grand scheme of things. Mioche and Ian Talbot – in this volume – note that Britain preferred to negotiate federal arrangements over partition, when this was practicable.[23] This is also supported by Dubnov's work on Reginald Coupland, seen as the architect of partition in Palestine, due to his work on the Peel Commission, who appeared to favour federal arrangements over partition in other parts of the British Empire such as India with a view to keeping the integrity of the Commonwealth intact.[24]

The claim that partition was a peculiarly British practice also tends to occlude partitions imposed by other powers in other places at other historical moments. Apart from Poland, partitioned by Austria, Prussia and Russia in 1772, 1793 and 1795, to preserve a 'balance of power',[25] there was the partition of Africa in the late nineteenth century that implicated all the European colonial powers as well as the United States of America.[26]

The focus on British imperial culpability also does not account for the partitions of Germany, Korea, Vietnam or Western Sahara that were all divided by a variety of states during the Cold War.[27]

As Kattan has demonstrated in his earlier work,[28] a broader approach to the history of partition demonstrates that it was a policy or technique of imperialism, which served different ends, depending on the circumstances of the moment. Thus, partition was employed as: (1) a method of allocating spheres of influence between great powers to maintain a balance of power; (2) a barrier to prevent the spread of subversive ideas or totalitarian doctrines; (3) a technique of decolonisation; and (4) a form of conflict resolution.[29] The partitions of Palestine and India in 1947 served a combination of these aims; they were techniques of decolonisation, forms of conflict resolution, and attempts to preserve order in the Middle East and South Asia by transferring power to what were perceived as loyal forces that would maintain friendly relations with the United Kingdom, while simultaneously preventing the emergence of dangerous political vacuums that could be exploited by hostile powers. Of course, events did not transpire as planned, and partition led to much misery and disorder, even contributing to future conflicts in both regions, but this was an unintended consequence of partition, not its aim.

The word partition has been mentioned much, but what does it mean? Dubnov has argued – in this volume – that partition was a modern phenomenon that led to the political division of geographical spaces into two states.[30] Like Dubnov, Sinanoglou also associates partition with twentieth-century imperial politics, describing the partition of Palestine as an evolving policy or technique that was used both to sustain imperial power, and to dismantle it.[31] O'Leary also described partition as a modern phenomenon in which a fresh border was cut through at least one community's homeland, creating at least two separate political units under different sovereigns or authorities.[32] In contrast, Talbot and Singh describe partition as more than a territorial division, but a 'division of minds'.[33]

Kattan, while agreeing that partition is both an imperial policy, and one that became associated with decolonisation in the twentieth century, describes partition as an *imposed boundary* that resulted in the creation of distinct sovereign units.[34] For Kattan, partition was a continuum; an imperial practice that predated the twentieth century. In his view, partition in the twentieth century was better understood as a *re-partition*, as by that time most of the world had already been colonized and subdivided between the colonial powers.[35] In the latter half of the twentieth century, partition was redeployed as a way of exciting territories during decolonization where irreconcilable differences had emerged in the colonies between competing national groups.

What distinguished partition from other boundary arrangements, whether it was viewed as a technique of imperialism, or of decolonization, was its *involuntary* nature.[36] It was not a boundary that was freely reached. In the case of imperial partitions, consultations were rare, and consent was inferred. In contrast, during decolonization consultations were undertaken by the departing colonial power in which the consent of one of the parties to partition was obtained through coercion or duress.[37] While the political representatives of the peoples may have consented to being divided in the final hour, they did not agree on the manner or the shape that partition took, which was left to the exclusive discretion of the departing colonial power.[38]

We can see this understanding of partition emerge in the cases of India and Palestine in 1947. In Palestine, as explained below, there was no real attempt to ascertain the wishes of most of its Arab inhabitants who remained implacably opposed to any form of partition that resulted in the establishment of a Jewish state at their expense, for both nationalist, as well as theological reasons.[39] In British India, the idea of Pakistan was initially proposed by the Muslim League and resisted by Congress, until the latter changed its mind in the final phases, although there remains disagreement as to whether the Muslim League's support for a Muslim homeland was tactical.[40] Certainly, its leaders did not desire partition in the form that it took – a motheaten subcontinent that entailed the vivisection of the Punjab and Bengal.

Partition and colonial policy in India and Palestine

This leads us to inquire into whether there were any connections between the partitions of India and Palestine and British colonial policy. Why did Britain partition Ireland, India, and propose partitioning Palestine, rather than establish a federation, its preferred mode of decolonizing territory? In other words, why was partition proposed in some situations, but not in others?

In her contribution to this volume, Amrita Shodhan argues that the builders of the British Empire imposed a colonial sociology in its overseas territories that divided the populations of these territories into national religious groups, which resulted in exacerbating divisions in heterogeneous societies like those in South Asia and the Middle East/West Asia who had to compete for political power and influence with the colonial authority.[41] Shodhan refers to the Government of India Act 1935, which created a structure of representation that required the forced homogenization of Muslims and Hindus. As a direct result, individuals and sectarian groups such as Christians, Parsis, Ahmadiyya's and Ismailis had to claim membership of larger groups to gain access and influence with the colonial authorities.[42] As Faisal Devji observed, 'the gradual extension of responsible government and the centralization of power in India meant that countrywide statistics about religious demography and ... equally expansive notions of religious identity came to displace the political pluralism of the past.'[43] Moreover, by dividing the communities into national religious groups, and then by offering these groups a measure of self-government, whether this took the form of separate electorates or a restricted franchise, political competition then ensued, which established the conditions that led to partition, as the principal parties could not agree on a shared future vision for the country.[44]

A similar phenomenon occurred in Palestine, where the British authorities established the Supreme Muslim Council and the Zionist Organization that would compete for political power throughout the duration of the mandate.[45] One of the consequences of dividing the population of Palestine into national *religious* groups was that Palestinian Christians initially joined forces with Palestine's Muslim community to oppose Zionism, with both communities even enlisting support from the Vatican, with the assistance of the local clergy, to make their concerns known to the Council of the League of Nations.[46] They even established an organization that was known as the 'Christian-Muslim Association' before it was outlawed by the British authorities.[47] From that moment, the British authorities – spearheaded by the first High Commissioner, Herbert Samuel, and his legal adviser, Norman Bentwich, established separate institutions for Christians and Muslims in the hope that this would confine Palestinian Muslim political expression to religious issues, with a view to pre-empting further challenges to British colonial rule 'from a multi-religious Palestinian Arab nationalist movement.'[48]

Although there is little doubt that these divide and rule policies were a hallmark of British imperialism, it would appear that religion was already a social distinction or demarcator before the British occupied Palestine, as evinced by the numerous religious institutions, courts, and charities in the country.[49] Article 15 of the League of Nations mandate for Palestine established '[t]he right of each community to maintain its own schools for the education of its own members in its own language', which could 'not be denied or impaired.'[50] These different schools in Palestine had the effect, as the Peel Commission noted, of creating 'seminaries of Arab nationalism.'[51] The same could have been said of the Jewish schools, which became centres of Jewish nationalism. Consequently, nationalism in Palestine developed along religious lines with most of the Jewish community supporting the establishment of a Jewish national home, which was opposed by most Palestinian Christians and Muslims.

Like Shodhan, Robson and Kattan draw parallels between British colonial policy and the emergence of a policy of partition. For Robson, a key moment was the decision taken early during the mandate by Samuel to suggest the establishment of a legislature based on parity with equal numbers of representatives of Christians, Muslims and Jews, even though the Jewish community comprised only 10 per cent of the population – a proposal that was swiftly, and unsurprisingly, rejected by the Arabs. The failure to establish a policy that satisfied the aspirations of all the communities in Palestine had the effect of creating separate spheres of public and social engagement between Arabs and Jews, contributing to partition. For Kattan, the key moment in the partitions of both India and Palestine were the attempts to establish representative institutions in India and Palestine in the mid-1930s. In Palestine, the House of Commons blocked the move, even though it only envisaged enfranchising a small number of people, and even though the legislature was prohibited from questioning the terms of the mandate.[52] The failure to establish representative institutions in Palestine was one of the reasons why the Peel Commission proposed partition, as the working basis of parliamentary government or democracy depended on 'common ground' between 'its different groups or classes to enable the minority to acquiesce in the rule of the majority'.[53] The Commission found this wanting in Palestine.

In India, the attempt to increase representation in government, as enshrined in the Government of India Act, 1935, led to disagreement and deadlock. The Congress and the Muslim League could not agree to share power in an independent India based on the Westminster system of parliamentary democracy. The League feared majority rule in which all power would be placed in the hands of the Congress with few safeguards for the Muslim minorities, which was outlined in a private memorandum submitted by the Muslim League to the Viceroy in 1940.[54] In other words, the problem in both India and Palestine was *systemic* and directly related to the institutions of governance, namely parliamentary democracy.

While the fear of majority rule may have been considered overblown in the immediate aftermath of the partition of India when the Congress adopted a benevolent policy towards its large Muslim minority, these fears appear to have proved prescient with the passage of time, especially following the rise of the Hindu right-wing Bharatiya Janata Party-led government and its policies towards the Muslim community since 2014 as explored in the chapter by Amit Ranjan.[55] The point is that in both India and Palestine, British policy led to a situation in which religious communities articulated a demand for a homeland to safeguard their identities.

As Talbot and Singh observed, the British rulers of India viewed the Indian subcontinent in terms of monolithic caste and religious identities that 'arose from the interaction between British sources of knowledge of native society and perceptions of the significance of religious identity arising from the place of Christianity and the Catholic–Protestant divide in contemporary European ideas'.[56] As mentioned, these religious differences were present before the British arrived in India and Palestine, but were exacerbated by the decision to extend self-government to them when the future identity of the state mattered.

Partitioning holy lands

Another similarity between the partitions of India and Palestine was their provenance as holy places or holy lands. Palestine is home to the holiest shrines of Judaism, Christianity and Islam, and it is therefore not surprising that adherents of these faiths take a keen interest in its affairs. India is also a holy land as it is home to significant Hindu, Buddhist, Jain and Sikh shrines.[57] Except for the Sikh community, which has important shrines in Pakistan, as explained in the chapter by Iqbal Singh Sevea, there is not the same level of emotional interest in the loss of a homeland in East Punjab by Hindus, Jains and Buddhists in what is now Pakistan.[58] This is even though Pakistan has some Hindu and Buddhist shrines, a few of which have been attacked, and even though prior to partition there existed large Hindu and Sikh communities in Lahore, Sialkot, Rawalpindi, Karachi and the North-West Frontier Province.[59]

The status of Palestine as a holy land is not often addressed in studies of partition but is given prominence in the chapters by Adraoui and Kumaraswamy. For devout Muslims, sovereignty over a sacred space like Bayt al-Maqdis (literally, the 'Holy House', a reference to Jerusalem, which is home to Al-Aqsa Mosque and the Dome of the Rock) cannot be divided. Following the conquest of Palestine by General Allenby and the abolition of the Caliphate by Mustafa Kemal Atatürk, the Founding Father of the Republic of Turkey, a Khilafat movement emerged in India that took a pro-Arab position in Palestine, and its members established a relationship of solidarity with the Mufti of Jerusalem who was responsible for taking care of Al-Haram ash-Sharif, one of the sacred shrines of Islam, which is also the holiest place in Judaism.[60] From 1936 until 1939, a major Arab uprising in Palestine was crushed by British troops and the leaders of the Arab political parties were killed or sent into exile, provoking indignation in British India and causing complications for the British Empire that was dependent on the Indian Army. As Jinnah stressed in his correspondence with the British Government, these soldiers were not to be used to suppress the rights of the Palestinian Arabs.[61]

As Cemil Aydin has observed, it was during the interwar years that a strong association between the Indian Muslim League and Palestinian Arab activists over the protection of the Muslim holy shrines in Jerusalem was articulated as a form of opposition to British colonialism.[62] These associations did not disappear after the Second World War. They influenced UN debates on self-determination in the 1940s when several countries in North Africa, the Middle East and Asia became independent members of the United Nations and established the Organisation of Islamic Cooperation (OIC) to foster the interests of the global Muslim community, referred to in Arabic as *al-Ummah*, in contradistinction to the British-inspired League of Arab States. Significantly, the OIC was established after an arson attack on Al-Aqsa Mosque in occupied East Jerusalem in 1969 by an Evangelical Christian.[63] The organisation has consistently taken the view that the partition of Palestine was unjust.

The role of institutions

Context is important in understanding partition. We can only really appreciate the significance of partition in India and Palestine in 1947 by taking a step back to consider them in tandem with the dramatic changes unfolding on the world stage after the Second World War when the United States eclipsed Great Britain as the dominant world power in global affairs. This was when new ideas about statehood, development and representative government emerged, surpassing older class-based ideas enshrined in the mandates system that considered some peoples perpetually unfit for self-government. The Soviet Union introduced the doctrine of self-determination into the corpus of international law that was to have a dramatic impact, not only on delegitimising colonialism, but also on accelerating the pace of decolonisation by giving economic, diplomatic and military support to the liberation movements.[64]

The changes that occurred after 1945 were profound and included the establishment of a pentarchy in the form of the United Nations Security Council that – it was envisaged – would secure world peace and enforce international norms, when these could be agreed. The newly established United Nations drafted a charter that called on its members to promote human rights and fundamental freedoms, no matter how self-interested their promotion may have been, and set out a framework for a managed end to colonialism.[65] A sense of these changes can be observed by comparing the 1937 Peel Commission's proposals to partition Palestine to the 1947 UN Partition Plan in General Assembly Resolution 181 (II).[66] Whereas the Peel Commission's proposal envisaged a forcible exchange of populations between Arabs and Jews and continued British rule, the UN's plan excluded both possibilities, and went even further by calling on the governments of the envisaged Arab and Jewish states to enshrine human rights safeguards in their constitutions and to outlaw the expropriation of private property.[67]

In her chapter on the 1947 UN Partition Plan for Palestine, Laura Robson stresses the importance of international institutions in trying to resolve national conflicts and the differing visions of the state-making capacities that emerged at the UN, with most European states favouring an interventionist strategy in colonial spaces. The British withdrawal from Palestine offered the UN a new institution uncertain about how to define itself or understand its true purpose, an opportunity to cast itself in a central role in the making and maintaining of a regional postwar order across the Middle East.[68]

In the case of India, different considerations applied, as it had been a British colony where the UN did not have jurisdiction. British postwar planning for India was therefore framed in terms of preserving the link with the United Kingdom within the Commonwealth, a voluntary association of independent countries. In the words of Harshan Kumarasingham, 'The Commonwealth was seen as an opportunity to justify and legitimise British power in the new world order.'[69] Both the Congress and the Muslim League leadership had vested interests in maintaining that link, at least in the early years, as they wanted the armoury of British rule, both military and political, to be transferred to the new independent states.[70]

The mechanics of partition

At this juncture it is worth reminding ourselves of how India and Palestine were partitioned. Technically speaking neither territories were unified political entities in 1947. In fact, with respect to India, with the exception of Punjab and Bengal that were divided, the rest of what became India was actually *united* (with the exception of Kashmir) in the sense that the different territories and princely states (such as Hyderabad and Junagadh) were amalgamated, whether by consent, coercion or force, to comprise one state that represented all the territories – initially called the Union of India (1947–50) and later (after 1950) the Republic of India. The actual partition line was drawn up by Sir Cyril Radcliffe, a British barrister, who travelled to India especially for that purpose.[71] But the precise location of the new borders were kept secret until two days after the new states had come into existence.[72] Prior to the division, an 'agreement' on the broad contours of partition had been reached by the British Government, represented by Lord Mountbatten, the Congress, represented by Jawaharlal Nehru, and the Muslim League, represented by Mohammad Ali Jinnah, although of the three leaders Jinnah was the most reluctant participant and appeared to have been presented with a fait accompli which he had little choice but to accept. The aim of partition was, according to the 3 June 1947 plan, to divide Punjab and Bengal by separating 'the contiguous majority areas of Muslims and non-Muslims'.[73]

In Palestine, which was a League of Nations mandate, the United Nations General Assembly provided powers for an international commission made up of UN officials to travel to Palestine to take over the administration of the country and make the necessary arrangements with the relevant parties to establish two independent Arab and Jewish states with a special regime for the city of Jerusalem.[74] The British Government, as the mandatory power, was expected to assist the Commission and work with the provisional Arab and Jewish governments. But the British Government only allowed a small advanced party from the Commission, headed by the Spanish diplomat Pablo de Azcárate, to enter Palestine a few weeks before it withdrew its administration.[75] Unbeknown to Azcárate, behind the scenes, senior British officials were engineering a situation that would result in a de facto partition of Palestine between the armed forces of the Jewish state and the Transjordanian Arab Legion, with the latter being led by loyal British officers.[76] Azcárate soon realised that without British assistance the Commission was powerless. When he appealed for armed forces from the United Nations to implement the Partition Plan, the Security Council could not agree on the practicalities.[77] Azcárate then warned the United Nations General Assembly that in the absence of forces adequate to maintain law and order in Palestine, the mandate would be left in chaos with widespread strife, violence and bloodshed breaking out all over the country between Arab and Jewish armed forces.[78] And this is precisely what happened. Palestine was not divided by the border established in the partition resolution but by ceasefire agreements concluded between the belligerents at the end of the war.

Contrasting the partitions of India and Palestine

There were also differences between the partitions of India and Palestine. The first has just been mentioned. As a Crown colony, the international community did not have a say in the fate of India's future, whereas Palestine's future was debated, and continues to be debated. This was because only two states (Israel and Transjordan) emerged from the partition violence in 1948. The Arab state that was expressly mentioned in UN General Assembly Resolution 181 – containing a plan of partition with economic union – was not one of these states. There were also other differences in terms of demographics and the sheer size of India, which is a subcontinent, whereas Palestine had just been an administrative district of the Ottoman Empire when it was occupied by the British Army in December 1917 before the Principal Allied Powers granted the Government of His Britannic Majesty a mandate over it.

Another difference was the way in which Britain transferred power in both places. As Ian Talbot observed, the Attlee government did not have to cope with conflicting arguments over India that existed with respect to Palestine or deal with US foreign policy interests.[79] In British India, unlike in Palestine, extensive conversations took place between British officials and representatives from the Congress, the Muslim League, and other parties, as to how the transfer of power would occur. The United Kingdom even went to the trouble of establishing Boundary Commissions for the two provinces, in which the parties were given an opportunity to present their views, even if they were not taken into full consideration by Radcliffe. In contrast, in Palestine there was little consultation between the United Kingdom and the Arab political parties. This was not just because the Arab Higher Committee and other Arab political parties – including the Arab Communist Party – were opposed to partition and boycotted any organisation that gave legitimacy to the idea, such as the UN Special Committee for Palestine (UNSCOP), which was established in 1947 to consider partition.[80] It was also because the establishment of representative government in Palestine would have put an end to British and League of Nations efforts to establish a Jewish homeland in Palestine as the legislature would have had an Arab majority that would have restricted Jewish immigration. Whereas a modicum of representative government was introduced to India in the Government of India Act, 1935, in the following year the British House of Commons vetoed a proposal to introduce representative government to Palestine.[81]

Another distinction between the partitions of India and Palestine was the quality of leadership in British India and the Jewish diaspora, and the lack of that leadership in Palestine. There were no statesmen in Palestine in the 1930s and 1940s with the qualities of Mohammad Ali Jinnah, Jawaharlal Nehru, Mahatma Gandhi or Zafrulla Khan in the case of India, or Chaim Weizmann, David Ben Gurion, Moshe Shertok or Menachem Begin, in the case of Israel. All these men were familiar with the ways of the British; they had been educated in the United Kingdom (in the case of Jinnah, Nehru, Gandhi, Khan and Shertok) or Germany, Switzerland, the major cities of the Ottoman Empire, and Poland (in the case of Weizmann, Ben Gurion and Begin). They had distinguished diplomatic, legal and political careers in which they had to deal with wide-ranging interlocutors from all walks of life. They had become familiar, through their overseas work and travels, with the rustle and tussle of parliamentary politics, the bureaucracy of the Foreign and Colonial Office, and the Empire's modus operandi in the colonies. They spoke various languages fluently, including English, the language of the British Empire, and were familiar with Western political thought. They also took a keen interest in the numerous peoples inhabiting other areas of the Empire, and not just their own narrow, sectarian spheres of interest.[82]

And above all, Jewish, Indian and Pakistani leaders had a degree of access to senior British officials that was not available to the Palestinian Arabs.[83] Of course, it did not help matters that Palestine's political elite had been systematically decapitated during the 1936–39 uprising, through arrests, imprisonment, deportations and executions, as Robson relates in her chapter, and as explored in the work of the Khalidis.[84]

A further difference between the partition of India and Palestine was that the UN Partition Plan for Palestine – although endorsed by the international community – was never actually enforced because the US did not want Soviet peacekeeping forces involved in the transfer of power.[85] The result was an armed conflict, or 'a war of partition', as Dubnov calls it.[86] In contrast, in India, partition was implemented according to a plan; and although the British failed to maintain law and order, armed conflict did not break out between India and Pakistan, except in Kashmir and Hyderabad.[87] During the war in Palestine, two-thirds of Palestine's Arab population were evicted or fled their homes, and the armies of Egypt, Transjordan and Iraq ended up occupying sections of the country that had been allotted to the Arab state in Resolution 181 (II), except for the City of Jerusalem that was divided between Jewish forces and the Transjordanian Arab Legion.[88] The transfer of power in British India was, in some respects, far messier than in Palestine, especially when considering the sheer numbers of people killed and displaced[89] – although as a proportion of the population, more people were displaced from Palestine than from Punjab and Bengal.[90] As Rephael Stern has noted in his work on partition, in common with India and Pakistan, 'the nascent Israeli state utilized its inherited British legal system to create, dispossess, resettle and rehabilitate refugees'.[91] While the Government of Israel allowed the Jewish refugees displaced in the fighting in 1948 to cross the ceasefire lines to take up residency in the new state from which they had been displaced, it put a stop to a return of Arab refugees who were prevented from returning to their homes, even though, in some cases, they had taken refuge just a few miles away from their properties.[92] Many of these refugees continue to live in camps in Jordan, Syria and Lebanon.

Finally, we must not also overlook the fact that whereas three states were established on the Indian subcontinent (India and Pakistan in 1947, and Bangladesh in 1971 – after a violent war of secession from the authorities in Islamabad, with the support of troops from India), in the Middle East, the Palestinian state envisaged in General Assembly Resolution 181 (II) was stillborn. An *independent* Palestinian state remains an aspiration. Only two independent states emerged from the partition violence in 1948: Israel and the Hashemite Kingdom of Jordan.

Consequently, those Palestinians who did not flee to these countries and who were not given citizenship by Israel or Jordan, remain stateless.[93] By

Introduction 15

way of contrast, former citizens of British India who migrated from India to Pakistan during and after partition were given citizenship of their new homelands,[94] and large landowners were given compensation in each state for abandoned properties.[95] This did not happen in Palestine. Few have been compensated, not even the effendi or merchant class, for the properties they were forced to leave behind in Palestine. Whereas partition in India is history (in the sense that it divided India into two independent states), in Palestine it remains a living reality.[96]

Background and volume outline

We begin our volume with a chapter on Lord Mountbatten, the last Viceroy of India, by Ian Talbot, who focuses on British strategic thinking during the transfer of power. For Talbot, partition was a pragmatic response to pressures from below arising from anticolonialism in the subcontinent. He provides a corrective to the argument popularised by Narendra Singh Sarila that partition served Western strategic interests in the emerging Cold War context, and that there was a conspiracy between a complicit Muslim League and the British Empire in viewing Pakistan as a military garrison.[97] He explains that Mountbatten did not touch down at Palam airport in Delhi on 22 March 1947 with a predetermined partition plan. Neither the new Viceroy nor the Attlee government abandoned the possibility of a return to the Cabinet Mission Plan with its three-tiered government providing autonomy to the Muslim-majority areas within an Indian Union. It was only after several weeks of extensive meetings with Indian politicians and opinion formers that Mountbatten became convinced that power-sharing was not possible. This was when partition became the main policy option. The India Office's longstanding resistance to partition was based not just on a negative assessment of Pakistan's future economic viability, but its defence weaknesses, as Britain would lose the Indian Army, strategic airfields, and the command of the Indian Ocean. British officials also believed that Pakistan would be vulnerable to the Soviet Union and China and that its financial resources would be hopelessly inadequate for defence requirements. It was only when Pakistan became inevitable that the Chiefs of Staff began to consider its strategic value. Talbot concludes by suggesting that a parallel could be made between the partitions of India and Palestine in that the withdrawal in both cases was accelerated amid a deteriorating law and order situation.

Like Talbot, Ayesha Jalal also wants to provide a corrective to popular accounts of partition, although her focus appears to be contemporary readers in India, Pakistan and Bangladesh. Nations need heroes and Pakistanis have a right to be proud of their greatest hero, the Quaid-i-Azam Mohammad

Ali Jinnah, but she cautions that popular memories also need to be informed by some bare facts and meaningful ideas. Jalal explains that Pakistanis have been constrained from engaging in an informed and open debate on whether their country merits being called Jinnah's Pakistan. Therefore, it is even more necessary to reassess the legacy of a man who is (almost) universally held responsible for a partition that he had assiduously tried avoiding. Rather than being an advocate of partition, Jinnah wanted to negotiate a constitutional arrangement based on a sharing of power between the Congress and the Muslim League representing Hindus and Muslims. While Jinnah's insistence on a national status for Indian Muslims became absolute after 1940, the demand for a separate and sovereign state was open to negotiation until the summer of 1946. He was very much aware that many members of the Muslim nation would reside in Hindustan as in the specifically Muslim homeland. The claim to nationhood was not an inevitable overture to separate statehood and his claim that the Muslims constituted a 'nation' was not incompatible with a federal or confederal structure covering the whole of India. But for the federal idea to be acceptable, the logic of majoritarianism had to be abandoned. With nations straddling states, the boundaries between them had to be permeable and flexible not impenetrable and absolute. The Pakistan that was foisted on Jinnah in the final hour was one that he had rejected on two separate occasions in 1944 and 1946. Pakistan was the price that had to be paid to enable the Congress to inherit British India's unitary centre and integrate the princely states. Jinnah remained a constitutionalist until his dying day. He had a very liberal upbringing in colonial Bombay, and an education at the British Bar. He was au fait with the ways of parliamentary democracy and was a skilled orator. He had a distaste for rabble rousers who made cynical uses of religion, which is ironic given Pakistan's postcolonial history.

From British India we turn to mandate Palestine with Laura Robson's chapter on the UN's role in partition. In contrast to Talbot and Jalal who want to correct popular misconceptions of partition in India and Pakistan, Robson's audience appears to be historians of international relations. She sees partition as an experiment in new forms of internationalism, which makes sense in Palestine's case, as it was a League of Nations mandate, in contrast to India, which was a Crown colony. Robson usefully highlights the different visions of the state-making capacities of the UN in 1947, with the Western states favouring an interventionist strategy, as opposed to the postcolonial states that opposed it. In 1947, UNSCOP's majority report recommended partition, whereas a minority, led by Abdur Rahman, the Commission's Indian rapporteur, and Zafrulla Khan, the Pakistani chair, favoured a federal solution, which ironically had been rejected by the Congress Party in India, as explored in Kumaraswamy's chapter. Robson explains that by accepting the idea that pluralism was problematic, UNSCOP's majority plan represented a continuation of League of Nation's concerns, in which they viewed themselves as having a special responsibility to ensure linguistic, religious and ethnic minority rights. Thus, the UNSCOP majority supported the premise of Jewish nationhood and mass settlement of what was left of Europe's Jews as a 'solution' to 'the Jewish problem'. UNSCOP's minority proposal, by way of contrast, privileged the concept of indigeneity over ethnic nationhood and favoured the creation of a pluralistic Palestinian state. It recognised Palestine as the common country of both indigenous Arabs and Jews, and accepted that both these people had an historic association with it. But this postcolonial vision of the future of Palestine was not to be, as the countries of Asia and Africa still constituted a small minority of the UN's members in 1947. Thus, the new UN in 1947, far from representing a new voice, accepted the League idea of ethnic national separation. It was not until 1960 that the new UN majority outlawed partition as a form of decolonisation in General Assembly Resolution 1514.

In the next chapter, by Mohamed-Ali Adraoui, we move from the hallowed halls of the UN to Syria, of which Palestine had once been an integral part, where the Syrian Muslim Brotherhood was watching events closely. Adraoui explains how the 1947 UN Partition Plan, despite its 'secular' institutional origins, boosted support for religious nationalism in Palestine and beyond. Adraoui's chapter is an important contribution to studies that look at partition exclusively through the lens of Paris or New York. This is on-the-ground-history, as opposed to institutional history. Adraoui, through his translation of their speeches from protests and despatches to the US Embassy, explains how the Brotherhood adopted a religious discourse that legitimised a radical shift in the way the struggle for Palestine was presented. He explains how the discourse that arose in opposition to partition played an important role in the rise of an exclusively religious understanding of the conflict. The more the UN Partition Plan was perceived to exclusively benefit the Jewish community, the more explicit the calls to jihad became: to resist oppression and external invasion by force of arms. Over time, the language of the protests shifted towards an impending religious conflict between the Muslims and their enemies, with every advocate of partition perceived as committing a crime against Islam. Therefore, every Arab and every inhabitant of a Muslim country had a duty to stand up against what the Muslim Brothers considered a forfeiture of Muslim rights to sacred land. Palestine, in the language of Hassan al-Banna, the Egyptian founder of the Muslim Brotherhood, was transformed from a local cause into a global one that affected all Muslims. Palestine was not just another part of the Arab world, but the religious and political property of any Muslim who had ever lived, and they had a duty to defeat those that usurped it. The adoption of the Partition

Plan by the UN was an important moment as it began the transformation of the conflict from one associated with the patrician classes and secular Arab nationalism to a new religious one.

From Syria we return to India and Palestine with two chapters that make direct comparisons to partition in both situations. The first chapter by Amrita Shodhan focuses on British imperial governance in India and Palestine. Shodhan argues that a common colonial sociology linked the two places enshrined in colonial laws, colonial administrators and policymakers. In contrast to Talbot, who only sees a commonality in the deteriorating law and order situation in Palestine and India in 1947, Shodhan sees much more commonality by taking a longer-term view of colonial governance. She sees the division of the population into national religious communities occurring because of the application of imperial/Roman law that was supposedly derived from the national and religious character of the population. After the 1857 rebellion and the assumption of rule by the Crown, when a large-scale overhaul of the legal system took place, a stringent application of Hindu and Muslim identities was imposed by British judges in Indian courts. The categorisation of the population into sharply defined religious groups resulted in individual members of sectarian groups like the Vaishnav or Khoja declaring themselves to be Hindus or Muslims to claim civil rights that allowed them to obtain property or make conjugal or inheritance arrangements. In a parallel development, numerous smaller, but significant, groups like the Sikhs, Buddhists and Jains were counted as falling under the broad umbrella of Hindu law. In Palestine, a similar phenomenon occurred, when the British administration established the Supreme Muslim Council and the Zionist Organisation. While, in 1936, formal electoral representation was curtailed by Parliament to prevent Arab majority rule, a religious-communal representation was made more effective establishing a dualist opposition: Arabs, Christians and Muslims on the one hand, versus Jews on the other. Thus, both the Indian National Congress and the Arab Executive became catchall national groups within which large numbers of smaller religious and ethnic groups were subsumed. A deep colonial sociology of native difference operated in the making of these categories, and native politicians operated with these ideas, adopting these categories of self-representation.

From Shodhan's deep dive into British colonial policy in India and Palestine we next turn to the work of P. R. Kumaraswamy who, like Robson, revisits the UN debates on the partition of Palestine in 1947. In contrast to Robson, Kumaraswamy looks at the role played in the debates by Indian and Pakistan politicians, who viewed the UN's Partition Plan through an Indian prism. In other words, he focuses on how Indian diplomats tried to make sense of the Palestine issue considering their own situation. In his view, India's support for the federal plan, which articulated a postcolonial vision of world order, was a sign of Indian naivety, as well as of moral equivalence since the Congress Party had rejected a similar plan (the Cabinet Mission Plan) for India. Kumaraswamy highlights the important role played by India's Muslim population in shaping New Delhi's perceptions of the Israel–Palestine dispute – such as the Khilafat movement that was influential in India in the 1920s. Kumaraswamy quotes a statement by Gandhi from 1921, when Gandhi was courting the support of Indian Muslims in which he insisted – in language reminiscent of Islamist groups like the Muslim Brotherhood addressed by Adraoui – that non-Muslims could not acquire sovereignty over Palestine as it was an integral part of the Arab world, although it is a holy land to Jews and Christians, as well as Muslims. Intriguingly, Gandhi claimed that the Jews could not receive sovereign rights in a place that had been held for centuries by Muslim powers by right of conquest without realising that the same logic could apply to large parts of India. But the idea that Palestine was an Arab state (with a Jewish minority) was not just a Muslim view. The Congress Working Committee, the highest decision-making body of the party, also visualised a free and democratic Arab state with adequate protection of Jewish rights. Like Adraoui, Kumaraswamy explains that one of the primary reasons why the Muslim world has failed to come to terms with the partition of Palestine is because the recognition of Israel poses a theological quandary for them.

From these comparisons between the partitions of India and Palestine in 1947, we next turn to their consequences, with Kattan drawing attention to the international law dimensions of the two partitions, in which he explains why both India and Pakistan voted against UN General Assembly Resolution 181 (II) that recommended a partition plan for Palestine when they had accepted partition as the price of independence from Britain. Ultimately, the partition of Punjab and Bengal was based on majority rule between Muslims and non-Muslims, but this principle was *not* put into effect in Palestine, where subdistricts with overwhelming Arab majorities were awarded to the Jewish state. Drawing on archival sources, Kattan explains how the Muslim League leaders aligned themselves with Palestinian Arab leaders in the 1930s in challenging British rule in Palestine, and even made inquiries with the Permanent Mandates Commission as to whether, as representatives of British India, they could challenge the legality of British policy in Palestine at the Permanent Court of International Justice (PCIJ). Their claim was that Britain's policy in Palestine was incompatible with its obligations under Article 22 of the Covenant of the League of Nations as Britain was not applying 'the principle that the well-being and development of such peoples form a sacred trust of civilisation'. Two decades later, in a manner that was striking in its resemblance to the Muslim League's inquiries in Geneva in the late 1930s, Ethiopia and Liberia lodged an application with the International Court of Justice, the PCIJ's successor, claiming that South Africa was not respecting its obligations under Article 22 of the Covenant by discriminating against its non-European citizens in South West Africa (now Namibia). One of the consequences of this flagrant deprivation of Palestinian democratic rights, and the perpetuation of minority rule in large parts of the colonial world, was that it paved the path for the emergence of an aggressive form of Third World nationalism that led to the development of irredentist forms of violent nationalism and anti-imperialism. While the call for majority rule was powerful in its simplicity as a rhetorical way of undermining imperialism in support of the right of self-determination at the UN, its drawback was that it gave birth to the notion of majoritarian democracy that led to the suppression of minorities.

From a deep dive into the comparisons of the partitions of India and Palestine in 1947 we next turn to Amit Ranjan's chapter that looks at the consequences of partition in South Asia – particularly for India, Pakistan and Bangladesh – which all came to espouse what he calls 'majoritarian nationalism'. For Ranjan, majoritarian nationalism contributes to a consensus among the larger group that their religions, customs and practices are better than those of the minorities. Accordingly, advocates of majoritarian nationalism believe that minorities have responsibilities to satisfy the demands of the majority community. But this, as Ranjan explains, is contrary to the principles of a multicultural democracy, whether the majority is expected to protect the rights of minorities living in their country. To support his argument that India, Pakistan and Bangladesh are majoritarian states with a bad record of protecting minorities, Ranjan focuses on the unresolved issues from partition, which he explains are communal in nature – regarding borders and citizenship. Although India is a secular republic on paper and although many Muslims have occupied some of the highest offices of the country, the situation has deteriorated since 2014 when the RSS-supported government encouraged Hindu radicals to capture the secular space. In contrast to India, Pakistan is explicitly an Islamic state, and its constitution reserves the offices of the President and Prime Minister for Muslims only. Ranjan argues that these provisions went against the principles of secularism envisaged by Pakistan's founders. It was only under General Zia-ul-Haq that Pakistan adopted all signs and symbols of Islam and became a fully Islamic state with detrimental consequences for its minorities. A similar phenomenon also occurred in Bangladesh, which adopted a secular constitution under Sheikh Mujibur Rahman. However, this changed following his assassination. General Ziaur Rahman, who replaced Mujibur Rahman, enacted the Political Party Regulation Act to clear the way for Bangladesh's Jamaat-e-Islami and other like-minded groups to participate in political activities in the country. This was also when the word 'secularism' was deleted from the Preamble of the Constitution and from Article 8, although the constitution was amended in 2011 by the Parliament so that the provision for secularism was restored.[98] Nonetheless, the words Bismillah-ar-Rahman-ar-Rahim (In the name of Allah, the Beneficent, the Merciful), which were inserted above the Preamble of the Constitution, remain in place. With the rise of majoritarian nationalism in India, Pakistan and Bangladesh the rights of minorities have fared badly. The situation in Jammu and Kashmir is a case in point as this is regarded by most Indians and Pakistanis as their own. As Ranjan observed, they are not bothered about the rights of the people living there. Like Israel, these countries could be described as 'ethnic democracies'.

It is the subject of Israel to which we turn next with a chapter by Arie Dubnov on the war of 1948, which he describes as a war of partition. Dubnov's readership appears to be young Israelis who 'are today subject to a project of state-sponsored denial and historical amnesia'. For Dubnov, partition was not a single, painful or traumatic act that had a clear beginning and an end. Rather, partition was a package deal with at least three critical elements: border making, state making and population transfer. In his view, partition was not a practical solution in Israel/Palestine or India/Pakistan as the reality on the ground did not correspond with the ethnonational phantasm of a nation-state that would emerge organically. Partition only intensified enmity and sedimented particularistic performances of exclusivist nationalism and incompatible religious differences, making these conflicts seem perpetual and intractable. Like Ranjan, Dubnov sees the subtext for partition as being based on what he calls the 'sinister logic of majoritarian democracy'. He explains how the 1948 War followed a familiar pattern of violence found in Ireland in the 1920s and South Asia in 1947 that blurred the distinction between combatants and non-combatants. These were hybrid civil wars, involving an amalgam of paramilitary forces and conventional armies with external support in the shape of foreign volunteers and funding. Reframing our understanding of the 1948 Palestine war as a war of partition reveals the striking similarity this conflict had to the violence triggered by partition plans in Ireland, India and Palestine. Partition created divided political spaces in which ethnonational separations were conceived as ongoing projects, demonstrated, for example, by the adoption of the controversial Nation-State Law in Israel in 2018. Partition jumps back out of dusty history books because it is unfinished business, which continues to shape the domestic and foreign politics of all these countries. Partition in Israel/Palestine and India/Pakistan remains a syndrome still in the making.

From Israel we travel to Pakistan with Iqbal Singh Sevea's chapter on Pakistan's attempts to construct a national identity in the aftermath of partition. To add complexity to the state's narrative, Sevea looks at the imposition of the Urdu language after partition, and the influence of Punjabi cinema. He explains that Urdu was promoted by Pakistan's founding fathers as languages like Bengali, Punjabi and Sindhi, although spoken widely, were associated with specific regions, and were thought to pose a threat to the cohesion of the newly formed state. East Pakistan, where Bengali was spoken, was at the forefront of resisting the imposition of the Urdu language. Anger at the imposition of Urdu was a catalyst to the mass protests in 1948, 1952 and 1971, with the latter leading to the secession of Bangladesh from West Pakistan. Also central to the identity of the new Pakistani state was Islam, which was presented as a unified system of belief that provided its adherents with a well-defined identity. This is the official position of the state as presented, for example, in school textbooks. However, when it comes to the realm of popular culture, a very different picture emerges. To illustrate how caste and regional identities still subsist, Sevea focuses on Punjabi cinema, and the legends of Maula Jatt and Dullah Bhatti, two Punjabi characters, who challenged the image of the quintessential hero in early Pakistani films that were depicted as educated, Urdu-speaking, morally upright, well-groomed and soft-spoken citizens. Maula Jatt, in contrast, was rural, loud, hypermasculine, violent, fluent in colloquial Punjabi, and had very little to do with the nation or state. These films, which were enormously successful in Pakistan and India, and these new heroes, reflected sociocultural developments in Pakistan in the 1970s, which celebrated the 'manliness' of rural folk. The only individuals depicted in these films wearing Western attire and speaking Urdu were the police, the judiciary and the medical profession, who were presented as being disconnected from the rural masses. Through Punjabi cinema, the region of Punjab was presented as one in open rebellion against the centralising and culturally imperialist power ruling from Islamabad. Thus, Sevea, like Ranjan and Dubnov, sees partition, not as primordial or unchanging, but as a constitutive historical moment that continues to shape the contemporary identities of the many peoples of South Asia.

We close the volume with an afterword by Penny Sinanoglou, who encourages us to think of partition as having occasioned not just immense physical and ideological violence and rupture, but also intense creation by establishing new names, new dwelling, new borders and new nations. She explains how the partitions of India and Palestine also partitioned history, with the successor states rewriting histories 'to tell stories of nascent, sometimes thwarted, other times victorious nations that were always there waiting to be revealed'. She focuses her afterword on three issues: narratives of speed, narratives of empire and partition as imperial inheritance. Regarding narratives of flight, Sinanoglou observes that a common narrative to both partitions is that of the 'shameful flight'. The forces of decolonisation through partition are seen as unfolding so quickly and violently that they are likened to natural disasters. Yet as she remind us, quoting Yasmin Khan, there was 'nothing inevitable about Partition and nobody could have predicted, at the end of the Second World War, that half a million people or more were going to die'.[99] Regarding narratives of empire, Sinanoglou explains that the presentation of definite and short timelines for withdrawal from both India and Palestine were tactical moves on Britain's part as they were 'meant to force the hands of various actors – the Muslim League, the Congress, Palestinian Arab and Zionist leaders, to say nothing of the United States and the new United Nations'. Finally, Sinanoglou draws attention to the way in which the scale of apparent disorder that precipitated and followed the mass dislocation and death of both partitions seems to have prevented many historians from considering the degree to which planning had been taking place for decolonisation and partition, in some cases for decades. Although the appearance of hasty deadlines and slipshod management may have damaged Britain's reputation for preserving law and order in the short term, 'in the longer term, partition allowed Britain to distance itself from the violence of empire and to develop strong relations with some of the successor states'.

Notes

1. See Ian Talbot and Gurharpal Singh, *The Partition of India* (Cambridge: Cambridge University Press, 2009); Yasmin Khan, *The Great Partition: The Making of India and Pakistan* (New Haven: Yale University Press, 2007); David Page, *Prelude to Partition: The Indian Muslims and the Imperial System of Control 1920–1932* (Oxford: Oxford University Press, 1999); Anita Inder Singh, *The Origins of the Partition of India* (New Delhi: Oxford University Press, 1987); Ayesha Jalal, *The Sole Spokesman: Jinnah, the Muslim League and the Demand for Pakistan* (Cambridge: Cambridge University Press, 1985, 1994); Joya Chatterji, *The Spoils of Partition: Bengal and India, 1947–1967* (Cambridge: Cambridge University Press, 2007).
2. See Penny Sinanoglou, *Partitioning Palestine: British Policymaking at the End of Empire* (Chicago: University of Chicago Press, 2019); Victor Kattan, *From Coexistence to Conquest: International Law and the Origins of the Arab–Israeli Conflict 1891–1949* (London: Pluto Press, 2009); Rashid Khalidi, *The Iron Cage: The Story of the Palestinian Struggle for Statehood* (Boston, MA: Beacon Press, 2007); Roza El-Eini, *Mandated Landscape: British Imperial Rule in Palestine 1929–1948* (Abindgon: Routledge, 2005); Yossi Katz, *Partner to Partition: The Jewish Agency's Partition Plan in the Mandate Era* (London; Portland, OR: Frank Cass, 1998).

3 T. J. Fraser, *Partition in Ireland, India and Palestine: Theory and Practice* (London: MacMillan, 1984).

4 See the chapters by Kate O'Malley, Lucy Chester and Penny Sinanoglou in Arie Dubnov and Laura Robson (eds), *Partitions: A Transnational History of Twentieth-Century Territorial Separatism* (Stanford, CA: Stanford University Press, 2019).

5 For previous studies see Bill Kissane, *The Politics of the Irish Civil War* (Oxford: Oxford University Press, 2005); Anthony Carty, *Was Ireland Conquered?: International Law and the Irish Question* (London: Pluto Press, 1996); Joseph M. Curran, *The Birth of the Irish Free State 1921–1923* (Tuscaloosa: University of Alabama Press, 1980); Michael Laffan, *The Partition of Ireland 1911–1925* (Dublin: Historical Association of Ireland, 1983); Nicholas Mansergh, *The Prelude to Partition: Concepts and Aims in Ireland and India* (Cambridge: Cambridge University Press, 1978).

6 Mark Mazower, *No Enchanted Palace: The End of Empire and the Ideological Origins of the United Nations* (Princeton, NJ: Princeton University Press, 2009); Susan Pedersen, *The Guardians: The League of Nations and the Crisis of Empire* (Oxford: Oxford University Press, 2015).

7 During the Cold War, references to the 'Third World' referred to those states that became members of the Non-Aligned Movement, not aligned with either the capitalist or communist blocs. Many of these states were non-European societies that had been colonised from the sixteenth century by the European empires, and which have gradually acquired political independence since the 1940s. See Antony Anghie, *Imperialism, Sovereignty and the Making of International Law* (Cambridge: Cambridge University Press, 2004, 2007 edition), p. 3.

8 See Victor Kattan, 'Self-determination as Ideology: The Cold War, the End of Empire, and the Making of UN General Assembly Resolution 1514 (14 December 1960)', in Luca Pasquet, Klara Polackova Van der Ploeg and Léon Castellanos Jankiewicz (eds), *International Law and Time: Narratives and Techniques* (Geneva: Springer, 2022), pp. 441–473.

9 On anti-colonial movements in the interwar years see David Kimche, *The Afro-Asian Movement: Ideology and Foreign Policy in the Third World* (Jerusalem: Israel Universities Press, 1973); Erez Manela, *The Wilsonian Moment: Self-Determination and the International Origins of Anticolonial Nationalism* (Oxford: Oxford University Press, 2007); Cemil Aydin, *The Politics of Anti-Westernism in Asia: Visions of World Order in Pan-Islamic and Pan-Asian Thought* (New York: Columbia University Press, 2007); Hakim Adi, *Pan-Africanism and Communism: The Communist International, Africa and the Diaspora, 1919–1939* (Trenton: Africa World Press, 2013); Michael Goebel, *Anti-Imperial Metropolis: Interwar Paris and the Seeds of Third World Nationalism* (Cambridge: Cambridge University Press, 2015); Luis Eslava, Michael Fakhri and Vasuki Nesiah (eds), *Bandung, Global History, and International Law: Critical Pasts and Pending Futures* (Cambridge: Cambridge University Press, 2017); Adom Getachew, *Worldmaking after Empire: The Rise and Fall of Self-Determination* (Princeton, NJ: Princeton University Press, 2019); Michelle Louro, Carolien Stolte, Heather Streets-Salter

and Sana Tannoury-Karam (eds), *The League Against Imperialism: Lives and Afterlives* (Leiden: Leiden University Press, 2020).
10 The role of the Soviets is explored in detail in Victor Kattan, 'Self-Determination in the Third World: The Role of the Soviets', *Jus Gentium: Journal of International Legal History* 8 (1) (2023), 87–144. See also Bill Bowring, 'The Soviets and the Right to Self-determination of the Colonized: Contradictions of Soviet Diplomacy and Foreign Policy in the Era of Decolonization', in Jochen von Bernstorff and Philipp Dann (eds), *The Battle for International Law: South–North Perspectives on the Decolonization Era* (Oxford: Oxford University Press, 2019), pp. 404–425. John B. Quigley, *Soviet Legal Innovation and the Law of the Western World* (Cambridge: Cambridge University Press, 2007), pp. 47–52, 143–147.
11 Kissane, *The Politics of the Irish Civil War*, pp. 51–52.
12 While the Jewish leadership of the Yishuv could not claim to represent a white Christian nation, culturally those who left Europe for Palestine did share a culture with the West. The 1937 Peel Commission made express mention of this, when distinguishing the European culture of Palestine's Jewish community from the Asiatic character of Palestine's Arab community. Consider, for example, the following description of the Jewish national home from the Commission's report: 'The literary output of the National Home is out of all proportion to its size. Hebrew translations have been published of the works of Aristotle, Descartes, Leibnitz, Fichte, Kant, Bergson, Einstein and other philosophers, and of Shakespeare, Goethe, Heine, Byron, Dickens, the great Russian novelists, and many modern writers … But perhaps the most striking aspect of the culture of the National Home is its love of music. It was while we were in Palestine, as it happened, that Signor Toscanini conducted the Palestine Symphony Orchestra, composed of some 70 Palestinian Jews … .' As an aside, the Commission added, 'there is Arab literature, of course, and Arab music, but the culture of Arab Palestine is the monopoly of the *intelligenzia*; and, born as it is of Asia, it has little kinship with that of the National Home, which, though it is linked with ancient Jewish tradition, is predominately a culture of the West.' See *Palestine Royal Commission Report Presented by the Secretary of State for the Colonies to Parliament by Command of His Majesty*, July 1937, Cmd. 5479, Chapter V, pp. 116–117, paras 7–8.
13 See the 'Declaration on the Granting of Independence to Colonial Countries and Peoples' in UN General Assembly Resolution 1514 (XV), 14 December 1960, at www.refworld.org/docid/3b00f06e2f.html (accessed 1 October 2022).
14 *Ibid*.
15 On the formation of Palestinian national identity, see Rashid Khalidi, *Palestinian Identity: The Construction of Modern National Consciousness* (New York: Columbia University Press, 1997). On Jordanian identity, see Joseph A. Massad, *Colonial Effects: The Making of National Identity in Jordan* (New York: Columbia University Press, 2001). On the formation of Jewish identity, see Shlomo Sand, *The Invention of the Jewish People* (London: Verso, 2010). On the formation of Indian identity, see Jawaharlal Nehru, *Discovery of India* (London: Penguin Classics, 2004); Sunil Khilnani, *The Idea of India* (London: Penguin, 2012).

On the formation of national identity in Pakistan, see Farzana Shaikh, *Making Sense of Pakistan* (New York: Columbia University Press, 2009); Ayesha Jalal, *The Struggle for Pakistan: A Muslim Homeland and Global Politics* (Cambridge, MA: Belknap Press of Harvard University Press, 2014). On the formation of national identity in Bangladesh, see Sheikh Mujibur Rahman, *Sheikh Mujibur Rahman: The Unfinished Memoir* (Dhaka: University Press of Bangladesh, 2012).
16 Fraser, *Partition in Ireland, India and Palestine*, p. 4.
17 Victor Kattan, 'Partition', *Oxford Public International Law: Max Planck Encyclopaedia of Public International Law*, at https://opil.ouplaw.com/view/10.1093/law-epil/9780199231690/law-9780199231690-e2189?prd=EPIL (accessed 1 October 2022).
18 Dubnov and Robson, *Partitions*, p. 1.
19 *Ibid.*, p. 4.
20 Antoine Mioche, 'India or North America? Reflections on Nicholas Mansergh's Partition Paradigm', *Éire-Ireland* 42 (2) (2007), 290–310. https://doi.org/10.1353/eir.2007.0022.
21 *Ibid.*, p. 305.
22 Lucy Chester, 'Close Parallels? Interrelated Discussions of Partition in South Asia and the Palestine Mandate (1936–1948)', in Dubnov and Robson, *Partitions*, pp. 128–153, at p. 129.
23 Isabelle Bour and Antoine Mioche, *Bonds of Union: Practices and Representations of Political Union in the United Kingdom (18th–20th Centuries)* (Tours: Presses universitaires François-Rabelais, 2005). See also Ian Talbot, 'The Mountbatten Viceroyalty reconsidered: personality, prestige and strategic vision in the partition of India' in this volume.
24 See Arie Dubnov, 'The Architect of Two Partitions or a Federalist Daydreamer? The Curious Case of Reginald Coupland', in Dubnov and Robson, *Partitions*, pp. 56–84, at p. 80. See also Golani's chapter in the same volume, in which he claimed that the real author of the Peel Commission's partition proposals was Chaim Weizmann, not Coupland. See Motti Golani, '"The Meat and the Bones": Reassessing the Origins of the Partition of Mandate Palestine', in Dubnov and Robson, *Partitions*, pp. 85–108.
25 See Victor Kattan, 'To Consent or Revolt: European Public Law, the Three Partitions of Poland (1772, 1793 and 1795) and the Birth of National Self-Determination', *Journal of the History of International Law* 17 (2) (2015), 247–281.
26 See Kattan, 'Partition'. On Africa specifically, see Thomas Packenham, *The Scramble for Africa* (London: Weidenfeld & Nicolson, 1991); H. L. Wesseling, *Divide and Rule: The Partition of Africa, 1880–1914* (Westport, CT: Praeger 1996).
27 Kattan, 'Partition'.
28 Kattan, 'Partition'. See also Victor Kattan, 'The Persistence of Partition: Border-making, Imperialism, and International Law', *Political Geography* 94 (April). https://doi.org/10.1016/j.polgeo.2021.102557.
29 Kattan, 'Partition', and examples mentioned.

30 See Arie M. Dubnov, 'Civil war, total war or a war of partition? Reassessing the 1948 War in Palestine from a global perspective' in this volume.
31 Sinanoglou, *Partitioning Palestine*, p. 15.
32 Brendan O'Leary, 'Analysing Partition: Definition, Classification, and Explanation', *Political Geography* 26 (8) (2007), 886–908, at 887.
33 Talbot and Singh, *The Partition of India*, p. 8.
34 See Kattan, 'Partition', para 2. See also Kattan, 'The Persistence of Partition'.
35 Kattan, 'Partition', section C.
36 *Ibid*, para 2.
37 *Ibid*.
38 *Ibid*.
39 For the theological reasons, see Mohamed-Ali Adraoui, 'Fighting for Palestine as a holy duty? The Syrian Muslim Brotherhood and the partition of Palestine in 1947' in this volume.
40 Jalal famously argued that Jinnah's support for partition was tactical, a claim she repeats in this volume.
41 See Amrita Shodhan, 'The communal question and partition in British India and mandate Palestine' in this volume.
42 *Ibid*.
43 Faisal Devji, *Muslim Zion: Pakistan as a Political Idea* (London: Hurst & Co., 2013), p. 52.
44 On the establishment of separate electorates for the Muslim communities see Page, *Prelude to Partition*.
45 On the establishment of the Supreme Muslim Council as a vehicle to channel Palestinian Muslim political energies into communal rather than nationalist expressions see Laura Robson, *Colonialism and Christianity in Mandate Palestine* (Austin: University of Texas Press, 2011), p. 61. More specifically, see Uri M. Kupferschmidt, *The Supreme Muslim Council: Islam under the British Mandate* (Leiden: Brill, 1987); Nicholas E. Roberts, *Islam under the Palestine Mandate: Colonialism and the Supreme Muslim Council* (London: I. B. Tauris, 2017).
46 See Sergio I. Minerbi, *The Vatican and Zionism: Conflict in the Holy Land, 1895–1925* (Oxford: Oxford University Press, 1990).
47 On the Christian-Muslim Association see Albert Hourani, 'Ottoman Reform and the Politics of Notables', in Albert Hourani, Philip Khoury and Mary Wilson, *The Modern Middle East: A Reader* (Berkeley: University of California Press, 1993), pp. 83–109; Ann Mosley Lesch, *Arab Politics in Palestine, 1917–1939: The Frustration of a National Movement* (Ithaca, NY: Cornell University Press, 1979); Abigail Jacobson, *From Empire to Empire: Jerusalem Between Ottoman and British Rule* (Syracuse: Syracuse University Press, 2011).
48 Robson, *Colonialism and Christianity in Mandate Palestine*, p. 45.
49 For instance, the Ottoman millet system also drew a distinction between religious communities. See Efrat Aviv, 'Millet System in the Ottoman Empire', *Oxford Bibliographies of Islamic Studies*, November 2016, DOI: 10.1093/OBO/9780195390155-0231.

50 Although the missionary schools in Palestine were established along national lines, they were primarily, though not exclusively, associated with the Christian communities. Antonius described these schools as a 'mixed blessing'. See George Antonius, *The Arab Awakening* (Philadelphia: J. B. Lippincott, 1939), p. 93. The Muslim community sent their children to religiously orthodox schools managed by the Ottoman authorities or by their own community where Arabic was the primary language of instruction. See Khalidi, *Palestinian Identity*, p. 48.
51 See *Palestine Royal Commission Report*, p. 340.
52 See *Proposed New Constitution for Palestine*, 12 March 1936, Cmd. 5119. See also HC Deb, 24 March 1936, vol. 310, cols. 1079–1150, at https://api.parliament.uk/historic-hansard/commons/1936/mar/24/Palestine (accessed 9 March 2023).
53 See *Palestine Royal Commission Report*, Chapter XVIII, p. 361, para. 11.
54 See Victor Kattan, 'The Empire Departs: The Partitions of British India, Mandate Palestine, and the Dawn of Self-determination in the Third World', *Asian Journal of Middle Eastern and Islamic Studies* 12 (3) (2018), 304–327. DOI: 10.1080/25765949.2018.1514173.
55 See Amit Ranjan, '"Unfinished" partition: territorial disputes, unequal citizens and the rise of majoritarian nationalism in India, Pakistan and Bangladesh' in this volume; Angana P. Chatterjee, Thomas Blom Hansen and Christophe Jafferlot (eds) *Majoritarian State: How Hindu Nationalism is Changing India* (London: Hurst, 2019).
56 Talbot and Singh, *The Partition of India*, p. 28.
57 Veena R. Howard, *Dharma: The Hindu, Jain, Buddhist and Sikh Traditions of India* (London: I. B. Tauris, 2017).
58 On the significance of Punjab to Sikhs, see Patwant Singh, *The Sikhs* (New Delhi: Rupa, 2002).
59 Ishtiaq Ahmed, *The Punjab Bloodied, Partitioned and Cleansed* (New Delhi: Rupa, 2011).
60 See M. Naeem Qureshi, *Pan-Islam in British Indian Politics: A Study of the Khilafat Movement, 1918–1924* (Leiden: Brill 1999).
61 When the British Government refused Jinnah's demand that a Muslim Indian delegation be represented at the Round Table Conference on Palestine in 1939, and to include Haj Amin al-Husseini, the Mufti of Jerusalem, in the negotiations, Jinnah threatened legal action and insisted that no Muslim troops serve in the British Army in Palestine. See the letters, minutes and telegrams exchanged in India Office Records and Private Papers at the British Library, File IOR/L/PO/5/38. On the policy of employment of Indian troops in Palestine in 1939 see IOR/L/WS/1/87. According to Tripathi, 60 per cent of the Indian Army in 1940 was Muslim: Amitava Tripathi, *Indian National Congress and the Struggle for Freedom: 1885–1947* (Oxford: Oxford University Press 2014), p. 274.
62 See Cemil Aydin, '"The Muslim World" Question during the Interwar Era Global Imaginary, 1924–1945', *New Global Studies* 10 (3) (2016), 345–372. https://doi.org/10.1515/ngs-2016-0018.
63 In 1969, Denis Michael Rohan, an Evangelical Christian, set fire to the pulpit of Al Aqsa Mosque. He believed he was given divine instructions to enable the

Jews of Israel to rebuild the Temple on the Temple Mount, thereby hastening the second coming of Jesus Christ. See M. Arkus, 'Rohan Changes Plea to Guilty in Trial on Al Aqsa Mosque Fire', *Washington Post*, 8 October 1969, p. A20. On the connection between the attack and the establishment of the OIC, see Saad S. Khan, 'Organization of Islamic Cooperation', *Oxford Bibliographies in Islamic Studies*, 2018. DOI: 10.1093/OBO/9780195390155-0120. On Jordan's special role in preserving the sacred character of the holy shrines in Jerusalem, see Victor Kattan, 'The Special Role of the Hashemite Kingdom of Jordan in the Muslim Holy Shrines in Jerusalem', *Arab Law Quarterly* 35 (5) (2021), 503–548. https://doi.org/10.1163/15730255-BJA10031.

64 See Christopher Andrew and Vasili Mitrokhin, *The World Was Going Our Way: The KGB and the Battle for the Third World* (New York: Basic Books, 2005).

65 See Chapters XI, XII, and XIII of the UN Charter. See also Mary Ann Heiss, *Fulfilling the Sacred Trust: The UN Campaign for International Accountability for Dependent Territories in the Era of Decolonization* (Ithaca, NY: Cornell University Press, 2020).

66 Compare the conclusions of the *Palestine Royal Commission Report* (Cmd. 5479, 1937) to United Nations General Assembly Resolution 181 (II) (29 November 1947) UN Doc. A/RES/180(II).

67 Again, compare the conclusions of the *Palestine Royal Commission Report* (Cmd. 5479, 1937) to United Nations General Assembly Resolution 181 (II) (29 November 1947) UN Doc. A/RES/180(II).

68 See Laura Robson, 'Partition and the question of international governance: the 1947 United Nations Special Committee on Palestine' in this volume.

69 Harshan Kumarasingham, 'The "Tropical Dominions": The Appeal of Dominion Status in the Decolonisation of India, Pakistan, and Ceylon', *Transactions of the Royal Historical Society* 23 (2013), 223–245 at p. 229.

70 Kumarasingham, 'The "Tropical Dominions"', pp. 232–242. See also Anita Inder Singh, 'Keeping India in the Commonwealth: British Political and Military Aims, 1947–1949', *Journal of Contemporary History* 20 (3) (1985), 469–481.

71 See Lucy P. Chester, *Borders and Conflict in South Asia: The Radcliffe Boundary Commission and Partition of Punjab* (Manchester: Manchester University Press, 2009); Joya Chatterji, *Bengal Divided: Hindu Communalism and Partition, 1932–1947* (Cambridge: Cambridge University Press, 2002).

72 Khan, *The Great Partition*, p. 3.

73 For the 3 June plan see the documents in Mian Muhammad Sadullah et al. (eds), *The Partition of the Punjab, 1947: A Compilation of Official Documents* (Lahore: National Documentation Centre, 1983).

74 UN General Assembly Resolution 181 (II), 29 November 1947.

75 Pablo de Azcárate, *Mission in Palestine, 1948–1952* (Washington, DC: Middle East Institute, 1966).

76 See Avi Shlaim, *The Politics of Partition: King Abdullah, the Zionists and Palestine 1921–1951* (Oxford: Oxford University Press, 1990); Eugene L. Rogan, 'Jordan and 1948: The Persistence of an Official History', in Eugene L. Rogan

and Avi Shlaim (eds), *The War for Palestine: Rewriting the History of 1948* (Cambridge: Cambridge University Press, 2001), pp. 104–124.
77 Confidential paper received by the UN Secretary-General from Azcárate, 13 April 1948, UN Archives, Memoranda to Secretary General, Series S-0624, Box 5, File 37, Acc. DAG13/3/1/01.
78 *Report of the United Nations Palestine Commission to the Second Special Session of the General Assembly*, 10 April 1948, UN Doc. A/532.
79 See Ian Talbot, 'The Mountbatten Viceroyalty reconsidered: personality, prestige and strategic vision in the partition of India' in this volume.
80 There were two communist parties in Palestine, one Jewish and one Arab. The Arab Communist Party in Palestine opposed partition even though the centre in Moscow supported it, demonstrating that opposition to partition in Palestine united communists, nationalists and members of the Islamic parties. See Musa Buderi, *The Palestine Communist Party 1919–1948: Arab and Jew in the Struggle for Internationalism* (Chicago: Haymarket, 2010).
81 The entire House, bar Willie Gallacher, the sole communist member, opposed it. See the statement by the Colonial Secretary William Ormsby-Gore in HC Deb, 21 July 1937, vol. 326, col. 2241.
82 As Lucy Chester explains, Indian politicians – both Muslims and Hindus – took a keen interest in Palestine's affairs; yet the same could not be said of Palestinian Arab politicians, who appeared to be more insular in their worldviews. See Lucy Chester, 'Close Parallels?', p. 144. Chester makes the point that the Arabs in Palestine and Egypt paid less attention to developments in India, and their journalists did not even know that Jinnah belonged to a different political party to the Mahatma Gandhi.
83 On the difficulties Palestinian leaders faced accessing British officials, see Lesch, *Arab Politics in Palestine*.
84 By the end of the three-year revolt in 1939, approximately 5,000 Palestinian Arabs had been killed, 10,000 were wounded and 5,670 were detained. See Appendix IV in Walid Khalidi (ed.), *From Haven to Conquest: Readings in Zionism and the Palestine Problem until 1948* (Beirut: Institute of Palestine Studies, 1987), pp. 846–849. See also Khalidi, *The Iron Cage*.
85 See Kattan, *From Coexistence to Conquest*, p. 159.
86 See Arie M. Dubnov, 'Civil war, total war or a war of partition? Reassessing the 1948 War in Palestine from a global perspective' in this volume.
87 Christopher Snedden, *Understanding Kashmir and Kashmiris* (London: Hurst, 2015); A. G. Noorani, *The Destruction of Hyderabad* (London: Hurst, 2014).
88 See, generally, Elad Ben-Dror, *Ralph Bunche and the Arab–Israeli Conflict: Mediation and the UN, 1947–1949* (New York: Routledge, 2016).
89 Ahmed, *The Punjab Bloodied*.
90 Approximately 85 per cent of the Arab population of Palestine was displaced from the territories that became part of the State of Israel. See Francesca P. Albanese and Lex Takkenberg (eds), *Palestinian Refugees in International Law* (Oxford: Oxford University Press, 2020), p. 35. See also the statistics in Janet L. Abu Lughod, 'The Demographic Transformation of Palestine', in Ibrahim

Abu Lughod (ed.), *The Transformation of Palestine: Essays on the Origins and Development of the Arab–Israeli Conflict* (Evanston: Northwestern University Press, 1971), pp. 139–163.
91 Rephael G. Stern, 'Uncertain Comparisons: Zionist and Israeli Links to India and Pakistan in the Age of Decolonization', *Law and History Review* 39 (3) (2021), 451–478 at p. 466.
92 See Kattan, *From Coexistence to Conquest*, p. 211.
93 The issue of Palestinian citizenship in Arab states is a little complicated due to inter-Arab politics. See, generally, Albanese and Takkenberg, *Palestinian Refugees*.
94 Niraja Gopal Jayal, *Citizenship and its Discontents: An Indian History* (Cambridge, MA: Harvard University Press, 2013).
95 Philips Talbot, 'The Rise of Pakistan', *Middle East Journal* 2 (4) (1948), 381–398, www.jstor.org/stable/4322009. Prashant Bhardwaj and Rinchan Ali Mirza, 'Displacement and Development: Long Term Impacts of Population Transfer in India', 2018. Project by University of California & NBER; Ilyas Chattha, 'Competitions for Resources: Partition's Evacuee Property and Sustenance of Corruption in Pakistan', *Modern Asian Studies* 42 (5) (2012), 1182–1211, https://doi.org/10.1017/S0026749X12000170.
96 Consider the partition proposal in Trump's deal of the century that envisaged partitioning the West Bank. See the conceptual maps in Appendix 1 in *Peace to Prosperity: A Vision to Improve the Lives of the Israeli and Palestinian People*, January 2020, at https://trumpwhitehouse.archives.gov/peacetoprosperity/ (accessed 9 March 2023).
97 Narendra Singh Sarila, *The Shadow of the Great Game: The Untold Story of India's Partition* (London: Constable & Robinson, 2005).
98 See Jahid Hossain Bhuiyan, 'Secularism in the Constitution of Bangladesh', *Journal of Legal Pluralism and Unofficial Law* 49 (2) (2017), 204–227, https://doi.org/10.1080/07329113.2017.1341479.
99 Sinanoglou quoting Khan, *The Great Partition*, p. 22.

Part I

The partition of British India

1

The Mountbatten Viceroyalty reconsidered: personality, prestige and strategic vision in the partition of India

Ian Talbot

Ritchie Ovendale's classic account of British policy towards Palestine in 1945–46 concludes that, 'It was impossible to divorce the question of partition in Palestine from partition in India. It was felt that if there was partition in the mandate, the Moslem case for partition in India would be strengthened.'[1] The contemporaneous partition policy in Palestine and India led Christopher Hitchens to argue that it was a peculiarly British practice at the time of imperial withdrawal.[2] Brendan O'Leary has questioned this assessment.[3] Nonetheless, he identified the British policies of indirect rule and the spread of representative government as creating the conditions for political institutionalisation of 'existing national, ethnic or communal cleavages'. This could move partition 'up the policy agenda' at the end of empire as a resolution of 'long-run conflict'.

This chapter supports O'Leary's views that partition was not 'a Liberal (with respect to Ireland) or Labour (regarding Palestine) enthusiasm'. Documentary evidence overwhelmingly suggests an official reluctance to divide and quit India. Strategic connections between partition in India and Palestine were far less clear cut than Ovendale asserts. Partition in both instances could however be seen as a means to extricate Britain from conflicts that threatened national prestige and aspirations to retain defence and economic interests after decolonisation. Expectations of 'neocolonial' power foundered both on the unanticipated aftermaths of partition in India/Pakistan and Palestine and on Britain's diminished postwar economic and military power.

The military and strategic dimensions to India's partition were however far more nuanced than Narendra Singh Sarila argues in his well-known work, *The Shadow of the Great Game*. He supports the notion that Pakistan was created following partition, because it served Western strategic interests in the emerging Cold War context. Sarila portrays India's partition as a conspiracy between a complicit Muslim League and a British administration intent on creating Pakistan with its potential strategic value as a military bastion.[4] This argument was echoed in Gurinder Chadha's controversial film *Viceroy's House* released at the time of the seventieth anniversary of partition. It shifted the British responsibility for partition from the Labour government and the final Viceroy Lord Mountbatten onto the figures of his Chief of Staff General (Pug) Ismay and the former Prime Minister Winston Churchill.[5] This chapter, with its focus on the Mountbatten Viceroyalty, argues that concerns regarding the impact of partition on the Indian Army led military planners to oppose partition until there was no alternative. Only then was thought turned to whether Pakistan, as a counterpart to Israel, could further Western security interests.

Aiyaz Husain has recently examined American and British strategic visions in Palestine and Kashmir.[6] He echoes Ovendale in revealing the serious differences between London and Washington with respect to Jewish migration to Palestine and the emergence of the new State of Israel. Like Sarila, he suggests that some British strategists saw Pakistan as a barrier to the Soviet Union's advance in South Asia. Husain does not however examine the extent to which developments in Palestine influenced the original British decision to divide and quit India.

This chapter argues that it is misleading to read back, Pakistan's post-independence strategic value into the British debates concerning its creation. Pakistan's geopolitical value was not a major issue in pre-independence thinking. Right up to the Indian politicians' acceptance of the Partition Plan in June 1947 civilian and military strategic reflection was concerned about the viability of a future Pakistan state, rather than its potential value as a military bastion. Moreover, as the chapter reveals, until their departure, the British viewed the subcontinent through a South Asian, rather than Middle Eastern, geographical lens. Indonesia loomed larger as a transregional interest than Palestine. Pakistan's strategic value only emerged in the context of its feared collapse, after the unforeseen partition-related massacres and the eruption in October 1947 of the Kashmir crisis.

Cabinet debates reflected the strategic shift. The decision to partition India had gained widespread support across government departments as well as party political divides. The Attlee government did not have to cope with the conflicting arguments over India that existed with respect to Palestine. Things changed rapidly after independence. There was an echo of the Commonwealth Office and Foreign Office earlier divide over Palestine. Attlee and Cripps continued their pro-India stance, supported by Mountbatten. The need to prop up Pakistan increased the influence of the Foreign Minister Bevin, who had previously played little role in Indian affairs, in comparison with his dominant position vis-à-vis Palestine. The 'pro-Pakistan lobby' included Britain's first High Commissioner in Karachi, Laurence Grafftey-Smith.

This chapter thus argues that, contrary to Sarila, a clear distinction must be made between British attitudes in the late colonial and early post-independence periods with respect to Pakistan's strategic value. It joins O'Leary in seriously questioning Hitchens' assumptions. It argues that partition was reluctantly adopted. The policy was primarily a pragmatic response to pressures from below arising from anticolonialism and communalism in the Indian subcontinent. Understandings such as Sarila's deny this agency.

Later episodes of British decolonisation in Asia and Africa indicate that if there was a 'peculiarly British practice', regarding decolonisation, it lay in the encouragement of federal arrangements, rather than partition. Whitehall may well have learned that partition in India had brought unintended consequences that exacerbated communal conflict and violence, rather than resolving it. Nonetheless, federations in former British colonial territories in for example west and southern Africa, and Malaya, rarely survived.

Partition reflected a desire to assure Britain's post-independence influence in India and thereby its continuation as an Asian power, rather than a response to mounting pressures in the Muslim Middle East, arising from the handling of the Palestine mandate. Britain, of course, had important oil and strategic interests there, and wished to maintain its standing with Arab countries, but this does not mean, as Ovendale suggests, that events in Palestine strengthened the prospects for Pakistan's emergence arising from a partition of India.[7] The partition of India was undertaken as part of a wider reassessment of how to maintain British informal influence and prestige in an Asian context of diminished economic and military resources, but continuing imperial commitments. This policy grasped the need to adjust Britain's role in the postwar world and represented an attempt to bring a 'Commonwealth moment' to decolonisation.[8]

The chapter will emphasise that partition was not the preferred policy choice. Indeed, it threatened wider imperial strategic goals – most notably, because it entailed the division of the Indian Army that had historically underpinned Britain's power in Asia. Certainly, Britain could not impose partition, if its wider South Asian interests were to be protected. There is a parallel here with the dilemma in Palestine. The difference is that Britain was able to secure the agreement of both Indian nationalists and Muslim separatists to partition. It would have been disastrous for Britain's strategic interests in Asia if the Indian National Congress had not accepted the decision which went against the organisation's long-term commitment to a united India.

The first section of this chapter examines how Mountbatten secured Indian agreement to partition. This is followed by a discussion regarding the reasons why the British Government had reluctantly agreed on the policy of partition. The chapter's third section examines Mountbatten's stage-management of independence and partition and how this served strategic British interests. The conclusion draws together the arguments, as well as suggesting possible areas of comparative research with respect to the partitions in Palestine and India.

Mountbatten and the Indian agreement to partition

In an earlier study on what I termed the 'pre-history' of the Viceroyalty, I argued how Mountbatten's wartime position as Supreme Commander of South East Asia Command assisted the later task of ensuring Britain left the Indian subcontinent on good terms with its future rulers.[9] He had established a rapport with Nehru following the Congress leader's visit to Singapore in March 1946. Mountbatten had moved the SEAC headquarters from Kandy to Singapore the previous autumn in order to have a closer oversight of his post-Japanese surrender tasks. Private correspondence reveals that he had already identified Nehru as a man who could be trusted, rather than as a 'nationalist troublemaker'.[10] Mountbatten's role as Supreme Commander had exposed him to the challenges of rising Asian nationalism and the need to respond constructively so as to substitute 'informal relationships' for empire.[11] The Labour government was aware of this flexibility and sought to use it in a process of decolonisation that contrasted markedly with contemporaneous French and Dutch rigidity in the face of anticolonial pressures.[12]

Mountbatten, in his role as Viceroy, formed much better working relations with Indian politicians than his rather 'stiff' predecessor Wavell had done. This was vitally important as the winding up of the Indian Empire was an important moment for Britain's postwar standing. The maintenance of British prestige was paramount. Mountbatten's charisma and public relations skills were to prove vital in establishing a narrative of achievement with respect to the transfer of power in India. The controversies surrounding the unforeseen human tragedy of the partition massacres and mass migrations, however, have obscured recognition of Mountbatten's contribution to a largely successful imperial exit from the purely British standpoint.

Critics blame Mountbatten for the appalling suffering that accompanied the partition. Indeed, Andrew Roberts argues that the administrative chaos, which accompanied a rapid transfer of power, precipitated the August 1947 massacres.[13] Roberts echoes contemporary critics when he links the advancement of independence from June 1948 to August 1947 to Mountbatten's personal impetuosity. Akbar Ahmed's description of Mountbatten as the 'first Paki-basher' similarly echoes contemporary criticism. It is vividly portrayed in a cartoon in the newspaper *Dawn* by Ajmal Hussain entitled 'EXPOSED: He is to be blamed'.[14]

Throughout the deliberations leading to the transfer of power, Mountbatten was assiduous in ensuring that key political players were onside to ensure London's desire for a departure on good terms with the Indian subcontinent's future rulers. The Viceroy's efforts to secure Nehru's agreement to the Partition Plan are well documented.[15] This sits awkwardly with the portrayal of an imperious Mountbatten forcing partition arrangements on 'reluctant' Indian politicians. If partition was, as some argue, a 'parting gift' from the British, it was one that the Congress high command readily accepted.

There was a convergence of British and Congress interests that eased Mountbatten's relations with Nehru, disregarding any personal dimension. This was just as well, as in reality Britain had little real power to transfer. The Congress had established a parallel ruling presence to the Raj. Although it had been chastened by the repression of the 1942 Quit India Movement, it was clear that Britain could not repeat this in peacetime. The February 1946 Bombay naval mutiny had revealed the extent to which British power was slipping away.[16] It had also warned the Congress that it could inherit a country on the brink of chaos. A speedy transfer of power was the best way to avoid this.[17]

Communal conflict also loomed large as a threat to India. The Congress investigated the March 1947 Rawalpindi Massacres in the previously relatively peaceful Punjab that claimed between 7,000–8,000 lives. The report worryingly discovered a high degree of planning and organisation.[18] The Dhanwantri and P. C. Joshi Communist Party pamphlet, 'Bleeding Punjab Warns', later reiterated this finding.[19] A fortnight before Mountbatten arrived in India, the Congress Working Committee called for the division of Punjab and Bengal if Pakistan was created.[20]

The Congress had always resolutely opposed the creation of a separate Muslim state, but political developments at the All-India, as well as local, level led the party's high command to reconsider. The Congress was glad to be free of a troublesome Muslim League presence. Its potentially disruptive impact on future nation-building projects, dear to Nehru's heart, had been displayed during the interim government in which the Congress leader had been a prime minister in waiting. When the Muslim League belatedly decided to join the government on 13 October 1946, the earlier smooth proceedings were disrupted. Rather than functioning as a coalition, the two parties acted as warring blocs.[21] Partition would thus remove a major irritant and enable the Congress to press ahead with nation-building tasks in the areas it controlled.[22] This factor, in addition to the realisation that

Muslims could not be compelled to remain in India, rather than it being a case of 'old men' in a hurry, explains how the Congress high command swallowed what Gandhi termed the, 'wooden loaf' of partition. Nehru, in a note to Mountbatten on 1 May, stated clearly that, 'We have accepted the partition of India in order to avoid conflict and compulsion.'[23]

Much has been written about Mountbatten's 'charm offensive' and the circumstances in which Congress reluctance regarding partition was overcome. The key was the convergence of Congress and the British around a partition scheme that minimised its impact on the political stability of the subcontinent. Jinnah was forced into a corner and ultimately had to accept a 'moth-eaten' Pakistan. The Congress and the British shared the concern that partition might result in the 'Balkanisation' of the subcontinent. From both their perspectives, there was to be only one partition, despite the hopes of Sikhs, Pakhtuns, Tamils and assorted princely rulers. Moreover, the division of India was to be accompanied by the partition of the non-Muslim-majority areas of Punjab and Bengal. Personalities aside, with this outcome in view, relations between Mountbatten and Jinnah were bound to be rockier than in the case of Nehru.

Certainly, Mountbatten and Jinnah were contrasting personalities with, at times, a prickly relationship. Mountbatten's vanity has been 'mythologised' as a key factor in this. Yet their relationship should not be viewed through the hindsight of the 1947 partition. Mountbatten recorded of an early meeting with Jinnah that, 'one and a half hours after the interview started he was joking, and by the end of our talk last night (6 April, when Jinnah stayed after dinner until half past midnight) the ice was really broken.'[24] It is only Ayesha Jalal, however, who has moved beyond a personality-driven explanation of the conflict between them that arose over the issue of the future Governor-General arrangements. Indeed, some of Mountbatten's well known vituperative remarks regarding the Quaid-i-Azam arose directly from Jinnah's announcement that he wished to be Pakistan Governor-General. Much more was at stake than the protagonists' vanity. Jinnah believed that Pakistan's sovereignty would be undermined if Mountbatten served after partition as joint Governor-General.[25] From Mountbatten's perspective the appointment would not only enable more time to resolve issues that had been left over by a speedy departure, it would politically underpin the close defence ties between the two countries which, as we shall see later, were a goal for a continued British imperial interest in Asia. Mountbatten was outraged not because of *amour propre*, but because, even before decolonisation, Jinnah was thwarting hopes for the Raj's successor states' continuing role in imperial defence.

Mountbatten has always received a bad press in Pakistan where he is seen as a partisan in support of India's interests at the time of partition.[26]

Writers have read back his stance as sole Governor-General in India into the Viceroy period. Mountbatten is thus especially seen as pro-India in the genesis of the Kashmir dispute. The issue of the Boundary Award to India of the Muslim-majority Gurdaspur district that provided access to Kashmir is frequently cited in this regard. This presupposes planning by Mountbatten in the absence of documentary evidence. In fact, the 'notional boundary' map which is used to prove Mountbatten's interference is less revealing than the fact that even during Wavell's Viceroyalty, Gurdaspur with its slight Muslim majority was being considered as part of India in any eventual partition. This had nothing to do with Jammu and Kashmir which had not surfaced at that time as a potential problem. It is tempting to see conflict over Kashmir as inevitable. Yet, just a matter of weeks before independence, Jinnah was privately negotiating with a British woman, Brenda Blencowe, to purchase her houseboat, *Mayflower*, on the Dal Lake at Srinagar.[27] Concern with Gurdaspur, despite its later strategic significance for India's road links with Kashmir, thus misses the mark. If Mountbatten influenced the Boundary Award at all to Pakistan's disadvantage, it was with respect to the Ferozepore *tehsil* (district).[28] This followed the threat of the Maharajah of Bikaner to accede to Pakistan, if the boundary placed the Ferozepore canal headworks in Pakistan control.

Britain and the decision to partition India

Mountbatten did not touch down at Palam airport in Delhi on 22 March 1947 with a predetermined partition plan. Neither the new Viceroy, nor the Attlee government, had abandoned the possibility of a return to the Cabinet Mission proposal with its three-tiered government providing autonomy to Muslim-majority areas within an Indian Union.[29] Despite the backdrop of violence and the Muslim League boycott of the Constituent Assembly, Mountbatten still hoped to resurrect these proposals. Even at his sixth staff meeting on 31 March, there was the desire to find a constitutional solution within the framework of the Cabinet Mission Plan.[30] Several weeks of extensive meetings with Indian politicians and opinion formers eventually convinced the Viceroy that this was out of the question.[31] Partition then became the main policy option. Mountbatten and his team turned its focus to how Indian politicians could agree on this. Britain could not impose partition if it wanted to wield influence in post-independence South Asia.[32]

The British clearly conceded partition to avoid civil war. Punjab, Bengal and parts of the United Provinces were badly affected by violence at the time of Mountbatten's arrival. Competing claims over territory, the settling of scores and the allure of loot were key driving factors, along with a sense of impunity on behalf of the perpetrators.[33] Worryingly, there was also a proliferation of paramilitary organisations trained and manned by ex-servicemen.[34] Indeed, recent scholarship has revealed a correlation in levels of partition-related violence and exposure of the population to active military service during the Second World War.[35]

Pakistan's birth coincided with an intensification of the violence partition was designed to avoid. This has led to criticisms, as we have seen, of Mountbatten's acceleration of the British departure. He has also been censured for ignoring the warnings sent from Sir Evan Jenkins, the Governor of Punjab. The region that was at the epicentre of the partition-related violence.[36] Nehru complained to the Viceroy that British officials in Punjab were not doing all in their power to prevent violence. He urged the introduction of martial law. Jenkins, who had struggled to impose authority after the first round of Punjab communal violence in March 1947, decided against this step, given the difficulties in taking decisive action.[37]

The British Governor was in an invidious position with a severely stretched administration, some of whose members were acting in a partisan manner. Jenkins had the disquieting experience of having his telephone tapped and confidential information passed on to Muslim League politicians.[38] Mountbatten did not press Jenkins, aware that the imposition of martial law in Punjab would further complicate the aim of a British departure on good terms with India's future rulers. The Viceroy instead supported his governor against Indian criticisms, at the same time as spelling out the need for Nehru's 'goodwill' in this 'critical transition period'.[39] Ultimately, Mountbatten was concerned more with the need for an All-India settlement than with the local situation in Punjab. This was not because of ignorance, or a personal agenda, as some critics have maintained, but because of the wider strategic imperatives that rested on a British departure on good terms with India's future rulers.[40]

It is important to realise, however, that although Punjab's future was settled in New Delhi, provincial politicians both influenced this process and had their own reasons for supporting division. State downsizing was a means by which local elites sought to cement power. Hindu and Sikh Punjabi leaders' demands for partition of their historic homeland forwarded Congress interests at a national level, as the spectre of an enlarged Pakistan that included the whole of Punjab threatened to extend the borders of the new state to the outskirts of Delhi. By early May, Jenkins had reluctantly concluded that the partitioning of Punjab, along with the division of India, was 'a means to reconciling irreconcilable people'.[41]

If partition was adopted in India, as in Palestine, in the name of conflict resolution, it also occurred to the backdrop of wider British strategic concerns. These were not however of the type Sarila envisaged. His understanding of

British and Muslim League complicity in partition reads back to 1947, Pakistan's later emergence as a military-dominated 'insecurity state'.[42] Until the eve of partition, British officials were pessimistic about Pakistan's prospects. The India Office's long-standing resistance to partition was based not just on a negative assessment of Pakistan's future economic viability, but its defence weaknesses. Officials believed that the new state would be vulnerable to both the Soviet Union and China. Pakistan's financial resources would be hopelessly inadequate for defence requirements. Notes produced in January and February 1946 saw defence as 'the crux' of the problem of partition.[43] Crucially the Chiefs of Staff shared this assessment. A couple of months later, they advised Attlee that Pakistan should only be accepted if there was no viable political alternative.[44] Frederick Pethick-Lawrence, the Secretary of State, summed up the British position in a broadcast on 16 May:

> The complete separation of Pakistan from the rest of India ... would in our view gravely endanger the whole of the country by splitting the army into two and by preventing that defence in depth which is essential in modern warfare. We therefore do not suggest the adoption of the proposal.[45]

Historically, Indian soldiers had underpinned British imperial power as far afield as New Zealand and Hong Kong. Indian troops fought on the Western Front, in Africa and in the Middle East during the First World War.[46] They were of immense importance to South East Asia Command during the Second World War. Around two and a half million Indians served in the allied cause.

Britain emerged exhausted from the second global conflict 'with the unenviable position of being the world's largest debtor nation'.[47] Nonetheless, it retained global responsibilities, with large troop commitments in Western Europe and the Middle East. As the government recognised, the dollar earnings of raw material exports from colonies in Africa and East Asia were necessary for the recovery of Britain's war-battered economy. The end of empire was not on the agenda. Where once, much of the Empire had been acquired to safeguard routes to India, now the independent subcontinent was expected to play a role in the British retention of its remaining empire – without which both national economic recovery and aspirations for global power would founder.

The Chiefs of Staff remained exercised by India's postcolonial role in Imperial Defence throughout the final year of British rule. In May 1946, General Claude Auchinleck pointed out that a united India could provide for its own defence in a way that a partitioned subcontinent could not.[48] The strategic dimension of the transfer of power was also appreciated by Wavell and Mountbatten in New Delhi and Bevin and Attlee in London.[49]

It was officially recognised that decolonisation would entail a 'great loss' if India ceased to be a linchpin in imperial defence. Ismay, six months before he accompanied Mountbatten to India to play 'the last chukka', had in a Chiefs of Staff Committee report for Attlee pointed out India's 'great manpower resources', its strategic airfields for 'attack on the industrial areas of the Urals and Western Siberia', as well as the maintenance of 'communications to the Far East' and naval bases 'important to our command of the Indian Ocean … (and) maintenance of our communications to South East Asia and the Persian Gulf'.[50]

It was only when Pakistan became inevitable that the Chiefs of Staff began to consider its strategic value. Sarila has seized on this 'evidence' for his argument.[51] Even so, it was not until the emergence of the Kashmir dispute in October 1947 that officials began to consider Pakistan, rather than India, as the linchpin for British interests beyond the subcontinent.[52] In the countdown to the transfer of power, the emphasis was rather on post-independence arrangements to enable both dominions to work together in collective security.

The closing months of the Mountbatten Viceroyalty are best understood as an attempt to square the circle of continuing British strategic interests and partition. This was to be achieved in part by ensuring that India and Pakistan joined the Commonwealth, and through the provision of a joint Governor-General for the dominions of India and Pakistan. The Empire was being transformed into the Commonwealth, and as the first non-white dominions India's and Pakistan's participation was regarded as important for the Commonwealth's future evolution.[53] Most importantly, Commonwealth membership would help tie in India and Pakistan to a wider imperial defence system.[54] It was this British wider strategic imperative that drove the aim to keep India in the Commonwealth, not, as some writers have maintained, Mountbatten's personal mission to do so.[55]

From the end of the Second World War, British planners increasingly saw the Commonwealth as 'a military entity'.[56] Indian membership would remove the necessity for a post-independence military treaty that would be essential for the security of British interests in the Far East and communications with Australia and New Zealand. A contingency plan was drawn up for Britain to retain the Andaman and Nicobar Islands, as outposts to Burma and Malaya, if India remained outside a Commonwealth defence system.[57]

As early as April 1947, Mountbatten prioritised keeping India in the Commonwealth as his 'most important and urgent single task'.[58] He rightly regarded India and Pakistan's Commonwealth membership as his greatest achievement as Viceroy. Consultations with Congress leaders convinced him that acquiescence could be secured if power was transferred quickly in 1947.

The accelerated pace of withdrawal was thus not only a response to communal pressures, but to ensure India and Pakistan joined the Commonwealth. Nehru in fact, in his first meeting with Mountbatten on 24 March, had maintained that 'he did not consider it possible, with the forces which were at work, that India could remain within the Commonwealth'.[59]

Commonwealth membership would provide mechanisms for military liaison with Britain and other dominions. There was also the need to coordinate defence at the subcontinental level. This was to be achieved through the establishment of a joint defence headquarters. Mountbatten had first suggested this to Nehru in May, likening the arrangement to that of the pre-1914 Austro-Hungarian Empire, which had separate armies, but a defence headquarters with the Emperor at its head.[60] General Claude Auchinleck was designated Supreme Commander of the divided British Indian Army, which was reconstituted into Pakistan and Indian forces. He was a member of the Joint Defence Council that was created on 15 August. It also comprised the defence ministers of India and Pakistan and Mountbatten the Governor-General of India, in his capacity as an independent chairman. Indian claims that Auchinleck was favouring Pakistan, as conflict mounted in Jammu and Kashmir, accelerated the winding up of the Joint Military Command structure in November 1947.

The eruption of conflict in Kashmir in October 1947 is widely regarded as part of the 'unfinished business of partition'. It is less acknowledged that it dealt a fatal blow to British strategic aspirations in South Asia. The presence of British officials in key positions in the Pakistan Government and in the Indian and Pakistan armies undoubtedly mitigated the first military conflict over Kashmir. There were in fact around 500 senior British officers in the Indian Army and over 1,000 in the Pakistan defence forces.[61] The nationalist backlash in both India and Pakistan, however, ended the prospects of collaboration with Britain in imperial defence. London's hopes that the subcontinent could still serve as a postcolonial 'oriental barracks' to underpin global British power died with the Pakhtun tribal invasion of the Kashmir Valley. It is beyond the scope of this book, but it is also important to acknowledge that both the Commonwealth's internal evolution along the lines that London hoped and Washington's post-1947 recognition of Britain's sphere of influence in the subcontinent were severely compromised by its two members' conflict over Kashmir.

'Oriental barracks' were sought elsewhere, first in the Suez Canal Zone and then in Aden.[62] In both instances, they had to be abandoned in the face of nationalist opposition. It was only in the late 1960s, however, that Britain finally called it a day as a military power east of Suez. This further supports the argument that London did not see Indian independence as part of an immediate postwar process of British decolonisation. Empire was to survive.

This strategy required the portrayal of the transfer of power as a triumph, rather than a defeat.

British prestige and Mountbatten's stage-managing of independence

The independence celebrations commenced in Karachi, the new capital of Pakistan, on 14 August. Some British newspapers were to contrast the 'curious apathy' in the city with the celebrations in New Delhi the next day. *The Times* correspondent took refuge in orientalist stereotypes to explain this state of affairs, linking it with the 'lethargic temperament of the "ordinary Sindhi"'.[63] In reality, there were large and enthusiastic crowds thronging the route, in what was described as the City of Flags, 'where cars hooted and bumped each other, people climbed lamp posts and stood on roofs or got jammed in the dense masses in the road'.[64]

Critics have claimed Mountbatten wasted precious time in his preoccupation with the Independence Day celebrations in New Delhi. There has been ridicule of his film star looks and love of uniform. More seriously, it has been claimed that he delayed publication of the Boundary Award so as not to spoil them. While uncertainty over the exact location of the border was a factor in the subsequent violence, we have already noted that the driving forces were far more complex. It is unrealistic to assume that an earlier announcement could have single-handedly forestalled the bloodletting. Mountbatten's preoccupation with the theatrical elements of the Independence Day events, including the flag lowering, the ceremonial ride through New Delhi and the media coverage, need to be considered in terms of Britain's wider strategic interests.

First and foremost, British prestige could not be undermined by the departure from India. Wavell's Viceroyalty was abruptly terminated because he persisted with proposals for what amounted to a staged withdrawal in response to the Congress–Muslim League constitutional impasse and growing conflict.[65] The Attlee government saw this breakdown plan policy as defeatist. Mountbatten was despatched to wind up the Indian Empire in such a way as it did not appear an ignominious defeat. This would neither play well with the domestic electorate, nor the international audience. London could not afford to display weakness to American opinion or that in the Empire, while it still harboured pretensions to global power.[66] The government's objectives were unequivocally stated in a Cabinet meeting on New Year's Eve 1946:

> The general feeling of the Cabinet was that withdrawal from India need not appear to be forced upon us by our weakness nor to be the first step in the dissolution of the British Empire. On the contrary, this action must be shown to be the logical conclusion ... of a policy followed by successive Governments.[67]

The Labour administration regarded Mountbatten as ideally suited for overseeing a narrative of independence as imperial fulfilment. He exuded glamour and had the royal connections (he was Queen Victoria's great-grandson) that would impress the princely order. Most importantly, he possessed a keen appreciation of the growing influence of good public relations and a media presence.[68] Wavell, in contrast, had been 'reticent', wholly lacking 'interest in a capacity for self-display'.[69]

Mountbatten, as Viceroy, continued the news management and film publicity that had accompanied his role in the wartime Burma campaign.[70] He commenced his office with a swearing-in ceremony in New Delhi in which, for the first time, 'film cameras whirred and flashbulbs went off'.[71] There was an even bigger media operation for the press conference that announced the Indian political leaders' acceptance of the 3 June Partition Plan. Mountbatten was concerned that there was a 'clear transmission' to England and the United States, as well as the Indian audience.[72] While he took pleasure in the plaudits his 'masterful' performance received, Mountbatten ensured that the Indian leaders' views received prominence. This was the way to maximise public support for partition.

Alan-Campbell Johnson, who was Mountbatten's press attaché, carefully managed the media. He had earlier accompanied Mountbatten as Air Publication Relations Officer, Combined Operations, and Recorder South East Asia Command.[73] Johnson cultivated relations with Indian and British news correspondents.[74] He could in this respect be termed the first spin doctor. In numerous publications and speaking engagements, throughout his life, he kept alive the Mountbatten 'legend', which he had helped create.[75] Johnson worked closely with A. H. Joyce, the adviser on publicity issues at the India Office.[76] He was also in close touch with Bob Stimson of the BBC in India. Mountbatten, who had met with Sir William Haley, the Director-General, saw such ties as important for being able 'to get the right stand on things'.[77]

Mountbatten was concerned that there would be no newsreel coverage of the Independence Day celebrations.[78] He turned to John Turner, who had been attached to South East Asia Command and had shot the film coverage of the Japanese surrender at Singapore.[79] It was released to six major companies (Paramount, Pathé, Gaumont British, Movietone, Universal and Metro) which had a potential worldwide audience of a hundred million people.[80] While Mountbatten was anything but camera shy, this was not merely his personal ego trip. He made it clear to London that Turner 'will be out here to publicize India and not the Viceroy'.[81] When the Managing Director of Gaumont British, Castleton Night, suggested that Turner could be used for purely private pictures, Mountbatten informed Sir Arthur Jarratt that 'we have no intention of doing this since I regard him out here as purely doing a job for the public'.[82]

Mountbatten ensured that Turner's expenses were paid, but refrained from appointing him to his staff to make the point that the cameraman was not in his personal service.[83] As a result of Turner's coverage, Gaumont British was to release 700 feet of film shot for the Independence Day celebrations. Paramount and Universal showed half of this, drawn not only from Turner's film but from the less experienced Indian cameraman P. Mohan and his brother Ved Parkash, who worked for Paramount News.[84]

Alan Campbell-Johnson reported that the celebrations 'went off very well from the publicity viewpoint'.[85] The coverage of cheering and joyful crowds in New Delhi, where Mountbatten was feted along with Nehru, reinforced the image that Britain was not in retreat but fulfilling a long-held promise to grant responsible government to a grateful Indian population. Mountbatten used his friendship with Nehru to reach a 'tacit agreement that the newsreels were not to film the lowering of the Union Jack anywhere'.[86] Subsequent coverage of the partition massacres partly undermined this carefully constructed narrative. Nonetheless, the sense of a fulfilment of Britain's imperial destiny in India persisted. It was part of a wider strategy to bolster an empire without India. The message was best summed up by the *Daily Herald's* report, which concluded that India was 'willingly relinquished' in a 'shining act of faith and justice'.[87]

Conclusion

The British transfer of power to the two dominions of India and Pakistan, like the earlier division of Ireland, was a response of imperial statecraft to intractable conflict in which religion formed a crucial element of political identity. However, Mountbatten's staff meetings and general correspondence do not reveal any reference to other partitions. This attests to the official reluctance to divide and quit India. We have seen that this was prompted by concerns about Pakistan's economic, and to a greater extent military, viability, as well as the desire to maintain India's administrative unity. There is no evidence for claims that before the handover of power Pakistan was conceived as a military bastion by the British. It is true that partition was viewed at times from a military perspective, but the disruption it threatened to the prospect of postcolonial India's involvement in an imperial military system formed a key argument against Pakistan. Partition was eventually accepted by the British and Indian leaders as a means to end communal conflict and ensure a rapid transfer of power on amicable terms.

The Mountbatten Viceroyalty remains controversial because of the disastrous massacres and migrations that accompanied the division of the

Indian subcontinent. Mountbatten's personality and his exaggerated claims in later life made him a target for ongoing criticism. He boasted to the authors Lapierre and Collins that, 'I had as great control of the Cabinet as I had over the leaders in India at the time.'[88] This chapter reveals that he was not the all-powerful arbiter of the subcontinent's fate. He had limited room to manoeuvre because of communal violence.[89] The situation in India at the time of Mountbatten's arrival was likened by Lord Ismay to 'a ship on fire in mid-ocean with ammunition in the hold'.[90]

Most importantly Mountbatten was implementing the British Government's strategy, not his own. He not only reported extensively to the Secretary of State in London, but also returned to Whitehall on 19 May 1947 for consultations on the revised Partition Plan with Attlee and the India and Burma Committee of the Cabinet. Its position from the outset of the Mountbatten Viceroyalty was that any exit strategy should both preserve British prestige and ensure that an independent India would continue to provide military assistance in Britain's defence of the Commonwealth. The American critic Stanley Wolpert portrays Mountbatten as imperiously bringing forward the British deadline for departure.[91] The Cabinet in fact fully approved this policy because it was seen as a means to meet its objectives.[92] Mountbatten, throughout his Viceroyalty, received powerful backing from Cripps and Attlee. Bevin, who was crucial with respect to British policy on Palestine, had a limited influence on Indian matters.

Mountbatten's lifelong fascination with film and almost endless capacity for self-publicity was turned to the nation's service in constructing a narrative of independence and imperial fulfilment.[93] This survived the shocks of the partition massacres in part because of what Pamela Mountbatten termed her father's 'operation seduction'.[94] The strategic nightmare of a hostile India was avoided. Britain's commercial interests continued to thrive in post-independence India until the downturn in the 1960s.[95]

At the time of independence, Pakistan was not thankful for partition in the way Ovendale suggests. There was a strong sense that Mountbatten had favoured India. This focused on the Boundary Award following the division of Punjab. While Mountbatten had forced Jinnah into a corner, over the Partition of Punjab and Bengal, the Quaid-i-Azam remained obdurate regarding the Viceroy's desire to serve as Governor-General of both dominions. This insistence, together with the unexpected ferocity of the partition-related massacres and the interlinked emergence of the Kashmir dispute, put paid to a hoped for 'Commonwealth moment' in Indian decolonisation.[96] Ultimately, British aspirations regarding the continuation of the subcontinent as an 'oriental barrack' proved unrealisable. Mountbatten returned to a naval career in a 'diminished Britain'. He continued through the remainder of his life to burnish the role he had played in the 'last chukka' of the Raj.

This re-examination of the Mountbatten Viceroyalty questions the extent to which British policy choices favoured the option of partition. Clearly partition in India was a reluctant response to diminishing British power, at a time of escalating communal conflict. It was London's, not just Mountbatten's, policy. Attlee only agreed to partition when it was clear that the Congress would own this in a way that did not jeopardise British political and strategic goals in postcolonial South Asia. Partition would not be imposed – certainly not in a way that privileged Muslim separatist interests. Indeed, Jinnah and the Muslim League were ultimately marginalised, along with regional interests in the key Punjab province, in the British drive for an All-India settlement. Pragmatic responses to historical contingencies arising from the Second World and its aftermath lay behind the decision to divide and quit India.

Does this then leave any room for the Indian partition in comparative scholarship? Should the Indian subcontinent's division in August 1947 be seen as a unique event which defies comparative historical and conceptual analysis? There remain several areas for exploration in a comparative approach to the Palestine and India cases of partition. To what extent did the 'winner takes all' Westminster system impact the separatist ideology of the Zionist Organisation and the Muslim League?[97] Why did partition not resolve communal conflict in India and Palestine?[98] Critics of the departure from India have referred to the reluctance to commit British troops for quelling communal violence in the run-up to partition and its immediate aftermath. This policy has been deemed 'callous'. The Punjab Boundary Force that was formed to maintain order comprised British officers and Gurkha troops among its contingent. It was no match for Muslim and Sikh war bands, and its capability was further undermined by the fact that the majority of the ordinary soldiers were drawn from the increasingly polarised Punjabi communities.[99]

Parallels can be drawn with the situation in the Palestine mandate where paramilitary forces were present in a similar context of diminished military resources. British soldiers were committed, unlike in India, with tragic outcomes as seen in the bombing by Irgun of the King David Hotel in Jerusalem in July 1946. Had the lesson been drawn that it was untenable to commit British forces in the midst of an escalating confrontation? There are also parallels when discussing the extent to which a speedy decolonisation in India and relinquishing the mandate in Palestine were tactical responses to deteriorating law and order. This threatened British standing and prestige in strategically and economically important regions for London's continuing global aspirations.

Finally, moving to the role of nationalists and their communal opponents, there is scope for comparative analysis between India and Palestine.

Revisionist historians have pointed to the Congress's underestimation of the Muslim League demands and the failure to accommodate the Indian Muslims' minority demands because of the commitment to a strong and modernising central government. This created the circumstances in which violence occurred, making partition a policy option for the outgoing imperial power. Can parallels be drawn with Palestine? Did Palestinian leaders make insufficient allowance for the ideas and interests of Zionists, thereby creating a conflict that led both the British and the UN to see partition as a policy resolution?

Notes

1. Ritchie Ovendale, 'The Palestine Policy of the British Labour Government 1945–6', *International Affairs* 55 (3) (1979), 431.
2. C. Hitchens, 'The Perils of Partition', *Atlantic Monthly*, March 2003, pp. 99–107.
3. See Brendan O'Leary, 'Analysing Partition: Definition, Classification, Explanation', *Political Geography* 26 (8) (2007), 886–908.
4. Narendra Singh Sarila, *The Shadow of the Great Game: The Untold Story of India's Partition* (New Delhi: HarperCollins, 2005).
5. G. Chadha (director), *Viceroy's House* (20th Century Fox, 2017). The film was heavily criticised by historians and writers. Fatima Bhutto termed it 'a servile Pantomime of Partition'.
6. Aiyaz Husain, *Mapping the End of Empire: American and British Strategic Visions in the Postwar World* (Cambridge, MA: Harvard University Press, 2014).
7. It should be noted here that concerns about the impact of the installation of a Jewish state in Palestine on India's 90 million Muslims needs to be set in a much longer historical context than 1945–46. The British Empire in important respects had always been a Muslim empire, making its rulers historically attuned to the potentially destabilising effects of transregional Islamic resentments.
8. Daniel Haines, 'A "Commonwealth Moment" in South Asian Decolonization', in Leslie James and Elisabeth Leake (eds), *Decolonization and the Cold War: Negotiating Independence* (London: Bloomsbury, 2015), pp. 185–202.
9. See Ian Talbot, 'The Pre-History of a Viceroyalty? Lord Mountbatten and South East Asia Command', in Ian Talbot (ed.), *The Independence of India and Pakistan: New Approaches and Reflections* (Karachi: Oxford University Press, 2013), pp. 164–186.
10. *Ibid.*, p. 176.
11. Mountbatten's accommodation to Asian nationalism led to clashes with Burma's Governor Reginald Dorman-Smith who had spent the Japanese occupation in exile at Simla. Talbot, 'The Pre-History of a Viceroyalty?', pp. 168–170.
12. Husain, *Mapping the End of Empire*, p. 150.
13. Andrew Roberts, *Eminent Churchillians* (London: Weidenfield and Nicholson, 1994), p. 89. The American author Stanley Wolpert is another trenchant critic

- see his book, *Shameful Flight: The Last Years of the British Empire in India* (New York: Oxford University Press, 2006).
14 Akbar S. Ahmed, *Jinnah, Pakistan and Islamic Identity: The Search for Saladin* (London: Routledge, 1997), p. 116. The cartoon by the 'painter of the East' appeared on 7 July 1948. Allegations about Lord Mountbatten regarding Sikhs and Boundary Award, L/PJ/10/119, India Office Records, British Library.
15 See Alan Campbell-Johnson, *Mission with Mountbatten* (London: Hamish Hamilton, 1985), p. 83 ff.
16 S. Banerjee, *The RIN Strike* (New Delhi: People's Publishing House, 1951); B. C. Dutt, *Mutiny of the Innocents* (Bombay: Sindhu Publications, 1971).
17 Telephone Message E. A. Simms to Intelligence Bureau 23 February 1946 in *Towards Freedom: Documents on the Movement for Independence in India 1946*, Vol. 1, ed. Sumit Sarkar (New Delhi: Oxford University Press, 2009), p. 83.
18 Report on the Recent Disturbances in the Punjab (March–April 1947), All India Congress Committee File No. G-10/1947, Nehru Memorial Museum and Library.
19 Dhanwantri and P. C. Joshi, *Bleeding Punjab Warns* (Bombay: People's Publishing House, 1947).
20 'Resolutions passed by the Congress Working Committee on 8 March 1947 at New Delhi', in *The Transfer of Power 1942-7*, Vol. 9: *The Fixing of a Time Limit 4 November 1946–22 March 1947*, ed. Penderel Moon (London: HMSO, 1980), Enclosure to Document 511, pp. 899–901.
21 For an assessment of Liaquat Ali Khan's 'People's Budget', see Raghabendra Chattopadhyay, 'Liaquat Ali Khan's Budget of 1947-8: The Tryst with Destiny', *Social Scientist* 16 (6/7) (1988), 77–89.
22 Judith M. Brown, *Nehru: A Political Life* (New Haven, CT: Yale University Press, 2003), pp. 167–168.
23 Nehru to Mountbatten, 1 May 1947, in *The Transfer of Power*, Vol. 10: *The Mountbatten Viceroyalty, Formulation of a Plan, 22 March–30 May 1947*, ed. Penderel Moon (London: HMSO, 1981), pp. 517–519.
24 Louis Mountbatten, 'Record of Interviews between Rear-Admiral Viscount Mountbatten of Burma and Mr Jinnah, 5 and 6 April 1947', in *The Transfer of Power*, Vol. 10: *The Mountbatten Viceroyalty, Formulation of a Plan, 22 March–30 May 1947*, ed. Penderel Moon (London: HMSO, 1981), pp. 137–139.
25 For further details see Ayesha Jalal, 'Inheriting the Raj: Jinnah and the Governor-Generalship Issue', *Modern Asian Studies* 19 (1) (1985), 29–53.
26 See Latif Ahmed Sherwani, *The Partition of India and Mountbatten* (Karachi: Council for Pakistan Studies, 1968).
27 The owner especially recommended it because of the spacious accommodation and high doors, which would give ease of entry to a tall gentleman like Mr Jinnah. She was prepared to sell the boat and the cook boat for Rs 28,000. Brenda Blencowe to M. A. Jinnah, 31 May 1947, in *Quaid-i-Azam Mohammad Ali Jinnah Papers*, First Series, Volume 2: *Pakistan in the Making: 3 June–30 June 1947*, ed. Z. H. Zaidi (Islamabad: Quaid-i-Azam Papers Project, National Archives of Pakistan, 1994), pp. 798–799.

28 See Lucy Chester, *On the Edge: Borders, Territory and Conflict in South Asia* (Manchester: Manchester University Press, 2008).
29 See Attlee to Mountbatten, 18 March 1947, Enclosure to Doc. 543, in *The Transfer of Power 1942–7*, Vol. 9: *The Fixing of a Time Limit, 4 November 1946–22 March 1947*, ed. Penderel Moon (London: HMSO, 1980), pp. 972–974.
30 Minutes of Viceroy's Sixth Staff Meeting – Addendum to No. 34, Uncirculated Record of Discussion No. 2, 31 March 1947, in *The Transfer of Power 1942–7*, Vol. 10: *The Mountbatten Viceroyalty, Formulation of a Plan, 22 March–30 May 1947*, ed. Penderel Moon (London: HMSO, 1981), pp. 49–51.
31 Full details can be accessed in: Records of Interviews with Lord Mountbatten March–April 1947, MB1/D69–70, Mountbatten Papers, University of Southampton.
32 Sucheta Mahajan argues to the contrary that Mountbatten forced partition on the Congress because of the Muslim League's insistence on Pakistan. Sucheta Mahajan, *Independence and Partition: The Erosion of Colonial Power in India* (New Delhi: Sage, 2000), pp. 290–291.
33 See Ian Talbot, 'The 1947 Partition Violence: Characteristics and Interpretations', in Radhika Mohamnram and Anindya Raychaudhri (eds), *Partitions and their Aftermaths: Violence, Memory, Living* (London: Rowman and Littlefield, 2019), pp. 1–23.
34 Ian Talbot, *Punjab and the Raj 1849–1947* (New Delhi: Manohar, 1988), p. 229. There were 58,000 members of the Hindu volunteer movement, the Rashtriya Swayam Sevak Sangh, in Punjab alone.
35 Saumitra Jha and Steven Wilkinson, 'Does Combat Experience Foster Organizational Skill? Evidence from Ethnic Cleansing during the Partition of South Asia', *American Political Science Review* 106 (4) (2012), 883–907.
36 See, for example, Jenkins to Mountbatten 30 July 1947, Note of a Long Talk with Giani Kartar Singh; Jenkins to Mountbatten 13 August 1947, MB1/D1 Mountbatten Papers, Special Collections, University of Southampton.
37 See Nick Lloyd, 'The Last Governor: Sir Evan Jenkins in the Punjab 1946–47', in Ian Talbot (ed.), *The Independence of India and Pakistan: New Approaches and Reflections* (Karachi: Oxford University Press, 2013), pp. 223–227.
38 Note by Abell, 26 March 1947, in *The Transfer of Power, 1942–7*, Vol. 10: *The Mountbatten Viceroyalty, Formulation of a Plan, 22 March–30 May 1947*, ed. Penderel Moon (London: HMSO, 1981), pp. 26–27.
39 Lloyd, 'Last Governor', p. 222.
40 For an Indian critique of Mountbatten's personal agenda, see Shashi Tharoor, *Inglorious Empire: What the British Did to India*, 2nd edn (London: Hurst, 2017), pp. 142–143.
41 Jenkins to Mountbatten, 7 May 1947, in *The Transfer of Power, 1942–7*, Vol. 10: *The Mountbatten Viceroyalty, Formulation of a Plan, 22 March–30 May 1947*, ed. Penderel Moon (London: HMSO, 1981), pp. 643–644.
42 Ian Talbot and Gurharpal Singh, *The Partition of India* (Cambridge: Cambridge University Press, 2009), pp. 161–163.
43 See Note by Taya Zinkin 18 January 1946, pp. 803–804, and Note 13 February 1946, pp. 951–961, both in *The Transfer of Power, 1942–7*, Vol. 6: *The Post-War*

Phase – New Moves by the Labour Government August 1 1945–March 22 1946, ed. Penderel Moon (London: HMSO, 1976).

44 Chiefs of Staff Meeting 12 April 1946, L/WS/1/1029, India Office Records, British Library.
45 Pethick-Lawrence Broadcast 16 May 1946, in *The Transfer of Power, 1942–7*, Vol. 7: *The Cabinet Mission 25 March–29 June 1945*, ed. Penderel Moon (London: HMSO, 1977), p. 593.
46 See Roger D. Long and Ian Talbot (eds), *India and World War I: A Centennial Assessment* (Abingdon: Routledge, 2018).
47 Paul Kennedy, *The Realities Behind Diplomacy* (London: Fontana, 1981), p. 18.
48 'Copy of a note by General Sir C. J. E. Auchinleck, concerning the Strategic Implications of the Inclusion of Pakistan in the British Commonwealth', 11 May 1946, MB1/D130/1, Mountbatten Papers, Hartley Library, University of Southampton.
49 On this see Anita Inder Singh, 'Imperial Defence and the Transfer of Power in India 1946–1947', *International History Review* 4 (4) (1982), 568–588; Anita Inder Singh, 'Keeping India in the Commonwealth: British Political and Military Aims 1947–49', *Journal of Contemporary History* 20 (3) (1985), 469–481.
50 Ismay to Attlee, 'Strategic Importance of India', 30 August 1946, PREM 8/467, National Archives, Kew.
51 On 12 May 1947, the Chiefs of Staff advised Attlee that Pakistan would be a 'tremendous' military asset to the Commonwealth. Chiefs of Staff Committee 12 May 1947, in *The Transfer of Power 1942–7*, Vol. 10: *The Mountbatten Viceroyalty, Formulation of a Plan, 22 March–30 May 1947*, ed. Penderel Moon (London: HMSO, 1981), pp. 789–792.
52 Husain, *Mapping the End of Empire*, pp. 96–102.
53 For a reflection on the importance of maintaining the Commonwealth connection and how this impacted on Mountbatten's response, see Y. Krishan, 'Mountbatten and the Partition of India', *History* 68 (February 1983), 22–38.
54 See 'C-in-C.'s Secretariat, Chiefs of Staff (India) Committee – Appreciation of the strategic value of India to the British Commonwealth of Nations (Final Paper), 13 July 1946, Enclosure to Doc. 26, in *The Transfer of Power*, Vol. 8: *The Interim Government 3 July–1 November 1946*, (ed.) Penderel Moon (London: HMSO, 1979), pp. 53–57.
55 See Alex von Tunzelmann, *Indian Summer: The Secret History of the End of an Empire* (New York: Henry Holt and Company, 2007), p. 167; Larry Collins and Dominique Lapierre, *Freedom at Midnight*, 4th edn (London: HarperCollins, 2017), p. 39: Nisid Hajari, *Midnight's Furies: The Deadly Legacy of India's Partition* (Boston, MA: Houghton Mifflin Harcourt, 2015), p. 93.
56 Singh, 'Imperial Defence', p. 572.
57 Hollis to Monteath 4 October 1946, in *Transfer of Power*, Vol. 8: *The Interim Government 3 July–1 November 1946*, ed. Penderel Moon (London: HMSO, 1979), pp. 661–662.

58 Viceroy's Staff meeting 19 April 1947, in *Transfer of Power 1942–7*, Vol. 10: *The Mountbatten Viceroyalty, Formulation of a Plan, 22 March–30 May 1947*, ed. Penderel Moon (London: HMSO, 1981), p. 329.
59 *Ibid.*; Record of an Interview between Rear-Admiral Viscount Mountbatten of Burma and Pandit Nehru, 24 March 1947, in *Transfer of Power 1942–7*, Vol. 10, pp. 11–13.
60 Singh, 'Keeping India in the Commonwealth', p. 472.
61 Rakesh Ankit, *The Kashmir Conflict: From Empire to the Cold War, 1945–66* (London: Routledge, 2016), p. 40.
62 See Jeffrey R Macris, *The Politics and Security of the Gulf: Anglo-American Hegemony and the Shaping of a Region* (Abingdon: Routledge, 2010), p. 116 ff.
63 Chandrika Kaul, '"At the Stroke of the Midnight Hour": Lord Mountbatten and the British Media at Indian Independence', *Te Round Table* 97 (398) (2008), 683.
64 *Ibid.*
65 Talbot and Singh, *The Partition of India*, p. 40.
66 See Robert Pearce, *Attlee's Labour Governments 1945–51* (London: Routledge, 1994), p. 62; Rhiannon Vickers, *The Labour Party and the World*, Vol. 1: *The Evolution of Labour's Foreign Policy, 1950–51* (Manchester: Manchester University Press, 2003), p. 164; Kenneth O. Morgan, *Labour in Power, 1945–1951*, 4th edn (Oxford: Oxford University Press, 1989), p. 193.
67 Cabinet Conclusions – Confidential Annex, India – Constitutional Position, 31 December 1946, CAB 128/8/8, National Archives, Kew.
68 Alan Campbell-Johnson retrospectively remarked that Mountbatten always wanted to 'popularise and in particular to photograph'. He was a believer in developing and using 'an image'. Alan Campbell-Johnson, *Mountbatten in Retrospect* (South Godstone: Spentech and Lancer, 1997), pp. 49–50.
69 Kaul, 'Midnight Hour', p. 685.
70 Talbot, 'The Pre-History of a Viceroyalty', pp. 178–181.
71 Campbell-Johnson, *Mission with Mountbatten*.
72 Chandrika Kaul, *Indian Independence, the British Media and Lord Mountbatten*, Occasional Publication 26 (1) (New Delhi: India International Centre, n.d.).
73 See Alan Campbell-Johnson, 'Mountbatten: The Triple Assignment, 1942–1948. A Recorder's Recollections', in *Mountbatten On the Record* (ed.) C. M. Woolgar (Southampton: Hartley Institute, 1997), pp. 1–21.
74 See Johnson to Joyce 25 June 1947, L/I/1/1456, India Office Records, British Library.
75 See Campbell-Johnson, *Mission with Mountbatten*.
76 Kaul, 'Midnight Hour', p. 688.
77 *Ibid.*
78 Viceroy to Listowel 16 July 1947, MSS.Eur.F.200/114.
79 John Turner, *Filming History: The Memoirs of John Turner Newsreel Cameraman* (London: British Universities Film and Video Council, 2001).

80 Alan Campbell-Johnson to Menon, 6 May 1948, Alan Campbell-Johnson Papers, MSS 350.A.3002, 3/2.5, University of Southampton.
81 Viceroy to the Secretary of State, Telegram 17 July 1947, Alan Campbell-Johnson Papers, MSS 350.A.3002, 3/2.5, University of Southampton.
82 Mountbatten to Sir Arthur Jarratt, 26 August 1947, MSS 350.A.3002, 3/2.5, University of Southampton.
83 Kaul, *Indian Independence*, p. 10.
84 Castleton Knight to Alan Campbell-Johnson 22 August 1947 MSS 350.A.3002, 3/2.5, University of Southampton.
85 Johnson to Joyce L/I/1/515, India Office records, British Library.
86 Kaul, *Indian Independence*, p. 3.
87 Kaul, 'Midnight Hour', p. 689.
88 Collins and Lapierre, *Freedom at Midnight*, p. 60.
89 See Ian Talbot, 'The Mountbatten Viceroyalty Revisited: Themes and Controversies', in C. M. Woolgar (ed.), *Mountbatten on the Record* (Southampton: Hartley Institute, University of Southampton, 1997), pp. 53–74.
90 Cited in Campbell-Johnson, *Mission with Mountbatten*, p. 221.
91 Wolpert, *Shameful Flight*, p. 1.
92 Clement Attlee, 'India Policy, Memorandum by the Prime Minister', 22 May 1947, in *The Transfer of Power, 1942–7*, Vol. 10: *The Mountbatten Viceroyalty, Formulation of a Plan, 22 March–30 May 1947*, ed. Penderel Moon (London: HMSO, 1981), pp. 949–951.
93 On Mountbatten's fascination with film and its role in his career, see Adrian Smith, 'Mountbatten Goes to the Movies: Promoting the Heroic Myth Through Cinema', *Historical Journal of Film, Radio and Television* 26 (3) (2006), 395–416.
94 Pamela Mountbatten and India Hicks, *India Remembered* (London: Anova Books, 2007), p. 66.
95 See M. Lipton and John Finn, *The Erosion of a Relationship* (London: Oxford University Press, 1975).
96 Haines, 'Commonwealth Moment', pp. 185–202.
97 See Kattan's suggestive analysis: Victor Kattan, 'The Empire Departs: The Partitions of British India, Mandate Palestine and the Dawn of Self-Determination in the Third World', *Asian Journal of Middle Eastern and Islamic Studies* 12 (3) (2018), 304–327. DOI: 10.1080/25765949.2018.1514173.
98 See Chapters 5 and 6 of Talbot and Singh, *The Partition of India*.
99 Robin Jeffrey, 'The Punjab Boundary Force and the Problem of Order, August 1947', *Modern Asian Studies* 8 (4) (1974), 491–520.

2

The paradigmatic partition? The Pakistan demand revisited

Ayesha Jalal

Nations need heroes and Pakistanis have a right to be proud of their greatest hero: the Quaid-i-Azam Mohammad Ali Jinnah. But popular memories too need to be informed by some bare facts and meaningful ideas. Fed on improbable myths and the limitations of the 'great man' approach to history, Pakistanis have been constrained from engaging in an informed and open debate on whether their country merits being called Jinnah's Pakistan. Is Jinnah at all relevant to the current Pakistani predicament? Even the most approximate answer requires training our sights on matters that most concern Pakistanis – rule of law and a balance between state institutions that is conducive to social justice, economic opportunities and peaceful coexistence. Fed on state-sponsored national yarns about the past, Pakistanis are at a loss how to settle matters of national identity and the nature of the state – democratic or authoritarian, secular or Islamic. The rise of Hindu majoritarianism in secular India and seemingly unending convulsions of religious bigotry in Islamic Pakistan is causing dismay, confusion and disenchantment across large sections of the citizenry across both sides of the international border demarcated in 1947.

This is why it is all the more important to reassess the legacy of a man who is universally held responsible for a partition that he had assiduously tried avoiding. To do so one has to go beyond the simplistic distinction between the secular and the religious on which so many of the national myths of India and Pakistan are based. 'Other men are lenses through which we read our own minds', the American philosopher Ralph Waldo Emerson once said, but the great man is one who 'inhabits a higher sphere of thought' and 'keep[s] a vigilant eye on many sources of error'.[1] Though sceptical of approaches to history restricted to studies of great men, it is difficult to disagree with Emerson, an ardent expositor of biography, that we can learn more from those who were truly great than those making a mockery of being great in our own times.

Over forty years of research and writing on Mohammad Ali Jinnah leaves me in no doubt that the tension between the creator's vision and where Pakistan stands today can help restore perspective on some of the key challenges now confronting us. There can be no dispassionate understanding of Jinnah's place in history without salvaging his political career from the cobwebs of prejudice and partisan comment about his role in India's partition. Restoring Jinnah to his proper place in history has faced methodological, not empirical, difficulties.[2] The 'great man' approach of his biographers, hagiographers and critics has obfuscated the extent to which Jinnah was shaped by larger dynamics in Muslim and Congress politics at both the provincial and the All-India levels. A skilful lawyer who earned the respect of his peers at the Bar, he imagined himself as someone who could bridge communitarian differences which, in his opinion, were the single biggest obstacle to India winning freedom. Fate deemed otherwise. Like a professional arbitrator, Jinnah argued the conflicting brief of his diverse Muslim constituents to the best of his ability. As a politician who had set his sights on wresting power from the British at the centre, Jinnah had to contend with the different pulls and pushes of Muslim politics in the provinces. Clashing interests of Muslims in provinces where they were in a majority and provinces where they were hopelessly outnumbered confounded the task. Jinnah not only tried reconciling differences among his own constituents but saw that an agreement with the Congress covering the whole of India would have to be found once the British conceded power at the centre. By becoming the Muslim spokesman, he hoped to negotiate a constitutional arrangement based on a sharing of power between the Congress and the Muslim League, representing Hindus and Muslims respectively.[3] Even 'great men' make history under certain constraints. Many find it remarkable that Jinnah 'made history' despite overwhelming odds. This explains the attention given to his role in the creation of Pakistan. If there has been a bit too much focus on the history Jinnah made, there is still much to be said about the history that made Jinnah.

The history that made Jinnah

The strikingly handsome Mahomedali Jinnahbhai was not yet sixteen when he stepped off the boat into a Britain bristling with the liberal ideas of John Morley, the British Liberal statesman, writer and newspaper editor. 'I grasped that liberalism', he confessed, 'which became part of my life and thrilled me very much.'[4] When not engrossed in study at law libraries or the British Museum, he went to the House of Commons to hear William Gladstone,

Joseph Chamberlain and Lord Balfour dilate on domestic and international policy. Jinnah's first brush with real politics came when Dadabhai Naoroji, the veteran Parsi leader of the Congress, entered the electoral fray in Britain as the Liberal candidate for Central Finsbury. Stung by Lord Salisbury's comment that Naoroji, a 'black man', could not possibly be the choice of the voters, Jinnah threw himself into the election campaign with a 'vengeance' and became 'an uncompromising enemy of all forms of colour bar and racial prejudice'.[5] Naoroji won by the slimmest of majorities, but the election of the first Indian to the British House of Commons was nothing short of a milestone. Jinnah sat transfixed in the Visitors' Gallery listening to the 'Grand Old Man of India' give his maiden speech, saluting the British tradition of free expression which had given an Indian like him the right to state his opinions 'openly and fearlessly'.[6] Acknowledging his debt to Naoroji, Jinnah noted that 'without free speech a nation is like a rose bush that is planted in a place where there is neither sunshine nor air'.[7]

After returning to India and starting a promising career as a lawyer in Bombay, Jinnah acquired a reputation in the legal fraternity for his no-nonsense attitude and quick temper. He could not suffer fools, and bullies less so. A committed constitutionalist of a moderate and liberal disposition, Jinnah developed an affinity for Gopal Krishna Gokhale whom he deeply admired and considered as his role model. The life of the moderate Congress leader was the best example of how 'a single man' could 'help his country and his people, and how millions could draw from him true leadership'.[8] After winning elections to the central assembly on a reserved Muslim seat from Bombay, Jinnah displayed his debating skills while proving to be a stickler for the rule of law. Among his abiding criticisms of the colonial state was its failure to enforce laws consistent with human dignity. He savaged the Rowlatt Act of 1919, which perpetuated wartime ordinances as peacetime legislations and denied Indians the right of habeas corpus. Jinnah resigned from the Imperial Legislative Council in protest, calling the Act an 'obnoxious' and coercive measure which no civilised government could pass during a time of peace. An 'overfretful and incompetent bureaucracy' that was 'neither responsible to the people nor in touch with real public opinion' had undermined the fundamental principles of justice and violated the constitutional rights of the people at a time when there was no real danger to the state.[9]

In a memorable speech in the central legislature, Jinnah made an impassioned defence of Bhagat Singh, who had hurled a bomb inside the same assembly building. The occasion was the young Sikh revolutionary's hunger strike in Lahore jail against prison conditions. Opposing the government's move to amend the Code of Criminal Procedure to break the hunger strike,

Jinnah castigated the British for seeking a statute establishing a general principle to score victory in a particular case:

> The man who goes on hunger strike has a soul. He is moved by that soul, and he believes in the justice of his cause. He is no ordinary criminal, who is guilty of a cold-blooded, sordid wicked crime.[10]

Describing himself as 'a patient cool-headed man', he told the colonial masters that thousands of patriotic young men outside were incensed by 'this damnable system of government, which is resented by the people'.[11] 'Is there today', he asked, 'in any part of the globe a civilized government that is engaged day in and day out, week in and week out, month in and month out, in prosecuting their people?'[12] Indians had taken to the bomb after 1906 because their aspirations had not been met.

There is no doubt that after the Muslim League's election debacle in 1937, Jinnah made a conscious effort to display his Muslim identity. On key public occasions, he donned the *sherwani* – the traditional Muslim dress – rather than his well-tailored Western suits, and made more of an effort to appear as a mass politician. This was in some contrast to the days when his oratorical powers were restricted to the quiet of council chambers in the central legislature. But the aloofness that characterised his earlier life did not give way to a new-found affinity with the teeming multitude. A champion of mass education as the key to the democratisation and freedom of India, Jinnah lacked the populist touch of a Gandhi.[13] Solitary in disposition, he used the distance between himself and his followers to command esteem and, most importantly, authority. Every bit the politician, Jinnah had a keen sense of timing and spectacle. Making the most of the adulation showered upon him by Muslims, he launched a powerful challenge against the Congress's claim to speak on behalf of All-Indians. However, even while banding with segments of the Muslim *ulema* for political purposes, he remained to the core a constitutionalist with a distaste for rabble rousers who made cynical uses of religion. He distanced himself from the humdrum of theological disputes about divinity, prophecy or ritual. 'I know of no religion apart from human activity', he had written to Gandhi on 1 January 1940, since it 'provides a moral basis for all other activities.' Religion for him was meaningless if it did not mean identifying with the whole of mankind and 'that I could not do unless I took part in politics'.[14] Jinnah's expansive humanism is in stark contrast with the shocking disregard for the freedom of religious conscience in the country he created, a result of the political gamesmanship resorted to by authoritarian rulers and the so-called ideologues of Islam in postcolonial Pakistan.

In terms of his most deep-seated political values and objectives, Jinnah was remarkably consistent throughout his long and chequered political career. He had begun his journey as a Congressman seeking a share of power for Indians at the All-India Centre. Since Muslims were a minority in the limited system of representation in colonial India, he became an ardent champion of minority rights as a necessary step towards a Hindu–Muslim concordat and Congress–League cooperation. The provincial bias in British constitutional reforms after 1919 tested the resilience of a centralist politician with All-India ambitions. As a constitutionalist of rare skill and vision, Jinnah tried reconciling communitarian and provincial interests while holding out an olive branch to the Congress. While his insistence on national status for Indian Muslims became absolute after 1940, the demand for a separate and sovereign state was open to negotiation until the late summer of 1946. Jinnah was acutely aware that almost as many members of the Muslim nation would reside in Hindustan as in the specifically Muslim homeland. As Zafrulla Khan had noted in his memorandum in 1940, a partition resulting in an exchange of population was 'utterly impracticable and would result in nothing but misery and suffering'.[15] The claim to nationhood was not an inevitable overture to completely separate statehood. An analytical distinction between a division of sovereignty within India and a partition of the provinces enables a precise understanding of the demand for a 'Pakistan'. On achieving Pakistan, Jinnah was categorical that equal citizenship and an assurance of minority rights would form the basis of the new state.

It was mainly religion as social demarcator rather than concerns with religion as faith, not the dream of an Islamic theocracy, which informed the All-India Muslim League's demand for a Pakistan in March 1940. In putting forward a claim to nationhood, Indian Muslims were decidedly revolting against minoritarianism, caricatured as 'religious communalism'. As Jinnah confessed, the idea of being a minority had been around for so long that 'we have got used to it ... these settled notions sometimes are very difficult to remove'. But the time had come to unsettle the notion since the 'word "Nationalist" has now become the play of conjurers in politics'.[16]

While the insistence on a national status for Indian Muslims was absolute, the demand for a separate and sovereign state and its relationship with a Hindustan containing almost as many Muslims remained open to negotiation until the late summer of 1946. The claim that Muslims constituted a 'nation' was not incompatible with a federal or confederal state structure covering the whole of India. But for the federal idea to be acceptable, the logic of majoritarianism and minoritarianism had to be abandoned and the fact of contested sovereignty acknowledged. In keeping with the better part of India's history, the overture to shared sovereignty enunciated by Jinnah and the League seemed the best way of tackling the dilemma posed by the absence of any neat equation between Muslim identity and territory. With 'nations' straddling states, the boundaries between them had to be permeable and flexible, not impenetrable and absolute. This is why Jinnah and the League were to remain implacably opposed to a partition of Punjab and Bengal along religious lines, even while furthering the cause of a political division of India between 'Pakistan' and 'Hindustan'.[17]

In one of the more unforgettable contemporary recollections of Mohammad Ali Jinnah, Beverley Nichols, in *Verdict on India*, described the lanky and stylishly dressed barrister as the 'most important man in Asia'. Looking every bit like a gentleman of Spain, of the old diplomatic school, the monocle-wearing leader of the All-India Muslim League held a pivotal place in India's future. 'If Gandhi goes, there is Nehru, Rajagopalachari, Patel and a dozen others. But if Jinnah goes, who is there?' Without the Quaid-i-Azam to steer the course, the Muslim League was a divisive and potentially explosive force that 'might run completely off the rails, and charge through India with fire and slaughter'; it might even 'start another war'. As long as Jinnah was around, nothing disastrous was likely to happen and so, Nichols quipped, 'a great deal hangs on the grey silk cord of that monocle'.[18]

If the British journalist overstated Jinnah's importance, he had put his finger on an essential piece of the subcontinental political puzzle on the eve of British decolonisation in India. Jinnah was a crucial link between the Congress and the Muslim League, which if broken could catapult India into disaster. While regaling journalists at a tea party in his honour at Allahabad in April 1942, two years after the formal orchestration of the demand for Pakistan by the Muslim League, Jinnah had emphatically denied harbouring the 'slightest ill-will' against Hindus or any other community. Drawing an analogy between himself and the first man to appear on the street with an umbrella, only to be laughed at and scorned by the crowd that had had never seen an umbrella before, he said self-assuredly, 'You may laugh at me', but the time will soon come when 'you will not only understand what the Umbrella is but ... use it to the advantage of everyone of you'.[19]

Jinnah's prediction that posterity would come to look kindly on the umbrella he had unfurled in the form of his demand for Pakistan remains unrealised. Confusing the end result with what he had been after all along, his admirers and detractors alike hold him responsible for dismembering the unity of India. But then, the Pakistan that emerged in 1947 was a mere shadow of what he had wanted. In the event it was, ironically enough, the Congress backed by the extreme right-wing Hindu Mahasabha which plumped for a partition of the two main Muslim-majority provinces of India, conceding a Pakistan which both in its shape and form had been rejected out of hand by its proclaimed architect on two separate occasions during the decade of the 1940s. Let down by his own followers, outmanoeuvred by the Congress and squeezed by Britain's last Viceroy, Jinnah was made to accept a settlement he had rejected in 1944 and 1946. His death in September 1948 deprived Pakistan of a much-needed steadying hand at the helm during an uncertain and perilous time. With no one of Jinnah's stature and constitutional acumen around to read the riot act, constitutional propriety and strict adherence to the rule of law were early casualties of the withering struggle between the newly created centre and the provinces, as well as the main institutions of the state.

The pity of partition

There has been a growing recognition among sections of the scholarly community in India that Pakistan was the price that had to be paid to enable the Congress to inherit British India's unitary centre and integrate the princely states.[20] History has a way of laying bare what is hidden or suppressed by individual and collective memory – an intrinsic unity in division that no amount of mechanical cartography can efface. Seventy years after partition and independence, and nearly fifty years since the separation of Pakistan's eastern wing and the establishment of Bangladesh, the long history that binds the subcontinent's diverse cultures and peoples into a whole has not receded into oblivion. It is, if anything, more present than ever, a veritable summons for those with daring to penetrate the veils that have been used to deny interconnections, whether in the name of region or nation.

Rammanohar Lohia recalled a private conversation in Noakhali with Nehru at the instance of Mahatma Gandhi in November 1946: 'Mr. Nehru spoke of the water, slime, bush and tree', Lohia wrote, 'that he found everywhere in East Bengal. He said that was not the India he or I knew and wanted with some vehemence to cut East Bengal away from the main land of India.' Lohia found this to be an extraordinary observation, and commented:

> These reasons of geography might under other circumstances prove how necessary it is for the Ganga and Jamuna plains to stay joined with their luxuriant terminus. But once the idea of partition came to be accepted as a condition precedent to India's freedom, no matter that the acceptance was still very private and not even communicated to Mahatma Gandhi, the geography of East Bengal could well become abominable.[21]

Much the same kind of thinking appears to have guided the view expressed at a major science conference held in Delhi in the early 1950s that the separation of Burma, India and Pakistan was a 'geological, geographical and economic crime' that flew in the face of nature and was unlikely to last for more than a century or two. The furies of nature have as yet failed to shake the resolve of the postcolonial states to uphold their hostile postures and reject calls for cooperation across arbitrarily drawn borders. It remains to be seen whether human nature or mother nature will have the final laugh.

'Whose blood is being shed with such heartlessness every day?', the Urdu short story writer Saadat Hasan Manto rued as he tried making sense of the independence celebrations in Bombay on 14 August 1947. Pakistan and India had been declared separate countries. There was public rejoicing: cries of 'Hindustan Zindabad' and 'Pakistan Zindabad' struck a discordant note with a frenzy of murder, rape and arson in the name of religion. Confused and disoriented, Manto could not decide whether India or Pakistan was his homeland. 'Where would they burn or bury the bones from which the vultures had stripped off the flesh of religion?' And now that they were free of servitude, what would the people of the subcontinent dream of? Would they have their own slaves now? To each of these big questions there was an Indian answer, a Pakistani answer and a British answer. The *batwara*, or partition, may have divided lives and drawn lines of blood in the hearts and minds of people. But the arbitrary lines drawn by the British on the map were not visible to anyone's eye. Some things could never be divided, like the common literary heritage of the subcontinent and bonds of friendship. The pity of partition was not that instead of one country there were now two – independent India and independent Pakistan – but that 'human beings in both countries were slaves, slaves of bigotry ... slaves of religious passions, slaves of animal instincts and barbarity'.[22]

Baffled by the furies let loose by the advent of a much-vaunted freedom, Manto left Bombay in January 1948 for Lahore with more questions than answers: 'Should we wash our hands of humanity?' 'Have we lost faith in that thing called conscience?', he wondered. Partition's unpardonable horrors were a blot on the face of humanity. The fanfare of official nationalism covered up the tragedy of partition with the result that human bestiality was finding perfect ground for nurture to become ever more audacious in its expression. Not a day passed without a human being getting killed by a fellow human being. 'Why are these few individuals so murderous', and 'why are their hearts and minds so possessed by murder and violence?'[23]

The fundamental questions Manto asked about the nature of the postcolonial transition continue to resonate today: Weren't the basic problems confronting Indians and Pakistanis the same? Was Urdu going to become extinct in India and what form would it take in Pakistan? Would Pakistan become a religious state? Would loyalty to the state confer citizens the right to freely criticise the government? The paradox of freedom from colonial rule in the subcontinent that Manto's discerning literary gaze captured so evocatively has mutated over the past seven decades into bewildering permutations and combinations. Partition may have become a distant memory for many and its invocations in public discourse limited to scoring points on the grid of patriotism. But its absent presences in everyday life across the great divide of 1947 are indicators of its historical significance, not merely as an event that occurred seventy years ago but a process that is very much part of the present. An ongoing process with neither end nor beginning, partition structures the postcolonial South Asian experience. An institutionalised form of dividing and disconnecting, partition has been the founding myth of postcolonial nation-states and ferrets out people, communities and linguistic cultures that were once historically indivisible. If there are multiple slippages, elisions and contestations in narratives about the great divide that occurred seventy years ago, there are strange silences about its constant re-enactments in the postcolonial nation-states of South Asia.

The god of nationalism

'The Nation [with a capital N]', Rabindranath Tagore had warned in his little book, *Nationalism*, in 1917, 'with all its paraphernalia of power and prosperity, its flags and pious hymns, its blasphemous prayers in the Churches, and the literary mock thunders of its patriotic bragging, cannot hide the fact that the Nation is the greatest evil for the Nation, that all its precautions are against it, and any new birth of its fellow in the world is always followed in its mind by the dread of a new peril.' As the self-love of Western nations danced to the clash of steel in the killing fields of Europe and the Middle East, the Bengali poet warned his fellow countrymen against the hubris of jingoistic pride that was embodied in the model of the modern nation-state:

> Keep watch, India…
> Let your crown be of humility, your freedom the freedom of the soul.
> Build God's throne daily upon the ample bareness of your poverty
> And know that what is huge is not great and pride is not ever lasting.[24]

While Tagore's songs have become the national anthems of two of postcolonial South Asia's nation-states, India and Bangladesh, the spirit of his message has remained largely unheeded.

Muhammad Iqbal, the Punjabi poet-philosopher who wrote in Urdu in the early twentieth century and is generally considered to be the visionary of Pakistan, had shared many of Tagore's concerns about the dangers of worshiping the god of nationalism. On the roots of conflict, however, Iqbal had a finer insight. In his considered view, it was nationalism that gave rise to the 'relativity of religions', the notion that religions were territorially specific and unsuited to the temperament of other nations. It was nationalism, and not religion, which by compartmentalising people into different nations was the source of modern conflicts.[25]

This point of view clashes with common perceptions of religion's all-pervasive role in South Asia. The tendency to interpret the complex politics of the subcontinent through the prism of essentialised religious communities locked in grim conflict since time immemorial gives a very distorted perspective on the subcontinent's conflicting politics of identity and discourses of contested sovereignty. Generating heated controversies among scholars quite as much as the political practitioners of postcolonial India, Pakistan and Bangladesh, the debate on the question of religion continues to be informed in significant measure by the colonial encounter and has been intrinsic to the social processes shaping the politics of democratisation and decolonisation in the region. Lying at the cutting edge of the politics of difference – that great builder of walls, both imaginary and real – religion's epistemological and historical meaning in colonial and postcolonial South Asia has to be fully grasped in all its multifaceted nuances and textures. Using religion loosely and uncritically, as so much of the discourse on the politics of the subcontinent is prone to do, is to become entangled in a web of hopeless confusion. We need to ask ourselves whether the category of religion, on which so many scholars have written meaningfully and perceptively, should continue to be used in blanket terms to describe the fault lines of freedom?

The binary opposition between secular nationalism and religious communalism is certainly inadequate for such an enterprise. Turning heterogeneities into homogeneities and conflicts into unities, both terms have given currency to a culture of labelling driven by shifting political agendas, not illuminated political dynamics in South Asia. Scholars of the subcontinent, though not its politicians and officialdom, have been seeking to go beyond the morass of the communitarian mode of analysis which had locked interpretations of the subcontinent's history and politics into a simplistic distinction between 'secular' and 'communal'. The dynamics of centre and region, as well as nationalism and religious communitarianism, in contemporary India and Pakistan plainly defy such neat distinctions.

It seems more prudent to take stock of the subcontinent's past and present without making facile distinctions between the religious and the secular, the emotional and the rational, or nationalist and communalist. Mental walls based on these binary oppositions have been quite as resolute in resisting a meaningful dialogue across the great divide of 1947 as the narrow interests fuelling the politics of national difference in the subcontinent. Disturbing these neat constructs of the mind allows for more creative approaches to not just the recent history but also the current political tendencies informing South Asia's trajectory in the twenty-first century. For purposes of conceptual clarity, it is useful to remind ourselves of the subtle but important difference between religion as faith and religion as a social demarcator of identity. While religion as faith can be seen to be a matter of personal belief, religion as social demarcator aims specifically at establishing boundaries with other communities. Tagore's critique of the aggressive nationalisms of modern nation-states along with his promotion of universalism was not devoid of a religious sensibility. Iqbal envisaged Islam as a universal religion which was neither national and racial, nor individual and private, but purely human. Religion as social demarcator, as both men knew from personal experience, was a mere label, not an accurate reflection of the religiosity of the individual believer, far less of the community or the 'nation'. Both men in their different ways affirmed the inextricable overlap between temporal and spiritual life. All human life is spiritual, Iqbal had argued. There was no such thing as a profane world. In their different ways, Tagore and Iqbal had pinpointed the dangers of letting religion as social demarcator appropriate the meaning, scope and spirit of religion.

The British decision to cap the welter of social identities constituting the colourful mosaic of India with the overarching category of religion had monumental consequences, particularly in regions like Bengal and Punjab where the politics of cultural differences required imaginative accommodations. The colonial penchant for defining majority and minority by privileging the religious distinction had profound political consequences. More a demarcator of social difference than a matter of faith, religion in late colonial India had manifestations that were more profane than sacred. Collapsing religion as difference with religion as faith has served to compound the ideological dilemmas of not only Islamic Pakistan but secular democratic India. Instead of translating Tagore's and Iqbal's ideas into practice, it has proved easier for the managers of the postcolonial states in South Asia to appropriate them for their respective national agendas. If the differences between Mohandas Karamchand Gandhi and Mohammad Ali Jinnah give a quintessential glimpse into the contrasts between the acknowledged fathers of independent India and Pakistan, the similarities between Tagore and Iqbal capture the as yet unrealised but potentially dynamic ability of these two congenital rivals to strike at some common chords. That potential unfortunately was not realised in the bitter endgame of the British Raj. As Manto had observed, 'previously religion used to reside in the heart, now it resided in caps' – whether the Gandhi or the Jinnah cap – 'long live caps'.[26]

A partition of India along self-professedly religious lines has lent a teleological tendency to the processes of historical retrieval. Religion, neither adequately problematised nor carefully contextualised, has contributed to the perpetuation of a most awkward binary opposition between 'nationalism' and 'communalism' separating the temporal from the spiritual realms. So what did religion as faith have to do with the politics of difference in late colonial India? Very little, it would seem, insofar as the main stumbling block to evolving a framework for a united India were power-sharing arrangements between members of different religious communities at the All-India level, as well as in key regions like Punjab and Bengal. Prior to the British conquest, relations between regional peoples and the sovereign power had never been defined wholly by religion. Despite a long history of creatively accommodating multiple levels of sovereignty, the renegotiation of the terms for sharing power in an independent India saw the privileging of a rigid and monolithic conception of territorial sovereignty based on a singular and homogenising idea of the 'nation'. An insistence on the unity of the 'nation', and the corresponding refusal to countenance internal differences, eventually paved the way for a partition of the subcontinent along ostensibly religious lines.

Conclusion

In grappling with the changing social and political dynamics shaping the nexus between religion and nation, as well as region and centre, the newly independent nation-states of India and Pakistan (and after 1971 also Bangladesh) have made selective appropriations of history to project their official nationalisms. While independent India embraced the ideal of a secular and inclusionary nationalism, Pakistan justified its creation by projecting a distinctive Islamic identity. While the claims and counterclaims of officially subsidised historians have freely invoked the partisan spirit to sustain the logic of their respective versions of nationalism, emotionally scarred memories of the loss of loved ones as well as homes and livelihoods have confounded the problem of separating myth from history in explaining why India was partitioned along mainly religious lines for the first time in its millennia-old history. The communitarian holocaust which accompanied the partition of India is often explained in terms of religious passions or 'communalism'. Yet even the ghastly violence in Punjab during 1947 had less to do with religion as such than a scramble over *zar* (wealth), *zameen* (land) and *zan* (women) within the patriarchal structures of rural society as the British Raj crumbled. That was what turned separating at close quarters into such a colossal human tragedy.[27] What does religion have to do with the killing of innocents?[28] One has to question a terminology that ends up implicating entire communities of religion with the bigoted and aggressive activities of the few.

Repeated suspensions of the democratic process by military regimes have ensured that, even after seven decades of independence, Pakistanis are bitterly disagreed on the principles and practices of constitutional government as well as the sharing of rights and responsibilities between state and citizen. So while there is no denying the centrality of Mohammad Ali Jinnah's iconographic location in Pakistani national consciousness, there is a gaping chasm between the nationalist icon and the savvy politician. Across the 1947 divide, clashing representations of Jinnah and his politics highlight the fissures in the Indian national imaginary. The unanimous rage that exploded as Indian nationalism, whether of the 'secular' or the 'communal' variety, against Jaswant Singh's book on the Muslim League leader is evidence of Jinnah's negative standing in the Indian psyche.[29]

Left to an adoring following in Pakistan and equally impassioned detractors in India, the clear-headed lawyer who never missed a cue has been reduced to a jumble of contradictions that mostly cancel each other out. Jinnah's demonisation in the Indian nationalist pantheon as the communal monster who divided mother India contrasts with his positive representation in Pakistan as a revered son of Islam, even an esteemed religious leader (*maulana*), who strove to safeguard Muslim interests in India. Misleading representations of one of modern South Asia's leading politicians might not have withstood the test of history if they did not serve the nationalist self-projections of both India and Pakistan.

The Quaid-i-Azam, who opposed the partition of Punjab and Bengal until mid-1947, was checkmated at the endgame of the Raj by the votaries of unitary and monolithic sovereignty. The precedent for such partitions had been set with the partition of the province of Ulster in the aftermath of the First World War. In that sense, the partition of India was not paradigmatic, but may have tilted the balance against a binational state and towards partition in Palestine. Jinnah's constitutional insights into the imperative of forging a new Indian union once the British relinquished power at the centre resonated well with a long South Asian political tradition of layered and shared sovereignties. The four decades since the end of the Second World War were the heyday of indivisible sovereignty across the globe. Since the late 1980s there has been a perceptible weakening in the hold of that dogma. Jinnah's legacy is especially pertinent to the enterprise of rethinking sovereignty in South Asia and beyond in the twenty-first century. If Pakistan and India can shed the deadweight of the colonial inheritance of non-negotiable sovereignty and hard borders which has been at the root of so many of their animosities, a South Asian union may yet come into being under the capacious cover of Jinnah's metaphorical umbrella. His hope that Hindus, quite as much as Muslims, would one day bless the memory of his name has not yet been unequivocally fulfilled. But moves in that direction have been in evidence more recently. The Indian Prime Minister, Atal Behari Vajpayee, made a point of visiting the venue where the Lahore

Resolution of 1940 was adopted by the Muslim League. This was followed by the Hindu nationalist leader Lal Krishna Advani's homage to the founding father of Pakistan at his mausoleum in Karachi. More than seven decades after partition, it is worth recalling the Bengali Congress leader Sarat Chandra Bose's obituary comment, paying 'tribute to the memory of one who was great as a lawyer, once great as a Congressman, great as a leader of Muslims, great as a world politician and diplomat and greatest of all, as a man of action'.[30]

Notes

1. Ralph Waldo Emerson, 'Uses of Great Men', *The Works of Ralph Waldo Emerson* (New York: Black's Readers Service, n.d.), p. 424.
2. There are several examples of works that take Pakistan's official narrative on Jinnah at face value or cherry-pick his public statements to counter his many critics. For a recent publication by a political scientist that relies primarily on Jinnah's various speeches and statements that are in the public domain rather than offering any new historical evidence, see Ishtiaq Ahmed, *Jinnah: His Successes, Failure and Role in History* (Gurgaon: Penguin Viking, 2020).
3. For an analysis of Jinnah's political strategy, see Ayesha Jalal, *The Sole Spokesman: Jinnah, the Muslim League, and the Demand for Pakistan* (Cambridge: Cambridge University Press, 1985).
4. Hector Bolitho, *Jinnah: Creator of Pakistan* (New York: MacMillan, 1955), p. 9.
5. Fatima Jinnah, 'A Sister's Recollections', in *Pakistan, Past and Present: A Comprehensive Study Published in Commemoration of the Centenary of the Birth of the Founder of Pakistan* (London: Stacey International, 1977), pp. 42–54, at p. 46.
6. Bolitho, *Jinnah*, p. 9.
7. Jinnah, 'A Sister's Recollections', p. 46.
8. H. V. Hodson, 'A Political Biography', in Jinnah, *Pakistan, Past and Present*, pp. 14–38, at p. 15.
9. *Speeches and Statements of the Quaid-i-Azam Mohammad Ali Jinnah [1911–34 and 1947–48]*, 2nd edn, ed. M. Rafique Afzal (Lahore: Research Society of Pakistan, 1973), pp. 112–113.
10. Syed Sharifuddin Pirzada (ed.), *The Collected Works of Quaid-e-Azam Mohammad Ali Jinnah, 1926–1931*, vol. III (Karachi: East and West Publishing Company, 1984–86), p. 390.
11. *Ibid.*
12. *Ibid.*, pp. 389–390, 399.
13. For biographical accounts of Jinnah, see Stanley Wolpert, *Jinnah of Pakistan* (New York: Oxford University Press, 1984); Yaseer Latif Hamdani, *Jinnah: A Life* (New Delhi: Pan Macmillan, 2020).

14 Jinnah to Gandhi, 21 January 1940, in Syed Sharifuddin Pirzada (ed.), *Quaid-i-Azam Correspondence* (Karachi: East–West Publishing, 1977), p. 98.
15 Zafrulla Khan, 'Separation Scheme', memorandum submitted to the Viceroy, March 6, 1940, Mss Eur F 125/135, Indian Office Library.
16 Jinnah's presidential address to the All-India Muslim League in March 1940, in Syed Sharifuddin Pirzada (ed.), *Foundations of Pakistan: The All-India Muslim League Documents, 1906–1947* (Karachi: National Publishing House Limited, 1970), vol. 11, p. 335.
17 For an analysis of Jinnah's political strategy, see Jalal, *The Sole Spokesman*.
18 Beverley Nichols, *Verdict on India* (London: Jonathan Cape, 1944), pp. 189–190.
19 *Speeches, Statements & Messages of the Quaid-e-Azam*, ed. Yusufi (Lahore: Bazm-e-Iqbal, 1996), vol. iii, p. 1559.
20 See Jalal, *The Sole Spokesman*; Sugata Bose, *Agrarian Bengal: Economy, Social Structure and Politics, 1919–1947* (Cambridge: Cambridge University Press, 1986); Joya Chatterji, *Bengal Divided: Hindu Communalism and Partition, 1932–1947* (Cambridge: Cambridge University Press, 1994); Semanti Ghosh, *Different Nationalisms: Bengal, 1905–1947* (New Delhi: Oxford University Press, 2017); Neeti Nair, *Changing Homelands: Hindu Politics and the Partition of India* (Cambridge, MA: Harvard University Press, 2011).
21 Rammanohar Lohia, *Guilty Men of India's Partition* (Allahabad: Kitabistan, 1960), p. 17.
22 Ayesha Jalal, *The Pity of Partition: Manto's Life, Times, and Work across the India–Pakistan Divide* (Princeton, NJ: Princeton University Press, 2013), pp. 129, 137.
23 *Ibid.*, p. 147.
24 Rabindranath Tagore, 'Sunset of the Century', in *Nationalism* (London: MacMillan, 1918), pp. 417–422.
25 Iqbal's response to Maulana Husain Ahmad Madani: Latif Ahmad Sherwani (ed.), *Speeches and Statements of Iqbal*, 4th edn (Lahore: Iqbal Academy Pakistan, 1995), p. 262.
26 Jalal, *The Pity of Partition*, p. 126.
27 On partition violence see Ayesha Jalal, *Self and Sovereignty: Individual and Community in South Asian Islam Since 1850* (London: Routledge, 2000), pp. 494–562.
28 For insightful accounts of the human tragedy of partition, see Urvashi Butalia, *The Other Side of Silence: Voices from the Partition of India* (Durham, NC: Duke University Press, 2000); Yasmin Khan, *The Great Partition: The Making of India and Pakistan* (New Haven, CT: Yale University Press, 2008).
29 Jaswant Singh, *Jinnah: India, Partition, Independence* (New Delhi: Rupa Publications India, 2009).
30 Sarat Chandra Bose, *I Warned My Countrymen*, ed. Sisir Kumar Bose (Calcutta: Netaji Research Bureau, 1968), p. 254.

Part II

The partition of Palestine

3

Partition and the question of international governance: the 1947 United Nations Special Committee on Palestine

Laura Robson

From its beginning, the modern state of Palestine served as a central venue for experiments in new forms of internationalism. In creating Palestine not only as a mandate territory but as a designated space for an externally sanctioned and supported European settler colonialism, the League of Nations was trying to demonstrate and ensure its own relevance: its members anticipated that the project of creating and defending a Jewish 'national home' in Palestine would cement the League's importance as a mediator and facilitator of Middle Eastern territory for the foreseeable future. This Palestinian role would become even more apparent in 1947, when the newly constituted UN seized on the idea of taking over the defunct League's role as political puppet master over Palestine. The task of deciding what would happen to Palestine following the British withdrawal offered the UN – a new institution uncertain about how to define itself or understand its own purpose – the opportunity to cast itself in a central role in the making and maintaining of a regional postwar order across the Middle East.

In 1947, the split United Nations Special Commission on Palestine, whose majority report recommended partition, was divided not only on the fate of Palestine itself, but on the role the UN would play in the postwar world. The proposal for a federated unitary state – supported, notably, by the Commission's India representative and prepared by the subcommittee's Pakistani chair – represented not only an alternative vision for the future of Palestine but a different and more limited vision of the state-making capacities of the newly formed UN. This chapter looks at Palestine as a locus of arguments about internationalism, sovereignty and external governance, arguing that the UN's decision for partition in 1947 represented a step towards a more interventionist state-building strategy for the 'Third World' whose ramifications would go well beyond Palestine itself.

The run-up to partition

The idea of partitioning Palestine arose in a global context, one that referenced both the partition of Ireland in 1921 and – perhaps especially – the Greek–Turkish population exchange of 1923, in which something like 1.2 million people were forcibly denationalised, moved and assigned new nationalities as part of a national and international scheme to promote ethnonational purity in the Ottoman successor states of Anatolia and the Balkans.[1] It also arose as a consequence of both local and international anxiety, arising on the local level from the strikes and protests of 1936–39 and on the European (and global) level from the spectre of impending war with Nazi Germany. Partition was far from a merely local 'solution' to a regional 'problem'; it was the consequence of an emerging consensus about the nature of a modern global order, made up of identifiable nation-states and economically and militarily dominated by the imperial powers.[2]

Some context is perhaps necessary here. Palestine had become a site for Zionist immigration – mainly from Poland, Romania and Russia – beginning in the late nineteenth century, as the tsarist state's persecutions of Jews increased in frequency and intensity.[3] Around the same time, there was a notably heightened awareness of Palestine in British imperial and domestic circles – as a potential strategic asset for the Empire, as a 'holy land' newly accessible to Protestant evangelicals interested in emerging forms of middle-class travel, and as a site of Jewish national ambitions.[4] Decades of this convergence of popular and political interest in Palestine culminated in the so-called Balfour Declaration, a letter written to the London-based Zionist leader Walter Rothschild in November of 1917 committing Britain to a position of active support for the Zionist goal of Jewish resettlement and a Jewish 'national home' in Palestine.[5] When, after the war, Palestine was assigned to Britain as a 'mandatory' possession – a not-very-convincing fig leaf for a new form of colonial control, to be overseen by the new League of Nations – this promise was incorporated into the mandate document, converting the Balfour letter from a declaration of administrative policy into an international legal commitment.

This was in some way the first iteration of a new imagining of international authority – in the form of both the British mandatory apparatus and the League of Nations overseeing it – that would be highly interventionist in nature, remaking not only modes of governance but also actual populations in the name of new visions of global order. The text of the document assigning the Palestine mandate to Britain was itself remarkably detailed in its vision of remaking Palestinian society to allow for not only a European Jewish presence but a Zionist governmental dominance, as a mode of preparation for a future Jewish demographic majority. It specified the maintenance of older

Ottoman forms of communally conscious government, but also stipulated an ethnically based hierarchy of political rights that would allow for the emergence of Jewish self-government without the simultaneous challenge of Arab self-rule. The League declared:

> The Mandatory shall be responsible for placing the country under such political, administrative and economic conditions as will secure the establishment of the Jewish national home, as laid down in the preamble, *and the development of self-governing institutions*, and also for safeguarding the civil and religious rights of all the inhabitants of Palestine, irrespective of race and religion.[6]

In other words, empire in the guise of internationalism would allow for the total political remaking of a post-Ottoman Palestine, in the explicit expectation that Jewish immigration would eventually make possible a demographically defensible Zionist-run state there.

And over the next couple of decades, the British approach to Palestine was indeed interventionist. Backed by a military force that eventually grew to more than 20,000 active service members, the mandatory government enforced a political, economic and social hierarchy in which members of the Yishuv (the European Jewish settler community) enjoyed a wide variety of privileges denied to the indigenous community, Muslims and Christians alike. The mandate promoted a variety of institutions of statehood for the Zionists: a legislative assembly known as the Vaad Leumi, the promotion of Hebrew as a national language, Jewish schools teaching a nationalist curriculum, a flag, and a police and security force, which tipped very close to a military wing. An attempt at a legislative assembly to include all the communities in Palestine fell apart as it became clear that the High Commissioner, the pro-Zionist Herbert Samuel, was envisioning a system of representation based on 'parity' – equal numbers of representatives for the Jewish community, making up roughly 10 per cent of the population, and the Arabs, making up roughly 90 per cent.[7] All these policies had the effect of creating almost entirely separate spheres for Arabs and Jews in Palestine, a tendency further reinforced by Labour Zionism's determination to create an all-Jewish labour force by refusing to employ Arabs in any capacity in Jewish settlements.[8] By the 1930s, the Zionist movement had acquired enough land that the refusal to employ Arab labour led to widespread dispossession among the Palestinian peasantry, many of whom had lost their livelihoods as tenant farmers to Zionist land sales and were now beginning to swell the population of urban slums ringing every major city in Palestine.[9]

The 1929 Western Wall demonstrations against Zionism, in which nearly 250 people were killed and hundreds more injured, proved only the beginning of the violence. In the spring of 1936, amid renewed negotiations over the makeup of a legislative assembly, an Arab general strike rapidly turned into huge demonstrations enveloping most of the country and leading the British to shore up their military presence and encourage the Yishuv to do the same. As they began to construct a plan and practice of 'counterinsurgency' – that is, a now-familiar mix of violent strategies targeting civilian communities, including assassinations, mass arrests, imprisonments without trial and the bulldozing of villages and cities[10] – they also appointed a royal commission to visit Palestine, determine the causes of the uprising, and make recommendations about future British policy – with the proviso that the Commission was not to question the underlying policy of the mandate.

The Commission was headed up by the Conservative former Secretary of State for India, Robert Peel, who was, however, already incapacitated by cancer and unable to direct the Commission fully. Real authority lay instead with one Reginald Coupland, an Oxford historian, who styled himself an expert on colonial conflict in a variety of settings.[11] Coupland and the rest of the Commission drew explicitly on the Irish and Greek–Turkish cases as justification for their new proposal for Palestine: partition into separate Arab and Jewish territories – not, as is often suggested, into two independent states, but rather one Jewish state and an Arab territory to be attached in some vague way to Transjordan. (As the report put it, 'two sovereign independent States would be established – the one an Arab State consisting of Trans-Jordan united with that part of Palestine which lies to the east and south of a frontier … the other a Jewish State consisting of that part of Palestine which lies to the north and west of that frontier'.)[12] This arrangement would be made possible by the forcible transfer of nearly 300,000 Arabs (and about 1,250 Jews) to create a Jewish majority in the proposed Jewish section.[13]

The Zionist leadership was disappointed with the territorial disposition proposed in the report, but pleased with the Commission's recommendation of partition – and especially with its advocacy for mandatory transfer, which Ben Gurion had not anticipated would 'yet' win acceptance among the British.[14] The Palestinian Arabs, on the other hand, viewed this as the most recent in a long line of colonial practices of violent dispossession; and when the contents of the report became generally known, the revolt moved from strikes and demonstrations to open rebellion, organised not by the political elites of the Arab Higher Committee but by grassroots activists among the peasantry.[15] Over the next two years, they wrested control of much of the Palestinian countryside from the British, who found themselves (on the eve of the war in Europe) having to deploy upwards of 20,000 troops to hold a territory less than a fifth of the size of England. In desperation, the metropolitan government replaced the High Commissioner with another colonial veteran willing to enact martial law in all its excess: Harold Mac-Michael, lately of the 'B' class mandate of Tanganyika. By the time the revolt was finally put down in 1939, the Palestinian Arab political elite had been systematically decapitated through arrests, imprisonment, deportations and executions; some historians estimate that 10 per cent of the male Palestinian population had been killed, arrested, wounded or deported.[16]

The partition scheme was abandoned for the time being. But as a militarily and financially exhausted British Empire planned its withdrawal from the mandate in 1947 – now, with not only Ireland and Greece but also India as examples on which to draw – the idea seemed, once again, to hold out some promise for an orderly postcolonial map in which Britain could retain some economic influence, if not its political authority.

Partition at the United Nations

In May 1947, following on the British imperial example, the United Nations put together a commission called the United Nations Special Commission on Palestine (UNSCOP), with the purpose of determining the future of Palestine following the British withdrawal. Under Zionist pressure, UNSCOP included no Arab or British representatives; its eleven members came from countries deemed to be neutral third parties to the conflict (though it is notable that of the eleven countries represented – Australia, Canada, Czechoslovakia, Guatemala, India, Iran, the Netherlands, Peru, Sweden, Uruguay, and Yugoslavia – three would eventually be subject to some form of partition). None of the members had any special knowledge of the conflict, and the Jewish Agency managed to convince the UN that they should visit some of the Displaced Persons camps in Germany and Austria, where Zionist propogandists were working overtime, as part of their research.[17] By contrast, the Palestinian political establishment (such as it was after its dismemberment during the revolt) boycotted the proceedings altogether, declaring that the UN had no jurisdiction over Palestine and the question could only be settled at an international court.[18] As the Palestinian lawyer Henry Cattan later wrote in his consideration of the legal aspects of the conflict, quoting another analysis:

> It is doubtful if the United Nations has 'a capacity to convey title', *inter alia* because the Organization cannot assume the role of territorial sovereign. Thus the resolution of 1947 containing a Partition plan for Palestine was probably *ultra vives*, and, if it was not, was not binding on member states in any case.[19]

The highly uneven presentation of evidence to the Commission featured all the main arguments Zionists had made use of over the past thirty years: the presentation of Palestine under the Arabs as underused 'wasteland', the promise of rapid mass development and modernisation, the feasibility of transfer on the Greek–Turkish model of the post-First World War period, and the impossibility of a pluralistic state in which majority rule would inevitably crush the political aspirations of the minority.[20] Speaking to UNSCOP, Ben-Gurion declared that a Jewish state would 'realize the maximum development of all the potentialities of Palestine; to cultivate as many millions of dunams as possible out of the 18 million which are at present uncultivated; to irrigate instead of 40,000 dunams as at present, at least 4,000,000'.[21] He emphasised the impossibility of European Jews living under an Arab government, with sharp reference to Europe's role in bringing European Jewry to this pass:

> a Jewish minority in an Arab State, even with the most ideal paper guarantee, would mean the final extinction of Jewish hope, not in Palestine alone, but for the entire Jewish people, for national equality and independence, with all the disastrous consequences so familiar in Jewish history ... The fate of the Jewish minority in Palestine will not differ from the fate of the Jewish minority in any other country, except that here it might be much worse.[22]

The Revisionist Zionist organisation Lehi – infamous as the perpetrators of the Deir Yassin massacre in April 1948 and the earlier assassination of the British Minister of State for the Middle East in Cairo in 1944 – went one stage further, highlighting not only the Greek–Turkish exchange but also the Allied-driven mass expulsions of ethnic Germans from Poland and Czechoslovakia (described, carefully, as 'population exchanges between friendly countries') as a possible model for clearing the Arabs out of a Jewish state.[23] The members of UNSCOP spent some weeks travelling around Palestine, meeting with members of the Zionist establishment as well as with representatives of less mainstream paramilitary branches like Irgun. They travelled in the Displaced Persons camps in Europe, and they tried to represent the Arab view by making a visit to Beirut, where they met with some Arab delegates from other surrounding countries as a kind of stand in for the Palestinian Arabs boycotting the proceedings.

Having absorbed the evidence presented to them, they eventually came to a conclusion agreed on by the majority of the Commission (with significant dissenters, to be discussed below): 'The claims to Palestine of the Arabs and Jews, both possessing validity, are irreconcilable ... among all of the solutions advanced, partition will provide the most realistic and practicable settlement.'[24] They proposed a partition plan inspired by the 1937 Peel Commission, dividing Palestine into three parts: an Arab state, vague in its details, to comprise 43 per cent of the mandate territory, including the highlands and one-third of the coastline; a Jewish state encompassing 56 per cent of the territory, including the northern coast, eastern Galilee and most of the

Negev; and a 'Corpus Separatum', including Jerusalem and its surrounds, which would be subject to some form of international authority. Like the Peel Commission's plan, such a division of territory suffered from a major demographic issue. One of UNSCOP's own subcommittees – made up of representatives from Afghanistan, Egypt, Iraq, Lebanon, Pakistan, Saudi Arabia, Syria and Yemen – produced a report composed mainly by Muhammad Zafrulla Khan and Fares al-Khoury which predicted that 'at the outset, the Arabs will have a majority in the proposed Jewish State'.[25] Mandatory transfer, though, had largely lost its appeal in the aftermath of a world war characterised by displacement of the most dramatic kind (despite the Allies' willingness to use it in the Soviet occupied zone); and the Commission, unlike its British counterpart a decade earlier, stopped short of recommending forcible removal.

UNSCOP's majority report's partition plan essentially represented a continuation of League concerns, policies and approaches. It accepted the idea that pluralism was inherently problematic and that the United Nations, like its precursor, had a special responsibility to ensure 'minority' rights, 'including the protection of the linguistic, religious and ethnic rights of the people' – further referencing the long-established colonial trope that this was somehow especially true for Palestine, 'in view of the fact that these two people live physically and spiritually apart, nurture separate aspirations and ideals, and have widely divergent cultural traditions'. Indeed, its reports included a 'Memorandum on Rights of Minorities in Palestine', which explicitly advocated for maintaining the mandate's 'status quo' approach and the remnants of the Ottoman system that gave religious communities control over personal status law.[26] It supported the premise of Jewish nationhood and mass resettlement of what was left of Europe's Jews as a 'solution' to what was still being called 'the Jewish problem'. And finally, it carried on the League's claim that such ethnonational conflicts indicated its successor's right, and indeed responsibility, to intervene to protect 'peaceful relations in the Middle East', declaring that 'Taking into account the charged atmosphere in which the Palestine solution must be effected, it is considered advisable to emphasize the international obligations with regard to peaceful relations which an independent Palestine would necessarily assume.'[27] The new United Nations, far from representing a new voice, had taken up the League's now decades-old legitimisation of the principle of ethnonational separation as well as its claim of the right to administer it.[28] But not all the Committee's members supported partition; three of them, representing India, Iran and Yugoslavia, proposed a different solution that would link the two communities in a 'federal' state and give the UN permanent control of Palestine's most important religious sites.[29]

The federal proposal versus partition

Given the general proliferation of scholarship around Palestine and the current interest in the so-called one-state solution, the almost total absence of literature discussing the 'minority' proposal for a federated binational state is little short of astonishing. Here, I will limit myself to two observations about this failed proposal: first, that its explicit rejection of Zionist-derived political premises surrounding ethnonationalism separatism pointed up the extent to which the United Nations General Assembly in general accepted a specifically ethnic and racialised conception of sovereignty in this new era of internationalism; and second, that it implied a much different and more limited role for the UN as arbiter of sovereignties and delimiter of borders than the one that actually emerged, particularly in the Middle East.

The federal proposal privileged the concept of indigeneity over a commitment to ethnic nationhood and declared real the possibility of a viable pluralistic state in Palestine. 'It is recognized that Palestine', the minority report stated, 'is the common country of both indigenous Arabs and Jews, that both these peoples have had an historic association with it, and that both play vital roles in the economic and cultural life of the country.'[30] Its authors went on to explicitly reject ethnic nationalism as the highest expression of sovereignty:

> Two basic questions have been taken into account in appraising the feasibility of the federal-State solution, viz. *(a)* whether Jewish nationalism and the demand for a separate and sovereign Jewish State must be recognised at all, costs, and *(b)* whether a will to co-operate in a federal State could be fostered among Arabs and Jews. To the first, the answer is in the negative, since the well-being of the country and its peoples as a whole is accepted as out-weighing the aspirations of the Jews in this regard. To the second, the answer is in the affirmative, as there is a reasonable chance, given proper conditions, to achieve such co-operation. ... The objective of a federal-State solution would be to give the most feasible recognition to the nationalistic aspirations of both Arabs and Jews, and to merge them into a single loyalty and patriotism which would find expression in an independent Palestine.[31]

Declaring that 'the moral and political prestige of the United Nations is deeply involved', the advocates of federalism tied the idea to the survival of a viable future regional and international order and denounced partition as an inevitable cause of future violence: 'It is important to avoid an acceleration of the separatism which now characterizes the relations of Arabs and Jews in the Near East, and to avoid laying the foundations of a dangerous irredentism there, which would be the inevitable consequences of partition in whatever form.'

The Indian representative Abdur Rahman wrote a commentary on the situation in Palestine in which he adopted a straightforward national view supporting the Arabs – arguing for the fundamental illegitimacy of the Balfour Declaration and the mandatory commitment to Zionist settlement – but also making a powerful case that the United Nations should not sully its mission by taking on the clearly imperial tasks of the League. The British in Palestine, he noted, had utterly failed to carry out the mandate's theoretical mission of 'preparing' the country for self-government, and had failed in every important measure of governance: 'The Administration of the mandatory Power does not seem to have done much during the last twenty-seven years in the way of uplifting the indigenous people of the country, a task which, as an agent of the mandatory Power, it was obliged to do ... No serious attempts seem to have been made to introduce measures which would have led to self-government'.[32] The mandate system had failed, and the UN had no mechanism, and indeed should not try to pursue an avenue, of taking up these old responsibilities. 'Nations had no right', Rahman wrote, 'to create a Mandate over Palestine without the consent of its inhabitants and to impose their will upon them.'[33] The new UN contained the possibility of a different kind of international governance, one that acknowledged the fundamental rights of former colonial subjects and refused to participate in their continued oppression: 'There are no means by which the international obligations in regard to mandates can be discharged by the United Nations.'[34] As a representative of the recently partitioned India, then, Rahman was making the case not so much that partition itself was an illegitimate political 'solution' (although doubts about it can be read into his comments) as that any settlement other than the complete termination of the mandate and the emergence of a binational state with an Arab majority would bring the new UN into disrepute, by associating it with the fundamentally imperial task of continuing the mandate. The minority report, then, viewed this settlement as consequential not only for Palestine and its Arab and Jewish residents but also for the nature of state sovereignty in the postwar global order and for the moral authority of the newly constituted United Nations.

Palestinians themselves, as Ghada Karmi has written, viewed partition as 'an outrageous assault on the integrity of their country and an undeserved gift to a newly arrived immigrant Jewish minority imposed on them'.[35] But many remained cautious about the idea of federation, which they correctly recognised as a vision deriving from earlier Zionist concepts of binationalism that had, by the late 1930s, clearly lost out in the negotiations over the nature of the movement.[36] Rather, many activists envisioned an outcome for Palestine not unlike the one depicted in the Palestine National Council's Resolution of 1971 that 'Palestinian armed struggle is not a racist or sectarian struggle against the Jews. Therefore the state of the future in a Palestine liberated from Zionist imperialism is the democratic Palestinian state, in which all who wish to do so can live in peace with the same rights and obligations and within the framework of the aspirations of the Arab nation to national liberation and full unity [with] emphasis on the unity of the people of both Banks of Jordan.'[37] Such visions bore certain resemblances to the federalist plan articulated in the UN's minority report; but, as Leila Farsakh points out, they also reflected a lack of engagement with its (or any) specifics. 'Historically', she writes, 'the Palestinian national movement has never seriously considered how to cooperate with Israeli Jews to bring about a single state' – a reality of the moment of partition as well as the subsequent decades.[38]

The majority report advocating for partition – ignoring both the absolute Palestinian rejection of partition and the existence within Zionism of other forms of thought about the necessity and nature of the nation-state – committed itself definitively to the cause of separatist ethnic nationalisms while explicitly refusing to address the origins of those movements.

> The basic conflict in Palestine is a clash of two intense nationalisms. Regardless of the historic origins of the conflict, the rights and wrongs of the promises and counter promises and the international intervention incident to the Mandate, there are now in Palestine some 650,000 Jews and some 1,200,000 Arabs who are dissimilar in their ways of living and, for the time being, separated by political interests … Only by means of partition can these conflicting national aspirations find substantial expression and qualify both peoples to take their places as independent nations in the international community and in the United Nations.[39]

There are a few things to note here. First, the disavowal of the colonial origins of the struggle in Palestine meant a reorientation of nationalisms as primordial and essential, marked by permanent 'dissimilarity' – language that reflected the approach of the British Peel Commission ten years before, and accepted the British elision of colonial responsibility for the conflict in Palestine. Second, the placing of such a concept of nationalism at the heart of the question of sovereignty – and, crucially, membership in the emerging brotherhood of nations – placed the UN itself in a new light, emphasising the nature of its membership as a collaborative of successful ethnic nationalisms and remaking its own role as one of arbiter and legitimiser of global national claims.

The rejection of the federal proposal, then, had consequences not only for Palestine itself but for the nature of international governance in general. In Palestine, the newly constituted UN was facing a crisis not only of postcolonial regional order but of self-definition: what sort of institution would it be, and how would it delineate and monitor its own membership?

The decision to partition Palestine, then, was taken not only on the basis of UNSCOP's consideration of local conditions – indeed, almost without reference to them – but in view of a much more general consensus on the part of the leading members of the General Assembly (and especially the new permanent members of the Security Council) that the UN, in order to justify its existence, would need to play a muscular role in the remaking of the global order. Partition offered the opportunity for the UN to intervene aggressively in Palestine: first by determining where the border would be, then by acting as the primary mediator and interlocutor among the various interests trying to renegotiate the issue (and, later, by serving as guardian of the hundreds of thousands of refugees created by the partition decision).[40]

Even more centrally, though, Palestine offered the opportunity for the United Nations to affirm to an anxious superpower constituency that it would uphold the absolute centrality and sole legitimacy of the nation-state as the fundamental locus of power in the postwar era. The decision to privilege ethnic nationalism above some form of pluralism in Palestine undoubtedly reflected the outsized influence Zionist leaders managed to exert on the Commission itself; but at a more fundamental level the UN was declaring itself on the side of a national order and reassuring its most powerful members that it had no intention of overturning or challenging the nation-state as the basic unit of global governance, whatever the political interests of its recently decolonised member states. Indeed, the partition resolution offered the opportunity to showcase the UN *enforcing* an ethnonational model of sovereignty from its position of international authority.

Conclusion

'The two-state solution', Ghada Karmi writes, 'is in fact a recent position for Palestinians, who always rejected the idea of partition as a device used by Britain and later the UN and Western states for accommodating Zionist ambitions in the country.'[41] Indeed, this view of the partition of Palestine was widely held across the Arab world in the two decades after 1948, a backdrop to these years' intense interest in non-national models of sovereignty: for instance, the Arab League and the broader cause of Arab nationalism, culminating in the short-lived United Arab Republic in the late 1950s, which took it as a fundamental assumption that nation-statehood was a tool of imperial oppression and that alternative modes of claiming independence could serve the region better. Such ideas were of course not limited to the Middle East but enjoyed a good deal of currency across the decolonising world, where varying conceptions of federalism were having a moment in anticolonial movements from the Caribbean to Africa.[42] For many Arab leaders in the post-1948 world, the UN's support for the forcible partition of Palestine – which in the end did not lead Palestinians even to the geographically truncated 'independent Arab state' originally envisioned but to permanent dispossession and statelessness – served to underline the ways in which postcolonial nation-statehood could serve an emerging neo-imperial world order.

But by endorsing partition and rejecting a federalist vision of sovereignty for Palestine, the newly constituted UN had clearly demonstrated that ethnic nationalism represented the only kind of claim to political sovereignty that would have a chance at being heard in the international arena. It is no surprise, then, that by 1967 many Palestinian leaders would come to see their best chance of regaining some of what they had lost as lying in the most intransigent kind of nationalism. By the 1970s, the Palestinian Liberation Organisation (PLO) was discussing the concept of an 'independent national state' that might not have to include the whole of historical Palestine. By the 1980s, partition was being quietly accepted as a reality around which the negotiations would be organised. In the long run, the lesson of 1947 – for the decolonising world in general and the Palestinians in particular – was that binational and federalist ideas could not coexist with the UN's most powerful actors' vision of the prevailing global order. In the brave new world of postwar international governance, segregationist ethnonationalism was the only game in town.

Notes

1 For more on the Greek–Turkish 'population exchange' of 1923, see especially Bruce Clark, *Twice a Stranger: The Mass Expulsions that Forged Modern Greece and Turkey* (Cambridge, MA: Harvard University Press, 2006); Renee Hirshon, *Crossing the Aegean: An Appraisal of the 1923 Compulsory Population Exchange between Greece and Turkey* (New York: Berghahn Books, 2004); Onur Yildirim, *Diplomacy and Displacement: Reconsidering the Turco-Greek Exchange of Populations, 1922–1934* (New York: Routledge, 2006).

2 For more on this point, see Arie M. Dubnov and Laura Robson, 'Drawing the Line, Writing Beyond It: Towards a Transnational History of Partitions', in Arie. M. Dubnov and Laura Robson (eds), *Partitions: A Transnational History of Twentieth-Century Territorial Separatism* (Stanford, CA: Stanford University Press, 2019), pp. 1–30.

3 For some useful overviews of the position of Jews in tsarist Russia, see especially Eugene Avrutin, *Jews and the Imperial State: Identification Politics in Tsarist Russia* (Ithaca, NY: Cornell University Press, 2010); Joshua Zimmerman, *Poles, Jews, and the Politics of Nationality: The Bund and the Polish Socialist Party in Late Tsarist Russia, 1892–1914* (Madison, WI: University of Wisconsin Press,

2004); Liliana Riga, 'Ethnonationalism, Assimilation, and the Social Worlds of the Jewish Bolsheviks in Fin de Siècle Tsarist Russia', *Comparative Studies in Society and History* 48 (4) (2006), 762–797.
4 On the connections between archaeological explorations and British military intelligence, see John James Moscrop, *Measuring Jerusalem: The Palestine Exploration Fund and British Interests in the Holy Land* (London: Leicester University Press, 2000).
5 The Balfour Declaration has been endlessly dissected by scholars, journalists, policymakers and interested amateurs; the literature on it is too extensive to be cited in full here, but for especially useful overviews of its making see Rashid Khalidi, *The Hundred Years' War on Palestine: A Century of Settler Colonialism and Resistance* (New York: Metropolitan Books, 2020); Walid Khalidi, *From Haven to Conquest: Readings in Zionism and the Palestine Problem until 1948* (Beirut: Institute of Palestine Studies, 1987); Maryanne Rhett, *The Global History of the Balfour Declaration* (New York: Routledge, 2016); Jonathan Schneer, *The Balfour Declaration: The Origins of the Arab–Israeli Conflict* (Toronto: Doubleday, 2010).
6 League of Nations Council, *Mandate for Palestine* (Geneva: League of Nations, 1922), p. 8.
7 See Laura Robson, *Colonialism and Christianity in Mandate Palestine* (Austin: University of Texas Press, 2011), chapter 2; Bernard Wasserstein, *Herbert Samuel: A Political Life* (Oxford: Clarendon, 1992); John Strawson, *Partitioning Palestine: Legal Fundamentalism in the Palestinian–Israeli Conflict* (Chicago: University of Chicago Press, 2010), chapter 2.
8 A policy that was influential though not always successful. See Barbara J. Smith, *The Roots of Separatism in Palestine: British Economic Policy, 1920–1929* (Syracuse, NY: Syracuse University Press, 1993); Jacob Metzer, *The Divided Economy of Mandatory Palestine* (Cambridge: Cambridge University Press, 1998); Zachary Lockman, *Comrades and Enemies: Arab and Jewish Workers in Palestine, 1906–1948* (Berkeley: University of California Press, 1996); Gershon Shafir, *Land, Labor, and the Origins of the Israeli–Palestinian Conflict, 1882–1914* (Cambridge: Cambridge University Press, 1989); Zeev Sternhell, *The Founding Myths of Israel: Nationalism, Socialism, and the Making of the Jewish State* (Princeton, NJ: Princeton University Press, 1998); Mark LeVine, *Overthrowing Geography: Jaffa, Tel Aviv, and the Struggle for Palestine, 1880–1948* (Berkeley: University of California Press, 2001).
9 The literature on British policy, Zionist development and Palestinian nationalism during the mandate years is extensive. There is an especially useful older literature on the topic from Palestinian scholars with direct experience of the British occupation; see especially Sami Hadawi, *Land Ownership in Palestine* (New York: Palestine Arab Refugee Office, 1957) and *Bitter Harvest: Palestine 1914–1967* (London: Saqi, 2000); A. L. Tibawi, *British Interests in Palestine* (Oxford: Oxford University Press, 1961) and *Anglo-Arab Relations and the Question of Palestine, 1914–1921* (London: Luzac, 1977). See also Rashid Khalidi, *The Iron Cage: The Story of the Palestinian Struggle for Statehood*

(Boston, MA: Beacon, 2006); Charles Smith, *Palestine and the Arab–Israeli Conflict*, 8th edn (Boston, MA: Bedford/St Martin's, 2013); Assaf Likhovski, *Law and Identity in Mandate Palestine* (Chapel Hill: University of North Carolina Press, 2006).

10 John Newsinger, *British Counterinsurgency, from Palestine to Northern Ireland* (London: Palgrave, 2002); Richard Andrew Cahill, '"Going Berserk": "Black and Tans" in Palestine', *Jerusalem Quarterly* 38 (2009), 59–68; Matthew Hughes, 'The Banality of Brutality: British Armed Forces and the Repression of the Arab Revolt in Palestine, 1936–39', *English Historical Review* 124 (507) (2009), 313–354. For an intriguing sketch of a transnational history of counterinsurgency, see Laleh Khalili, 'The Location of Palestine in Global Counterinsurgencies', *International Journal of Middle East Studies* 42 (3) (2010), 413–433.

11 On Coupland's background and the origins of his political ideas, see especially Arie M. Dubnov, 'The Architect of Two Partitions or a Federalist Daydreamer? The Curious Case of Reginald Coupland', in Arie. M. Dubnov and Laura Robson (eds), *Partitions: A Transnational History of Twentieth-Century Territorial Separatism* (Stanford, CA: Stanford University Press, 2019), pp. 56–84.

12 League of Nations, *Summary of the Report of the Palestine Royal Commission* (Geneva: League of Nations, 1937).

13 See maps of this plan in Arie. M. Dubnov and Laura Robson (eds), *Partitions: A Transnational History of Twentieth-Century Territorial Separatism* (Stanford, CA: Stanford University Press, 2019).

14 Yossi Katz, *Partner to Partition: The Jewish Agency's Partition Plan in the Mandate Era* (London; Portland, OR: Frank Cass, 1998), pp. 85–87. The longer history of Zionist transfer plans for the Palestinians is explored in detail in Nur Masalha, *Expulsion of the Palestinians: The Concept of 'Transfer' in Zionist Political Thought, 1882–1948* (Washington, DC: Institute for Palestine Studies, 1992).

15 On the revolt of 1936–39, see especially Ted Swedenburg, *Memories of Revolt: The 1936–1939 Rebellion and the Palestinian National Past* (Minneapolis: University of Minnesota Press, 1995); Matthew Hughes, 'From Law and Order to Pacification: Britain's Suppression of the Arab Revolt in Palestine, 1936–39', *Journal of Palestine Studies* 39 (2) (2010), 6–22; Laila Parsons, 'Soldiering for Arab Nationalism: Fawzi al-Qawuqji in Palestine', *Journal of Palestine Studies* 36 (4) (2007), 33–48; Kenneth Stein, 'The Intifada and the 1936–39 Uprising: A Comparison', *Journal of Palestine Studies* 19 (4) (1990), 64–85. Some more general accounts that include discussions of the revolt can be found in Weldon Matthews, *Confronting an Empire, Constructing a Nation: Arab Nationalists and Popular Politics in Mandate Palestine* (London: I. B. Tauris, 2006); Bayan al-Hut, *Qiyadat wa-al-mu'assasat al-siyasiyya fi Filastin, 1917–1948* (Beirut: Mu'assasat al-dirasat al-filastiniyya, 1981); Ann Mosely Lesch, *Arab Politics in Palestine, 1917–1939: The Frustration of a National Movement* (Ithaca, NY: Cornell University Press, 1979).

16 Rashid Khalidi, 'The Palestinians and 1948: The Underlying Causes of Failure', in Eugene Rogan and Avi Shlaim (eds), *The War for Palestine: Rewriting the*

History of 1948 (Cambridge: Cambridge University Press, 2001), pp. 12–36. On the violence of the British response, and casualty numbers, see also Jacob Norris, 'Repression and Rebellion: Britain's Response to the Arab Revolt in Palestine of 1936–39', *Journal of Imperial and Commonwealth History* 36 (1) (2008), 25–45.

17 For some investigations of Zionist activism in the camps, see Margarete Myers Feinstein, *Holocaust Survivors in Postwar Germany, 1945–1957* (Cambridge; New York: Cambridge University Press, 2010); Miriam Rürup, 'The Citizen and its Other: Zionist and Israeli Responses to Statelessness', *Leo Baeck Institute Yearbook* 59 (1) (2014), 37–52; Michael Marrus (ed.), *The End of the Holocaust* (Westport, CT: Meckler, 1989); Avinoam Patt, '"The People must be Forced to go to Palestine": Rabbi Abraham Klausner and the She'erit Hapletah in Germany', *Holocaust and Genocide Studies* 28 (2) (2014), 240–276.

18 UN Doc. A/364 Add. 1, 1947, UN Archives (UNA).

19 Henry Cattan, *Palestine in International Law: The Legal Aspects of the Arab–Israeli Conflict* (London: Longman, 1978), p. 78.

20 Elad Ben-Dror, 'The Success of the Zionist Strategy vis-à-vis UNSCOP', *Israel Affairs*, 8 January 2014, 1–21.

21 David Ben-Gurion address to UNSCOP, 4 July 1947, in United Nations, *United Nations Special Committee on Palestine* (Geneva: United Nations, 1947), vol. 3, pp. 8–23.

22 *Ibid.*

23 Memorandum from Lohamei Herut Yisrael (LEHI) to UNSCOP, 26 June 1947, reprinted in Ruth Gavison (ed.), *The Two-State Solution: The UN Partition Resolution of Mandatory Palestine: Analysis and Sources* (New York: Bloomsbury, 2013), pp. 51–157.

24 Report to the General Assembly of the UN Special Committee on Palestine, 3 September 1947, at https://www.un.org/unispal/document/auto-insert-179435/ (accessed 24 March 2023).

25 Report of Sub-Committee 2, 11 November 1947, reprinted as United Nations, *The Partition of Palestine 29 Nov 1947: An Analysis* (Beirut: Institute for Palestine Studies, 1967), p. 32.

26 Memorandum on Rights of Minorities in Palestine, 1947, Box S-0609-0001, II, UNSCOP Papers, UNA.

27 Report to the General Assembly of the UN Special Committee on Palestine, 3 September 1947.

28 This is a particularly important point to emphasise because many scholars have looked at the emergence of UN policy as a rejection of the League's focus on collective rights via the minorities treaties and the beginnings of a new regime of *individual* human rights; see especially the work of Mark Mazower, 'Minorities and the League of Nations in Interwar Europe', *Daedalus* 126 (2) (1997), 47–63; 'The Strange Triumph of Human Rights, 1933–1950', *Historical Journal* 47 (2) (2004), 379–398; 'Two Cheers for Versailles', *History Today* 49 (7) (1999), 8–14. In fact, while this shift in emphasis did indeed constitute an important break between the League and the UN, there were other ways in which the UN

represented a continuation of League philosophies and policies – like its ongoing interest in 'solutions' of ethnic separation and partition, which continued to feature prominently in UN policy through the twentieth century. The Dayton Accords of 1995, for instance, legitimised and formalised the ethnic cleansing and population exchanges that had taken place in Bosnia and Herzegovina during the war. On this point, see especially Linde Lindkvist, *Religious Freedom and the Universal Declaration of Human Rights* (Cambridge: Cambridge University Press, 2017), chapter 6.
29 The federal proposal can be found in UN Doc. A/364, 1947, UNA.
30 Report to the General Assembly of the UN Special Committee on Palestine, 3 September 1947.
31 *Ibid.*
32 Abdur Rahman, special note to UNSCOP, in appendix to *Report to the General Assembly*, vol. 2. (Lake Success, NY: United Nations, 1947), p. 38.
33 *Ibid.*
34 *Ibid.*
35 Ghada Karmi, 'The One-State Solution: An Alternative Vision for Israeli–Palestinian Peace', *Journal of Palestine Studies* 40 (2) (2011), 63.
36 *Ibid.*, pp. 67–68.
37 Palestine National Council, 8th Session, 'Interim Political Program of the Palestine Revolution', available in *The International Encyclopedia of the Palestine Question*, at www.palquest.org/en/historictext/16262/palestine-national-council-8th-session-interim-political-program-palestine-revolution (accessed 13 March 2023).
38 Leila Farsakh, 'The One-State Solution and the Israeli–Palestinian Conflict: Palestinian Challenges and Prospects', *Middle East Journal* 65 (1) (2011), 64.
39 Report to the General Assembly of the UN Special Committee on Palestine, 3 September 1947.
40 See Laura Robson, 'Refugees and the Case for International Authority in the Middle East: The League of Nations and UNWRA Compared', *International Journal of Middle East Studies* 49 (4) (2017), 625–644.
41 Karmi, 'The One-State Solution', p. 63.
42 On some of the iterations of federalism in the era of decolonisation, see Jason Parker, *Brother's Keeper: The United States, Race, and Empire in the British Caribbean, 1937–1962* (Oxford: Oxford University Press, 2008).

4

Fighting for Palestine as a holy duty? The Syrian Muslim Brotherhood and the partition of Palestine in 1947

Mohamed-Ali Adraoui

Although many scholars view the Israeli–Palestinian dispute as the epitome of clashes between religious powers fighting for a sacred cause serving a divine purpose, the partition of mandatory Palestine emerges from a much more complex pattern of reasoning.[1] However, a certain historiography still gives prominence to the simplistic interpretation of the conflict, according to which the Israeli–Palestinian confrontation derives from the ever-increasing influence gained over the years by religious movements at the expense of more secular, nationalist forces, who were primarily fighting for a Jewish or Muslim sovereignty over mandatory Palestine, but shied away from using religious imaginary to generate support.[2]

Indeed, an historical analysis of the partition of Palestine after the Second World War in 1947[3] confirms that Islamist movements, and most notably the Muslim Brotherhood-inspired movements of the 1930s that existed in a large number of Arab countries (Egypt, Syria, Sudan),[4] played a prominent role in anti-Zionist protests. Their opinion about the perceived misappropriation of the sacred land of Palestine, which they believed belonged to its historic inhabitants, the Palestinian Arabs, gained considerable ground among Arab and Muslim militants. And yet, the symbolic ascendancy of the Muslim Brotherhood's discourses and the influence of its political actions during the 1947–48 partition of Palestine, was anything but exceptional. In fact, this Islamist reaction needs to be considered as one piece of a larger puzzle that made up the opposition to the loss of Palestine. The deeply religious rhetoric and the promotion of a holy Muslim society that were propagated during the protests organised by the Syrian and Palestinian Muslim Brothers who had been most affected by the international community's 'unjust' backing of a Jewish state, should not detract from the collaborations they simultaneously built with a wide range of Arab militants.

This chapter sheds light on the ways in which the Muslim Brotherhood handled the 1947 partition of Palestine, how they organised in order to first prevent it, and then reacted to what they perceived to be a grievous political and religious attack against the rights of the Islamic 'community/ Nation' (*al-Ummah*). The intervention of Zionist Jews as a third party in the process of decolonisation in a region that had been considered as a land of Islam for centuries undoubtedly led many to believe that the rest of the world was betraying each and every Muslim.[5]

To better understand the specific role played by Islamic actors and the influence of their speeches and political actions among the broader opposition to the 1947 partition of Palestine, this chapter frames the mobilisation of the followers of the Palestinian and Syrian Muslim Brotherhood as a nationalist reaction dressed up in religious language. In so doing, we aim to uncover the ways in which they have defined, conceptualised and led the fight against oppression in Palestine as a religious duty. This chapter also aims to illustrate how, through a religious discourse, the Syrian Muslim Brotherhood opposed the partition of Palestine, thereby legitimising a radical shift in the way the struggle for Palestine was presented, which played an important role in the rise of an exclusively religious understanding of the conflict.

Against the background of the international recognition accorded to three new entities (a Jewish state, an Arab state and Jerusalem as an international city), the opposition to the perceived loss of Palestine also represents a key element in the evolution of Islamic ethics. Indeed, the Muslim Brothers based in the Middle East have always stood out as the most virulent opponents of the loss of the century-old birthplace of Arab and Muslim identity. Even if, from the onset of their foundation in Egypt, then part of the British Empire,[6] the Muslim Brothers drew their ideological tenets from late nineteenth-century reformism, and despite their refusal to apologise for their radical religious and political actions, the fact remains that they were not acting in a vacuum and toughened their stance in light of historical events.

This meant that in the immediate post-Second World War context, marked between the 1950s and the 1970s by the impending collapse of European colonialism, the conflict in Palestine was a key element behind the Brothers' dramatic shift towards liberating formerly colonised Muslim countries. These Islamist advocates believed that the partition of Palestine was more than an ill-fated, anti-imperialist struggle that did not bode well for Muslim believers. Rather, they saw the partition as a clear victory for the enemies of Islam (as a religion and a community) that was standing in the way of its divine mission on earth: fighting for truth. Consequently, anyone who obstructed the Islamist forces' way of freeing Palestine was thought of as an enemy of God.

In terms of methods, the analysis presented here takes a closer look at the attitudes, declarations and actions of the representatives of the Muslim

Brotherhood who took part in denouncing the partition of Palestine in 1947 and tried to obstruct it in every possible way.

The special attention given here to the Syrian Muslim Brotherhood derives from the large amount of archival resources made available at the Syrian desk in the US State Department collections for researchers interested in the contemporary history of the Middle East.[7] Furthermore, as the twentieth-century stronghold of Arab nationalism and Islamism, the former territories under the French mandate for Syria and the Lebanon that make up the Levant[8] provide an excellent location to study the Islamic response to the perceived slight to an entire religion. Newly available archives offer valuable insights into the discourses and reactions of Members of Parliament affiliated with the Muslim Brotherhood regarding the loss of Palestine and its aftermath. These insights, although limited when compared with the scope of verbal and physical hostile reactions that took place, nonetheless provide a privileged view into the ideological tenets that fuelled the Islamist movements' rapid expansion and increasing legitimacy: the loss of Palestine, the treason of some of the leading Muslim actors, and the perceived conspiracy against Islam.

Examining the Muslim Brotherhood's opposition to the partition of Palestine in 1947 allows us to look at the mobilisations that took place in November 1947 and the following months to understand how the Brotherhood reacted to the partition process at the United Nations that embodied, in their eyes, the loss of historic and divine sovereignty. From this vantage point we analyse the long-term consequences of the partition for Islamist ideology to the present day.

The Muslim Brotherhood in Syria: some insights

The Syrian branch of the Muslim Brotherhood was founded in the mid-1940s when Mustafa As-Siba'iy and Muhammad Mubarak Al-Tayyib, two close friends of Hasan al-Banna (1906–49), the Egyptian founder and main theorist of the Muslim Brotherhood, established an offshoot of the Brotherhood in their country. Sharing with the Egyptian founder the same principles and political outlook, the Muslim Brotherhood in Syria, right after the country won its independence in 1946, turned out to be relatively influential, especially in the urban areas. Some other political organisations (such as the communists and nationalists) were significantly more popular. However, the Muslim Brothers represented a religiously dynamic movement and recruited its members from merchants, professors, blue-collar workers and public servants in cities like Damascus and Aleppo.[9]

Although the Muslim Brothers were not present in mandatory Palestine until the late 1940s,[10] the Brotherhood in Egypt and Syria were concerned with events in Palestine. The Syrian Muslim Brotherhood, before it was banned in 1963, in the aftermath of the Baathist coup, played a significant role in Syrian political life, both domestically and externally. To appreciate how the Muslim Brotherhood dealt with the events surrounding the UN Partition Plan, it is necessary to revisit events in Syria in the final months of 1947.

The great strike in support of Palestine

In October 1947, the Damascus Committee of the Muslim Brotherhood organised a series of strikes and protests aimed at pressing the great powers to vote against the UN Partition Plan.[11] Every Syrian was urged to take action to stop the partition. The most remarkable mobilisation took the shape of a general strike that was held on 3 October 1947. The Muslim Brothers' parliamentary leaders, along with other political parties (including nationalists and liberals), called on their supporters, and every Arab and adherent of Islam, among whom were many students, to strictly oppose the plan.

The 3 October general strike was religious to a large extent. The participants joined in the protest after the midday Friday prayer at the Umayyad Mosque in Damascus. Many students took part in the 10,000-strong protest that began after the representatives of the Muslim Brotherhood had taken the floor. The Muslim Brotherhood MP Muhammad Mubarak, who wore a white turban that day to highlight the importance of the occasion, gave a speech that invoked God, his prophet, and jihad, to legitimise the fight against the vote in favour of partition. Feisal Al-Azmeh, a younger leader, adopted a stronger political tone and called on all Western countries to halt the partition of Palestine. He also called on Saudi Arabia to follow an action plan to the same end. Incidentally, the action plan bore an uncanny resemblance to later Arab–Israeli conflicts as it raised the threat of an oil and trade war against any Western country that did not pay heed to Arab and Muslims' demands: 'One word from Ibn Saud can save Palestine. One decision by the Syrian Parliament can also help. The Arab king and the Syrian Parliament can help by cancelling and refusing the oil agreement with the Americans and force them to stand with the Arabs on the Palestine question.'[12] A telegram with similar content written by Mustafa As-Siba'iy from the Committee for the Defence of Palestine was also read out on 3 October 1947. The creation of this committee, in which Muslim Brothers also took an active role, preceded with the 6 October appeal of the Damascus Committee. Interestingly, this offshoot of the Cairo-based Arab Higher Committee, in which the Egyptian Muslim Brotherhood was quite influential, illustrated the close-knit communications that the Syrian opponents of partition had established with the other political and religious forces of the Arab world. This suggests that the Syrian Muslim Brothers' openness towards cooperating with other Arab forces was anything but exceptional, since every Arab country agreed that the seriousness of the situation warranted a united appeal. Here is an excerpt from that telegram:

> Syria strikes today in harmony with the other countries of the Arab world in protest against the decisions of the Committee of Inquiry [the United Nations Special Committee on Palestine or UNSCOP], announces its determination to defend the Arabism, unity, and independence of Palestine by all available offensive and defensive means. Syria also announces its determination to boycott economically, culturally, and politically those countries which support Zionism. We do not accept anything less than the establishment of an Arab state in Palestine.[13]

Similar protests that the Muslim Brotherhood helped organise in Syria's largest cities were marked by the same fits of anger and fiery speeches threatening war as a last resort to prevent the pending catastrophe of partition. In Aleppo, for instance, the local representative of the Muslim Brotherhood said the following to the crowd: 'A Jewish state in Palestine will only be established on the skulls and bodies of the Arabs.'[14] Its counterpart who led the protest in Hama was heard saying: 'Palestine awaits bloodsheds. She is hungry and will not revive unless the mountains and the valleys are flooded with Zionist blood.'[15] In Jalkhad, in the southern part of the country, also on 3 October, the Brothers' slogans followed the same line: 'We, thousands of demonstrators, volunteer to rescue it (Palestine) from the claws of criminal Zionism by force of arms.'[16]

The more the UN Partition Plan for Palestine was perceived to only benefit the Jews, the more explicit the calls to jihad became: to resist oppression and external invasion by force of arms. In other words, the language of the protests shifted over time towards an impending religious conflict between the Muslims and their enemies: every advocate of the partition was thereby committing a crime against Islam. Gradually the 'Islamic' undertone of the Brotherhood's reaction stood out among the unanimous opposition in the Arab and Muslim world against the vote in favour of the UN partition resolution that crossed partisan lines.

A growing fear of partition: the appeal of the Damascus Committee

The first political and religious militant organisations were created in Lebanon and Syria in the late 1930s. They were followers of al-Banna, the founder of the Brotherhood in Egypt. Structured around a network called 'Muhammad's Youth' (*Shabab Muhammad*), these organisations gathered young activists interested in the new style of preaching that originated from Egypt where many had studied at the University of Cairo where they familiarised themselves with the Brotherhood's thought. These associations formed part of a larger social fabric that marked the emergence of the Muslim Brotherhood in Syria.[17] There the Brotherhood gained representation in Parliament where it promoted al-Banna's project to further the legal and cultural Islamisation of all Muslim societies aimed at countering the perceived alienation caused by the lack of respect for Islamic ideals.

The parliamentary members affiliated with the Muslim Brotherhood took the lead in organising the protests against the forthcoming United Nations resolution that contained the Partition Plan for Palestine. That plan was the majority recommendation of UNSCOP (that was addressed in Laura Robson's chapter), which was established on 15 May 1947. The strategy devised by the Muslim Brotherhood was to mobilise every movement that made up the Syrian political spectrum to work together to thwart the Partition Plan as a violation of Muslim rights.

From the outset, the Syrian Muslim Brotherhood not only emphasised the fact that the fate of Palestine was a holy duty grounded in the paramount importance of the Holy City of Jerusalem, they also exhorted everyone, not just the religious forces, to come and help fight the UN Partition Plan that they believed would result in the dispossession of the Palestinian Arabs. Every Arab and every inhabitant of a Muslim country, not just Islamist militants, was deemed to have a duty to stand up against what they considered a forfeiture of Muslim rights to the Holy Land.

The 6 October 1947 appeal of the Damascus Committee laid out a transnational strategy according to which Muslim Brothers were to raise the alarm about the unfolding conspiracy, across nonpartisan lines. The leading representatives of Syria's main political parties[18] joined this appeal that called upon everyone to sacrifice their lives for the greatest holy Arab cause to defend Palestine, and to condemn the Zionists' wrongdoings as a jihad:

Noble Nation,

Arab Palestine today crosses the most critical stage in its history and is exposed to the greatest danger ever threatening it: Zionism.

The United Nations Organization will give its word on Palestine in the coming few days.

This nation has always struggled and fought for the purpose of maintaining the Arabism of Palestine and has been generous in sacrificing blood and money to resist Zionist tyranny and British colonization.

Today, you are called to renew your sacrifices and to resume the Jihad for the defense of this holy land, which is the first Kiblah (point towards which the Muslims turn their faces in prayer) and the third sacred place.

The world expects [to hear] your word. Announce your opinion clearly and courageously that you will not accept a substitute for the Arabism of Palestine, and that you strongly disapprove of the cruel recommendation of the Committee of Inquiry which would make Palestine Jewish.

The Provisional Committee for Defense of Palestine in Damascus in answer to the appeal of the Arab Higher Committee calls upon you to express your anger against the plots planned for Palestine, to share with the other Arab countries by sending out the cry of Justice in a general strike tomorrow (Friday), and calls upon you to meet following the prayer of Friday at the Umayyad Mosque to take decisions which will be transmitted to the United Nations Organization and to the various states.

You will undoubtedly listen to the appeal of duty. Damascus the giant fighting city which has always embraced the Palestine cause shall be, this time, as it has always been, the advance guard for the assistance of Palestine.

Long live Palestine, free and Arab.[19]

Contemporary understandings of *al-Nakba*

The Brotherhood's view, according to which Muslims were the sole victims of what would soon be named the 'catastrophe' *(al-Nakba)* can be contrasted with the more non-discriminatory language employed by Munir Ajlani, the then Syrian Minister of Education, in his speech delivered at the University of Damascus on 30 November 1947, the day after the UN vote, to rally students, Muslims and Christians alike, against the Arabs' oppressors:

> The Zionists with their money and intrigues, were able to convince great powers, especially America, Russia, and France to decide on the Partition of Palestine for their interests. It is your duty now to tell your people that Palestine is a dear part of Syria and the Arabs. It is both sacred to the Muslims and Christians, the Zionists will never be able to take it except over the bodies of every Muslim and Christian Arab in all the Arab countries.[20]

He implored the students:

> Let us stand together in one line, firm and united, without any other party or religious difference in mind, to get to our single aim which is the liberation of Palestine and the conservation of its Arabism in spite of the great world conspiracy against us. You, students, are the enlightened group and you have to extend your energy and patriotism to all the people. Warn them against the massive catastrophe that is threatening our community.[21]

Notice here that the term *Nakba* carried a broader meaning associated with the recognition of the creation of the State of Israel as an embodiment of the loss of Arab sovereignty over Palestine, as opposed to the way it is used in contemporary Israeli–Palestinian historiography to refer to the tragic expulsion of some 800,000 Palestinians from their land by Israeli forces in 1947–49. What was referred to as the main source of evil according to the Arabs fighting for Palestine at that time, was first and foremost the loss of territory, before mention was made of the fact that hundreds of thousands of people were being forced to leave their birthplace (although, in November 1947, the expulsion of the Palestinians had not yet begun). The loss of this specific territory was considering an amputation of Arab identity.

In contrast, here is the analysis developed on 29 November 1947 in *An-Nasr* (Victory), a newspaper close to the Syrian Muslim Brothers, to explain what was at stake in the Partition Plan:

> Americans, Britons, Russians, Jews, and collaborators! You have left out logic, law, or rule when you decided to plot against Palestine which does not belong to any of you. Palestine's people did not want you to interfere in their own affairs and ask by what right you do.
>
> Palestine with all the Arabs and Muslims mocking your efforts do not care a bit for your comedy. Stop working so hard day and night for a question which does not belong to you and take it easy. Your decisions will remain ink on scraps of paper and will not be able to divide Palestine.
>
> Fools and dopes. The boundaries of Palestine are not mountains, rivers, stones, and lines, but ranks of faithful men ready for sacrifice. Every Arab and Muslim will fight for and defend the holy shrines in Jerusalem. Do as you please, and work as hard as you can, but the key to the question is not yours. It is here in our country and in our hands. Come and take it if you can; but you cannot. If you are willing to start a war, we accept the challenge. We are ready for a new crusade which will prove greater and more effective than the first crusade. We shall give you people who like to die, and who believe, if they die, that they are martyrs going to God's paradise. Every man, every woman, and every child believe that Jihad is a duty more important than prayer and fasting. Can you stand with your armies and deadly weapons? Come and try.[22]

Similarly, the MPs affiliated with the Muslim Brotherhood demonstrated a particularly gritty determination when the Syrian Parliament voted unanimously to rule out the implementation of the new UN-backed Partition Plan on 1 December 1947. The Muslim Brothers were among the keenest advocates of the allocation of a £2 million emergency aid plan for Palestine, and of the anticipatory enforcement of a mandatory conscription. The contributions of one Muslim Brother to the decision-making process behind the vote, Ma'ruf Dawalibi, an Aleppo parliamentary representative, is worth mentioning here. One of the thirty members of Parliament who stepped up voluntarily to take part in anti-partition protests, Dawalibi exhorted Arabs and Muslims to summon up the courage to confront Western powers based on the fact that a righteous war brings victory: not unlike the Yugoslavs who successfully resisted the all-powerful Nazi Germany in 1941–42.[23]

Enlarging the field of protest: the anti-US riots in Damascus

On 30 November 1947, moving from words to deeds, the diplomatic delegations of some of the partition-friendly countries were assailed by organised groups. Reports of calls to violence can be found in the Western powers' diplomatic correspondence that was suspected by the Brothers of aiding and abetting this anti-Arab and anti-Muslim conspiracy. In one telegram, the US Embassy in Damascus mentioned the anti-partition protests that took place on 30 November and apportioned blame for the violent outbursts to 'agitators from the Muslim Brotherhood' who were responsible for the overall radicalisation of the opposition to the Partition Plan. Consider the following excerpt from the telegram:

> The violent aspects of this reaction on November 30, 1947, were directed primarily against the American delegation …, although the French and Belgium delegations received some attention. The American Legation was stoned, three automobiles were burned, the building was forcibly entered, and the American flag was torn down and burned. The mob, about 2,000 strong men, which attacked the Legation was led by members of the Muslim Brotherhood and by student nationalists.
>
> By Sunday morning, November 30, 1947, Damascus had received the news of the vote in favor of partition which had been taken the previous evening by the United Nations Assembly and the politically conscious elements of the population were automatically on strike. When students arrived at schools Sunday morning, they were met by agitators from the Brotherhood and with exhortations from their own teachers … The students carried placards demanding that schools be converted into army training camps.[24]

Even though these riots had been interpreted as a sign of clear radicalisation, and more precisely of the influence of the Muslim Brotherhood, the US support for the Partition Plan was never questioned and there was no indication that it would abandon the Plan.[25] The main lesson when it came to the Muslim Brotherhood in Syria and the issue of Palestine was the recognition that the Islamist movement was popular and was able to mobilise the masses. At the national level, the Muslim Brothers were now being taken seriously by Western interests and policies. In the broader Middle East, some comparisons with the views of other US embassies towards the Muslim Brotherhood can also be observed. For instance, as early as 1944 the US Embassy in Cairo distributed a report dealing with what it called the 'fanatical Muslim Brotherhood', which it described as potentially very violent. In fact, the first report ever sent from the US Embassy in Cairo about the Muslim Brotherhood was in response to a letter written by some of the Brotherhood's leaders to the US Ambassador asking the US to oppose the growing Jewish influence in Palestine. The report, dated 29 April 1944, shed light on the Muslim Brotherhood, its ideology, and its activities, with a focus on its violent potential.[26] It appeared that for US diplomats based in the Middle East the Palestinian issue was one of (possibly) the most essential matters for which the US developed an interest in the activities of the Muslim Brotherhood.

The declaration of Jihad on 17 December 1947

Reactions against the partition of Palestine expanded well beyond the parliamentary arena, as the Brotherhood were drawing ideas from the religious field to call the whole *Ummah* to take action to preserve the Arab and Islamic sovereignty of Palestine. The most remarkable of these reactions was the 17 December 1947 Declaration of Jihad, which came on the heels of the UN Partition Plan. It was written by the League of Islamic Scholars (*Rabita al-'Ulama*) which was then considered the highest Syrian religious authority, and which mainly consisted of specialists of Quranic studies. Besides the board president, Abul-Khayr Midani, three of the nine members that formed the League's board of directors belonged to the Muslim Brotherhood: Mustafa As-Siba'iy (already mentioned), Mustafa Az-Zarqa (Professor of Law at the Syrian University) and Muhammad Shaqfah (MP for the city of Hama).

The declaration, which was backed by Grand Mufti Muhammad Shukri Al-Istiwani and the Qadi of Syria (in charge of the Shari'a court) Muhammad Aziz Al-Khan, portrayed the partition of Palestine as a declaration of war addressed to all Muslims, who, in turn, had no other choice but to retaliate in the name of their faith. In fact, the declaration offers a new understanding of jihad, which is first and foremost defensive, and aimed at fending off an external attack: 'The field of Jihad and eternity is open to you [true believers] ... it is the duty of all Arabs and Muslims to oppose the realization of partition of Palestine by all the force, weapons, arms, men, and money that they possess.'[27]

Jihad was also made mandatory to ward off the creation of the State of Israel that was supported by the US, the Soviet Union, the United Kingdom and France, and was said to have originated in the ancient crusades before it was invoked against nineteenth-century colonialism.[28] Furthermore, the declaration was explicit about the use of arms to expel the foreign body from the land of Islam. It spoke to the 'true believers' and reminded them of their duty to go to Palestine to lead the fight against the theft of this land. There was no excuse for every able-bodied believer to evade the fundamental task to protect holy Palestine.

The most noteworthy element of the declaration was the fact that it enjoined true believers to dissociate themselves from, and condemn, any group that did not join the religious resistance to free Palestine, although it did not name the more secular communist and nationalist forces that would not comply. In fact, the declaration introduced, for the first time, a hierarchical system that arranged people in Syrian society in a graded order according to their dedication to the 'true' Islam, namely: the fight for Palestine. While it would be wrong to assume that this idea was specific to the Muslim Brothers, and that it was not shared by other dignitaries within the League, it nonetheless remained a key and topical element of the Brotherhood's doctrine at the time.

In the thought developed in Egypt by al-Banna, it was stated that the strength of one's faith derived from taking part in jihad to preserve Islamic sovereignty over Palestine. In one of his epistles, *Engagement for Palestine*,[29] the founder of the Brotherhood illustrated the new grammar by which the 'Islamic cause' had to be defended. He was explicit about the legitimacy of the conflict that was 'usurping' the rights of the Muslims in Palestine:

> Muslims worldwide, Palestine is the first line of defence and the first strike already represents half of the battle. Those who are fighting over there are only defending the future of your country, your lives and your families, as though they were defending their lives, their country and their families! The cause of Palestine is not the cause of the East, nor the cause of the Arab nation only, but is the cause of both Islam and the people of Islam.
>
> There is no need to dwell on the rights of the Arabs in Palestine. There is no reason to expose or explain these rights. There is also no point of talking, making speeches or writing articles. The time has come for action! Protest at any opportunity and by all means. Cut off opponents to the Islamic cause, whatever their nationality or their identity. Make financial donations to poor families, to homes that have been ruined and to the courageous fighters. Get involved if you can. No one has an excuse. Because nothing prevents us from activity, if only weakness of faith.[30]

Even though this epistle has not been quoted much in Islamist literature, the idea that Palestine is no less an Islamic cause is still at the heart of the Brotherhood's ideology. The Muslim Brothers have played a key role in this major doctrinal shift that turned Palestine into a topic of concern for the whole Islamic community by highlighting the religious dimension of the land. This cause, according to the Muslim Brotherhood's founder, now represented the most crucial and sacred reason for fighting. Palestine is no longer a part of the Arab world only, but the religious and political property of any Muslim who has ever lived. Having lost one of their most holy territories, every Muslim has the duty to defeat the people who are said to have usurped this land.

The Muslim Brotherhood's defence of Palestine

The UN Partition Plan for Palestine represented a break in the imaginary of Islamic movements as the moment when hostility solidified towards actors targeted for 'usurping' sovereignty over Muslim lands and symbols. The result was that the partition of Palestine transformed a primarily religious *disputatio*[31] into a plural and widespread antagonism, involving 'religious nationalism',[32] in which considerations of theology, geopolitics and identity were interwoven. The intellectual categories called upon since then have been used to justify a disparate conflict involving both religious argumentation and strategic confrontation. Jews, seen foremost and even exclusively as depositaries of a 'religion of the book' (as recognised in the sacred scriptures), have thus been included, since the apostolate of Mohammed, in debates about the management of religious otherness. As believers in a message subsequently recognised and surpassed by Islam, Muslim clerics and leaders have granted a specific status to the Jewish community, with certain rights and duties.[33] Therefore, the notion of antisemitism appears to be simply irrelevant when it comes to characterising how Jews have been historically treated in Muslim-ruled territories, at least for centuries. Although far from being equivalent to full and equal citizenship as is, for instance, observable in contemporary liberal democracies, Jewishness was conceived and dealt with principally as a religious affiliation involving belonging to a community with rights and duties that were meant to ensure Islamic primacy. As highlighted by Bernard Lewis,[34] the emergence of antisemitism in the Arab East is due to Arab intellectuals and political leaders whose main influence was Europe at a time when the Arab world experienced prominent changes in the cultural, economic and social spheres, making an elimination agenda likely. Lewis argues that the influence of the Islamic sphere should not be seen as linked to a form of endogenous hatred for Jews. The end of the nineteenth century witnessed a huge change in the aftermath of European colonisation, making a large part of representations of Jewishness evolve towards Judeophobia and then antisemitism. As summarised by Lewis: 'The influence of Europe and specifically European anti-Semitism prepared the ground and planted the seeds of the new Arab anti-Semitism.'[35] In his study of how Semites and anti-Semites have interacted, Lewis even mentions, when describing Sayyid Qutb's vision of Jews, that this was incorporated within the framework of 'the War against Zionism'.[36] Consequently, there seems, in his view, to be a specific historicity of anti-Jewish hatred supported within Islamic radicalism.

As Jewish colonisation spread all over Palestine, the Muslim Brothers emphasised a new conception of religious and political sovereignty that still prevails today within radical Islamic movements, starting with Hamas.[37] First of all, Palestine is an exceptional territory due to its intrinsically sacred nature. If, as al-Banna explains in his writing, no landmark of *Dar al-Islam* ('Domain of Islam') could be surrendered to foreign control,[38] it is even more vital to defend regions that house sanctuaries[39] of the *Ummah* like Palestine. Since Palestine is *Waqf*,[40] (a land held in sacred trust for the use of the Muslim community), the 'traditional' rules of property are null and void. As stated in Hamas' 1988 charter (Article 11), Palestine is a sacred land for all Muslims for all times and shall never be relinquished at any price at risk of committing a serious sin. A state can, of course, possess a territory just like a private operator, but in the present case the Palestinian political nation cannot claim the classical nationalist right to oversee a religious and political land whose property, responsibility and defence belong, in reality, to the Islamic nation and motherland of believers. While the Brotherhood's preaching insists on the need to liberate (by force if necessary) the land of Islam, al-Banna is clear as concerns making this specific struggle the peak of jihad which he legitimises as an armed solution to a detrimental situation for Muslims. The liberation of Palestine is, as a result, a sacred unique cause, while the enemies of this project are also the enemies of Islam.[41] The fight thus becomes metaphysical, as it involves a heteronomous dimension, with its justification coming from another world whose rules are set by God rather than by human beings.

The type of animosity directed towards Jews demonstrated by the founder of the Brotherhood is undoubtedly linked to the establishment and expansion of a Zionist home in Palestine,[42] which he reacted against by clearly targeting Zionist Jews, accusing them of harbouring an imperialist plan against the *Ummah*. This resulted in a political Judeophobia, and a significant break with Sayyid Qutb (1906–66), whose view of the Jewish question is marked by antisemitism (Jews for what they are, not for what they do), which became a fundamental issue for Salafist-Jihadist movements. Questioned by a *Times* correspondent in Cairo on 1 August 1948,[43] al-Banna stated that 'the Arabs must throw the Jews living on their territory (the land of Arabs) into the sea'. The next day al-Banna accepted an interview with the *New*

York Times[44] in which he attempted to correct his statement by affirming that this was just a way of speaking and that his thoughts went out to the settlement of Jews in the empty lands of Australia out of sympathy for the uprooted Jewish people, which didn't prevent him from finding it 'inhuman that they would settle in a region where they would make its inhabitants [speaking of the Arabs] who had been living there for thousands of years homeless'.[45]

Radicalising to an even greater extent the heritage of al-Banna, at a time when the State of Israel had become an undeniable reality, was Qutb, another leading member of the Muslim Brotherhood, who stood out by systematising a Judeophobia that was synonymous with the convergence of all contemporary forms of hostility towards Jews. If the historical driving force of Qutb's vision remains 'the Israeli shock' experienced by Arab societies in 1947–49, which opened up a space for the radicalisation of a number of fundamentalist and radical Islamic movements,[46] this Egyptian thinker is distinguished by systematising a framing of the question of Palestine rooted in injustice. The conflict that opposes 'Israelis' and 'Palestinians/Arabs' is, according to Qutb, in reality an antagonism between 'Jews' and 'Muslims'. The struggle over sovereignty of the Holy Land is only the visible side of the cosmic and ahistorical confrontation between believers of 'the true religion' and a Judaism that is the ultimate symbol of the betrayal of God. In this respect, Judeophobia becomes political antisemitism since it is not only a negative way of essentialising Jews, but also, and especially, of constructing them as the ontological enemy of Islam. In a work that is key for understanding this view, which mixes theological anti-Judaism, political Judeophobia and metaphysical antisemitism, titled *Our Struggle Against the Jews* (1950), Qutb explains the foundations and manifestations of what appears to him to be an ontological hatred of Jews towards Muslims.[47]

According to Qutb, 'the Jew' is the ultimate enemy and doubly dangerous because he is deemed theologically 'wrong' and politically treacherous. Unlike Christians, whose beliefs are certainly thought to be wrong and who can thus also be thought of as enemies of Islam, Jews are characterised by a form of betrayal that makes the struggle in Palestine particular. Moreover, they are believed to act in secret, which enables Qutb to describe the Jewish conspiracy (*al-Muamara al-Yahudiyya*) as the primary and most effective manifestation of the anti-Islamic plan, of which the creation of the State of Israel is at once a means and an end. Mixing strength and weakness, the Jews, with their hatred of Muslims, were historically able to wait for the right time in order to weaken the *Ummah*, when they were finally able to bring down the Muslims (at least temporarily) thanks to strategic intelligence. Islamist generations must therefore draw on their original faith in order to lead the final conflict which will politically re-establish the flouted rights of their religion, but which will also announce the end of time since bringing down the Jews bears a fundamental eschatological dimension. In his work *Milestones*, published in 1964,[48] Qutb went as far as to claim that the Jews had corrupted the Muslim states, including some of the political leaders of the *Ummah*. The theft of Palestinian land was thus not the only manifestation of their desire to cause damage; Qutb also mentioned that the introduction of usury in Muslim societies was a means of 'transferring all of the wealth of humanity into [the Jews'] hands'. This was in addition to being morally driven by the desire to 'put an end to the (healthy) limitations imposed by faith and religion'.[49]

Conclusion

To conclude, it turns out that the Islamist conceptualisation of the Palestinian issue, even though initially mainly nationalist and inclusive, progressively turned into a more radical and exclusive ideology. To put it in different terms, although the initial Muslim Brothers, as seen in the Syrian case, were dedicated to defending Palestine as a holy cause by targeting Western countries for supporting a people that were seen as usurpers, Islamists and Jihadists have increasingly been adding a new adversary to the equation, which is the 'traitor'. If Palestine had been lost, this is also because Islam was given up by some fellow believers, and for now, in this regard, they have to lead a fight not only against the Jews and their allies but also against the 'so-called' Muslims accused of betraying Palestine. It turns out that political Islam has become more radical and less likely to compromise than many Arab nationalists, at least until the last decade, when some leaders within Hamas started to accept the fact that a Palestinian state could be accepted over only part of mandatory Palestine.[50] Nevertheless, examining how the partition of this land has been viewed and understood by the Muslim Brothers in Syria demonstrates that beginning in the 1940s there was a potential for religious radicalisation that, of course, needs to be understood in its historical context. From its initial role as a nationalist force opposing the partition of Palestine, as well as a movement that saw Islam as a political nation facing a tremendous danger, the Muslim Brothers played a major role in both the reinforcement of the defence of the Palestinian cause as well as constituting a factor of its fragmentation.

Notes

1 For a presentation of the many interpretations of this conflict, see: Avi Shlaim, *Israel and Palestine: Reappraisals, Revisions, Refutations* (London: Verso, 2010).

2 Neil Caplan, *The Israel–Palestine Conflict: Contested Histories* (Oxford: Wiley Blackwell, 2011); Benjamin Beit-Hallahmi, 'Religion and Nationalism in the Arab–Israeli Conflict', *Il Politico* 38 (2) (1973), 232–243.
3 Sami Hadawi, *Palestine Partitioned: 1947–1958* (New York: Arab Information Center, 1958).
4 Barry Rubin (ed.), *The Muslim Brotherhood: The Organization and Policies of a Global Islamist Movement* (Basingstoke: Palgrave Macmillan, 2010).
5 Walid Khalidi, *From Haven to Conquest: Readings in Zionism and the Palestine Problem until 1948* (Beirut: Institute of Palestine Studies, 1987).
6 Although the largest Arab country had officially become independent (in 1922) by the time the association of Muslim Brotherhood (*Jam'iyat al-Ikhwan al-Muslimun*) was created, the United Kingdom retained control over the Egyptian state and its social apparatus until the 1950s. This seminal organisation of Islamism is founded on a unique purpose to reintroduce Islam (deemed to have been abandoned by most Muslim populations throughout the world) as the fundamental norm (be it identity-related, legal, social or political) in order to reunify the *Ummah* and bring it under the direction of a single authority: the Caliphate. These elements also fed into a fight against colonialism that was widely supported by every movement in Egyptian society at the time.
7 All the excerpts mentioned in this chapter come from declassified sources at the US State Department. See RG: 59 General Records of the Department of State 1947–1949 Central Decimal File from 390d.1115/12–241 to 890d.00/12–447, Box no 800. National Archives at College Park, Maryland, United States.
8 A. L. Tibawi, *A Modern History of Syria, Including Lebanon and Palestine* (New York: St Martin's Press, 1969).
9 Raphaël Lefèvre, *Ashes of Hama: The Muslim Brotherhood in Syria* (Oxford: Oxford University Press, 2013); Dara Conduit, *The Muslim Brotherhood in Syria* (Cambridge: Cambridge University Press, 2019).
10 Ziad Abu-Amr, *Islamic Fundamentalism in the West Bank and Gaza: Muslim Brotherhood and Islamic Jihad* (Indianapolis: Indiana University Press, 1994). Izz ad-Din al-Qassam was a Sufi, and a religious nationalist, but was not organically connected to the Muslim Brotherhood. See Basheer M. Nafi, 'Shaykh 'Izz Al-Din Al-Qassam: A Reformist and A Rebel Leader', *Journal of Islamic Studies* 8 (2) (1997), 185–215.
11 UN General Assembly Resolution 181 (II), 29 November 1947.
12 CDF 890d.5045/10-647. 6 October 1947.
13 *Ibid.*
14 *Ibid.*
15 *Ibid.*
16 *Ibid.*
17 Joshua Teitelbaum, 'The Muslim Brotherhood in Syria, 1945–1958: Founding, Social Origins, Ideology', *Middle East Journal* 65 (2) (2011), 213–233.
18 Munir Malki, member of the Arab Popular Party; Salahiddin Bitar, member of the Arab Resurrection Party; Zeki Al-Khatib, Damascus Deputy and member

of the Popular Parliamentary Group; and Mustafa As-Siba'iy, Inspector General of the Muslim Brotherhood Association.

19 Enclosure to Despatch no. 790 dated 6 October 1947, from American Legation, Damascus, Syria.
20 CDF 890d.5045/10-647. 6 October 1947.
21 *Ibid.*
22 *Ibid.*
23 *Ibid.*
24 CDF 890d.00/12-147. 1 December 1947.
25 However, the US abandoned its support for partition in April 1948. See Victor Kattan, *From Coexistence to Conquest: International Law and the Origins of the Arab–Israeli Conflict 1891–1949* (London: Pluto Press, 2009), p. 166.
26 For an in-depth analysis of the history of the US connection with the Muslim Brotherhood in Egypt, see Mohamed-Ali Adraoui, 'The United States and the Egyptian Muslim Brotherhood: Understanding a Chaotic History', *Georgetown Journal of International Affairs*, 9 May, 2019, at https://gjia.georgetown.edu/2019/05/09/egyptian-muslim-brotherhood-part-i/ and https://gjia.georgetown.edu/2019/05/12/egyptian-muslim-brotherhood-part-ii/ (accessed 16 December 2019).
27 CDF 890d.00/12-147. 1 December 1947.
28 For a closer look at the meaning of military jihad as a tool for defending Muslim lands at a time of colonial predominance, see David Cook, *Understanding Jihad* (Berkeley: University of California Press, 2005).
29 Hasan al-Banna, *Five Tracts of Hasan al-Banna (1906–1949): A Selection from the Majmu'at Rasa'il al-Imam al-Shahid Hasan al-Banna* (Berkeley: University of California Press, 1978).
30 *Ibid.*, p. 79.
31 Clerics and thinkers representing Abrahamic religions opposing each other throughout the centuries in order to assert the truthfulness of their views. While these kinds of conflicts, doctrinal at first, perfectly coincided with repressing and hating a religion and its followers (medieval anti-Judaism in Europe, expulsion of Spanish Muslims after 1492, etc.), the dispute is an autonomous field of political practices since it is primarily directed towards the exchange of religious arguments. Initially a scholastic debate, the *disputatio* can serve as a pretext for political and identity hostilities but its first function is indeed religious controversy and demonstration. See Marc R. Cohen, *Under Crescent and Cross* (Princeton, NJ: Princeton University Press, 2008).
32 One can thus note that, despite the assumed desire to break with the nationalist forms of allegiance to a country then in vogue, the pan-Islamism of the time must also be seen as an acculturation of Muslim thinkers who were pushed to theorise religion in 'nationalist' terms. Thus, the *Ummah* is conceptualised as needing a recognised territory (in large part comparable to pan-Germanism or pan-Slavism) with the aim of being directed by a sole and unique political-religious power (the Caliphate).
33 Generally expressed by the term *dhimmi*, from the name of the tax paid by confessional groups subject to temporal Islamic powers in exchange for their

protection. While the aim of such a measure is not equality between believers of different religions, Judeophobia is not the main motivation. The management of the Jewish question is primarily part of a policy of diversity management responsible for maintaining the legal and symbolic precedence of Islam. See Anver Emon, *Religious Pluralism and Islamic Law: Dhimmis and Others in the Empire of Law* (Oxford: Oxford University Press, 2012).
34 Bernard Lewis, *Semites and Anti-Semites* (New York: W. W. Norton and Company, 1999 [1986]); Bernard Lewis, *The Jews of Islam* (Princeton, NJ: Princeton University Press, 2014 [1984]).
35 Lewis, *Semites and Anti-Semites*, p. 164.
36 *Ibid*.
37 The Arabic term for 'enthusiasm' and an acronym for the Islamic Resistance Movement officially founded in 1987, whose charter specifies the need to defend Palestine not only as the land of the Palestinian people but also as a landmark of Muslim territory. Such an ideological construction should not be surprising given that this movement is a manifestation of the Muslim Brotherhood in Palestine. See Azzam Tamimi, *Hamas: Unwritten Chapters* (London: Hurst, 2006).
38 Mohamed-Ali Adraoui, 'Borders and Sovereignty in the Islamist and Jihadist Thought: Past and Present', *International Affairs* 93 (4) (2017), 917–935.
39 This is in the case of Palestine the Al-Aqsa Mosque and the Dome of the Rock, visited by Muhammad according to Islamic tradition.
40 This term refers to a perpetual donation made by an individual to a public entity. The good that is given becomes inalienable. For Islamists, Palestine, as a sacred land, is a gift of God (who put the sacred sites there) to the *Ummah*, whose separation from it would be a sin. Palestine thus cannot escape its status, and even less so people who are claiming a different religion such as Judaism. The *Ummah* only manages the usufruct since God keeps the fructus which he allows Muslims to enjoy. Therefore the defence of a good described as *Waqf* in theory goes to any Muslim. See Pascale Gazaleh (ed.), *Held in Trust: Waqf in the Islamic World* (Cairo: American University in Cairo Press, 2011).
41 Abd al-Fattah El-Awaisi, *The Muslim Brothers and the Palestine Question: 1928–1947* (London: I. B. Tauris, 1998).
42 The Brotherhood movements have been violent, as shown by the creation of the special organisation (*al-Tanzim al-Khass*), a fighting section of the movement that was the main vector of armed contingents against Jewish combat units (paramilitary ones such as the Haganah or terrorist ones such as the Lehi) which were present in Palestine from this era until the Arabic defeat in 1949. It is nonetheless important to specify that the Muslim Brotherhood does not have the monopoly on hostility towards the Jewish national project, as shown by the action of the Grand Mufti of al-Quds Amin Al-Husseyni, organiser of the Jerusalem Muslim Congress from 6–17 December 1931, during which he attempted to warn his religious peers about the growing establishment of Jewish communities in Palestine. His efforts were key in the triggering of the Arab Revolt several years later (1936–39). See Gilbert Achcar, *The Arabs and*

the Holocaust: The Arab–Israel War of Narratives (New York: Macmillan, 2011).
43 El-Awaisi, *The Muslim Brothers and the Palestine Question*.
44 *Ibid*.
45 *Ibid*.
46 At the same time, following the split with their original movement, some Palestinian Muslim Brothers created the *Hizb al-Tahrir* ('Party of Liberation'). Founded in November 1952 in Jerusalem at the instigation of the cleric Taqidine Al-Nabhani (1909–77), it was an Islamist force with a transnational ambition whose first objective was the liberation of Palestine, before working to re-establish the Caliphate. See Reza Pankhurst, *Hizb Ut-Tahrir: The Untold of the Liberation Party* (Oxford: Oxford University Press, 2015).
47 James Toth, *Sayyid Qutb: the Life and Legacy of a Radical Islamic Intellectual* (Oxford: Oxford University Press, 2013); John Calvert, *Sayyid Qutb and the Origins of Radical Islamism* (New York: Columbia University Press, 2009); Olivier Carré, *Mysticism and Politics: A Critical Reading of Fi Zilal Al-Qur'an by Sayyid Qutb (1906–1966)* (Leiden: Brill, 2003).
48 Sayyid Qutb, *Milestones* (Cairo: Kazi, 1964).
49 Qutb furthermore links the immorality that he observed during his stay in the United States at the end of the 1940s to the action of rich Jews who were, in his view, interested in furthering the moral decay of American society in order to dominate it. See Sayyid Qutb, *The America Which I Saw* (Cairo: Al-Risala, 1951).
50 Issued on 1 May 2017 in Doha by Khaled Meshaal, this document consists in an acceptation of a Palestinian state that would fall within the borders that existed before 1967, before Israel took control of the West Bank, Gaza and the whole of Jerusalem. However, the document offers no recognition of 'the Zionist enemy' (the expression that is used by Hamas to describe Israel). Khaled Meshaal also highlights that 'Hamas affirms that its conflict is with the Zionist project, but not with the Jews because of their religion.' To access the document in full, see 'Hamas in 2017: The Document in Full', *Middle East Eye*, 2 May 2017, www.middleeasteye.net/news/hamas-2017-document-full (accessed 16 December 2019).

Part III

The partitions of India and Palestine compared

5

The communal question and partition in British India and mandate Palestine

Amrita Shodhan

In this chapter, the superficial similarity between the partitions of India and Palestine are probed and examined to reveal the structures of knowledge and the mentalities of governance that treated the populations of the two lands very similarly. It demonstrates the links in British imperial governance of both places, in the context of partition, and asks whether making these connections can give us a new perspective on the divisions that still occupy India–Pakistan and Palestine–Israel today.

There has been a small spate of academic writing comparing partitions, especially the Irish, Palestinian and Indian partitions, beginning with the early work of T. G. Fraser in 1984, Schaeffer in 1999, followed by publications in quick succession in the mid-2000s by Deschaumes, Ivekovic, Forman, Kedar and Chester, and most recently by Robson in 2017 and Kattan in 2018.[1] This body of work looks at the many different aspects of partition, including the similarities in the ideology of the departing colonial power (Fraser, Schaeffer, Deschaumes et al.), the similarities in the personalities involved in partition (Fraser), the ideologies of minority nationalisms (Devji and Mufti), the nature of the colonial and international administration that required a transfer of populations as a prelude to partition (Robson), or who argued that partition was the result of the systemic failure of representative government in divided societies (Kattan). Yet others, like Cleary and Greenberg, have looked at the similarities resulting from the consequences of partition.[2]

This chapter focuses on the partitions of mandate Palestine and British India that happened in quick succession under the auspices of Great Britain and the international community of the United Nations. There are many points of comparison between the two partitions, from their planning to their execution, as well as consequences and human experiences. In this chapter, I focus on the genealogy of one common understanding prevalent at the time, which was that the population of each country was divided into two opposing political groups. The opposition between the groups led to 'deadlock', the term most famously used by Reginald Coupland, the Beit Professor of Colonial History at Oxford University.[3] The deadlock caused by the implacable opposing positions taken by two rival communities – Hindu and Muslim in India and Jew and Arab in Palestine – led to partition. It was assumed that partitioning the land and creating homelands for these rival groups would lead to the cessation of violence between the communities.[4]

This chapter draws attention to the limited history of the governance structures in both places that generated the two groups of Arab and Jew, Hindu and Muslim, in Palestine and India. Comparing the developments of these communities in India and Palestine reveals a pattern of governance that contributed to the division of communities. The creation of these groups required the elision of multiple groups who may have not identified with either group.[5] Older histories have accused the imperial rulers of 'divide-and-rule' policies. However, I suggest that partition was not merely the result of a Machiavellian imperial policy, but also a colonial sociology that generated structures of governance wherein community identities became the most legitimate identities for individuals in both places. Other genealogies for the creation of these nationalised political/communal blocks can be sought in the diverse history and multiple developments in ideology and mobilisation. While the latter developments have been studied better and discussed, the structures of governance have not been directly linked to the political developments. In India, especially, the governance structures were established before these political developments. Thus, the identities of Muslim and Hindu develop in a non-political or apolitical environment of 'understanding and governing' or 'counting' the population. In mandate Palestine, the development and mobilisation of community identity occurred in a more political environment as seen in the work of Palestinian scholars like Muslih, Khalidi and Huneidi, among others.[6]

This chapter begins by examining colonial governance and its role in consolidating the diverse religious, linguistic and ethnic groups that lived in India and Palestine into two antagonistic national groups. I next examine the various plans for representative government that encompassed these groups. Then, I look at the imperial precedents that accepted partition as a workable governance solution for the transfer of power from Britain to the national groups. Finally, I examine how the partition solution is represented as a failure of local groups to reconcile their differences, thus compelling the departing imperial rulers (and the international community in the case of Palestine) to suggest partition and sharing the land.

The division of the population into national religious communities

The division of the population into national religious communities occurred in both British India and mandate Palestine in similar conditions of colonial governance, applying similar structures of knowledge or ontologies embedded in colonial policies. Dubnov and Robson have recently published a work comparing the partitions of Ireland, India and Palestine, in which they describe many of the processes of partition that are comparable. They accept that colonial sociology generated 'a re-imagining of often-intermingled Hindu and Muslim populations as distinct and separate political communities'.[7] However, their focus was on twentieth-century history of nationalism whereby Hindus and Muslims engaged in imperialist and internationalist[8] schemes of self-determination and nationhood. They locate some of the politics of nationalism, like the politics of Zionism, in an imperial background. Their focus on the liberal imperialist designs to federate the communities and ethnicities in self-governing states is a much-needed corrective to the narratives that locate partitions in the demands from the grassroots. However, their focus on the international context of the nation-state form obscures the nature of the 'community' that was nationalised.

The question of national, religious or ethnic communities is most often characterised as 'politicised communities'. In these cases, the community is pitted against the state in a Manichean duality with the community described as a primordial-intimate collective, whereas the state is a political collective. Thus, in many studies, political, economic and electoral processes are held responsible for 'producing' and making politically active, already pre-existing religious identities,[9] without considering how individuals were identified with a broad, homogenous religious community. While the discourse on identity normalises these identifications, whereby a person is either Hindu or Muslim, Jew or Christian or Muslim or Arab by birth, we know that the broad categories have multiple sub-affiliations that varied by sect, language, ethnicity and so on. Yet, in law and governance, individuals had to present themselves as members of a unitary community defined primarily by religion as though it were fixed, unchanging and undebatable. While the broad categories and identity labels existed before the advent of colonial rule, I suggest that the legal and governance processes in both India and Palestine were the most basic structures that rendered the subsects and affiliations, local governance of individuals in community law-ways, ineffective. Individuals and sectarian groups had to claim membership in larger groups recognised by the colonial authorities to gain access to colonial governance, laws and power.[10] Thus, we must consider the forms of colonial legality that privileged the making of these groups.

Communal colonial sociology of governance

The sociology of colonial knowledge that developed over the years of colonial legal and political organisations reduced a plethora of small community groups to fundamentally defined singular religious groups in both British India and mandate Palestine. Comparing the histories of these different and singular communal definitions gives important insights into colonial ontologies and opens up questions regarding these constructions. These comparisons also demonstrate the systematic nature of the construction, and break down the sense of the unique quality to the particular experiences in Palestine and in India.

In India, the process of creating singular and fundamentalist definitions of communities is older and has been better documented than in Palestine. Extensive studies on the Indian census, riot reporting, adjudication and representation in government demonstrate that numerous communities with varying caste, religious and class, or 'fuzzy' identities, were coalesced into singular fundamentally defined religious groups: Hindu and Muslim.[11]

In Palestine, research on British colonial administration has not looked at the sociology of knowledge in quite the same way. However, work by Yair Wallach, Roberto Mazza, Assaf Likhovsky and others have shown the presence of multiple communities from late Ottoman times.[12] In British accounts, these are reduced to 'Jewish', 'Christian' and 'Muslim' communities initially. Likhovsky suggests that, from the mid-1930s, British reckoning in Palestine changed from a religious identification to a national one, whereby the Christians in Palestine were counted with the Muslims as Arabs, and the Jews were treated as a separate nationality.[13] In this account, the Christians were seen as Arab and the political representation of the population of Palestine was categorised into two distinct categories of Arab and Jew.

Briefly examining the Palin Commission report on the riots in Jerusalem in 1920 and the Haycraft Commission of inquiry into the Jaffa riots of 1921, we can see the making of the category Arab as inclusive of Muslims and Christians. The Palin Report kept the religious groups as the basic relevant units of the population, and yet it frequently used the term 'Arab' to speak of both Christians and Muslims. For example, speaking of the local population it says, 'the vast majority of the local population, both Muslim and Christian is actually a mix of local tribes and ... rooted in the soil'.[14] The statistics regarding those injured and killed in the riots are presented by religious group – Jews, Muslims and Christians – but there is a tendency to club the Muslim and Christian statistics together – as in 'the total number of non-Jews affected being 8 – i.e. 6 Moslems and 2 Christians'.[15] In contrast to this, in the report published a year later by the Honourable Justice Haycraft, the Chief Justice of Palestine, on the riots in Jaffa in 1921, there was no attempt to distinguish between the Muslim and Christian individuals. The statistics presented are only about Jewish and Arab categories.[16] Sherene Seikaly notes that a survey of family budgets by a medical officer, W. J. Vickers, in 1943 begins with the separate categories of Muslim and Christian, but abandons them for a single group of 'Arabs' as he found little difference among them.[17] Seikaly warns that the invisibility of Palestinians in much colonial statistics was a component of the broader condition of settler colonialism.[18]

Any discussion of the 'colonial construction' of communities begs the very valid question of the self-descriptions of the populations in these categories. All the categories – Hindu, Muslim, Arab, Jewish – were used by the locals themselves in their self-identification. In Palestine, for example, the Christian community considered themselves Arabs, given their shared history in Palestine and common language with the Muslims. The British Government's support for the Zionist project, which by the terms of the Balfour Declaration and the mandate categorised these communities into 'Jews' and 'non-Jews', was also a factor that brought these religious groups together in opposing Zionism. On the other hand, the settler colonial project itself required the 'malicious simplification of Arab and Jew'.[19] However, the making of political blocks of these communities required a marginalisation of every other identifier for individuals. Looking at the governance record – of laws, of reports on riots, etc – provides the locations where the marginalisation of multiplicity occurs without explicit political intentions. Thus marginalisation occurred separately from the political mobilisation. In India, this is seen more clearly in a period prior to the political mobilisation. In Palestine, the non-political marginalisation of community identities occurred simultaneously with the political developments.[20] As I explain below, in India the various different group identities were classified as sects of Hinduism or Islam, and as such became insignificant in the eyes of the colonial ruler. Individual members of sectarian groups like the Vaishnav or Khoja had to declare themselves as Hindu or Muslim to claim their civil rights that allowed them to obtain property, or make conjugal or inheritance arrangements, defend themselves from libel, etc.

Colonial sociology of law

Besides the many locations like the riot reports cited above, the census, and other locations in India that I alluded to earlier, I suggest a primary locale for this understanding of 'native' identity is the arena of law. Here, I draw on my work on Indian caste-religious communities and on the work of Assaf Likhovski on law in Palestine.[21] These studies document that the multiple regime of laws and communities permitted in early colonial administration gave way to a system that consolidated the laws in two main categories – in India Hindu and Mohammedan laws, and in Palestine Jewish and Ottoman laws. While the argument for India is better made, further research is required to flesh out the development in Palestine.

India

Roman law thinking (as opposed to common law) lay behind British legal institutions in India, starting in 1772 with Lord Hastings, and was behind the revival of Hebrew law in Palestine, as well as the Tanzimat Ottoman reforms in the nineteenth century. In the British administration of India, William Jones (1746–94) was the first judge of the Supreme Court at Fort William, Calcutta (appointed in 1783). He had to identify the laws by which to settle disputes, and in pursuit of this he compiled and caused to be compiled various statutes on personal laws. Bernard Cohn has noted his correspondence with Lord Cornwallis where he referred to Cornwallis as the Indian Justinian, the emperor of the sixth-century Roman Empire who is known for commissioning the codes of law, and himself as the Indian Tribonian, the jurist who supervised the law code. Cohn explains how Roman imperial precedent was also cited by the early Indian judiciary as providing the models for governing India. To honour this self-image, partaking of the fascination of his age with all things imperial and Roman, Jones's supporters placed a statute of him in a toga in St Paul's Cathedral, with the Institutes of the Law of Manu under his hand. The statues of Lord Hastings, the first Governor-General of India, show him dressed as a Roman senator in a toga, and one of Lord Cornwallis, his successor, dressed as a Roman emperor. These were made in 1830, but stand today in the Victoria Memorial, Kolkata.[22]

Thus it was Roman law, which recognised the national laws of their subject populations, that provided the model for Lord Hastings as the first Governor-General in 1772. He proclaimed that the state would apply 'Mohammedan' and 'Gentoo' (derived from gentile, which applied to the Hindus) laws to the respective people. In practice though, the courts recognised much caste and customary laws of the smaller groups along with the religious laws of 'Hindus' and 'Muslims'. This can be seen in Perry's early reporting of case law in the Bombay Presidency.[23]

Palestine

In Palestine, the mandate regime that was relinquished in 1948 was preceded by a three-year period of military government under the British Army at the end of the First World War. During the period of this occupation, from 1917 to 1920, the British administration promised to promote the settlement of Jewish colonists in Palestine, and in pursuit of this object oversaw the systematic policy of establishing a 'national home'.[24] The British mandatory authorities continued to apply many of the laws of the former Ottoman rulers of Palestine, in which the idea that personal law matters should be determined by the religious law of the group to which the individual belonged prevailed. This Ottoman legal system was developed after the Tanzimat reforms. These reforms also employed the Roman law thinking that identified the laws as deriving from the national and religious character of the population, especially in personal law matters. Thus, the Ottomans established a regime of religious personal law with millet and religious courts for recognised religious communities. The British administration continued to support the religious courts for the adjudication of personal matters. The civil administration was responsible for the enforcement of the decisions of these religious courts. The separation of civil law matters from personal law matters was familiar to the British from their colonial administrations elsewhere – especially in India.[25]

Early administration of multiple legal jurisdictions

In India, from the 1830s, we find that there was a secularisation and reform of the legal administration. With this there was a decline in caste-based law and 'law of the defendant' or customary law regimes. After the 1857 rebellion and the assumption of rule by the Crown, there was a large-scale overhaul of the legal system.[26] After this reorganisation there was a more stringent application of the singular 'Hindu' and 'Muslim' identities in Indian courts. With the growth of legal codification and procedures, the occasions for the application of customary law of the particular community, as well as caste law, declined and became an area that was a residual category. Thus individual sectarian and caste members had to identify themselves as either Muslim or Hindu to access and enforce rights through the legal system. This happened because the court denied and reduced the rights of the small local religious and caste bodies to govern their members in matters that were seen as belonging to the civic public sphere.[27] The reduction of this plurality required that individuals presented themselves as members of the fundamentally defined communities[28] of either Muslim or Hindu. Shazia Ahmad shows this same process in the development of Ahmadiyya Muslims as apostate groups in Punjab from 1872 to 1939. She concludes that the sectarian interpretation of Islamic law by the Ahmadiyyas was incompatible with the notion of Anglo-Mohammedan law in British India.[29]

In a parallel development, numerous smaller but significant groups like the Sikhs, Buddhists and Jains were counted as falling under the broad umbrella of Hindu law.[30] As Metcalf concludes, 'By the end of the nineteenth century this insistence that India was divided into two opposed religious communities shaped the way not only the British, but increasing numbers of Indians, viewed their society.'[31]

Likhovski documents a similar regularisation of multiple communities in Palestine. In the case of the Jewish communities of Palestine, he notes how the British mandatory authorities refused to recognise the demands from the Orthodox old Yishuv to have separate Hasidic courts. He documents how the Supreme Court was 'at first' composed by a presiding British judge with three Palestinian members – Jew, Christian and Muslim – but in 1945 had 'two native ones, a Jew and an Arab'.[32] He also notes that despite the separate tribal courts for the Bedouin of the Negev, in a popular discussion the Bedouin were understood as 'original' Arab groups.[33] Thus, multiple different communities, like the Druze and the Bedouin, were identified as Arab.

This brief comparison suggests that a common pattern of colonial sociology of law became the norm in both India and Palestine whereby state courts dealt with individuals as members of singularly defined religious groups administered by experts. Thus, where in an earlier period castes may have been assembled in an Indian provincial court to provide a statement of the law, in the regularised British court after the 1860s experts in Hinduism provided the definition of Hindu and a dispute would be adjudicated accordingly by a British judge. In the latter case, no dispute was allowed as to what constituted Hinduism. Similarly, Islam was also dealt with through experts and textual references. In Palestine, millet courts as well as state courts administering personal law of religions, rather than separate sectarian courts or consular courts administering justice by members of the community, became the norm. Bentwich suggests that in the early period, when matters of personal status of foreigners were concerned, the British president of the court was authorised to invite the consul or representative to sit as an assessor for the purpose of advising the court on the personal law.[34]

For the Muslims, Bentwich notes that the Supreme Muslim Council, presided over by the Mufti Al-Hajj Amin al-Husayni, was established in 1921 to supervise the Muslim religious courts and charitable trusts. This body was the singular Muslim body that was to deal with the multiplicity of Muslim sects in Palestine. The Jews or congregation of Jews that did not follow the official rabbinical congregation would be exempted from the religious court and tried by civil courts. Separate religious courts were not set up for them.[35]

The legal practice of reducing sectarian courts and amalgamating different groups under general categories defined by experts based on a historical textual argument generated a broad disembodied identity to which individuals had to show allegiance. The broad identities the state recognised, whether it was Hindu and Muslim in India, or Jew and Arab in Palestine, were treated as non-justiciable. The religious identity was defined such that it could be discoverable 'in fact' by a British judge on the basis of texts and experts. Thus, the identity was fixed rather than debated, and membership was determined by demonstration of 'recognised' observances rather than declaration of belief. This can be termed identitarian. A broad category of 'Hindu' was created in law, applying to groups that were quite different from each other. Likhovski's account demonstrates that developments in mandate Palestine reflected the Jewish and Arab nationalists' designs to unify their communities under law. This required the reinterpretation of self in law among all three actors on the judicial scene – the British judges and Jewish and Arab lawyers, as well as the litigants who came to the courts.[36]

Strategies of representation

Besides the operation of singular religious groups as identitarian bodies in legal governance, the colonial government employed these larger identities for organising representation to effect a legal, if not orderly, living. Colonial governments were headed by the Governor-Generals in India and the High Commissioner in Palestine, with authority devolving on them from the Crown. They initially ruled with the help of a council that was advisory, with representatives on the council chosen to represent the various native interest groups. The later progress of these councils to legislative assemblies in India is different from the history in Palestine, however, as I shall argue, the effect of the extension of electoral representation in India, and the curtailment of such representation in Palestine was similar in creating identitarian structures of governance.

In India

Nominated members to governing bodies were the only means of including popular representation until the introduction of municipal boards in 1882, and then extended to the upper levels of government with every decennial reworking of the Government of India. The idea of involving locals in provincial governance got a boost in 1909 after the extensive agitations following the 1905 partition of Bengal.[37] Elections to provincial councils were introduced with a very limited franchise. In the Government of India Act, 1909, 'Muslims' were allocated separate electorates for electing their own representatives in certain provinces. A decade later, by 1918, these separate electorates were considered to provide self-government for religious and other minority groups, and the separate electorates were extended to Sikhs in Punjab, Indian Christians in Madras, Anglo-Indians in Madras and Bengal, and Europeans in five provinces, along with the Marathas in the Bombay Presidency and non-Brahmins in Madras. The scheme of separate electorates was further extended in the Government of India Act, 1935 by including Europeans in all provinces, making separate provisions for women.

The communal divergence between Muslim and Hindu was accentuated in the representation as the Depressed Classes came to be included in the category of 'general', often glossed over as Hindu. B. R. Ambedkar, the leading champion of the rights of the Depressed Classes, vigorously challenged the inclusion of these groups as Hindus in the general category.[38] Thus, the structure of representation that developed by 1935 required a forced homogenisation among Muslims as well as Hindus. Representation by religious community has been seen to provide for the division of the body politic by religion in India and to be the direct cause of the development of communal politics.[39]

In 1946, a delegation from the British Cabinet offered a new scheme of federation for the provinces, with a central federal council that would have representation such that equal numbers of Muslims and Hindus would be represented and there would be parity between the communities. This is commonly referred to as the Cabinet Mission Plan. The Muslim League accepted the plan with the proviso that the Congress Party also agree to it. This acceptance has been interpreted as proof that the League was willing to settle for parity in government rather than an independent country.[40] This plan once again presented two religious groups, Muslim and Hindu (encompassing other minorities), as somehow best representing the total population of India. The reservation and separate representation systems were all devised to overcome the problem of representation of minorities in a majoritarian democratic system associated with the Westminster model that was employed to secure popular government in India.[41]

In Palestine

The British mandatory authority was responsible for developing Palestinian representative institutions. Herbert Samuel, on being appointed High Commissioner, announced in 1921, in the wake of the Jaffa riots, that Britain was considering a partially elected legislative council. This legislative council was described in the Palestine Order in Council of August 1922. It provided for a high commissioner to be advised by a local council, a majority – (twelve out of twenty two) of whose members would be elected representatives. Of these, not less than two were to be Christian and two Jewish.[42] This structure did not please the Zionist Commission as it would give a distinct majority to the Arab population and might work to prevent the establishment of the national home promised by the Balfour Declaration and reinforced by the mandate. The Zionist commission wanted to be represented in any representative scheme on a par with the Arab population, despite being a small minority (7 per cent) of the total population. The Palestine Arab Congress also boycotted the elections of the council. While Herbert Samuel shelved the proposal as unworkable, it was again raised in 1936 by Arthur Wauchope, then High Commissioner. The scheme of representative government was defeated in Parliament in London, again on the grounds that majority Arab rule would not enable the fulfilment of British policy, which was to establish a national home for the Jewish people in Palestine.[43] Thus, the High Commissioner continued to rule by decree, until the end of the mandate.

While most governmental duties were retained by the British administration, 'communal' governance related primarily to the administration of religious courts and matters related to the community. As outlined in Churchill's 'White Paper on Palestine, 1922', the Zionist Executive was assigned the role in assisting the implementation of 'measures to be taken in Palestine affecting the Jewish population ... and the Chief Rabbinate for the direction of the religious beliefs'.[44] To parallel the Jewish organisations, and to replace the Ottoman supervision of religious Muslim courts and trusts (*waqfs* – charitable organisations), the British created the position of the Grand Mufti and, in 1921, the Supreme Muslim Council. The Council was to control religious courts, the appointments of all *qadis* (heads of these courts), trusts and *waqfs*.[45] Khalidi notes how, politically, this appointment was employed to present the Grand Mufti as the Palestinian Arab representative to counter the power of the Zionist Commission or the Zionist Executive. Thus, in the matter of representation in administration too, while formal electoral representation was curtailed, a religious-communal representation was made effective, creating a dualist opposition. The Christian patriarchates continued to represent the Christian groups in Palestine.

In these formulations of schemes for governance individual subjects of the state were represented by perceived group interests. The important groups were the fundamentally defined singular religious groups of Jewish, Muslim and Christian 'communities'. The British chose religious-communal representation in the schemes of government in Palestine, rather than the national representation as individual adults. While national groups like the Muslim–Christian Associations and the Palestine Arab Congress and its offshoot, the Arab Executive, existed, none of them established a structure that could lead to the formation of a state.[46] As in India, but with the greater importance of a British colonial Zionist policy, the idea of colonial 'difference' governed the choice of representation, ruling out any possibility of universal adult franchise.[47] As Lord Minto said, when promulgating the 1909 reforms to the Government of India Act that was addressed above, 'what India required was a "constitutional autocracy which binds itself to govern by rule", and which invites to its councils "representatives of all the interests which are capable of being represented".'[48]

I would like to add the caveat that governance was only one field in which singular communities were structured. Processes within the population also aided this coalescing of communities. The separate electorates for Muslims discussed above, for representing them in local government, were responding to deals between the main political parties – the All-India Congress and the Muslim League – made in 1916, as well as to the demands for separate electorates raised by the All-India Muslim League (1906). The Legislative Council proposal by Herbert Samuel was also responding to the nationalist slogans raised by Arab and Zionist Jewish groups in Palestine.

Large singular groups were constructed as the main 'actors' in both Palestine and India at around the same time, and these groups become nationalised in their political personas but in quite different ways. The Zionists in Palestine and the Muslim League in India were drawn into a religious nationalist position claiming to represent a minority or oppressed group. The category of the majority national group was less clearly religious. Both the Indian National Congress in India and the Arab Executive were the catchall national groups within which a large number of small religious and ethnic groups got subsumed. In India, the Sikhs, Jains, Depressed Classes and indigenous tribals across the subcontinent were counted with the Hindus, and in Palestine the Christian, Druze, Alawis and Bedouin were subsumed within the category of 'Arab'. Thus, a generalised 'majority' was created in opposition to the nationalised minority.

Partition plans

Another area of comparison and similarity were the various partition plans proposed for both locations. These have been studied separately by a number of scholars, but comparative work is rare. In both locations, partition was not the first solution, but was presented as a solution of last resort to solve an intractable governmental situation of two opposing groups refusing to come to any terms to share power.

We saw above the making of identitarian blocks, generated both by the basic structures of legal administration as well as representational practices in public policy and politics. Despite these groups and their aspirations to nationhood, in neither case was the initial demand for power accompanied by the notion of a division of the land.

In India

Separate provinces for Hindu and Muslim-majority populations were suggested as early as 1924 by Hindu nationalist and Congress leader Lala Lajpat Rai. After suggesting four provinces that had a Muslim majority in the north and west and east, he wrote: 'It should distinctly be understood that this is not a united India. It means a clear partition of India into a Muslim India and a non-Muslim India.'[49] The Muslim League talked about two nations from 1930 onwards. The most eloquent ideological description of communal life in India is the poet Iqbal's 1930 presidential speech to the annual conference of the Muslim League.[50] This was, arguably, the first articulation of the demand for separate states by the All-India Muslim League. In the run-up to partition, though, the League and Jinnah referred to the demand for separate states raised at the annual meeting of 1940 in Lahore as definitive of their idea of partition.[51]

Even after making the demand for a separate state, the Muslim League continued to ask for separate representation to ensure parity in government beyond demographic swamping by the majority. This was highlighted subsequent to the elections of 1937 in India, when the Congress did not accommodate the defeated Muslim League members despite a pre-election agreement in the provincial legislative assemblies.[52] These elections were followed by a mass contact campaign by both parties among the Muslim masses. With the onset of war in 1939, the Congress members resigned from the provincial assemblies and the provincial government reverted to the British appointed governors.

In 1942, the war administration in Britain tried to win favour and Congress support for the war in India, by sending Sir Stafford Cripps to negotiate terms for the postwar transfer of power. The liberal party in government also supported a study by Coupland, a liberal imperialist, at around the same time, to come up with 'innovative' solutions to the problem of transferring power during a British withdrawal from India. I will examine these proposals below.

In Palestine

The Arab Executive rejected communal representation in 1922 in much the same terms as the Indian National Congress, as a betrayal of the democratic principle. The language of the two 'majority groups', calling for a denial of communal self-determination and the establishment of universal suffrage, can be examined to see how the conflicts over different justifications of sovereignty led to the impasse deemed 'ungovernable' in 1947–48.

Models of governance like cantonisation and federation, both permitting power-sharing, existed in both locations, indicating a collective resolution of ways of living together differently. Sinanoglou has looked at various early suggestions of cantonisation proposals from the late 1920s and more concrete published proposals from 1935. She looks at these plans as precursors to partition.[53] However, one might suggest that they represented a way of identifying *living together* differently.

Roza El-Eini's work suggests that Douglas G. Harris, Commissioner on Special Duty and Irrigation Engineer in Palestine, who had served as a member of the committee looking at the partitioning of Sindh from the Bombay Presidency in 1931 in India, brought his experience of working in India to bear in his proposals for the separate finance, irrigation and boundary committees for partitioning Palestine. His detailed proposals contained statistics on sharing water, electricity and public finances, and subventions as legal ways for states to help each other to be independent and separate. Thus, he prepared the ground for looking at partition as *living separately* as a realistic possibility. His proposals fed into the 1937 Peel Commission, which recommended partition for Palestine. Harris used the plans and experience of partitioning the province of Sindh from Bombay within the Indian state as the model to work out a territorial partition.[54] Here the problem of partition was not seen as an identity issue as much as a question of viability of the state. The common connections between the two places of India and Palestine cannot be ignored in this case. The example suggests that the Palestine partition proposal could be better understood if we explore the links with the Sindh–Bombay Presidency partition.[55] I suggest that the manner of working out the separation of Sindh from Bombay province provided a pragmatic language to speak about partition. The Sindh partition was advocated on communal grounds, but accepted on the grounds of 'administrative reorganisation and financial viability of the province'. The comparison is crucial to understanding the 'logistical' aspects of partition, rather than the identitarian politics we have been looking at above. Harris used his experience in Sind to suggest the parameters within which separate states could be created in Palestine.

Personal linkages between partition in India and Palestine

Another link in the partition plans for India and Palestine is in the person of Reginald Coupland. As mentioned earlier, he was the Beit Professor of Colonial History at Oxford University and he served in various public positions. Coupland was a member of the Round Table, a liberal colonial pressure group that helped in developing colonial policy. T. G. Fraser[56] first drew scholarly attention to his work on the partitions of Palestine and India, though Sinanoglu has shown how near contemporaries also linked Coupland to the conception of partition.[57] The prominence given to his role has been disputed by Sinanoglou's exhaustive study. It demonstrates, as does El-Eini's study detailing the Palestine administration's role, that the role of Coupland was less important than suggested by Fraser, or believed by contemporaries, in proposing partition as the solution for dealing with divided societies.[58] However, Sinanoglu does note that Coupland's authorship of the Peel Commission report does make the argument for partition eloquent and convincing.[59] Recently his role has been re-examined by Arie Dubnov. He focused on Coupland's liberal imperialist ideology, concluding that a federal structure was the best solution for India, securing local autonomy with national oversight. Such a federally united India would join in a British commonwealth of nations, similar to the Durham plan that gave Canada's disparate groups a way to live together in the Commonwealth.[60] I examine Coupland's role below, again briefly, to tease out the implications of his suggestions for India.

Coupland was appointed by the Secretary of State for India, Lord Amery, to come up with a bold and credible alternative plan for India in 1941. First he went to India in the winter of 1941–42 and travelled widely to study the Indian problem. On his return to Oxford wrote a three-volume report that detailed the history, current issues and future suggestions for the problem of Indian governance.[61] As he was in India, he was detailed to assist the new constitutional initiative in the form of Sir Stafford Cripps's Mission to India in March 1942. Coupland's role in Cripps's offer to the Indian public remains unclear as his own account hardly describes what he said to Cripps.[62] However, Cripps and Coupland, and Lord Amery who nominated the latter, were similar in their thoughts and views about empire. They were all liberals and associated with the Round Table group – who advocated a federal structure for the Empire, such that the nations would have home rule over their regions, but would be joined in a federal structure as a commonwealth.[63] This stand was expressed in Cripps's offer as related by Abul Kalam Azad, when Cripps promised a 'national government' in India immediately. Hodson has also recounted this offer as he was a participant in the negotiations in his role as Reforms Commissioner in India.[64] The liberals, represented by Coupland in his reports on India published in 1942, 1944, and to his restatement in 1946, laid out how the disputes in India should not lead to partition. He presented a strong argument for a federal solution on behalf of the British Government.[65] Coupland suggested a federation of three provinces in most of his writing, but in his 1942 article, 'The Indian Deadlock', he suggested that 'South India' should form a fourth provincial grouping. In the federal centre of these four provinces – two

Muslim dominated and two Hindu dominated – the two religious groups would be equal partners.[66]

As Coupland said in his 1944 article, the problem of governance in India was not one of British attitudes but Indian differences between Hindu and Muslim – more specifically, between the Congress Party and the Muslim League.[67] He made the same observation in the Peel Report about Arabs and Zionists.[68] As clearly shown by Fraser, Coupland indicated that certain types of societies that had primary English membership could learn to live with divisions and differences, as in Great Britain, South Africa and Canada, but not societies that were from a different racial background. He had to accept that Ireland, in this case, was a tragic exception.[69] Thus, despite the federal solution to the Indian problem suggested by Coupland, in all of his numerous articles and the three-volume *Report on the Constitutional Problem*, he expressed the real fear that the differences among Indians were irreconcilable. He predicted civil war several times in his essays.[70] The federal solution he suggested was also an attempt to geographically separate the communities that were seen as warring.

Laura Robson's excellent study documents the policy of geographically separating communities and transferring populations in the post-imperial states of Europe in the late nineteenth and, more extensively, early twentieth century and after the First World War. She convincingly argues how partition works to further the imperial aims of generating 'client' states and populations in regions that the imperial states were to govern over the nineteenth and, more especially, twentieth century. She looked at the politics of 'protection' of minority rights that led to extensive population transfers. She analyses the British policy of 'favouring' the minority in mandate Palestine as well, generating a strong nationalised, territorial claim as a result of arming and supporting Zionist settlement during the mandate period.[71] In the same light, Indian nationalists have often criticised the colonial policy of 'divide and rule' in India, leading to the encouragement of diametrically opposed Muslim League and Congress politics – and even that Pakistan would serve a strategic function in Asia that a socialistic Congress-led India would not.[72] This claim, popularised by writers like Narendra Singh Sarila, is challenged in the chapter in this volume by Ian Talbot who argues that the defence strategy only emerged after partition was accepted by all the parties, and was not some Machiavellian motivation for partition.

While strategic concerns might explain British policy in both places, these alone cannot account for the popular support for the policy and the nature of local politics that played a role in the making of partition. As demonstrated above, there is a reason to compare the local politics and the nature of the ideology behind the partition decisions as well. As argued by Kattan, the role of ideology in the formation of national identity, and the defining role played by structures of governance, may provide a more solid explanation for the absence of a common ground between the Zionist and Arab groups and Muslim League and the Congress.[73] He suggests that the functioning of a representative system of government, based on the Westminster model, was contingent not only on a parliamentary majority, but also on common group consciousness that was found wanting in mandate Palestine and British India. Thus the aspirations for a homogenous community achieving nationhood could not be reconciled with the representative form of government in a plural society.

In addition, the role of colonial officials and their contribution to the development of policy cannot be ignored either. For example, Roza El-Eini has documented the importance of Douglas E. Harris, an officer who first worked in India, and then in Palestine. She has noted that other members of the Indian Civil Service had worked in Palestine as well, and suggests that the strategies that worked in India were imported to Palestine via members of the Palestine administration. The Palestine administrators' 'ascendant role' in the partition plans can be viewed from the Peel Commission through the Anglo-American Committee and UNSCOP's plan.[74]

Conclusion

This chapter suggests that colonial structures of governance – legal and representational – generated a construction of identitarian religious and ethnic groups. Thus, the legal and representational treatment of religious groups and communities was not a suppression of the narrative of community, but rather a consistent deployment of this narrative to strengthen the supreme authority of the colonial state. This is not to suggest that the terms Hindu, Muslim, Arab and Jew were not employed to speak of the multiple sects and linguistic and other groups that existed in the two places, before British colonial administration. However, the consistent employment of identitarian governance meant that smaller polities, separately organised sectarian groups, had to define themselves with reference to the unitary community to access governmental schemes and legal protections.

The same identities were also nationalised and politically mobilised in the two places by the local populations. The history of this latter political process has been more often written about. The rise of nationalism, and the consolidation of religious political parties that claimed to be the singular representative of the Jewish communities of Palestine, and the Muslims of India, are important processes whose parallels have been examined by Devji as well as Aamir Mufti. Both have suggested similar processes of minority nationalist ideology in colonial conditions.[75] In both cases, the construction of a religious identity is centred on the political quest of homeland and denuded of geographical or historical referents. Devji shows that western Indian merchant Shia leadership dominated a Sunni Muslim League. In the early days of the Muslim League, sectarian identities were unimportant – as shown also in the case of Sir Muhammad Zafrulla Khan. Zafrulla Khan was a prominent League member who belonged to the Ahmadiyya sect, considered today to be apostate. Ahmad's study, quoted above, demonstrates that this seeming political change regarding the position of Ahmadiyyas has long roots in Anglo-Mohammedan law that entailed the construction of impermeable social boundaries between communities in India.[76]

Thus, despite the importance of political developments that aided and made the identitarian groups stand off on the streets of India and Palestine, I would like to draw attention to the arena of governance where such identities developed and were effectively and authoritatively deployed on individual subjects of the state – at the time not citizens. The categorisation of British Indians and mandate Palestinians into two opposing blocks as the normalised understanding of the 'local populations' of these two places occurred very prominently in the legal arena and in the political representation of people. A deep colonial sociology of native difference operated in the making of these categories. 'Native' politicians also operated with these ideas, adopting these categories for self-representation.

What of the consequences of these categories? The adoption of these unitary categories of fundamentally defined nationalised religions legitimated the conquest and settlement strategies adopted at partition. Thus the Muslim League National Guard felt that territory assigned to Pakistan belonged only to Muslims and may be cleared of all non-Muslims, and a similar view was held by the Sikh *jathas* (armed group) and Hindu volunteer gangs of the Rashtriya Swayamsevak Sangh. The Border Security Force soldiers and the local administration in Punjab also became involved in this mentality of conquest.[77] A similar mentality of conquest pervaded the *Nakba* and the British withdrawal of Palestine.[78] The extent of violence was also compounded by the British refusal to govern in both places. The role of the British during the violence in the final days of the Raj is only just coming under scrutiny.[79] The mere exercise of colonial governance that divided local society in India and Palestine was not the sole actor in the mode, operation and experience of partition. Yet, without understanding and accounting for such governance, it would be difficult to understand why and how so many individuals who identified with small sectarian groups ended up as members of larger communal identitarian bodies.

Does the making of these connections and comparisons across the two states help us address the partitions that still occupy the countries today? This chapter is an attempt to unpick the unitary identities by historicising them and locating them in British governance of the territories under their control. This unpicking can unlock the multiplicity that lies hidden in politically mobilised unitary identities.

Notes

1 T. G. Fraser, *Partition in Ireland, India, and Palestine: Theory and Practice* (New York: St Martin's Press, 1984); Robert Schaeffer, *Severed States: Dilemmas of Democracy in a Divided World* (Lanham, MD: Rowman and Littlefield, 1999); Smita Jassal and Eyal Ben-Ari (eds), *The Partition Motif in Contemporary Conflicts* (New Delhi: Sage, 2007); Ghislaine Deschaumes and Rada Ivekovic (eds), *Divided Countries, Separated Cities: The Modern Legacy of Partition* (New Delhi: Oxford University Press, 2003); Geremy Forman and Alexandre Kedar, 'From Arab Land to "Israel Lands": The Legal Dispossession of the Palestinians Displaced by Israel in the Wake of 1948', *Environment & Planning D: Society & Space* 22 (6) (2004), 809–830; Lucy Chester, 'Boundary Commissions as the Tools to Safeguard the Interests at the End of Empire', *Journal of Historical Geography* 34 (2008), 494–515; Ranabir Samaddar (ed.), *Reflections on Partition in the East* (Calcutta: Vikas Publishing, 1997); Victor Kattan, 'The Empire Departs: The Partitions of British India, Mandate Palestine, and the Dawn of Self-Determination in the Third World', *Asian Journal of Middle Eastern and Islamic Studies* 12 (3) (2018), 304–327. See also Aamir Mufti, *Enlightenment in the Colony: The Jewish Question and the Crisis of Postcolonial Culture* (Princeton, NJ: Princeton University Press, 2007); Faisal Devji, *Muslim Zion* (Cambridge, MA: Harvard University Press, 2013); Farzana Shaikh, 'Faisal Devji, *Muslim Zion: Pakistan as a Political Idea*', *South Asia Multidisciplinary Academic Journal* (2015), at http://journals.openedition.org/samaj/3846; Laura Robson, *States of Separation: Transfer, Partition, and the Making of the Modern Middle East* (Oakland, CA: University of California Press, 2017).
2 Jonathan D. Greenberg, 'Divided Lands, Phantom Limbs: Partition in the Indian Subcontinent, Palestine, China, and Korea', *Journal of International Affairs* 57 (2) (2004), 7–27; Jonathan D. Greenberg, 'Generations of Memory: Remembering Partition in India/Pakistan and Israel/Palestine', *Comparative Studies of South Asia and Middle East* 25 (1) (2005), 89–110; Joe Cleary, *Literature Partition and the Nation State: Culture and Conflict in Ireland, Israel and Palestine* (Cambridge: Cambridge University Press, 2002).
3 Reginald Coupland, 'The Indian Deadlock', *Pacific Affairs* 17 (1) (1944), 26–37, at www.jstor.org/stable/2751994.
4 For the Indian partition, see the news items quoted in Yasmin Khan, *The Great Partition: The Making of India and Pakistan* (New Haven, CT: Yale University Press, 2007), p. 5, fn 10. For Palestine, the agreement regarding partition was much less sanguine. However, UK Prime Minister Mr Attlee and others in his cabinet hoped that an announcement that the UK government intended to relinquish the mandate would produce salutary results. See the Conclusions of

the Cabinet meeting 20 Sep. 1947, The National Archives, Cabinet 76 (47) ref. CAB 128/10/27. This is also referred to in Chester, 'Boundary Commissions', p. 512.
5 Other minority groups that did not fit the narrative of the two major opposing blocks, like the Christians and Parsis in India, were considered irrelevant to the partition decision and will not be examined in this chapter.
6 Sahar Huneidi, *A Broken Trust: Herbert Samuel, Zionism and the Palestinians* (London: Tauris Academic Studies, 2001); Rashid Khalidi, *The Iron Cage* (Oxford: Oneworld Publications, 2006); Muhammad Muslih, *The Origins of Palestinian Nationalism* (New York: Columbia University Press, 1988).
7 Arie Dubnov and Laura Robson, 'Introduction', in their edited *Partitions: A Transnational History of Twentieth-Century Territorial Separatism* (Stanford, CA: Stanford University Press, 2019), p. 13. I thank Arie Dubnov for sending along his newly published chapter and book introduction just as I was finishing this chapter.
8 This coincidence of internationalist and imperialist is very well argued in Robson, *States of Separation* as well as in Dubnov and Robson, 'Introduction'.
9 For a clear formulation see Kumkum Sangari, 'Politics of Diversity: Religious Communities and Multiple Patriarchies', *Economic and Political Weekly*, December 1995, 3288–3292.
10 For a more extensive argument see my *A Question of Community: Religious Groups in Colonial Law* (Kolkata: Samya, 2001); also 'Legal Formulation of the Question of Community: Defining the Khoja Collective', *Indian Social Science Review* 1 (1) (1999), 137–151.
11 Bernard Cohn, *Colonialism and its Forms of Knowledge: The British in India* (Princeton, NJ: Princeton University Press, 1996; ACLS Humanities E-Book); Sudipto Kaviraj, 'The Imaginary Institution of India', in Partha Chatterjee and Gyan Pandey (eds), *Subaltern Studies*, vol. 7 (Delhi: Oxford University Press, 1992); Gyan Pandey, *The Construction of Communalism in Colonial North India* (Delhi: Oxford University Press, 1990).
12 Roberto Mazza, 'Transforming the Holy City: From Communal Clashes to Urban Violence, the Nebi Musa riots in 1920', in Ulrike Freitag, Nelida Fuccaro, Claudia Ghrawi and Nora Lafi (eds), *Urban Violence in the Middle East: Changing Cityscapes in the Transition from Empire to Nation State* (New York; Oxford: Berghahn Books, 2015), pp. 179–194; see also Roberto Mazza, *Jerusalem: From the Ottomans to the British* (London: Tauris Academic Studies, 2009); Yair Wallach, 'Jerusalem Between Segregation and Integration: Reading Urban Space through the Eyes of Justice Gad Frumkin', in S. R. Goldstein-Sabbah and H. L. Murre-Van Den Berg (eds), *Modernity, Minority, and the Public Sphere: Jews and Christians in the Middle East*, Leiden Studies in Islam and Society (Leiden: Brill, 2016), pp. 205–233; Yair Wallach, 'Rethinking the Yishuv: Late-Ottoman Palestine's Jewish Communities Revisited', *Journal of Modern Jewish Studies* 16 (2) (2017), 275–294.
13 Assaf Likhovski, *Law and Identity in Mandate Palestine* (Chapel Hill, NC: University of North Carolina Press, 2006), p. 38.

14 *Report of the Court of Enquiry into the Riots in Jerusalem during Last April, 1920* (Palin Report), 3, unpublished report, Port Said, see https://en.wikisource.org/wiki/Palin_Report (accessed 13 March 2023). Victor Kattan, *From Coexistence to Conquest: International Law and the Origins of the Arab–Israeli Conflict 1891–1949* (London: Pluto Press, 2009), pp. 83–86 discusses both these riots.
15 *Report of the Court of Enquiry, 1920*, p. 76.
16 Colonial Office, Great Britain, *Palestine: Disturbances in May, 1921: Reports of the Commission of Inquiry with Correspondence Relating Thereto* (Haycraft Commission) (London: HMSO, 1921). Thanks to Penelope Sinanoglou for this reference and for responding so generously to my queries on the 1920/21 disturbances.
17 Sherene Seikaly, *Men of Capital: Scarcity and Economy in Mandate Palestine* (Stanford, CA: Stanford University Press, 2015), p. 94. She notes the difficulty the colonial officials had in counting and differentiating between people and races.
18 Sherene Seikaly, 'Men of Capital in Mandate Palestine', *Rethinking Marxism* 30 (3) (2018), 412.
19 Edward Said, 'Zionism from the Standpoint of its Victims', *Social Text* 1 (1979), 7–58, at 14.
20 See Laura Robson, 'Partition and the question of international governance: the 1947 United Nations Special Committee on Palestine' in this volume for a discussion of labour Zionism and the politics around the creation of separate spheres in mandate Palestine.
21 Shodhan, *A Question of Community*; Likhovski, *Law and Identity*.
22 See Bernard Cohn, 'Law and the Colonial State in India', in his *Colonialism and its Forms of Knowledge*, pp. 57–75, at pp. 30, 67.
23 Erskine Perry, *Cases Illustrative of Oriental Life and the Application of English Law to India, decided in H.M. Su* Erskine Perry, *Cases Illustrative of Oriental Life and the Application of English Law to India, decided in HM Supreme Court at Bombay* (London: Law Bookseller and Publisher, 1853), pp. 123–124. He says, 'It was believed erroneously that the population of India might be classified under the two great heads of Mahommedan and Gentoo, ... the main object was to retain to the whole people lately conquered their ancient usages and laws ...'.
24 There are many histories of this process, but for our purposes see Huneidi, *A Broken Trust*.
25 Likhovski, *Law and Identity*, pp. 23–24, 27, 37, 215. See also Norman Bentwich, 'The Legal System of Palestine under the Mandate', *Middle East Journal*, 2 (1) (1948), 33–46.
26 The East India Company governed India from approximately 1764 (dates vary for different parts of the country) to 1857. In 1857 there was a major rebellion and the government of India was taken over by the Crown directly, managed through their representative, the Viceroy. From 1858 to 1869 there were major changes in legislation with the codification of many aspects of legal procedure and laws.

27 See Shodhan, *A Question of Community*, p. 6; also see Shodhan, 'Legal Formulation'; Amrita Shodhan, 'Caste in the Judicial Courts of Gujarat – 1800–1860', in Edward Simpson and Aparna Kapadia (eds), *Idea of Gujarat: History, Ethnography and Text* (Hyderabad: Orient Black Swan, 2010), pp. 32–49.
28 Communities were defined on the basis of fundamental texts – thus Hindu communities were seen as those that followed the prescriptions of texts – which were also selected as foundational texts of Hinduism; for Islam the Koran was seen as the fundamental text and Muslim practices had to claim continuity with the Koranic prescriptions.
29 Shazia Ahmad, 'A New Dispensation in Islam: The Ahmadiyya and the Law in Colonial India, 1872 to 1939' (PhD dissertation, SOAS, University of London, 2015), at http://eprints.soas.ac.uk/id/eprint/20372 (accessed 13 March 2023).
30 Flavia Agnes notes the slow, case-by-case process of working out how Sikhs, Jains, Buddhists and many tribal groups were seen as governed by Hindu law, modified to their own peculiar customs, if any. Flavia Agnes, *Law and Gender Inequality: The Politics of Women's Rights in India* (New Delhi: Oxford University Press, 1999), p. 24. See also M. P. Jain, *Indian Legal History 2006* (n.p.: Lulu Press, 2014).
31 Thomas Metcalf, *Ideologies of the Raj* (Cambridge: Cambridge University Press, 1994), p. 148.
32 Likhovski, *Law and Identity*, p. 29.
33 *Ibid.*, pp. 39–40.
34 Bentwich, 'The Legal System of Palestine', pp. 35–36.
35 *Ibid.*, pp. 36–37. Though he gives a different explanation for the setting up of the Supreme 'Moslem' Council, I focus here on the work that the Council was tasked with.
36 Assaf Likhovski, 'Arab', in *Law and Identity*, throughout the book but especially see p. 213.
37 Sumit Sarkar, *Modern India, 1885–1947*, Cambridge Commonwealth Series (Basingstoke: Macmillan Press, 1989).
38 For a discussion of the politics of the Poona Pact between the fasting Gandhi and B. R. Ambedkar, see B. R. Ambedkar, *What Congress and Gandhi Have Done to the Untouchables* (Bombay: Thacker and Co., 1945). Also see Sekhar Bandyopadhyay, 'Transfer of Power and the Crisis of Dalit Politics in India, 1945–47', *Modern Asian Studies* 34 (4) (2000), 893–942.
39 See the excellent study of this argument in James Chiriyankandath, '"Democracy" under the Raj: Elections and Separate Representation in British India', *Journal of Commonwealth & Comparative Politics* 30 (1) (1992), 39–63. doi: 10.1080/14662049208447624.
40 Most extensively argued by Ayesha Jalal, 'Jinnah's Pakistan and the Cabinet Mission Plan', in *The Sole Spokesman: Jinnah, the Muslim League and the Demand for Pakistan* (Cambridge: Cambridge University Press, 1985), pp. 174–207.
41 See the general discussion of the clash of ideas of representation v. liberal democracy in Kattan, 'The Empire Departs', especially pp. 4–8.

42 George V of the United Kingdom, 'The Palestine Order in Council, 1922', Part III, para 19 and attached to it 'Palestine Legislative Council Election Order, 1922', para 12, UNISPAL (n.d.): 8, 29. www.un.org/unispal/document/auto-insert-196295/ (accessed 18 January 2015). Also see the discussion by Elie Kedourie, 'Sir Herbert Samuel and the Government of Palestine', *Middle Eastern Studies* 5 (1) (1969), 59–60. www.jstor.org/stable/4282274.
43 Kattan, 'The Empire Departs', pp. 12–14.
44 Winston Churchill, 'British White Paper of June 1922', (n.p. Yale University, 2008), at http://avalon.law.yale.edu/20th_century/brwh1922.asp, retrieved 02/07/2014 (accessed 13 March 2023).
45 Kedourie, 'Sir Herbert Samuel and the Government of Palestine'; Khalidi, *The Iron Cage*, pp. 31–64.
46 Khalidi, *The Iron Cage*, pp. 58–63.
47 See Laura Robson, 'Partition and the question of international governance: the 1947 United Nations Special Committee on Palestine' in this volume for a further discussion of the mandate authority's support for differential development of Zionist and Arab governance structures.
48 Quoted in Metcalf, *Ideologies of the Raj*, p. 224. See also Thomas Metcalf, 'Preface', in *Ideologies of the Raj*, pp. ix–xi for a discussion of the idea of colonial difference and its central place in the ideology of rule.
49 Lala Lajpat Rai, 'The Hindu–Muslim Problem (1924): Some Suggestions for Political Improvement', part 11, in Vijaya Chandra Joshi (ed.), *Lala Lajpat Rai: Writings and Speeches*, vol. 2, 1920–1928 (Delhi: University Publishers, 1966), p. 213. Reproduced by Frances Pritchett with notes on her website, 'South Asia Resources', at www.columbia.edu/itc/mealac/pritchett/00islamlinks/txt_lajpatrai_1924/11part.html (accessed 13 March 2023).
50 Muhammad Iqbal, 'Presidential Address to the Muslim League – 1930', in Syed S. Pirzada (ed.), *Foundations of Pakistan: All India Muslim League Documents 1906–1947*, vol. 2: 1924–1947 (Karachi: National Publishing House, 1970), pp. 153–171.
51 See M. K. Gandhi, Mohammad Ali Jinnah and Nawabzada Liaquat Ali Khan, *Jinnah-Gandhi Talks: September, 1944: Text of Correspondence and Other Relevant Documents Etc.: Foreword by Nawabzada Liaquat Ali Khan* (Delhi: All India Muslim League, 1945).
52 Mushirul Hasan, *India's Partition: Process, Strategy and Mobilization* (Delhi; Oxford: Oxford University Press, 1993), pp. 9–15 has a long discussion on this refusal of the Congress to accommodate Muslim League members in government in 1937. The pre-election agreement is mentioned on p. 9.
53 Penelope Sinanoglou, 'British Plans for the Partition of Palestine 1929–1938', *Historical Journal* 52 (1) (2009), 131–152.
54 Roza El-Eini, 'The Partition Plans', in *Mandated Landscape: British Imperial Rule in Palestine 1929–1948*. (London: Routledge, 2006), pp. 314–379, at pp. 317, 320–324.
55 Sindh became an independent region when the Government of India Act 1935 partitioned it from the Bombay Presidency and gave it a separate legal status

from 1 April 1936. This partition created separate provinces within a national union, hence it was different from the later separation of nation states. While the movement to separate Sindh from a majority Hindu province of Bombay became a political movement of Muslims wanting partition in the 1920s, it was initiated in 1913 by Harchandrai Vishnindas, and supported by Ghulam Mohammed Bhurgri, along with Shaikh Abdul Majid and Diwan Gidumal (Hindu and Muslim politicians and merchants). Their initial argument was that this would provide protection for Sindhi traders from the more prosperous Bombay traders. Adeel Khan, *Politics of Identity: Ethnic Nationalism and the State in Pakistan* (New Delhi: Sage, 2005), p. 132. The Financial Inquiry Committee that sat from July to September 1931 to look into the separation question was primarily concerned with the financial viability of Sindh. During its hearing, the communal divide was breached and evidence supporting separation was received from some Hindus as well as Muslims. Mani Shankar Aiyar, 'The Historical Dimension', *Confessions of a Secular Fundamentalist* (UK: Penguin, 2006), chapter 3 (n.p.).

56 T. G. Fraser, 'Sir Reginald Coupland, The Round Table, and the Problem of Divided Societies', in Andrea Bosco and Alex May (eds), *The Round Table: Empire, Commonwealth and British Foreign Policy* (London: Lothian Foundation, 1997), pp. 407–419.

57 Sinanoglou, 'British Plans', pp. 134–135.

58 El-Eini, 'The Partition Plans', p. 320, fn 31, 32 says that contrary to various Israeli scholars, specifically Yossi Katz, *Partner to Partition: The Jewish Agency's Partition Plan in the Mandate Era* (London; Portland, OR: Frank Cass, 1998) and Itzhak Galnoor, *Partition of Palestine* (New York: SUNY, 1995), 'Prof. Reginald Coupland did not have such a singular influence on the Commission's final partition plan. Input is evident from various sources, including the mandatory government, Arabs and Jews and shows that Coupland was open to ideas.' Sinanoglou, 'British Plans', pp. 131–152.

59 Sinanoglou, British Plans', p. 135.

60 Arie Dubnov, 'The Architect of Two Partitions or a Federalist Daydreamer: The Curious Case of Reginald Coupland', in Arie Dubnov and Laura Robson (eds), *Partitions: A Transnational History of Twentieth-Century Territorial Separatism* (Stanford, CA: Stanford University Press, 2019), pp. 56–84, especially pp. 64, 80.

61 Fraser, 'Sir Reginald Coupland', pp. 407–419 has a detailed account of how he was appointed to the job by Lord Amery, then Secretary of State for India to the bipartisan war cabinet.

62 Reginald Coupland, *The Cripps Mission* (London: Oxford University Press, 1942).

63 Fraser, 'Sir Reginald Coupland'; Dubnov, 'The Curious Case' as well as Coupland's many writings and speeches on the issue of India, especially his 'Indian Deadlock', pp. 26–37. Reginald Coupland, 'Alternative Scheme to Pakistan, March 1944', extracted from his *Report on Constitutional Problem*, vol. 3, 'Future of India', 1942 and repeated in *India – A Restatement*, 1945, in Maurice Gwyer and A.

Appadorai (eds), *Speeches and Documents on the Indian Constitution 1921–1947*, vol. 2 (Bombay: Oxford University Press, 1957), pp. 467–478.
64 H. V. Hodson, *The Great Divide: Britain–India–Pakistan* (London: Hutchinson, 1969), pp. 99–104.
65 Very well argued and presented by Dubnov, 'The Curious Case'.
66 Coupland, 'Indian Deadlock', p. 36.
67 Coupland, 'Indian Deadlock'.
68 Kattan, 'The Empire Departs', pp. 12–14.
69 Fraser, 'Sir Reginald Coupland', pp. 408–410.
70 Coupland, *The Cripps Mission*, p. 27; Coupland, 'Indian Deadlock', p. 28.
71 Robson, *States of Separation*.
72 A. R. Desai, *The Social Background of Indian Nationalism* (Mumbai: Popular Prakashan, 1966); Jawaharlal Nehru, *The Discovery of* India (New Delhi: Penguin, 2004; first published 1947), pp. 418–426. Narendra Singh Sarila, *The Shadow of the Great Game: The Untold Story of India's Partition* (London: Constable, 2006).
73 Kattan, 'The Empire Departs'.
74 Roza El-Eini, *Mandated Landscape: British Imperial Rule in Palestine 1929–1948* (Abindgon: Routledge, 2005), pp. 367–368.
75 Devji, *Muslim Zion*; Mufti, *Enlightenment in the Colony*.
76 On the impact of law in the making of Ahmadiyya identity, see Ahmad, 'A New Dispensation in Islam'.
77 Swarna Aiyar, '"August Anarchy": The Partition Massacres in Punjab, 1947', in D. A. Low and Howard Brasted (eds), *Freedom Trauma, Continuities: Northern India and Independence* (New Delhi: Sage Publications, 1998), pp. 15–38; Ian Copland, 'The Master and the Maharajas: The Sikh Princes and the East Punjab Massacres of 1947', *Modern Asian Studies* 36 (3) (2002), 657–704; Indivar Kamtekar, 'The Military Ingredient of Communal Violence in Punjab, 1947', *Proceedings of the Indian History Congress* 56 (1995), 568–572. Ian Talbot, 'The Mountbatten Viceroyalty reconsidered: personality, prestige and strategic vision in the partition of India' in this volume also refers to the presence of nearly 58,000 members of the Hindu volunteer movement the RSS in Punjab alone (fn 34).
78 Eugene L. Rogan and Avi Shlaim (eds), *The War for Palestine: Rewriting the History of 1948*, 2nd edn (New York: Cambridge University Press, 2007).
79 Yasmin Khan, 'Out of Control? Partition Violence and the State in Uttar Pradesh' (pp. 36–59) and Pippa Virdee, 'Partition and the Absence of Communal Violence in Malerkotla' (pp. 16–35), both in Ian Talbot (ed.), *The Deadly Embrace: Religion, Politics and Violence in India and Pakistan 1947–2002* (New Delhi: Oxford University Press, 2007).

6

India's dilemmas of pragmatism v. principles: Nehru's preference for a partitioned India but a federal Palestine

P. R. Kumaraswamy

While the acceptance of a communal partition in the Indian subcontinent was a collective majority decision of the Congress Party, Jawaharlal Nehru (Prime Minister of the Interim government from September 1946 and of free India from 15 August 1947) was the architect of the federal plan for Palestine. His approach towards colonial situations and partition as a possible solution to communal problems in India and Palestine highlighted his dichotomy between pragmatism necessitated by the politico-territorial immediacy of the Indian condition and moral posturing facilitated by geographical distance. Having achieved independence through communal partition, he was urging the Jews and Arabs of Palestine to coexist under one political authority through accommodation and cooperation. The federal plan was not only a sign of Indian naivety regarding international diplomacy, but also a reflection of its duality; political pragmatism was confined to the subcontinent while moral eloquence was visible and useful elsewhere. The duality towards the two partitions was compounded by the uncritical adulation of the federal plan by various Indian scholars and writers.[1]

The roots of the dichotomous Indian approach to communal partition can be traced to the early 1920s, when amid the Khilafat struggle (1919–24) the Indian nationalists expressed a position that gradually culminated in free India advocating a federal Palestine as its solution nearly three decades later. The Khilafat Movement, which sought to preserve and perpetuate the thirteen-century-old caliphate, played a crucial role in the evolution of the Indian understanding of, and response towards, the unfolding crisis in Palestine following the Balfour Declaration of 1917 which pledged British support for a Jewish national home in Palestine.

For centuries, the Muslims of the subcontinent were indifferent to the institution of caliphate and instead paid allegiance to various Muslim rulers and dynasties that had governed vast areas of northern India since the twelfth century. There is no evidence to suggest that the Indian Muslims looked up to the caliphs for allegiance, and for its part Islamic histography rarely discussed India's vast Muslim community. Firmly entrenched in power, the Muslim rulers also did not need the support or endorsement of caliphs for legitimacy. Things began to change in the nineteenth century when British rule ended the Mughal dynasty (1526–1857), with its last ruler Bahadur Shah Zafar (1837–57) being deposed and exiled to Burma (now Myanmar) and India coming under direct control of the British Crown in 1858.

The fall of the three-century-old Mughal dynasty was devastating for the Indian Muslims and forced them to look for solace and comfort elsewhere. The Ottoman Empire, which encompassed vast swaths of territories in the Middle East, emerged as the symbol, hope and personification of Islamic glory. Capturing this sudden discovery of the Caliphate by the community, historian Jadunath Sarkar observed that the Ottoman ruler becoming the 'spiritual head' of Indian Muslims was 'the creation of the late nineteenth century' and an outcome of 'a political pan-Islamic movement' due to the gradual 'absorption of all sovereign Muslim states by the Christians'.[2] As a result, towards the end of the nineteenth century Ottoman Turkey 'began to loom large in the imagination of Indian Muslims ... (and) had become a symbol of the glorious past of Islam'.[3] In other words, so long as the Mughals were at the helm of affairs, the Indian Muslims did not look to caliphs in foreign lands. The loss of Muslim rule, especially the Mughal dynasty, compelled them to look outside the country for solace and comfort.

Sir Syed Ahmed Khan, one of the leaders of the reformist movement, aptly summed up the dilemma facing the Indian Muslims when he said:

> When there were many Muslim kingdoms, we did not feel much grief when one of them was destroyed; now that so few are left, we feel the loss of even a small one. If Turkey is conquered that will be a great grief, for she is the last of the great powers left to Islam. We are afraid that we shall become like the Jews, a people without a country of our own.[4]

Therefore, so long as there were local Islamic dynasties, the Muslim masses of India were indifferent towards the caliphs and the various Islamic dynasties in the Middle East and beyond. There was no political need or emotional compulsion for the rulers and masses alike for an external legitimacy or endorsement. Likewise, Muslim dynasties in India did not figure in the traditional Islamic histography.

Palestine and Indian Muslims

The political importance of the Indian Muslims was first recognised by the Grand Mufti of Jerusalem in the early 1920s when he sought to steer the

Palestinian problem. Recognising the insurmountable challenges posed by Jewish immigration and unfavourable British mandate administration, he sought to expand the Palestine question into a larger challenge facing the Muslim masses in the region and beyond. Pledging to renovate the dilapidated Al-Aqsa Mosque, al-Husseini launched a fundraising campaign among the Muslim communities in the region and beyond.[5] British India, which had the largest Muslim population at that time, drew his attention, and he sent a three-member delegation comprising his distant uncle Jamal al-Husseini (also the Secretary of the Arab Executive), Mufti of Haifa, Muhammad Murad, and a sheikh of Al-Aqsa, Ibrahim al-Ansari, to India in 1923–24. The delegation travelled to different parts of India to persuade rich and philanthropic Muslim rulers and businesspeople to elicit generous contributions and managed to raise £22,000, not an inconsiderable amount in the 1920s. Out of this, £7,000 came from the Nizam of the southern princely state of Hyderabad.[6]

Meanwhile, al-Husseini met the Ali brothers, prominent figures in the Khilafat Movement, during the hajj pilgrimages in 1924 and 1926,[7] and younger brother Mohammed briefly visited Jerusalem in 1928.[8] In 1929, an Indian Muslim delegation took part in the International Wailing Wall Commission where Mohammed Ali delivered 'one of the three closing speeches for the Muslim side before the commission'.[9] The following year, the Mufti travelled to Cairo 'to meet the Ali Brothers and members of the Indian Muslim delegates on route from India to London to participate in the London Round Table Conference'.[10] The Mufti made his first and only visit to India in July 1933 as the guest of the Nizam of Hyderabad.[11]

These contacts between al-Husseini and the Ali brothers took an interesting turn in January 1931 when the Mufti offered to inter the body of Mohammed Ali, who had died earlier that month in London, within the precincts of Haram al-Sharif in Jerusalem. The proposal came when the family members were planning to carry the body to his ancestral home in Rampur, in present-day Uttar Pradesh. Accordingly, the funeral of Mohammed Ali was held in Jerusalem on Friday 23 January 1931.[12] The Mufti's gesture was 'an acknowledgement of the Indian leader's long support for the Palestine cause, but it also had the appearance of a calculated measure towards turning Jerusalem into a pan-Islamic capital'.[13] A few months later, Shaukat Ali, who became an ardent supporter of the Mufti, played a key role in the Jerusalem Conference organised in December.[14]

Simultaneously, in the early twentieth century, Ottoman Turkey came 'to occupy a place in the minds and hearts of large sections of the Muslim community, which it had not done during the long centuries of Muslim rule in India'.[15] During the closing stages of the First World War the Indian Muslims were anxious over the future of the Ottoman Empire, the last

Islamic empire at that time whose sultan also held the office of caliph, the spiritual-temporal leader of the Sunni Muslims. This was when the pan-Islamic Khilafat Movement was born.[16]

Mahatma Gandhi, who was emerging as a principal leader of the nascent anti-British agitation, viewed the pan-Islamic sentiments among the Indian Muslims as an opportunity to establish a multiconfessional anticolonial movement, and plunged the Congress Party into embracing the Khilafat Movement.[17] He embraced an explicitly pan-Islamic agenda to promote the much-needed but absent Hindu–Muslim unity in the nationalist movement. Gandhi recognised that the Indian National Congress could be neither 'Indian' nor 'national' without the substantial participation of the Muslim masses. Not everyone was happy with Gandhi's strategy; Nirad Chaudhuri, for example, observed: 'by allying itself with the Khilafat Movement, the Congress had encouraged the most retrograde form of Islamic group consciousness'.[18] Despite misgivings, Gandhi's goal of communal unity overwhelmed any possible opposition and he plunged the Congress Party into the pan-Islamic struggle and even emerged as its leader.

Amid the Khilafat phase, Gandhi adopted Islamic history, motifs, logic and terminologies to view, understand and depict Palestine and its political claims within the Arab–Islamic narrative, and argued that Palestine was an integral part of the *Jazirat-ul-Arab* (literally, Island of Arabia or the Arabian Peninsula).[19] According to historian Mushirul Hasan, Indian Muslims had a broader territorial canvas for *Jazirat-ul-Arab* and it encompassed 'Constantinople, Jerusalem, Medina and above all Mecca, with its Baitrullah, the focal point of daily prayers and the annual hajj'.[20]

Making his first reference to the problem in March 1921, Gandhi declared that Britain 'would not dare have asked a single Muslim soldier to wrest control of Palestine from fellow Muslims and give it to the Jews'.[21] A month later, he was more forceful:

> The Muslims claim Palestine as an integral part of *Jazirat-ul-Arab*. They are bound to retain its custody, as an *injunction* of the Prophet. But that does not mean that the Jews and the Christians cannot freely go to Palestine, or even reside there and own property. What non-Muslims cannot do is to acquire *sovereign jurisdiction*. The Jews cannot receive sovereign rights in a place which has been *held for centuries* by Muslim powers by right of religious conquest. The Muslim soldiers did not *shed their blood* in the late war for the purpose of surrendering Palestine out of Muslim control. I would like my Jewish friends to impartially consider the *position of the seventy million* Muslims of India. As a free nation, can they tolerate what they must regard as a *treacherous* disposal of their sacred possession?[22]

A number of Gandhi's assertions and historical claims are open to challenge, but it was clear that through these statements, which came nearly four years after the Balfour Declaration, he categorically ruled out a Jewish national home in Palestine.

Gandhi's views on Palestine gradually became the position of the Congress Party, and though the party did not endorse an explicitly religious paradigm in the post-Khilafat phase, the contours of its Palestine policy were firmly in place. Palestine, for Indian nationalists, was Arab, and would remain so. Meanwhile, the failure of the Khilafat struggle and the abolition of the Caliphate by Kemal Atatürk in 1924 led to a temporary lull in Congress interests in Palestine; but as the Arab–Jewish violence intensified, especially after the Arab Revolt of 1936, the Congress Party began visualising the future of that mandate territory. By then, the Palestine question has become a domestic political battle between the Congress Party and the Muslim League.[23]

As the war clouds were hovering over Europe, in December 1938 the Congress Working Committee (CWC), the highest decision-making body of the party, met in Wardha and expressed its sympathy for the 'plight of Jews in Europe'.[24] But at the same time it deplored that 'in Palestine, the Jews have relied on British armed forces to advance their special claims and thus aligned themselves on the side of British imperialism'. Urging the Arabs and Jews to cooperate, the CWC visualised as its solution a 'free democratic State in Palestine with adequate protection to Jewish rights'.[25] This proved to be the forerunner for the federal plan when India became a member of the United Nations Special Committee on Palestine in 1947, which was addressed in Laura Robson's chapter.

India and UNSCOP

Though still a British colony, India was a founding member of the United Nations and Jawaharlal Nehru became the head of the interim government in September 1946. In early February 1947, unable to manage its contradictory promises to the Jews and Arabs, the British Government, headed by Clement Attlee, asked the UN to appoint a committee and determine the future political status of mandate Palestine. This led to the convening of the First Special Session of the UN General Assembly on 28 April, which lasted until 15 May 1947. While nominating Asaf Ali – its ambassador in Washington – for the session, New Delhi instructed him to 'obtain ... India's membership on the fact-finding Committee'.[26]

Things did not go as India had planned. During the two-week-long deliberations of the Special Session, Asaf Ali articulated the pro-Arab position of the Indian nationalists and at times went overboard and criticised the mandate power. Reflecting on Asaf Ali's role in the Special Session, Nehru was candid: 'Though you balanced your observations, when there are many observations, they are apt to irritate one party or the other needlessly as they appear to have done sometimes.'[27] It had diplomatic consequences when the General Assembly was discussing the composition of the proposed committee; India was not among the nine members proposed by the US and Chile that were endorsed unanimously. Seeking a broader and more balanced representation, the composition of UNSCOP was increased to eleven, with representations from Asia and the South Pacific. In the subsequent contest, India defeated Siam (now Thailand) and Australia narrowly defeated the Philippines. Thus, India became a member of UNSCOP.

In the selection of its nominee for UNSCOP, the Indian civil service was candid and felt that the government should quickly find 'a *suitable Indian Muslim* with *legal knowledge*'.[28] Though no specific reasons were given, both these criterions are interesting. Both before and after independence, Indian leaders, elites and mainstream critics wrapped and presented the official policy on Palestine through secular-nationalism, anticolonialism and anti-imperialism. Any suggestions of an Islamic dimension to Indian policy were rejected, ridiculed and vilified, as an agenda-driven exercise of the Hindu right. Hence, the officials recommending 'a suitable Indian Muslim' for UNSCOP was one of the rare official admissions of the Islamic dimension of India's Palestine policy. As discussed elsewhere, since the early 1930s, the Palestine issue had become a political contest between the Congress Party and Muslim League for the support and loyalty of Indian Muslims.[29] Hence, proposing a Muslim to represent India in UNSCOP was logical and even inevitable.

Likewise, the preference for a person 'with legal knowledge' perhaps indicates the Indian preference or understanding of UNSCOP's terms of reference. Whether one supports the rights of Arabs or Jews, Palestine was a political issue, more so because the United Nations is a body of and for sovereign entities. States are legally recognised political entities and their decisions are always political. It appears that the Indian Government viewed the future of Palestine also as a legal issue, and hence opted for a person 'with legal knowledge'. The choice fell upon Sir Abdur Rahman, a judge in the Punjab High Court, to represent India in UNSCOP.

After their initial deliberations in New York, UNSCOP members arrived in Palestine and heard the testimonies, mainly from the Jewish representatives. The Arab parties in Palestine had boycotted UNSCOP contending that its terms of reference were flawed and unjust. The UN Committee had a special meeting in Beirut to listen to the views of the neighbouring Arab states. Abdur Rahman went to Amman to meet the then Emir Abdullah of

Transjordan who refused to go to Beirut for the meeting with UNSCOP. In August, a subcommittee was sent to the Displaced Persons Camps in Europe which held the Jewish refugees of the Second World War. UNSCOP finalised its report in Geneva on 1 September 1947, and submitted it two days later.

As India was being elected to the UN body, Asaf Ali flagged the prevailing mood in the General Assembly that the nominees to the committee should be 'free from interference by nominating government' and 'will not (repeat not) be subject to direction by their governments'.[30] Had this been the case, there was no need for Nehru to aspire for India's membership of the Committee, even before the commencement of the Special Session. Hence, to avoid any confusion, upon nominating Sir Abdur Rahman, Nehru stated that the latter 'will function as the representative of India on this committee and will naturally refer to us any particular matter that you think should be cleared up'.[31]

The impending partition back home kindled Rahman's doubts over the legal position of India after the scheduled British withdrawal. He began seeing himself as the nominee of the UN 'although on the recommendation of the Indian Government, *at a time when India was a member of the United Nations*'.[32] Through this interpretation, Rahman was challenging the legality of India being a founding member of the UN and its status after the British withdrawal. Infuriated by this reading, in early July Nehru reminded Rahman that 'India was chosen as one of the countries to be represented on the Special Committee. The nomination of the representative from India was done by the Government of India and not by the United Nations.'[33]

Another disagreement cropped up in early August 1947, just days before India's partition. In the light of the impending formation of two sovereign entities out of the British Empire – namely India and Pakistan – Rahman feared that India 'would not continue to be a member of the United Nations and I would consequently not be entitled to represent India on the Committee'. Therefore, Rahman offered to present his views 'in a sealed cover with the Chairman of the Committee on the 14th of August (on the eve India's partition and Pakistan's independence) to ask him not to open it until the report of the Committee was ready'. With the benefit of hindsight and Nehru's rebuke one can say that, despite being a legal luminary, Rahman appeared to lack a clear understanding of UN membership. Upon its independence, India became the successor state of British India, which signed the UN Charter in San Francisco on 26 June 1945, while Pakistan became a member of the UN on 30 September 1947 (although legally the position was not clear at the time, and a legal opinion was sought by the UN Secretariat on the issue).[34]

The last and far more severe challenge came on 14 August 1947, the day Pakistan became independent and hours before India's own freedom. Swayed by the prevailing Arab position on this issue, Rahman made a strong case for a unitary Palestine and felt that there were only two realistic options before UNSCOP – namely, partition or unitary state – and he rejected the federal option as 'unworkable'.[35] This was the final straw for Nehru, and amid the post-partition riots, on 22 August, a week after India's independence, Rahman was instructed to abandon his unitary Palestine option and was directed to propose a 'middle course what maybe theoretically just and what is factually practicable' (*sic*) and propose a federal Palestine and not 'a democratic unitary Palestinian state' as Rahman had suggested.[36] Materials currently available on this issue do not shed light on the details of Rahman's plan or how it differed from the federal plan suggested by Nehru. Indeed, as early as on 23 April, even before the composition of the UNSCOP report was finalised, Nehru's government felt that the solution to the Palestinian problem 'must lie on the lines of the Arab state with the inclusion of an autonomous Jewish area'.[37] This has been the traditional position of the Congress Party vis-à-vis Palestine, especially since the late 1930s.

In short, India was elected to UNSCOP in mid-May 1947 when it was legally a British colony, but gained independence when the UNSCOP report was finalised. As the UNSCOP report was being prepared, the subcontinent was partitioned along communal lines and the erstwhile Congress–Muslim League tussle over Palestine was transformed into Indo-Pakistani political rivalry as the UNSCOP report was debated in the Second Annual Session of the UN General Assembly from 16 September to 29 November 1947. Throughout this period, especially from May to September 1947, Nehru shaped, guided and determined the Indian position in UNSCOP.

A comparison between the federal plan for Palestine and India's partition

If the UN Partition Plan was a compromise between exclusive Arab and Jewish nationalisms, the federal plan was midway between partition and a unitary Palestine.[38] While the details of both the plans are extraneous to our analysis, it is useful to examine and compare some of the salient features of the federal plan with India's own partition. First, Britain presided over both partitions; in one case it was a colonial power and in the other the mandatory administration. In the latter case, the British did not have exclusive jurisdiction to terminate the mandate or enforce a partition because it needed the consent of the UN to modify the mandate's status. Furthermore, Britain referred the Palestine issue to the UN primarily because of its incompatible and irreconcilable promises to the Arabs and Jews – to the Arabs under the Husayn–McMahon Correspondence (1915–16), according to which Britain was alleged to have pledged Palestine and its holy shrines to the protection of the Sharif of Mecca, and to the Jews under the Balfour Declaration. This made the process of partition more complex in Palestine than in India.

Second, the partition of India was negotiated and agreed among the parties who had differing worldviews; the Congress Party represented the idea of a diverse but inclusive India, while the Muslim League championed Pakistani nationalism. Though it was initially opposed to the division, eventually the Congress – the bigger of the two parties – accepted communal partition as a price for India's independence. In Palestine, partition was proposed and endorsed by the UN but was accepted only by the Jews. This resulted in both partitions charting a different trajectory; India and its nationalists were quick to come to terms with Pakistan, and even the Jan Sangh, which championed *Akhand Bharat* (greater or undivided India), eventually came to terms with the partitioned subcontinent. This was not the case in Palestine. The Arabs, the majority party, vehemently opposed the idea of partition, and the Palestinian-Arab-Islamic recognition of the Jewish state has been slow, painful and, in some sense, incomplete. The Muslims were the rulers of the lands, except for the Crusader Period (1095–1291), and at the time of the Balfour Declaration 'non-Jewish' Arabs constituted 90 per cent of the population of Palestine. The Arabs saw granting of sovereign rights to immigrant Jews as unjust and unacceptable.

Third, there is an Islamic dimension to the problem, which makes recognition of Israel a theological quandary. Palestine had been under Muslim sovereignty since the armies of Second Caliph Umar laid siege to the City of Jerusalem and captured it. Initially, Jerusalem was also the first *qibla* (direction of Muslim prayer) until it was changed by the Prophet Mohammed to the Ka'aba in Mecca. The construction of Al-Aqsa, which was completed in 705 AD, and the veneration of Al-Haram ash-Sharif as the third holiest site in Islam, on top of the pre-Islamic, non-Islamic and un-Islamic Second Jewish Temple, forms a core for the Arab-Islamic reluctance to come to terms with Israel. As a result, even seven decades later a vast majority of the countries belonging to the Organisation of Islamic Cooperation, as well as a host of Islamist groups and organisations, do not accept Israel's legitimacy on theological grounds. For them, Palestine has been historically part of the Islamic *waqf* (endowment) and hence cannot be ceded in full or in part to non-Islamic control or sovereignty, even within a peace settlement. This is the position of the Muslim Brotherhood, for example, as explored at length in the chapter by Mohamed-Ali Adraoui.

Fourth, in the Indian subcontinent mutual agreement resulted in India being partitioned into two sovereign states: India and Pakistan. In the case of Palestine, only one side – the Jews – accepted the UN partition proposal. The Arabs of Palestine, as well as the neighbouring Arab countries, rejected it. While it benefitted from the partition, Israel was not solely responsible for the absence of an independent Arab Palestinian state in 1948 or afterwards. Backed by the Arab states, the Palestinian leadership under al-Husseini declared the All-Palestine Government (APG) on 22 September 1948 in Gaza City.[39] A Mufti-led government took over on 1 October and was recognised by all the independent states of that time, except Transjordan (later the Hashemite Kingdom of Jordan) which controlled eastern Palestine (the West Bank). The formation of the APG spurred King Abdullah to sponsor the Jericho Conference in December that year, and formalise the annexation of the West Bank on 24 April 1950. Though the Arab states disagreed with this move they did not act against Jordan or suspend its membership from the Arab League.

Fifth, the response of the majority parties to the partitions was also different. A section of Indian nationalists, especially Mahatma Gandhi, vehemently opposed the idea of India's partition, but eventually the Congress Party came to terms with it as the price for independence. This was not the case in Palestine, and the majority Arab party refused to consider even India's suggestion for greater autonomy for the Jews under the federal plan, let alone the partition along religious-national lines. Reflecting on these differences, Nehru lamented on 4 December 1947:

> [The Arab States were] so keen on the unitary state idea and were so sure of at any rate preventing the partition or preventing two-third majority in favour of partition, that they did not accept our suggestion. When, during the last few days, partition somehow suddenly became inevitable and it was realized that the Indian solution was probably the best ... a last-minute attempt was made in the last 48 hours to bring forward the Indian solution *not by us but those who wanted a unitary state*. It was then too late[40]

Indeed, rejecting the Indian plan was the only thing that the Jews and Arabs agreed on in 1947.

Sixth, in both cases, the dominant minority populations – Muslims in India and Jews in Palestine – viewed partition as the only option that would guarantee their dignity and satisfy their future political aspirations. There were dissenting voices among Muslims in India and Jews in Palestine but, in both cases, a significant portion of them were in favour of a communal partition. At the same time, the response of the majority groups was different; partition was grudgingly accepted in India but vehemently opposed by the

Arabs of Palestine. Above all, in both cases the Muslims were a major party; in one case it was a section of the leadership which demanded partition, and in the other the entire Muslim and Christian Arab community – both inside and outside Palestine – was opposed to partition and to the idea of Jews being given any political rights over Palestine. The Arab Muslims had another argument against non-Muslims or *dhimmi* being given sovereignty over a land that remained under Muslim rule for centuries. As People of the Book, Jews (as well as Christians) were to be protected; but political Zionism demanded political rights of equality over Islamic *waqf* land. As historian S. M. Burke put it: 'While the device of dividing the country provided the only means of real freedom to the Indian Muslims, the very word partition was anathema to Muslims elsewhere.'[41] One should, however, be rather cautious in accepting his observation as it was valid for the Muslim League and not for the Muslim masses of the undivided India. Otherwise, India would not have become the home to the second largest Muslim population on the globe after Indonesia.

Seventh, there is one significant similarity in both the partitions. The Congress Party, especially Nehru, never came to terms with the distinct nationalism of the Muslims in India and Jews in Palestine. While its territorial nationalism is understandable, the Congress could not accept the underpinnings of minority nationalism in both cases.[42] The ideological opposition to religion-centric nationalism was more vividly demonstrated in India's position vis-à-vis Palestine. Though their presence in India is often traced to the immediate aftermath of the destruction of the Second Temple in 70 AD, the Jews never had a sizeable presence in the country. Estimates suggest there were about 20,000 Jews between the two world wars, composed largely of Jews fleeing from Europe and, according to the 2011 census, there were only 4,650 Jews in a country of 1.2 billion people.[43] This microscopic Jewish population and the large Muslim population – the largest in the world during British rule – meant that India and its nationalists never understood Jewish history, their centuries of suffering, and their longing for statehood. Even the educated continue to believe that *dhimmi* is a sociocultural arrangement of equality and political egalitarianism. On the contrary, as Gandhi's approach in the early 1920 highlighted, the Indian nationalists viewed Jewish claims to Palestine primarily through an exclusively Islamic prism.

As a result, Indian nationalists, especially Gandhi and Nehru, never understood Zionism and viewed it primarily as a religious nationalism which was seeking the help of, or benefitting from, British colonialism, and resorting to violence to further its political objectives in Palestine. Indeed, days after Kristallnacht, Gandhi observed: 'Palestine belongs to the Arabs in the same sense that England belongs to the English or France to the French.'[44] The Japanese and Nazi connections of a section of the nationalists led by Subhas Chandra Bose to overthrow British rule rarely figure in Indian discussions on Palestine. Even Nehru was harsher on the imperial connections of the Zionists, but was less critical of the Japanese and Nazi connections of Bose.

However, viewing the demands of Pakistani nationalism through a religious prism led to other problems. Conceding to the League's demands of Muslims being a separate and distinct 'nation' because they adhere to a different religion would open a Pandora's box and instigate similar demands from other religious, ethnic, social and cultural groups, and vindicate Winston Churchill's prognosis of India being nothing more than a transient idea. Hence, the Congress and its leaders had no choice but to oppose 'religious nationalism' both in India and in Palestine. At the same time, geographical proximity made it easier for India to come to terms with Pakistan than distant Palestine and hence, for over four decades, it followed a policy of recognition-without-relations vis-à-vis Israel.[45]

Eighth, Nehru's envoy in UNSCOP adopted a dual position vis-à-vis both the partitions. In his public statements and private notes, Sir Rahman followed the traditional line of the Congress Party and vehemently opposed the idea of religion-based nationalism, as he viewed Zionism. He was not prepared to accept the entry of religion in political discourses and as the driving force behind nationalism. Advocating the federal plan as directed by Nehru, Rahman observed that 'it is important to avoid an acceleration of the separatism which now characterizes the relations of Arabs and Jews in the Near East, and *to avoid lying the foundations of a dangerous irredentism there*, which would be the inevitable consequences of partition in whatever form'.[46] If the Zionist demand for statehood in Palestine were granted, he warned, Jews everywhere would be accused of practicing 'double loyalty'. Upholding the principle of self-determination, Rahman argued that it would be difficult to 'refuse the majority, the right of forming the government'.[47] Reflecting the prevailing view of his government in India, he argued that 'it is impossible to forget that the Jews as a whole are not a nation but only a community which follows a particular religion ... Moreover, the so-called nationalism is of too recent a growth to be any value ... there is no reason why political considerations should be mixed up with religious considerations and why political rights in a state should be confused with religious rights.'[48] Indeed, Rahman was making a statement in the UN that ran contrary to the religion-centric nationalism spearheaded by Mohammad Ali Jinnah, and was arguing that democracy meant the rule of the majority and Church and State are distinct and separate entities and spheres of influence.

Subsequently, however, Rahman made a personal choice that raises doubts over these eloquent arguments in the United Nations against religion-based nationalism. In his memoirs, Guatemalan representative in UNSCOP, Jorge García-Granados, referred to Rahman's worries over 'the safety of his family in the post-partition riots in India'.[49] Shortly after submitting the UNSCOP report, Rahman emigrated to Pakistan, a state formed on the logic similar to Zionism,[50] and retired as a judge of Pakistan's Federal Court.[51] At the UN, Rahman's rejection of the Partition Plan was accompanied by his passionate arguments of religion not constituting distinct nationalism or nationhood; but when it came to the Indian subcontinent, Rahman could not internalise the same logic. By emigrating to Pakistan he reflected the dilemma facing the Muslim League: partition was necessary in India, but a sacrilege in the Islamic lands of Palestine.

Nehru's duality

The outlines of Nehru's federal plan were communicated to Abdul Rahman during India's partition and reiterated on 22 August, a week after the British departure. Having gone through a communal division, Nehru was suggesting a different option for Palestine. A more generous justification could be that the Indian leader wanted the Arabs and Jews of Palestine to avoid the trials and tribulations of the Hindu–Muslim communal discord and seek coexistence. However, Nehru's inability to walk the talk on 'religious nationalisms', as he saw the Muslim and Jewish nationalist demands in India and Palestine respectively, cannot be ignored lightly.

Unlike the Partition Plan for Palestine, Nehru's federal plan was rejected by both the parties to the conflict; the Arabs felt it gave more rights to the immigrating Jews than they deserved, while the Jews felt it granted them civil and municipal rights when they were aspiring for political rights and sovereignty. Rejecting Nehru's plan, ironically, was the only issue that the Jews and Arabs agreed on in 1947. Reflecting this mood, the UN General Assembly never discussed the Indian plan; it appointed two committees, and only one of them discussed the partition plan. The other subcommittee, interestingly headed by Muhammad Zafrulla Khan of Pakistan, which became a member only on 30 September (weeks after the submission of the UNSCOP report), discussed and endorsed the unitary plan which was not proposed by UNSCOP.[52] If the international academic community did not take note of the federal plan, Indian writers and scholars never addressed the question of its rejection by the Arabs.[53] As referred to earlier, Nehru also lamented the Arab rejection of his federal plan.

The primary failure of the federal plan and its rejection by the Arabs was India's inability to read the pulse of the United Nations. The majority partition plan had the support of seven out of eleven members of UNSCOP, while the Indian plan was endorsed only by Iran – the only Muslim country of the UN Committee – and the then Yugoslavia. Moreover, when the partition resolution was put to the vote on 29 November 1947, Yugoslavia abstained, and India was one of three non-Muslim states – Cuba and Greece being the other two – to vote against the majority, along with ten Arab and Islamic countries. Overruling Rahman's original suggestion for a unitary Palestine, which the Arab states preferred to the federal plan, indicated that Nehru was not in tune with the ground realities in the Middle East.

As far back as April 1947, India recognised the importance of the Palestinian issue and aspired for membership of the proposed committee, even before the commencement of the First Special Session of the UN General Assembly. At the same time, it failed to see Palestine as a political question that required a solution which had a wider acceptance. India neither recognised the mood of the Arab countries nor the sentiments of the UN General Assembly, but adopted a naive attitude towards the federal plan and its acceptance. Its failure to secure some Arab support resulted in the Indian plan never being discussed in the UN or by the wider academic community. With its impending independence, the Palestinian issue was a major diplomatic test for India and a degree of utopianism was unavoidable; indeed, shortly after the partition vote, Nehru unilaterally referred the Kashmir issue to the UN in the naive hope that the international community would endorse the validity of his claims and arguments.

The federal plan did not reflect the ground realities in Palestine either. Arab–Jewish relations were far more hostile and unbridgeable than the Hindu–Muslim relations in the subcontinent. The UNSCOP majority proposed partition also because of the irreconcilable nature of the communal situation in Palestine. Indeed, Rahman informed Nehru that 'government service, the Potash Company (on the Dead Sea) and the Oil Refinery (in Haifa) are almost the only places where Arabs and Jews meet as co-workers in the same organization'. To his bewilderment, Rahman found out that 'even the communists ... are divided into two parties, one Jewish and the other Arabs'.[54] Such deep divisions meant that superhuman efforts would be needed to make the federal plan work, more so when Britain was not prepared to shoulder any responsibility to 'implement' the UNSCOP proposals or to stay in Palestine beyond 15 May 1948.

Above all, the federal plan exposed the fundamental contradictions between Nehru's positions on partitioning India and Palestine. He was advocating a proposal for Palestine that he and the Congress Party were not ready to practise in the Indian context. Hindu–Muslim relations were tense, but were far better than the Arab–Jewish situation in Palestine, even though the

Indian partition was followed by riots in which an estimated million people were killed on both sides. Still, the conditions for interreligious coexistence under one political unit were indefinitely better in India than in Palestine. Hindu–Muslim coexistence was not merely a political slogan of the Congress Party but a lived and living reality in many parts of India. Thus, a federal option was more feasible in India than in Palestine. Despite these advantages, partition became inevitable and unavoidable in India. Without recognising these differences and difficulties, Nehru advocated a federal Palestine even after accepting a partitioned India.

Conclusion

When he unfurled the tricolour in the Red Fort, Jawaharlal Nehru recognised and came to terms with the irreconcilable Congress–League positions regarding the communal divisions of India. Still, a few days later he was advocating a plan whereby he visualised that Arabs and Jews would coexist side by side under one political arrangement. What prevented Nehru and the Congress Party from considering a similar option by Mahatma Gandhi that avoided the partition of India? Partition and federation were Nehru's preferred options for India and Palestine respectively; having achieved Indian independence through partition, he was urging the Arabs and Jews of Palestine to live under one roof through accommodation and cooperation. Thus, the federal plan was not only a sign of Indian naivety but also a reminder of its duality; its political pragmatism was confined to the subcontinent, but moral eloquence became prominent in distant Palestine. Therein lies the irony of Nehru's stand vis-à-vis the two partitions.

Notes

1 For example, M. S. Agwani, 'The Palestine Conflict in Asian Perspective', in Ibrahim Abu-Laghod (ed.), *The Transformation of Palestine* (Evanston, IL: Northwestern University Press, 1971), pp. 443–462; B. N. Mehrish, 'Recognition of the Palestinian Liberation Organisation; An Appraisal of India's Policy', *Indian Journal of Political Science* 36 (2) (1975), 137–160; Bansidhar Pradhan, 'India's Policy towards the PLO', in Riyaz Punjabi and A. K. Pasha (eds), *India and the Islamic World* (New Delhi: Radiant, 1998), pp. 65–83.
2 Quoted in B. R. Nanda, *In Search of Gandhi: Essays and Reflections* (New Delhi: Oxford University Press, 2002), pp. 86–87.

3 *Ibid.*, p. 87.
4 Sir Theodore Morison, 'Muhammadan Movements', in John Cumming (ed.), *Political India, 1832–1932: A Cooperative Survey of a Century* (London: Oxford University Press, 1932), pp. 95–96.
5 Omar Khalidi, 'Indian Muslims and Palestinian Awqaf', *Jerusalem Quarterly* 40 (2009), 56.
6 Yehoshua Porath, 'Al-Hajj Amin al-Husayni, Mufti of Jerusalem: His Rise to Power and Consolidation of His Position', *Asian and African Studies* 7 (1971), 212–256; H. A. R. Gibb, 'The Islamic Congress at Jerusalem in December 1931', in Arnold J. Toynbee (ed.), *Survey of International Affairs* (London: Oxford University Press, 1934), pp. 99–109.
7 Uri M. Kupferschmidt, 'The General Muslim Congress of 1931 in Jerusalem', *Asian and African Studies* 21 (1) (1978), 129.
8 Maoz Azaryahu and Yitzhak Reiter, 'The Geopolitics of Interment: An Inquiry into the Burial of Muhammad Ali in Jerusalem, 1931', *Israel Studies* 20 (1) (2015), 34. https://doi.org/10.2979/israelstudies.20.1.31.
9 Kupferschmidt, 'The General Muslim Congress of 1931 in Jerusalem', p. 129.
10 Azaryahu and Reiter, 'The Geopolitics of Interment', p. 34.
11 Khalidi, 'Indian Muslims and Palestinian Awqaf', p. 56.
12 Azaryahu and Reiter, 'The Geopolitics of Interment'.
13 Basheer M. Nafi, 'The General Islamic Congress of Jerusalem Reconsidered', *Muslim World* 86 (3–4) (1996), 246.
14 Kupferschmidt, 'The General Muslim Congress of 1931 in Jerusalem'. Nafi, 'The General Islamic Congress of Jerusalem Reconsidered'.
15 Nanda, *In Search of Gandhi*, p. 87.
16 Gail Minualt, *The Khilafat Movement: Religious Symbolism and Political Mobilization in India* (New York: Columbia University Press, 1982); A. C. Niemeijer, *The Khilafat Movement in India, 1919–1924* (The Hague: Brill, 1972).
17 B. R. Nanda, *Gandhi: Pan-Islamism, Imperialism and Nationalism in India* (New Delhi: Oxford University Press, 1989).
18 Nirad C. Chaudhuri, *The Hand, Great Anarch, 1921–1952* (London: Addison Wesley Longman, 1987), p. 39.
19 P. R. Kumaraswamy, *Squaring the Circle: Mahatma Gandhi and the Jewish National Home* (New Delhi: Knowledge World for ICWA, 2018).
20 Mushirul Hasan, *Nationalism and Communal Politics in India, 1885–1930* (New Delhi: Manohar, 1994), pp. 112–113.
21 CWMG, *Collected Works of Mahatma Gandhi*, vol. 19 (New Delhi: Publications Divisions, 1958 ff.), p. 530.
22 *Ibid.* (emphasis added).
23 Kumaraswamy, *Squaring the Circle*, pp. 111–134.
24 A. Moin Zaidi (ed.), *Immutable Policy of Friendship and Cooperation: The Foreign Policy of the Indian National Congress during the Last Hundred Years* (New Delhi: Indian Institute of Applied Political Research, 1985), p. 52.
25 *Ibid.*, p. 52.

26 NAI, 'Foreign Office Telegram to Asaf Ali, 24 April 1947' (MEA F-2(16)-UNO-1/47, 1947).
27 'Jawaharlal Nehru to Asaf Ali, 14 May 1947', *Selected Works of Jawaharlal Nehru*, Series II, vol. 2 (New Delhi: Nehru Memorial Museum Library, n.d.), p. 497.
28 NAI, 'H. C. Beaumont to S. E. Abbott, 22 May 1947' (MEA F-2(16)-UNO-1/47, 1947).
29 Kumaraswamy, *Squaring the Circle*, pp. 111–133.
30 NAI, 'Asaf Ali to Foreign Office, 14 May 1947' (MEA F-2(16)-UNO-I/47, 1947).
31 'Jawaharlal Nehru to Abdur Rahman, 22 May 1947', *Selected Works of Jawaharlal Nehru*, Series II, vol. 2, pp. 474–475.
32 NAI, 'Abdur Rahman to Jawaharlal Nehru, 25 June 1947' (MEA F-2(16)-UNO-I/47, 1947).
33 NAI, 'Jawaharlal Nehru to Abdur Rahman, 10 July 1947' (MEA F-2(16)-UNO-I/47, 1947).
34 For the legal opinion see https://legal.un.org/ilc/documentation/english/a_cn4_149.pdf (accessed 13 March 2023).
35 NAI, 'The Official Summary of Abdur Rahman's Reports, 10 September 1947' (MEA F-2(5)-UNO-I/47, 1947).
36 NAI, 'Foreign Office to Abdur Rahman, 23 August 1947' (MEA F-2(16)-UNO-I/47, 1947). This appears to be a reminder of an earlier message from Nehru asking Rahman to withdraw the memorandum that he had prepared earlier.
37 NAI, 'Foreign Office to Asaf Ali, 23 April 1947' (MEA F-2(16)-UNO-I/47, 1947).
38 Details of the Indian plan can be found in Agwani, 'The Palestine Conflict in Asian Perspective'; Mehrish, 'Recognition of the Palestinian Liberation Organisation'.
39 Avi Shlaim, 'The Rise and Fall of the All-Palestine Government in Gaza', *Journal of Palestine Studies* 20 (1) (1990), 37–53.
40 Jawaharlal Nehru, 'Constituent Assembly Debates, Volume I, Session II, Col.1261', 4 December 1947 (emphasis added).
41 S. M. Burke, *Pakistan's Foreign Policy: An Historical Analysis* (London: Oxford University Press, 1973), p. 66.
42 See Victor Kattan, 'The Empire Departs: The Partitions of British India, Mandate Palestine and the Dawn of Self-determination in the Third World', *Asian Journal of Middle Eastern Studies* 12 (3) (2018), 304–325.
43 Express News Service, 'Maharashtra Accords Minority Status to Jewish Community', *Indian Express*, 22 June 2016, at https://indianexpress.com/article/india/india-news-india/maharashtra-accords-minority-status-to-jewish-community-2867911/ (accessed 22 March 2023).
44 P. R. Kumaraswamy, 'The Jews: Revisiting Mahatma Gandhi's November 1938 Article', *International Studies* 55 (2) (2018), 146–166, https://doi.org/10.1177/0020881718768345.
45 P. R. Kumaraswamy, *India's Israel Policy* (New York: Columbia University Press, 2010).

46 UNSCOP, 'UNSCOP Report, Vol. 1' (New York: United Nations, 1947), p. 58.
47 UNSCOP, 'UNSCOP Report, Vol. 2' (New York: United Nations, 1947), p. 45.
48 UNSCOP, 'UNSCOP Report, Vol. 1', pp. 42–45.
49 Gorge Garcia-Granados, *The Birth of Israel: The Drama as I Saw it* (New York: Alfred A. Knopf, 1949), p. 9.
50 P. R. Kumaraswamy, 'The Strangely Parallel Careers of Israel and Pakistan', *Middle East Quarterly* 4 (2) (1997), 31–39.
51 Jawaharlal Nehru, *Selected Works of Jawaharlal Nehru*, Series II, vol. 1, 572n.
52 UNGA, 'Ad Hoc Committee on the Palestine Question: Report of Sub-Committee 2', 11 November 1947.
53 Mehrish, 'Recognition of the Palestinian Liberation Organisation'.
54 NAI, 'Abdur Rahman to Jawaharlal Nehru, 15 June 1947' (MEA F-2(16)-UNO-I/47, 1947).

Part IV

The consequences of partition for South Asia, the Middle East and beyond

7

The partitions of India and Palestine and the dawn of majority rule in Africa and Asia

Victor Kattan

The partition of the Indian subcontinent in August 1947 that led to the birth of Pakistan and the independence of India might be said to be both triumphant and traumatic. The same might be said of the attempt to partition Palestine in November 1947, which led to the birth of Israel, but has yet to lead to the creation of an independent Palestine. These partitions have produced a vast scholarship, although comparative studies of the partition of British India and the United Nations' proposal to partition Palestine have produced very little in the way of comparative work.[1] Yet, the partitions of British India and mandate Palestine make useful comparisons, not only because they were administered by the same power, but also because they occurred within months of each other in the early stages of the Cold War. Significantly, India and Pakistan voted against UN General Assembly Resolution 181 (II) of 29 November 1947 (hereafter 'the UN Partition Plan for Palestine'), even though their leaders accepted the partition of the Indian subcontinent as the price of independence.

To understand why both India and Pakistan could oppose the partition of Palestine, after its leaders had acquiesced to partition in the Indian subcontinent, it is necessary to take a closer look at events preceding these partitions and the arguments that were formulated at the United Nations with respect to the debate on the partition of Palestine. It will be seen that Muslim League, Indian and Palestinian nationalists foreshadowed the emergence of self-determination in Africa and Asia through their insistence on transferring power to the majority community during decolonisation. While the Congress agreed with the principle of majority rule as the basis for the creation of Pakistan – i.e., the secession of the North-West Frontier Province, Sind and Baluchistan – it made an exception for the provinces of Punjab and Bengal, which were to be partitioned, even though both provinces had a Muslim majority.[2] The Congress and the League's disagreement concerned the *standard* as to which Punjab and Bengal would be partitioned, and whether majority rule was to be applied to the provinces, or to the divisions and sub-units of those provinces. The League originally envisaged that the whole of Punjab and Bengal would form part of a northern federation of Muslim-majority provinces tied loosely to an All-Indian federal centre; it did not desire partition, but had little choice but to accept this, when it was demanded by the Congress Working Committee in March 1947, and subsequently adopted as policy by the British Government. In the end, Sir Cyril Radcliffe, the umpire, divided the provinces by the *thana* – that is, territory under the jurisdiction of a single police station – which was the smallest unit for which the census had published data, while also taking into account other factors such as irrigation, railways, security concerns, infrastructure and the location of important holy shrines.[3]

The reason why the Congress Party in India and the Muslim League in Pakistan both opposed the partition of Palestine was because what the United Nations proposed to do in Palestine was the very opposite of what happened in India. Whereas majority rule formed the basis for the creation of Pakistan, and for the division of Punjab and Bengal, this principle was explicitly denied to the Arabs of Palestine. In contrast to the situation in Punjab and Bengal, which were divided between Muslims and non-Muslims by the smallest and most accurate geographical unit for which there was published data, the UN allotted whole subdistricts to a Jewish state, even where the Arab population was the overwhelming majority.

In 1939, senior leaders of the Muslim League made inquiries as to whether India could challenge the legality of British colonial policy in Palestine at the Permanent Court of International Justice (PCIJ) in a manner that was highly reminiscent of a later challenge against minority rule at the International Court of Justice (ICJ), the PCIJ's successor, during the South West Africa Cases (1960–66). In 1947–48, Egypt, Iraq and Syria also tried to challenge the legality of British colonial policy and the constitutionality of the UN Partition Plan for Palestine in 1947–48 by requesting an advisory opinion from the ICJ, but these attempts failed to garner sufficient support in the General Assembly. The flagrant deprivation of Arab democratic rights in the formulation of the UN Partition Plan for Palestine, and the means for their peaceful redress, inadvertently paved the path for the emergence of an aggressive form of Third World nationalism based on majority rule that would lead to the development of atavistic, irredentist and 'subterranean' forms of violent nationalism, Islamism, and anti-imperialism.[4] In Palestine, this found expression in the charters of the Palestine Liberation Organisation and Hamas.[5]

Additionally, after the partitions of 1947, a group of Muslim-majority states from North Africa, the Middle East, South Asia and Southeast Asia joined the United Nations and played a pivotal role in promoting self-determination in Africa and Asia with support from the communist bloc at the UN, which culminated in the adoption by the UN General Assembly of the seminal Declaration on the Granting of Independence to Colonial Countries and Peoples in December 1960.[6] The drawback of their call for majority rule and the immediate transfer of power was the advent of majoritarian democracies and dictatorships and their suppression of minorities, which was to have a profound and lasting influence on the postcolonial world.

Comparing and contrasting the partitions of India and Palestine

The origins of partition in British India and mandate Palestine both lay in British colonial policy and challenges to that policy that was inspired by the anticolonialism of the Soviet Union following the October Revolution in 1917 and the United States entering the world stage at the Paris Peace Conference.[7] When the United Kingdom began to consider plans to steadily devolve power to India and Palestine by granting its peoples self-government in the 1930s, a competition for political power opened. The leaders of the Muslim League and British supporters of the Zionist project in Palestine were concerned with these developments because as representatives of minorities they would lose out in a political system where the winner takes all. This is because in the Westminster system of parliamentary democracy sovereignty is vested in Parliament and exercised by a cabinet selected by the winning party.

Accordingly, as organisations that represented minorities in Palestine and India in the sense in which these communities were tabulated in official censuses in these territories at the time (i.e., within the borders of the British Raj and those of mandate Palestine), the leaders of the Muslim League and the Zionist Organisation favoured partition plans by claiming to be nations entitled to self-determination in independent self-governing states carved out of India and Palestine. In other words, all the main groups in India/Pakistan and Israel/Palestine (that is, the leaders of the Congress, the Muslim League, the Zionist Organisation and Palestinian Arab Higher Committee) *desired majority rule in some form.*[8]

Their disagreement was over how majority rule would be exercised, and specifically, *who* would be entitled to claim it, and over which *territory* this principle would apply. Whereas the Congress supported majority rule, irrespective of race or religion, the Muslim League was primarily concerned with the Muslim community. In Palestine, the Zionists supported majority rule for the Jewish community, and the Arab community's conception of majority rule was primarily aimed at the Arab community (primarily Arabic-speaking Muslims and Christians). For Indian and Palestinian nationalists, the territorial unit was the whole of the Indian subcontinent and mandate Palestine, where they formed a majority of the population as a whole, whereas the Muslim League demanded sovereignty in specific areas of India, especially the northwest and the northeast of the subcontinent, where Muslims were more populous. The Zionist Organisation desired sovereignty over the coastal plains of Palestine, from Gaza to Acre, where the most fertile lands were located, and the area around Jerusalem.[9]

The difference between the claims of the Muslim League and the Zionist Organisation was that the Jewish community in Palestine in 1947 was a minority in all of Palestine's subdistricts, except for the Jaffa subdistrict where Jews had a majority because it included the cities of Tel Aviv and Peta Tikva (although the port had an Arab majority), but the Jaffa subdistrict was too small to establish a viable Jewish state.[10] The Muslim populations of Punjab and Bengal, in contrast, were not only the overall majorities of both provinces, but during the proceedings prior to the partition it was agreed that a distinction would be made between those sub-units where the Muslims were a majority, and those where they were a minority.[11] In other words, majority rule remained the basis of the partition of the Indian subcontinent, but in Punjab and Bengal the unit of measurement was not the provinces or districts *but their sub-units*.[12] This was done to prevent the whole of Punjab and Bengal from joining Pakistan.

What was proposed for Palestine was different. As a direct result of the Holocaust, the European states that numerically dominated the UN as it was constituted in 1947 were determined to grant the Jewish people a state of their own in Palestine, even in those subdistricts where Jews were distinct minorities. This included Beersheba, where the Jewish population in 1947 was less than 1 per cent of the whole, while the Arab population was 99 per cent.[13] Despite this enormous population disparity, most members of the UN Special Committee for Palestine (UNSCOP) awarded the subdistrict to the Jewish state.[14] But if UNSCOP had applied the same logic or standard that led to the partition of British India – namely majority rule – *even by its sub-units*, then most of Palestine should have remained Arab.

Finally, whereas provincial elections were held in India in 1946–47, and referendums were organised in disputed sections of the provinces in 1947,[15] no elections were ever held in Palestine. Although an attempt was made to organise an election in Palestine in 1923, it envisaged a system based on parity, even though the Arab population at that time outnumbered the Jewish population by nine to one.[16] All attempts to establish a legislature in Palestine failed to garner British support because a legislature with an Arab majority would have taken steps to block the establishment of a Jewish homeland in Palestine by restricting Jewish immigration.

The partition of British India

When one speaks of the partition of India it ought to be remembered that one is really speaking of the partition of Punjab and Bengal.[17] The 3 June Partition Plan, approved by the British Government, provided that the demarcation of these provinces was to be undertaken 'on the basis of ascertaining the *contiguous majority areas* of Muslims and non-Muslims'.[18] The plan also instructed the Commission to take 'other factors' into account.[19] What is striking about the 3 June Plan is that, for the first time in the history of British imperial policy, the notion of majoritarianism – i.e. distinguishing rights to territorial sovereignty on the basis of whether a specific religious group formed the majority in an allotted territory – was *explicitly* spelt out in an instrument of government policy.[20]

Jawaharlal Nehru (1889–1964) and the Indian National Congress (established in December 1885) claimed to represent all Indians, irrespective of caste or religion, and it initially sought to amalgamate all the princely states, as well as those parts of British India with majority Muslim populations, into a single territorial unit that would be ruled from the centre. 'Though predominantly Hindu in membership', explained Nehru, 'the Congress had large numbers of Muslims on its rolls, as well as all other religious groups like Sikhs, Christians, etc. It was thus forced to think in national terms. For it the dominating issue was national freedom and the establishment of an independent democratic state.'[21]

In contrast, Mohammad Ali Jinnah (1876–1948) and the Muslim League claimed to represent Indian Muslims, whom it viewed as a separate political community. Established in 1906 by the Aga Khan and the landlords of Bengal, one of the central demands of the League was for Muslims to be treated as a separate political unit by the colonial power. Sir Syed Ahmed Khan, one of the Muslim community's earliest advocates, argued on the basis of his reading of J. S. Mill's views on representative government that Liberalism presupposed an ethnically and religiously homogenous society in which there was a basic harmony of interests.[22]

The Government of India Act, 1935 and the failure of statutory safeguards

The foundations of the Congress–League split that paved the path for partition in 1947 may be traced to the passing of the Government of India Act, 1935 (the 'GOI Act 1935'), which widened the franchise from 7 to 35 million people.[23] The GOI Act 1935 created constitutional safeguards in the interest of minorities so that provincial governors were invested with special powers to overrule their ministers when they deemed such intervention as being in the interest of a minority in the province.[24] However, after the 1937 elections, when the Congress obtained majorities in seven non-Muslim-majority provinces, it refused to form ministries because they feared that the governors would nullify the responsibilities of the ministries to their respective legislatures by intervening on the ground to protect the interests of the Muslim minority. This brought about a deadlock which was only resolved by a gentleman's agreement that the governor's special powers would not be utilised to justify the intervention in the day-to-day administration of the provinces by the ministries.

According to Muhammad Zafrulla Khan (1893–1985), who was the sole Muslim member of the Executive Council of the Viceroy of India, the gentleman's agreement in effect meant the nullification of the safeguard by which the Muslims laid great store, and demonstrated the futility and practice of statutory safeguards.[25] These fears were exacerbated by Nehru's refusal to accommodate League leaders unless they joined the Congress, and this increased their apprehension that the Congress would ignore the interests and views of Muslims in an independent India. Essentially, the GOI Act 1935 'heightened Muslim-minority anxieties and fears of Hindu domination'.[26] This was further accentuated when the Congress leaders 'enforced cow protection and the use of Hindi'.[27]

On the eve of the Second World War, and in opposition to the British Government's decision to go to war against Germany without consulting the Congress or issuing a declaration promising India freedom after the war, members of the Congress resigned from the Government in the provinces en mass. In addition, the Congress's front-rank leaders were detained by the British authorities until 1945.[28] Ironically, their resignations and the detention of the Congress's high command reduced British dependence on the Congress Party, and paved the way for the Muslim League to fill the political vacuum, which Jinnah did with great skill and acumen.[29]

The Muslim League opposes the 'Pakistan Scheme'

On 13 March 1940, Jinnah met with the Viceroy, the Marquess of Linlithgow, and expressed his fear of Hindu-majority rule when the British left. One week before Jinnah had met the Viceroy, Zafrulla Khan, one of Jinnah's closest advisers, submitted a 32-page memorandum advocating a 'separation scheme' to the Viceroy.[30] The memorandum articulated Jinnah's two-nation theory, but it did *not* advocate what was called the 'Pakistan Scheme' because the latter implied an exchange of populations 'entailing expense, misery, suffering, and horror ... on the scale that it would be necessary in India to discard the scheme at once'.[31] In the League's view, the 'Pakistan Scheme', as its supporters called it, was 'utterly impracticable and would result in nothing but misery and suffering and can, therefore, make no contribution towards the solution of India's problems'.[32] You cannot get a more clear-cut statement from the Muslim League opposing the partition of India than that.

Significantly, the separation scheme, which was advocated in the memorandum, *explicitly ruled out* a population transfer. It did not favour partition. Rather, the League wanted a scheme that would 'secure for India a status equal to that of the free nations of the world' while guaranteeing 'for the different sections of the population equal opportunities and means of advancement'.[33] The separation scheme that was advocated in the memorandum consisted of two *federations* (not independent states) with a northeastern federation compromising Bengal and Assam, and a northwestern federation comprising Punjab, Sind, the North-West Frontier Province, Baluchistan and the Frontier tribal areas.[34] The rest of India could constitute itself into a federation or federations, as it desired. There would be customs, railways, and defence conventions concluded between the federations.[35] The system was based on a series of treaties that would maintain the unity of India, but that would grant significant autonomy to the federations. The minorities in each of the federations could remain where they were, and their rights were to be safeguarded by reciprocal treaties exchanged between the federations.[36] 'The great merit of this scheme', the memorandum explained, 'is that it does away with any question of exchanges of populations and contemplates the retention in certain measures of the unity of India in those matters in which unity is essential and would prove beneficent'.[37] Complete liberty would be granted in matters of religion throughout the federation, subject only to the general law regulating public order and morality.[38]

The memorandum explained that the League was opposed to the establishment of a single unitary Indian state with a central Constituent Assembly because it would be dominated by Hindu-orientated political parties when the British left. This would result in the 'ruthless domination of the majority',[39] which was 'bound ultimately to lead to civil war',[40] and the 'setting up of a totalitarian Hindu State in India'.[41] The memorandum then drew attention to the age-old problem of the Westminster system of parliamentary democracy:

> The Central Legislature, by whatever name it is described, would have the power to legislate for the whole of the Central field without check or restriction and would be at liberty to repeal and amend such Acts of Parliament as apply to India. The Central Executive would be completely responsible to the Central Legislature and would exercise complete control over the armed forces of India. At any time, after the Dominion Constitution comes into operation, India would be at liberty to part company with the remaining British Commonwealths, to proclaim its complete independence and set up a Constituent Assembly or any other device that may appeal to the Central Legislature to frame a completely new constitution for India.[42]

The memorandum added: 'It is inherent in a Dominion Constitution of the Statute of Westminster type that the Dominion Legislatures are at liberty to convert a Dominion Constitution into a republic or a dictatorship or any other type of sovereign government that appeals to it.'[43]

A particular point of concern for the Muslim League was the communal problem, which caused its authors much anxiety and was addressed at length in the memorandum.[44] Clearly, the League's leaders were paying attention to what the leaders of the Hindu Mahasabha, like Dr B. S. Moonje, who was expressly mentioned in the memorandum, were saying.[45] The view was expressed in the memorandum that '[t]he attitude of the ordinary Hindu towards the Muslims is that Islam has stolen these millions from the fold of Hinduism and that these millions must be brought back into the fold'.[46] It was also complained that there were 'large quarters in big towns in India where it is impossible for a Muslim to rent accommodation, let alone be permitted to acquire property'.[47] In the ideology of the Hindu Mahasabha, the Muslims in South Asia were alien conquerors and cultural usurpers, and their mass conversion to Hinduism was envisaged as part of a Hindu renaissance.[48]

Nehru understood the Muslim demand for special treatment, although like most members of the Congress he was suspicious of them and was firmly of the opinion that the genuine emergence of nationalism did 'not come to a nation or a community from mere numbers, or special seats in legislatures, or protection given by outsiders'.[49] Rather, 'It [came] from within and from the cooperation and goodwill of comrades in a common cause. The minorities in India will not flourish by being spoon-fed from above but by their own merits and strength.'[50] But Nehru had no answer to the League's fear of what was called the communal problem.[51]

Distinguishing Muslim League and Zionist claims to India and Palestine

One week after Jinnah's meeting with Linlithgow, and after the Viceroy had seen Zafrulla Khan's memorandum, Jinnah spoke before an estimated crowd of 100,000 in a presidential address to the twenty-seventh session of the League, staking his claim for a Muslim homeland.[52] Rejecting the notion that the Muslims were just a minority, Jinnah asserted: 'The Musulmans are a nation by any definition.' He pointed out that, 'even according to the British map of India, we [the Muslims] occupy large parts of this country where the Musulmans are in a majority – such as Bengal, Punjab, N.W.F.P., Sind and Baluchistan'.[53] In other words, in those areas where Muslims were populous, they were not a minority, but a majority, with a long-established cultural and social history in the form of a nation.

This point is important to emphasise when making comparisons between the partitions of India and Palestine in 1947, because unlike the Muslim population of British India, the Jewish community in Palestine was a minority in nearly all of Palestine's subdistricts. In other words, the claim to a Muslim homeland advanced by the Muslim League in Pakistan was quite different to the claim advanced by the Zionists that were *in the process of colonising Palestine*. In Palestine, there were no large contiguous areas settled by Jews before 1947 as there was in northwest and northeast India where Muslims had been settled for centuries. While it may be legitimately questioned whether the Muslims of northern India formed a 'nation',[54] and while both Jews and Muslims were minorities in Europe and India, the League's claim to establish a Muslim homeland in India could not be replicated in Palestine. The numbers did not permit it. Of course, the fatal flaw with any partition based on majority rule is that it ignores the claims of minorities. This included the Sikh community who bore the brunt of partition because they lacked a majority in any district of Punjab that could form the territorial basis for a separate state, as the Sikh population was evenly divided between East and West Punjab.[55] Even so, the main Sikh political party, the Shiromani Akali Dal, accepted the 3 June Partition Plan, in the hope that the Punjab Boundary Commission would take into account 'other factors' in drawing the boundary, other than just demography, which was a weak point for the Sikhs.[56]

The point is that the League's claim to establish a Muslim homeland in northern India in those areas of the subcontinent where there were contiguous Muslim-majority areas was quite distinct from Zionist claims to Palestine. The Muslim League was not proposing to colonise the Hindu-majority areas of India. Accordingly, the identification of Pakistan as a 'Muslim Zion' only existed in the minds of certain individuals, but it could not be replicated in the conditions that existed in Palestine in 1947 without displacing Palestine's Arab majority.

The road to partition

At the heart of the ideological divide that emerged between the Congress and the League in the 1930s and 1940s were their different philosophical approaches to nationhood and the question of representation in a political system that vested power in parliamentary majorities. The Congress leadership had been influenced by the revolutionary experiences in the US and Europe in the eighteenth century and by the revolution in Russia in 1917, and it sought to establish a centralised nation-state ruled from Delhi as a strong parliamentary democracy based on the principle of majority rule.[57] As Nehru explained, the Congress Party had been influenced 'by the ideas of the

French and American revolutions, as also by the constitutional history of the British Parliament', in addition to 'the influence of the Soviet revolution'.[58]

But these ideas were alien to the League which did not look to the US or Europe or Russia for inspiration. For the Muslim League, majority rule and the West's history of nationalism was extraneous. In terms of looking at the Indian subcontinent as a single political unit, Jinnah 'repeatedly and categorically dismissed the suitability of applying the principles of arithmetic to the problem of representation'.[59] If, however, it was recognised that the Indian Muslims were a nation entitled to self-determination, then he was prepared to accept that based on arithmetic, Muslims were entitled to majority rule *in those areas where they formed the majority*. Indeed, majority rule based on a religious distinction – between Muslims and non-Muslims – was to be the principal argument for partition and would find direct expression in the 3 June 1947 Partition Plan approved by the British Government.

After the Second World War, the Labour government in London warmed to the idea of giving India complete independence, but the British Government did not think the members of the existing legislature reflected the views of the Indian people as to whether India should be divided or remain one independent nation. This was because the central assembly had been elected in 1934 and the provincial legislatures in 1936. Accordingly, it was thought necessary to have new elections.[60] Although the Congress Party won a spectacular victory in the elections, it failed to dislodge the Muslim League's hold on the Muslim population. According to Khushwant Singh, the League went to the polls on the issue of Pakistan and won every single Muslim seat in the central legislature.[61] Even in the provinces – except for North-West Frontier Province – the League obtained 90 per cent of the Muslim vote. As Singh observed, 'non-Muslims wanted a united India; Muslims wanted India to be divided to make Pakistan'.[62]

To preserve the unity of British India, the British Government came up with the Cabinet Mission Plan in 1946. This sought to create three autonomous zones: the northeast (comprising the provinces of Bengal and Assam), the northwest (comprising Punjab, the Frontier, Baluchistan and Sind), and the centre (comprising the remaining Provinces). These zones would be tied into a federation responsible for defence, foreign affairs, currency, communications and federal finance. At the end of ten years, the first or second zone, or both, could opt out of the federation and become independent.[63] In essence, the plan would have been an attempt to forestall partition and came very close to Zafrulla Khan's separation scheme that he put to the Viceroy in 1940 and that was articulated by Jinnah in the Lahore Resolution. The Congress and the League were effectively being offered a ten-year reprieve to see if they could agree to share power in a united India. This time around the League accepted the plan, but the Congress rejected it.⁶⁴ In other words, as late as 1946 the League was prepared to accept a federation and power-sharing with the Congress. Only if the Cabinet Mission Plan failed would the League take steps to form an independent Muslim homeland, but the League remained opposed to a hard border and population transfer.

But the Congress high command rejected the Cabinet Mission Plan because it wanted to create a strong centralised government in India, and parity with the League would have prevented that.⁶⁵ In the words of Joya Chatterji, 'the Congress high command wanted a swift transfer of power to a strong central government, firmly under its control. The Muslim League's demands for group autonomy and parity at the centre were seen by the Congress as the main obstacle to achieving this goal.'⁶⁶ The creation of Pakistan – the 'Pakistan Scheme' that the League had categorically ruled out in no uncertain terms to the Viceroy in 1940 – had become inevitable. As Sardar Patel, Nehru's powerful Home Minister, commented in a debate in the Bengal Chamber of Commerce in January 1950: 'We agreed to partition *because we saw the alternative was worse*. Therefore, we agreed to it, but at the same time we made a condition that we can only agree to partition if we do not lose Calcutta.'⁶⁷ Partition was imposed in haste, and with disastrous human consequences.

The partition of Palestine

Britain's administration of Palestine differed considerably from its hold over India. This was because, in Palestine, Britain had become obliged to encourage Jewish immigration on a large scale pursuant to the policy in the Balfour Declaration of 2 November 1917, according to which the British Government was to use its 'best endeavours' to facilitate the creation of a Jewish national home in Palestine.⁶⁸ British interest in facilitating the colonisation of West Asia had long been connected to the trade routes to India following the creation of the Suez Canal, which became an important strategic outpost along with Cyprus, Egypt, the Sudan and Yemen. As home to holy places sacred to Christianity, Judaism and Islam, Palestine had long attracted the interest of theologians, travellers and missionaries, but in the dispute over the status of Palestine after the partition of the Ottoman Empire in 1918, it was Zionism that had the greatest impact.

Zionism differed from many of the other nationalist movements claiming self-determination in the twentieth century (including that of the Muslim League) because, prior to the insertion of the Balfour Declaration into the text of the British mandate of Palestine, the Jewish national movement had no territory, no *terra sancta*, in its control or exclusive possession.

And before the creation of Israel in 1948, and the expulsion of Palestine's Arab inhabitants, Palestine's Jewish inhabitants were never a majority of Palestine's population, nor owners of a majority of the land. In 1918, the population of Palestine was 93 per cent Arab and 7 per cent Jewish; most Jews spoke Arabic.[69] While the Jewish community dramatically increased their numbers during the British mandate when they were fleeing European persecution, especially in the 1930s, they never became a majority of the population before 1948, and they remained a minority community in all of Palestine's subdistricts – except for the Jaffa subdistrict.[70] With regard to land ownership, the situation was even starker. According to British statistics on land ownership as late as 1945, in every single subdistrict of Palestine most of the land in private ownership remained Arab – *including in Jaffa*.[71] Moreover, Zionism needed the support of Great Britain, then one of the world's greatest colonial powers (the 'British bayonet' as Gandhi, Jinnah and Nehru used to say) to nurture and support the development of a Jewish national home in Palestine. This explained why the Zionist movement favoured partition plans because they would grant sovereignty to a Jewish state.[72] The only point of disagreement among the various Zionist groups was the extent of that sovereignty and the shape a Jewish state would take in the boundaries established by partition.[73] Conversely, the Arab population of Palestine opposed partition because, as the majority population in private ownership of most of the land, they desired independence in a single unitary state.

The development of British and Jewish partition plans in Palestine was made problematic by the size of Palestine's Arab majority, which prevented the British Government from establishing representative self-governing institutions in Palestine as required under the mandate.[74] It was feared that a representative legislative assembly that would reflect the interests of the indigenous Arab majority would take steps to block the Zionist project by restricting immigration. Accordingly, from the beginning of the mandate until the outbreak of the Second World War, Britain, in the words of Rashid Khalidi, 'rejected the principle of majority rule, or any measure that would have given the Palestinian Arabs majority control over the government of Palestine'.[75]

Parliament opposes majority rule

In 1936, in an attempt to placate Arab opinion, Sir Arthur Wauchope, the British High Commissioner of Palestine, submitted a proposal to establish self-governing institutions in Palestine, but the plan encountered vehement opposition in the British Parliament because it would empower the Arab majority, seemingly in contravention of British policy as expressed in the Balfour Declaration. As William Ormsby-Gore, the Colonial Secretary, observed, the entire House, bar Willie Gallacher, the sole communist member, was opposed to the High Commissioner's plan to establishing self-governing institutions in Palestine.[76] As Winston Churchill recognised: 'If you have an Arab majority ... you will have continued friction between the principle of the Balfour Declaration and ... the wishes of the Arab majority. I should have thought it would be a very great obstruction to the development of Jewish immigration into Palestine and to the development of the national home of the Jews there.'[77]

Due to the opposition expressed in Parliament to the prospect of establishing representative government in Palestine, and to the recent arrival of thousands of Jews fleeing persecution in central Europe, the leaders of the Palestinian national movement, who viewed these recent arrivals with alarm given British policy in the Balfour Declaration, declared a six months' strike. There followed an armed rebellion, mostly targeting British troops (the 1936–39 Arab revolt), that triggered a proposal to send a Royal Commission of Inquiry (called the 'Peel Commission', after its chairman) to Palestine to examine the causes of the disturbances.[78]

According to the terms of reference provided to the Commission, it was not to question the underlying policy of the Balfour Declaration that encouraged the very immigration that led to the violence. The Commission was therefore precluded from recommending a solution based on majority rule that would vest political power in the Arab masses. Accordingly, it concluded that the only solution was partition:

> About 1,000,000 Arabs are in strife, open or latent, with some 400,000 Jews. There is no common ground between them. The Arab community is predominantly Asiatic in character, the Jewish community predominantly European. They differ in religion and language. Their cultural and social life, their ways of thought and conduct are as incompatible as their national aspirations. These last are the greatest bar to peace.[79]

In reaching the conclusion that the only solution to the 'Arab–Jewish conflict' was partition, the Commission claimed that the concept of a single Palestinian citizenship was a 'mischievous pretence' since neither Arabs nor Jews had any sense of service to a single state.[80] Accordingly, the Commission expressed its opinion that democracy could not flourish in Palestine because it lacked a homogenous population that was essential for representative government to work:

> the successful working of representative government requires that the population concerned should be sufficiently homogeneous. Unless there is common ground enough between its different groups or classes to enable the minority to acquiesce in the rule of the majority and to make it possible for the balance of power to readjust itself from time to time, the working basis of parliamentary government or democracy as we understand it is not there.[81]

Ironically, this was the same theory of representative government articulated by the Muslim League in India. Its application to the Indian subcontinent formed one of their principal fears: that in a single unitary independent India, the Congress could establish a totalitarian Hindu state. This is why the League insisted that the British Government recognise communal groups.

In explaining why representative government was not appropriate for Palestine, the Commission referred to the 'most patent example of this in present-day politics', which was 'the impossibility of uniting all Ireland under a single parliament; and that the gulf between Arabs and Jews in Palestine is wider than that which separates Northern Ireland from the Irish Free State'.[82] Clearly, the way in which the British elite viewed the conflict in Palestine and administered the mandate was affected by what Khalidi described as 'a worldview rooted in their earlier colonial experiences, notably in Ireland and India'.[83] And 'this was a worldview that almost invariably perceived colonized societies in religious and communitarian rather than in national terms, and as profoundly divided internally rather than as potentially unified'.[84]

The attempt to refer the Palestine dispute to the Permanent Court of International Justice

Whatever the intentions of the authors of the Balfour Declaration may have been from 1917 to 1922, the British Government considered that all of Palestine's inhabitants were entitled to self-government by 1939 when it published its White Paper, where it was declared that the objective of His Majesty's Government was the establishment of 'an independent Palestine state ... in which the two peoples in Palestine, Arabs and Jews, share authority in government in such a way that the essential interests of each are shared'.[85] The White Paper did not come out of the blue. It was formulated after an assessment of British policy brought about by the Arab Revolt and the changing geopolitical situation before the outbreak of the Second World War.[86]

Prior to the publication of the White Paper, the British Government had convened a Round Table Conference with a view to establishing a plan for Palestine following the termination of the mandate to which both Jews and Arabs were invited. The Arab states called on the United Kingdom to 'abrogate' the mandate and replace it by 'a treaty similar to that concluded with Iraq'.[87] While India was not represented at the conference, Jinnah sent a Muslim League delegation to London to advice the Arabs on the sidelines, a tactic that would be repeated at the UN in 1947. By 1939, Jinnah had emerged as one of the most influential leaders – in London's eyes – because he did not oppose the war effort like his counterparts in the Congress Party, who would be imprisoned for their disloyalty.[88] Accordingly, British leaders listened closely to what Jinnah said, including his demand for a Muslim homeland.[89]

Jinnah demanded that Britain allow the Mufti of Jerusalem, Haj Amin al-Husseini, and a Muslim League delegation to be officially represented at the constitutional talks on the future of Palestine at the Round Table Conference in London. When Whitehall refused Jinnah's demands, he threatened legal action and insisted that no Muslim troops serve in the British Army in Palestine.[90] At the time, 60 per cent of the Indian troops serving in the British Empire were Muslim.[91] The Viceroy took Jinnah's threats seriously, but did not yield.[92] The Mufti and the Muslim League delegation was not represented at the conference.

But this was not the whole story, for despite not being invited, a Muslim League delegation travelled to London in February 1939 comprised of senior members, including Abdur Rahman Siddiqi, Member of the Legislative Assembly of Bengal, and Choudhry Khaliquzzaman, Member of the Legislative Assembly of the United Provinces, to offer the Arab leaders informal advice on the sidelines of the Round Table Conference.[93] Khaliquzzaman advised the Palestinian Arabs to accept the 1939 White Paper, even though it allowed for Jewish immigration to Palestine for a further ten-year period, because once Palestine was given self-government, the British authorities were likely to ignore the views of the minorities, as they had done in India, when the Viceroy had allowed the Congress to violate the safeguards for the Muslims in the GOI Act 1935.[94] Khaliquzzaman's sage advice was ignored by the Arab delegation, and they rejected the White Paper thinking that time was on their side.[95]

In addition to meeting British officials and politicians in London, Siddiqui and Khaliquzzaman sent an official memorandum protesting British policy in Palestine to the Secretary of State for India, the Secretary-General of the League of Nations, and the President of the Mandates Commission.[96] The five-page memorandum was titled 'Statement of Indian Muslim views on Palestine'.[97] Among other matters, the statement complained about the history of British rule in Palestine, which 'left no room for doubt' that the United Kingdom had 'not only failed to protect, much less to advance, the interests of the people placed under its charge as a trust of civilization'.[98] It was questioned whether Britain had divested itself of responsibility for good government by having bought into Palestine large numbers of Jewish immigrants and 'transferred all its functions of trusteeship to the immigrants'.[99] 'Such a devolution of power', the statement continued, 'was never contemplated and has been questioned by the Arab and the Muslim World repeatedly and continually.'[100]

After delivering this statement, the delegation travelled to Geneva for discussions with League of Nations officials, including Edouard de Haller,

Director of the Mandates Section.[101] According to the report of their visit,[102] which they presented to Jinnah on their return, the delegation enquired whether India could take up Palestine's case at the Permanent Court of International Justice, since Palestine was 'debarred under League rules and regulations'.[103] The reason why Palestine could not 'sue' the British Empire directly was because the jurisdictional clause of the Palestine mandate only provided the court with such jurisdiction, 'if any dispute whatever should arise between the Mandatory *and another member of the League of Nations* relating to the interpretation or the application of the provisions of the mandate'.[104]

In the view of the Muslim League, the British Government was not administering the mandate in accordance with Article 22 of the Covenant of the League of Nations, which required Britain, as the mandatory power, to apply the principle that 'the well-being and development of such peoples form a sacred trust of civilisation'. This was because Britain was privileging Jewish rights over those of Palestine's Arab population and was not administering the mandate for the 'well-being and development' *of all of Palestine's inhabitants*. In other words, the League was proposing to challenge the idea that self-government could be denied to the majority community in Palestine. Implicitly, they were challenging the idea of minority rule. This argument was striking in its similarly to a later complaint by Ethiopia and Liberia at the International Court of Justice, the successor to the Permanent Court of International Justice, when they challenged South Africa's apartheid policy in South West Africa.[105]

Intriguingly, the arguments raised in the 1939 statement were reiterated at the UN in 1947 by Abdur Rahman and Zafrulla Khan, when they opposed UNSCOP's plan to partition Palestine.[106] Egypt, Syria and Iraq proposed referring several questions to the International Court of Justice for an advisory opinion; the questions were similar to those raised in the report submitted by the Muslim League to the British Government and the League of Nations in 1939.[107]

The debate on Palestine at the United Nations

On 26 November 1947, the world community met at the UN to debate the merits of the Partition Plan for Palestine after it was drawn up by one of the subcommittees established by the General Assembly.[108] The Arab delegations were disorganised and did not do a good job of challenging UNSCOP's majority plan. It fell to Pakistan, which had recently been admitted to the UN as a new member state, to articulate their cause. As Zafrulla Khan, who had been appointed head of Pakistan's delegation to the UN, recalled:

The Arab delegates also spoke at length and some speeches were indeed studied with solid arguments but the eloquence was by and large emotional and the speakers spent most of their time in a vain effort to prove that the Jews coming to settle in Palestine were not the descendants of Abraham and belonged to a Russian tribe named Khazar whose forefathers in a distant past had converted to Judaism. The Arab cause in all its aspects was so strong and just that to support it with such irrelevant arguments amounted to weakening it. It appeared as if the Arab delegates had not organised their speeches or martialled their arguments under a central direction. Whatever came to anyone's mind he blurted it out.[109]

Zafrulla Khan would have been aware, when criticising the Arab argument that the Jews immigrating to Palestine were not the descendants of Abraham as they belonged to a Russian tribe named Khazar, that many of the Muslims of the Indian subcontinent had once been Hindus before they converted to Islam.[110] Even Jinnah, the founding father of Pakistan, had 'his origins in a western Indian trading caste, with its largely Hindu background and culture'.[111] Zafrulla Khan's own community had originally been Hindu.[112] In the course of time, his extended family had embraced Islam, certain others had become Sikhs, and only two remained Hindus, although during his grandfather's era 'more than twelve generations of our forebears had been Muslims'.[113] Given Zafrulla's family background, one can appreciate why the communal problem in India and the exclusivist ideology of Hindutva concerned him.

Prior to the UN debate, Zafrulla Khan had been appointed Chairman of subcommittee 2 of the Ad Hoc Committee on the Palestine Question that was asked to consider alternatives to partition.[114] As both the chairman *and the rapporteur* of the committee, Khan drafted most of the report, which raised serious questions about the statistical data the UNSCOP majority had used to endorse its conclusion to divide Palestine into a Jewish state and an Arab state. This was because UNSCOP had not included the Bedouin community in its population statistics for the Jewish state. When the Bedouin community (some 127,000 people) was accounted for, there would actually have been an *Arab majority* in the Jewish state.[115] The committee also thought the establishment of a Jewish state along the lines suggested by the UNSCOP majority would economically suffocate the Arab state and devastate its citrus industry, as it included in the territory of the Jewish state the best agricultural land, leaving the Arab state burdened with uncultivatable mountainous regions.[116] The UNSCOP majority placed Palestine's two ports – Haifa and Jaffa – in the territory of the Jewish state (in the final plan, the UN majority decided to create an Arab enclave around Jaffa *port*, presumably due to its Arab majority and the need for the Arab state to have an outlet to the sea).[117] At the time the port of Haifa was the terminal of the

Iraq oil pipeline and the point of entry of all international trade into Palestine. The UN majority wanted the port to be wholly within the territory of the Jewish state.[118]

Zafrulla Khan had become adept at reading maps and population statistics, as only three months previously he had been given a week's notice to make the case for partition before the Punjab Boundary Commission.[119] He was subsequently asked, at the end of October 1947, that is, one month before the UN voted in favour of the UN Partition Plan for Palestine, to chair subcommittee 2 on the Palestine Question. As chairman and rapporteur of the subcommittee, Zafrulla Khan was furnished with the latest statistical data by the British authorities. With his command of this data, he was able to make mincemeat of UNSCOP's majority proposal, which he did with great skill and acumen, even causing the subcommittee to modify its plan through the sheer force of his arguments.

Speaking before the UN plenary in New York City, Zafrulla Khan made short shrift of the claim that Palestine was a haven for the survivors of the Holocaust in the refugee camps of Europe by highlighting the hypocrisy of Western immigration policies when they *restricted* Jewish emigration from Europe during the Shoah (1933–45).[120] After taking the moral high ground, Khan then concentrated on the details of the plan. He pointed out that there were 1,300,000 Arabs in Palestine and 650,000 Jews – with room wanted for more Jewish immigrants – and that the problem had supposedly become insoluble, which is why the UNSCOP majority envisaged giving the Jewish state most of the land. Since the UN majority was of the view that it was not right for the Jews to form a minority in a single unitary or federal Arab state, it was being suggested that the only fair solution was partition and the establishment of two states – an Arab state, with Jerusalem as a corpus separatum, and a Jewish state. The boundaries were drawn accordingly and the draft Partition Plan envisaged establishing an Arab state with only 10,000 Jews in it and almost 1,000,000 Arabs. However, the population of the Jewish state, according to the figures provided by the UNSCOP majority,[121] envisaged a Jewish state with 498,000 Jews and 435,000 Arabs. This prompted Khan to question whether the minority problem had really been solved: 'Jews are not to live as a minority under the Arabs, but the Arabs are to live as a minority under the Jews. If one of these is not fair then neither is the other; and if one is not a solution, the other is not.'[122]

Zafrulla Khan then turned his attention to boundaries, pointing out that the Jewish population only constituted 33 per cent of the population of the whole area of Palestine within its mandate borders, and the Arabs 67 per cent, and yet 60 per cent of the total area of Palestine was to go to the Jewish state – which he thought was hardly fair or equitable. He then mentioned a document which had been circulated to members of the subcommittees by the United Kingdom representative prior to the debate showing that, of the irrigated, cultivable areas, 84 per cent would be in the Jewish state and only 16 per cent in the Arab state.[123] In the Negev, the inequity was even starker – where Arabs owned 14 per cent of the land and the Jews only 1 per cent – and yet the whole of the Negev was to be awarded to the Jewish state. Moreover, there was an Arab population of over one hundred thousand inhabiting the Negev, and a Jewish population of only one thousand, yet the Jewish state was to be awarded the lot.[124]

Zafrulla Khan also criticised the UN for ignoring the wishes of the majority of the inhabitants of Palestine in proposing to implement the Partition Plan against their will.[125] This argument had also been made by Sir Abdur Rahman, the Indian representative, in his dissent from the UNSCOP's majority proposal, when he suggested that in accordance with the international principle of self-determination, 'the affairs of a country must be conducted in accordance with the wishes of the majority of its inhabitants'.[126] As Henry Cattan, the Palestinian lawyer and representative of the Arab Higher Committee at the UN in 1948, pointed out, not all the Jews that immigrated to Palestine in the 1940s had acquired Palestine citizenship; yet they were being given more rights than citizens.[127] Moreover, the Jews who settled in Palestine never owned the majority of the land until after the creation of Israel, when this land was confiscated by the Jewish state and given to Jewish refugees from Europe.[128]

India and Pakistan vote against the UN Partition Plan for Palestine

Despite the partition of the Indian subcontinent, India voted with Pakistan against the UN General Assembly Resolution to partition Palestine in 1947, as did every single Arab country.[129] Vijayalakshmi Pandit, Nehru's sister, who in 1947 was India's Ambassador to the UN, explained in a cable to her brother that the Arab demand for national independence in Palestine was the same as the Congress's claim to represent India. This was why India, in her opinion, had to support the Arab claim to Palestine: 'The Arab demand is based on the same principle of right of self-determination and freedom, which Congress in India has always fought for. India's support of the Arab demand will also therefore be ideologically consistent.'[130]

The only Indian national movement that supported the partition of Palestine in 1947 consisted of the leaders of the Hindu Mahasabha, some of whose members were implicated in the assassination of Mahatma Gandhi in 1948. Vinayak Damodar Savarkar, a former president of the Hindu Mahasabha, applauded the UN Partition Plan, although he regretted that the Jews were not granted the whole of Palestine.[131]

As P. R. Kumaraswamy noted in his chapter, Nehru paid close attention to the debates on the partition of Palestine and actively intervened, diluted, modified and even dictated his views to the Indian representative at the UN when UNSCOP was considering a federal scheme for Palestine prior to the debate on partition.[132] It was as though Nehru wanted to implement the federal scheme in Palestine that had similarities to the Cabinet Mission Plan which had been rejected by the Congress as a solution to the Hindu–Muslim divide in India.[133] The Cabinet Mission Plan that the Congress rejected, and the federal plan for Palestine that was initially opposed by the Palestine Arabs in favour of a single unitary state, closely resembled Zafrulla Khan's (misnamed) 'separation scheme' (6 March 1940) that envisaged a federation for British India.

Nehru and Zafrulla Khan – from opposite sides of the political spectrum – could distinguish India's partition from the UN's proposal to partition Palestine because the majority of Palestine's Jewish population were recent arrivals coming to Palestine in the 1920s and 1930s whose claim to Palestine was viewed as being as tenuous as that of any other immigrant community. In India, the overwhelming majority of the population was rooted to the soil. India was never a location of mass European migration. Not so in Palestine where British policy led to a fundamental transformation of the population that also affected its very identity as an Arab country. In Palestine, partition along the lines of India, by dividing the Jews from non-Jews, was not possible because the Jewish population in 1947 only had a majority in one of Palestine's sixteen subdistricts (Jaffa) and was a minority landowner in all subdistricts. In British India, elections were held in 1936, 1945 and 1947, albeit on a restricted franchise. In contrast, throughout Britain's administration of Palestine no elections were ever held.

During the last years of the mandate, Britain vacillated between partition and a federal system for Palestine, as it had done in India, but in the end British leaders could not make up their minds what to do in Palestine, and hastily ended the mandate. As the report of subcommittee 2 that was chaired and drafted by Zafrulla Khan warned: '[t]he forcible creation of a Jewish State within the heart of the Arab world, would constitute a serious factor of disturbance, not only within the boundaries of Palestine, but would also jeopardise the peace and international security throughout the Middle East'.[134] This was because the creation of a Jewish state would come into being against 'the bitter opposition of the Arabs of Palestine and of the inhabitants of the adjoining countries', and would thus create and give rise to an outbreak of hostilities which 'it may become extremely difficult to control'.[135] This warning was prophetic, but it fell on deaf ears. Few Western diplomats were willing to listen or take seriously the concerns expressed by diplomats from the Indian subcontinent in 1947. Yet a few months after these words were written, the UN Palestine Commission, headed by the Spanish diplomat Pablo de Azcárate, that was tasked with implementing partition, warned that in the absence of forces adequate to maintain law and order in Palestine after the termination of the mandate, 'there would be administrative chaos, starvation, widespread strife, violence and bloodshed in Palestine, including Jerusalem'.[136]

This is precisely what happened, and the creation of Israel in 1948 was born of war with the surrounding Arab states that were opposed to the establishment of a Jewish state in Palestine. The war resulted in the expulsion of some 750,000 Palestinian Arabs (three-quarters of the Arab population of Palestine) from what they regarded as their ancestral homeland.[137]

Conclusion

The partitions of India and Palestine in 1947 were geopolitical earthquakes that had major consequences. At the diplomatic level, India and Pakistan emerged as independent states determined to end colonialism elsewhere by transferring power to indigenous majorities, which they articulated at the UN in the 1940s and 1950s where they also discredited apartheid in South Africa.[138] In 1952, a group of mostly Muslim-majority states submitted a letter to the UN Secretary-General insisting that the question of the race conflict in South Africa resulting from the policies of apartheid of the Government of the Union of South Africa be included in the agenda of the General Assembly.[139] The publication of this letter marked a milestone as it changed the tone of subsequent UN resolutions on apartheid. This was because all previous UN resolutions criticising South Africa had been exclusively concerned with the treatment of Indians in South Africa.[140] After the publication of this letter, subsequent UN resolutions broke the connection to Indian South Africans by criticising South Africa's apartheid policy for discriminating against all non-white South Africans, including indigenous black Africans who constituted the vast majority of the population.[141] In a resolution adopted by the UN General Assembly in December 1952, which made express reference to the letter signed by the group of mostly Muslim-majority states, the General Assembly declared that:

> in a multi-racial society harmony and respect for human rights and freedoms and the peaceful development of a unified community are best assured when patterns of legislation and practice are directed towards ensuring equality before law of all persons regardless of race .... and when economic, social, cultural and political participation of *all racial groups* is on a basis of equality.[142]

At the subterranean level, the violent movement of people caused by large-scale human suffering in India and Palestine also lead to the emergence of atavistic forms of violent nationalism and anti-imperialism, with the first clashes occurring over Kashmir – which Zafrulla Khan was quick to criticise before the UN Security Council, where he called for a plebiscite and opposed an Indian proposal to partition the state.[143] Yet Devji has argued that Zafrulla Khan's arguments criticising the partition of Palestine at the UN in November 1947 were 'disingenuous' because of what was happening to Punjab in that very month, when millions of people were butchered and displaced.[144] But we must remember that Zafrulla Khan categorically opposed partition and population transfer when the two-nation theory was articulated in his memorandum to the Viceroy in 1940.[145] Senior League leaders like Zafrulla Khan and Khaliquzzaman always envisaged a large non-Muslim minority in their Muslim federation, or failing that Pakistan, if only to prevent the future leaders of India from oppressing its Muslim minority.[146] With regard to the events of 1947, Zafrulla condemned them unequivocally, describing the greater part of Punjab as 'a scene of unmitigated savagery', when 'greed, lust and carnage reduced human beings below the level of beasts'.[147] As argued earlier in this chapter, it may be questioned whether there was a contradiction between the Muslim League's support for *two nations within a federal India* and Pakistan's support for the recognition of an Arab state in Palestine, since they were both based on majority rule. It was not the Muslim League that called for dividing Punjab and Bengal, but the Congress. According to Zafrulla Khan's recollection, Mountbatten's insistence on dividing Punjab and Bengal drove Jinnah 'quite mad'.[148] While Jinnah can be criticised for succumbing to the demand for partition in the end, it may be questioned whether his consent was freely given. Devji's reference to Zafrulla's lack of concern for the migration of Jews to Palestine from the Arab world also seems misplaced.[149] This was because Jewish emigration did not occur *simultaneously* with the adoption of the UN Partition Plan for Palestine on 29 November 1947, as happened in Punjab. There was no 'population exchange' between Arabs and Jews in 1947 or 1948.[150] Jewish emigration to Palestine came in waves, for various reasons, *after* the expulsion of 750,000 Palestinians from their homes, and after Israel was admitted to the UN.[151]

India's contribution to the freedom struggle is well known and justly celebrated. Less told is Pakistan's role. In the 1940s and 1950s, several Muslim-majority states joined the UN, including Indonesia, Jordan, Libya, Malaysia, Morocco, Sudan and Tunisia.[152] Prior to their independence, Pakistan had used its position as an independent state to assertively and publicly attack the policies of the colonial powers 'inside and outside the United Nations on the questions of Indonesia; the Italian colonies of Libya,

Eritrea and Somaliland; Morocco and Tunisia; and support[ed] ... Egypt and Iran in their disputes with Britain'.[153] As Zafrulla Khan explained to Pakistan's Constituent Legislative Assembly in 1952 when he was Pakistan's Foreign Minister:

> whenever there is a question of liberty and independence from imperialism or opposing colonialism or pushing forward a people's march towards freedom, Pakistan is always to the fore and second to none whether it is the case of a Muslim country or it is the case of a non-Muslim country. So long as it is the case of a people awaiting its independence, we have always supported it.[154]

Thirteen years after the UN had recommended the partition of Palestine in November 1947, a more diverse General Assembly, whose composition had been transformed with the addition of countries from Africa and Asia as a direct result of the decolonisation process spearheaded by India, Pakistan and the Soviets, was now of the view that partition would be contrary to the UN Charter unless it reflected the will of the people.[155]

There was, however, a gloomier end to this story. For the Founding Fathers of Pakistan did not survive for long. Jinnah died a few months after partition, and Zafrulla Khan was removed from office because he was an Ahmadiyya Muslim, a supposedly 'heretical Islamic sect'. He subsequently moved to The Hague where he became a judge of the International Court of Justice. The identification of Pakistan as an *Islamic state* that Zafrulla Khan had assiduously advocated in the 1940s had a major drawback, as non-Orthodox Muslims could now be condemned, if not killed, by the new rulers of Pakistan for not being 'proper Muslims'.

In *The Agony of Pakistan*, published in 1974, Zafrulla Khan reflected on the situation in his adopted homeland, where a succession of dictators had ruled from 1958–71 (Zafrulla resigned as Foreign Minister of Pakistan in 1954). He realised there was little to celebrate, especially following the war of 1971, when East Pakistan broke away from West Pakistan causing much death and destruction. Although Zafrulla was unwilling to concede that the establishment of Pakistan as an Islamic state was misconceived because the 'beneficent values of Islam' applied to 'Muslims and non-Muslims', he did accept that Islam was 'besmirched, dishonoured and disgraced by the misbehaviour of Muslims' during the war against East Pakistan.[156] In his view, '[t]he entire ideology of Pakistan, its very *raison d'être*, were falsified and exposed to ridicule at the hands of those who had claimed that they were their exponents and guardians'.[157] He contrasted the claims and proclamations of the forties, when Pakistan was established, with the 'miserable failure of the opening seventies'.[158]

The sad irony is that a few months after Zafrulla had penned these words, the Constitution of Pakistan was amended by the government of Prime

Minister Zulfiqar Ali Bhutto so that it now declared the Ahmadis – like Zafrulla – *non-Muslims*.[159] Thus, Zafrulla, despite the pivotal role he played in the creation of Pakistan in 1947, as the man who gave content and structure to Jinnah's two-nation theory, had his identity as a proud and devout Muslim taken away from him by the new leaders of his adopted homeland.[160]

Clearly, advocating majority rule for a specific community to overcome a minority problem through territorial fragmentation was problematic as the new majority established as a result of that fragmentation would find another minority to oppress, absent constitutionally enforced safeguards and a meritorious bureaucracy that applied the rule of law impartially and effectively. Ultimately, as Zafrulla concluded in his 1940 memorandum to the Viceroy, 'the real solution of the communal problem lies in the hands of the communities themselves'.[161]

Zafrulla Khan's concerns about Pakistan could have also been expressed about events in the Middle East, after the shattering loss of Palestine in 1948, and what was left of it in 1967, followed by the rule of hard men and the military in Israel,[162] Egypt, Syria, Iraq, Algeria, Libya and Sudan, in which opposition to these regimes was often expressed through religious organisations, especially the mosques, which could not be so easily shut down.[163] Unsurprisingly, given this context, opposition to government oppression was often (although not exclusively) articulated through a religious discourse, as most recently expressed during the Arab Winter of 2012 and subsequently. These events led to the development of a form of postcolonial Arab nationalism that had no place in its conception of the Arab Nation for the very few Jews that remained in the Middle East and North Africa in the 1960s and 1970s.[164] Clearly, the consequences of partition in India and Palestine in 1947 continue to shape the politics of both places, which have not recovered from the traumas of the past.

Notes

1. For exceptions see T. J. Fraser, *Partition in Ireland, India and Palestine: Theory and Practice* (London: MacMillan, 1984); Joe Cleary, *Literature, Partition and the Nation-State: Culture and Conflict in Ireland, Israel, and Palestine* (Cambridge: Cambridge University Press, 2002); Arie Dubnov and Laura Robson (eds), *Partitions: A Transnational History of Twentieth-Century Territorial Separatism* (Stanford, CA: Stanford University Press, 2019).
2. The Sylhet district of Assam joined Pakistan following a referendum.
3. Occasionally, Radcliffe followed village boundaries as in Kasur *tehsil*. See Lucy P. Chester, *Borders and Conflict in South Asia: The Radcliffe Boundary Commission*

and the Partition of Punjab (Manchester: Manchester University Press, 2009), p. 78. For the partition of Bengal, see Joya Chatterji, 'The Fashioning of a Frontier: The Radcliffe Line and Bengal's Border Landscape, 1947–52', *Modern Asian Studies* 33 (1) (1999), 185–242; Joya Chatterji, *The Spoils of Partition: Bengal and India, 1947–1967* (Cambridge: Cambridge University Press, 2007), p. 59.

4 For the colonial context see Peter Sluglett and Victor Kattan, *Violent Radical Movements in the Arab World: The Ideology and Politics of Non-State Actors* (London: Bloomsbury, 2019), pp. 2–5. For the rise of Islamist movements after 1947 see Mohamed-Ali Adraoui, 'Fighting for Palestine as a holy duty? The Syrian Muslim Brotherhood and the partition of Palestine in 1947' in this volume.

5 See Article 19 of the PLO's 1968 Charter: 'The partition of Palestine in 1947 and the establishment of the State of Israel are entirely illegal, regardless of the passage of time, because they were contrary to the will of the Palestinian people and to their natural right in their homeland, and inconsistent with the principles embodied in the Charter of the United Nations; particularly the right to self-determination.' Compare this to Article 18 of Hamas's 2017 Charter: 'The following are considered null and void: the Balfour Declaration, the British Mandate Document, the UN Palestine Partition Resolution, and whatever resolutions and measures that derive from them or are similar to them. The establishment of "Israel" is entirely illegal and contravenes the inalienable rights of the Palestinian people and goes against their will and the will of the Ummah; it is also in violation of human rights that are guaranteed by international conventions, foremost among them is the right to self-determination.'

6 General Assembly Resolution 1514, 14 December 1960, paras 5 and 6. See also Victor Kattan, 'Self-Determination as Ideology: The Cold War, The End of Empire, and the Making of UN General Assembly Resolution 1514 (14 December 1960)', in Luca Pasquet and Klara van der Ploeg (eds), *International Law and Time: Narratives and Techniques* (Geneva: Springer, 2022), pp. 441–473.

7 For literature on this period, see Erez Manela, *The Wilsonian Moment: Self-Determination and the International Origins of Anticolonial Nationalism* (Oxford: Oxford University Press, 2007); Cemil Aydin, *The Politics of Anti-Westernism in Asia: Visions of World Order in Pan-Islamic and Pan-Asian Thought* (New York: Columbia University Press, 2007), pp. 128–141; Michael Goebel, *Anti-Imperial Metropolis Interwar Paris and the Seeds of Third World Nationalism* (Cambridge: Cambridge University Press, 2017).

8 The Zionist Organisation had a problem in this regard, given the sheer population disparity between Arabs and Jews in Palestine, with Arabs forming not just the majority of the population of Palestine as a whole, but also the majority of the population in nearly all of Palestine's subdistricts, which is why senior leaders of the Zionist Organisation gave serious thought to proposals to 'encourage' the Arab population to leave, including by compulsory transfer. See Nur Masalha, *Expulsion of the Palestinians: The Concept of 'Transfer' in Zionist Political Thought, 1882–1948* (Washington, DC: Institute for Palestine Studies, 1992).

9 Of course, there were other Jewish groups in Palestine, such as the Revisionists, which demanded sovereignty over all of Palestine, even including Transjordan, but they were not part of the mainstream Zionist Organisation at the time the UN was considering partitioning Palestine in 1947. The Jewish Agency told the UN in no uncertain terms that they accepted the partition of Western Palestine as the price of independence. See the statement by Moshe Shertok, 127th meeting, UN Doc. A/C.1/SR.127, 27 April 1948, 108.

10 The estimated population of the Jaffa subdistrict as at 31 December 1946 was 295,160 Jews and 114,130 Arabs. This estimate was provided by the (British) Palestine Administration. See the statistics furnished by the British government to the subcommittee 2 in Ad Hoc Committee on the Palestinian Question, Report of Sub-Committee 2, UN Doc. A/AC.14/32, 11 November 1947, Appendix 2, at p. 64.

11 For population statistics, see the Definition of Pakistan by Districts in the Mody-Matthai memorandum (Appendix to No. 428) in Nicholas Mansergh and Penderel Moon (eds), *The Transfer of Power 1942–7, Volume VI, 1 August 1945–22 March 1946* (HMSO, 1970–83), p. 966.

12 The Muslim League wanted the subunit to be approximated to the districts or subdistricts of Punjab and Bengal, whereas the Congress wanted it to be based on the *thana*, an even smaller subunit. In the end, Radcliffe adopted the *thana*. See Chatterji, *The Spoils of Partition*, p. 40, fn 52.

13 See the statistics furnished by the British government to the subcommittee 2, UN Doc. A/AC.14/32, pp. 41–43. See also the map in Appendix 2 of the same document.

14 Official Records of the Second Session of the General Assembly, Supplement No. 11, *United Nations Special Committee on Palestine, Report to the General Assembly*, Volume 1 (Lake Success, NY, 1947), UN Doc. A/364, 3 September 1947, pp. 47–58 (hereafter the UNSCOP Report).

15 On the results of the provincial elections in 1946, see Ian Talbot and Gurharpal Singh, *The Partition of India* (Cambridge: Cambridge University Press, 2009), pp. 35–36. On the elections of the Bengal Assembly in June 1947, see Chatterji, *The Spoils of Partition*, p. 20. A referendum was also held in the Sylhet district of Assam.

16 The High Commissioner proposed establishing a semi-elected Legislative Council composed of the High Commissioner as President, with twenty-two members, ten of whom would be British officials, and twelve elected members, which would have included two Jews. See Mogannam E. Mogannam, 'Palestine Legislation under the British', *Annals of the American Academy of Political and Social Science* 164 (1) (1932), 48–49.

17 See Articles 1 and 2 of the Indian Independence Act, 1947. 10 & 11 Geo. 6. Ch. 30.

18 Statement by His Majesty's Government in Mian Muhammad Sadullah et al. (eds), *The Partition of the Punjab, 1947: A Compilation of Official Documents*, Vol. I (Lahore: National Documentation Centre, 1983), pp. 4–10 at p. 6 (emphasis added).

19 *Ibid.*
20 This contrasted with the partition of Ireland in 1920, where greater weight was given to the views of Irish landowners in drawing the boundary. Majority rule was *not* the basis for the partition of Ireland. This was because only four of the six counties that formed what became known as 'Northern Ireland' had unionist majorities, while two – Tyrone and Fermanagh – had nationalist majorities. If the same standard of majority rule that was applied in India had been applied to Ireland, Northern Ireland would have been limited to four counties.
21 Jawaharlal Nehru, *The Discovery of India* (New Delhi: Penguin, 2004; first published 1946), pp. 422–423.
22 *The Pioneer*, 5 October 1893, cited in Syed Sharifuddin Pirzada (ed.), *Foundations of Pakistan: All-India Muslim League Documents: 1906–1947*, Vol. I (Karachi: National Publishing House, 1970), p. xxxvii.
23 Anita Inder Singh, *The Origins of the Partition of India* (New Delhi: Oxford University Press, 1987), pp. 1–44.
24 Muhammad Zafrulla Khan, *The Agony of Pakistan* (Oxford: Kent Publications, 1974), p. 13.
25 *Ibid.*, pp. 13–14.
26 Talbot and Singh, *Partition of India*, p. 32.
27 *Ibid.*
28 *Ibid.*, p. 35.
29 *Ibid.*
30 See 'Separation Scheme' by Sir Zafrulla Khan. Indian Office Library Mss Eur F 125/135. The memorandum was submitted to the Viceroy on 6 March 1940.
31 *Ibid.*, p. 11 (emphasis added).
32 *Ibid.* (emphasis added).
33 *Ibid.*, p. 12.
34 *Ibid.*
35 *Ibid.*
36 *Ibid.*, pp. 13–25.
37 *Ibid.*, p. 13 (emphasis added).
38 *Ibid.*, p. 23.
39 *Ibid.*, p. 3.
40 *Ibid.*
41 *Ibid.*, p. 4.
42 *Ibid.*, p. 5.
43 *Ibid.* India became a republic in 1950.
44 *Ibid.*, pp. 6–10.
45 *Ibid.*, p. 7.
46 *Ibid.*
47 *Ibid.*, p. 9.
48 A. Dirk Moses, *The Problems of Genocide: Permanent Security and the Language of Transgression* (Cambridge: Cambridge University Press, 2021), p. 367 – referring to the writings of Vinayak Damodar Savarkar (1883–1966),

the leader of the Hindu Mahasabha, and author of *Hindutva: Who is a Hindu?* (1923).
49 Jawaharlal Nehru, *Selected Works of Jawaharlal Nehru*, vol. 8 (New Delhi: Orient Longman, 1976), p. 127.
50 Ibid.
51 See, for example, his rather dismissive and cursory treatment of the communal issue in Jawaharlal Nehru, *Glimpses of World History* (New Delhi: Penguin, 2004), p. 840. See also Aamir Mufti's perceptive critique of Nehru's views on Muslim 'separatism' in chapter 3 of his book, where he explores the relationship between the writings of Nehru and Abul Kalam Azad, who were imprisoned by the British in adjoining cells along with other senior leaders of the Congress during the Second World War. See Aamir R. Mufti, *Enlightenment in the Colony: The Jewish Question and the Crisis of Postcolonial Culture* (Princeton, NJ: Princeton University Press, 2007), pp. 129–139.
52 Presidential Address of Mr M. A. Jinnah, All-India Muslim League, Twenty-Seventh Session, Lahore, March 22–24, 1940, in Pirzada, *Foundations of Pakistan*, pp. 325–349.
53 Ibid., p. 335 (emphasis added).
54 See Faisal Devji, *Muslim Zion: Pakistan as a Political Idea* (London: Hurst & Co., 2013).
55 Talbot and Singh, *Partition of India*, p. 43.
56 Ibid., pp. 43–44.
57 Ayesha Jalal, *The Sole Spokesman: Jinnah, the Muslim League and the Demand for Pakistan* (Cambridge: Cambridge University Press, 1985), p. 273 quoting Patel demanding majority rule.
58 Nehru, *The Discovery of India*, pp. 420–421.
59 Farzana Shaikh, 'Muslims and Political Representation in Colonial India: The Making of Pakistan', *Modern Asian Studies* 20 (3) (1986), 548.
60 Khushwant Singh, *A History of the Sikhs, Volume 2: 1839–1974* (Oxford: Oxford University Press, 1987), p. 255.
61 Ibid., p. 256.
62 Ibid.
63 Zafrulla Khan, *The Agony of Pakistan*, p. 28.
64 See the sources cited by Zafrulla Khan, *The Agony of Pakistan*, pp. 28–33.
65 Jalal, *The Sole Spokesman*, pp. 241–293. Chatterji, *The Spoils of Partition*, pp. 64–65. Talbot and Singh, *Partition of India*, p. 38.
66 Chatterji, *The Spoils of Partition*, p. 14.
67 Zafrulla Khan, *The Agony of Pakistan*, p. 60 (emphasis added).
68 See 'The Balfour Declaration' in John Norton Moore (ed.), *The Arab–Israeli Conflict*, Vol. 3: *Documents* (Princeton, NJ: Princeton University Press, 1974), pp. 31–32.
69 See Justin McCarthy, *The Population of Palestine: Population History and Statistics of the Late Ottoman Period and the Mandate* (New York: Columbia University Press, 1990), Table 2.2., p. 26. Nearly all Christians, Muslims and Jews spoke Arabic and would have self-identified as Arabs before British rule.

See Menachem Klein, *Lives in Common: Arabs and Jews in Jerusalem, Jaffa, and Hebron* (London: Hurst & Co., 2014), pp. 19–64.
70 See the statistics published by subcommittee 2, UN Doc. A/AC.14/32, pp. 41–43 and Appendix 2 of the same document.
71 See Ad Hoc Committee on the Palestinian Question, Summary Record of the Thirty-Second Meeting, Lake Success, New York, Monday, 24 November 1947, UN Doc. A/AC.14/SR.32, 25 November 1947, paras 67–68.
72 Yossi Katz, *Partner to Partition: The Jewish Agency's Partition Plan in the Mandate Era* (London; Portland, OR: Frank Cass, 1998), pp. 17–18.
73 The Zionist Congress rejected the Peel Partition Plan in 1937 because they did not agree with specific provisions in that plan, not because they opposed the principle of partition. See Katz, *Partner to Partition*, pp. 19–20.
74 See Penny Sinanoglou, 'British Plans for the Partition of Palestine, 1929–1938', *Historical Journal* 52 (1) (2009), 131.
75 Rashid Khalidi, *The Iron Cage: The Story of the Palestinian Struggle for Statehood* (Boston, MA: Beacon Press, 2007), p. 35.
76 HC Deb, 21 July 1937, vol. 326, col. 2241.
77 HC Deb, 24 March 1936, vol. 310, col. 1114.
78 See *Palestine Royal Commission Report Presented by the Secretary of State for the Colonies to Parliament by Command of His Majesty, July, 1937*, Cmd. 5479 (London: HMSO, 1937).
79 *Ibid.*, p. 370, para. 5.
80 *Ibid.*, p. 371, para. 5.
81 See Chapter XVIII, *Palestine Royal Commission Report*, p. 361, para. 11.
82 *Ibid.*
83 Khalidi, *The Iron Cage*, p. 53.
84 *Ibid.*
85 *Palestine: Statement of Policy, Presented by the Secretary of State for the Colonies to Parliament by Command of His Majesty, 1 May 1939*, Cmd. 6019 (London: HMSO, 1939).
86 See, for example, *Military Lessons of the Arab Rebellion in Palestine, 1936, General Staff, Headquarters, the British Forces, Palestine & Transjordan, February, 1938*, at 7. WO 191/70 TNA. See also *Palestine Defence Policy: Military Aspects of Partition. Memorandum by the Minister for Co-ordination of Defence*, 1937–38. CAB 104/5. TNA; HC Deb, 22 May 1939, vol. 347, cols 1938–1954. See further Yehoshua Porath, *The Palestinian Arab National Movement: From Riots to Rebellion 1929–1939* (London: Frank Cass, 1977), pp. 277–281.
87 See H. G. L. and H. K., 'The Palestine Conferences in London', *Bulletin of International News* 16 (4) (1939), 9.
88 On Jinnah's rise, see Jalal, *The Sole Spokesman*, pp. 45–46. The Viceroy, rather cunningly, anticipated that the Congress would resign from the ministries, and *six months before* the war, persuaded Parliament to give him powers to take over and run the provinces if the need arose. As a result, a new section (Section 126A) was added to the Government of India Act, 1935. On Nehru's

imprisonment, see Amales Tripathi and Amitava Tripathi, *Indian National Congress and the Struggle for Freedom: 1885–1947* (Oxford: Oxford University Press 2014), p. 276.
89 Jalal, *The Sole Spokesman*, pp. 45–50.
90 On Jinnah's request to attend the Round Table Conference in 1939, see the letters, minutes and telegrams exchanged in India Office Records and Private Papers at the British Library, File IOR/L/PO/5/38. On the policy of employment of Indian troops in Palestine in 1939, see IOR/L/WS/1/87.
91 See Tripathi and Tripathi, *Indian National Congress*, p. 274.
92 See the policy of employment of Indian troops in Palestine, IOR/L/WS/1/87, Indian Office Records.
93 Rahman Siddiqui became Governor of East Pakistan. Khaliquzzaman succeeded Jinnah as President of the Muslim League in 1948. In his memoir, *Pathway to Pakistan*, Khaliquzzaman mentions his trip to London, Paris and Milan in 1938–39, but does not mention his meetings with League officials in Geneva. See Choudhry Khaliquzzaman, *Pathway to Pakistan* (London: Longmans, 1961), pp. 198–211.
94 Khaliquzzaman, *Pathway to Pakistan*, pp. 202–203.
95 Despite Arab opposition, the British government pressed ahead with implementing the White Paper by restricting Jewish immigration and banning land sales to Jews. The White Paper effectively repudiated the 1917 Balfour Declaration, as it implied that the Jewish national home called for in that declaration had been established in Palestine. The Palestinian Arabs opposed the White Paper as they wanted *immediate* independence.
96 See *Statement of Indian Muslim Views on Palestine submitted to the British Government through the Right Honourable The Secretary of State for India by The All-India Muslim League Palestine Delegation*, dated 10 February 1939. The document is included in 'Palestine: Round Table Conference', London, 1939.
97 *Ibid.*
98 *Ibid.*, p. 5.
99 *Ibid.*, pp. 5–6.
100 *Ibid.*, p. 6.
101 De Haller disabused them of the idea because he explained that the great powers were no longer interested in the League and had started to settle their differences outside the organisation. This was sage advice as Germany, Italy and Japan had already left the League by then, and the Soviet Union would invade Finland later that year. The Permanent Court held its last wartime session in the Hague in February 1940, before the German invasion of the Netherlands: 'Correspondence with individuals and Associations'. Mandates section. Registry no. A 37120/668. Reference code: R4078/6A/668/37120. Geneva: League of Nations Archives.
102 See 'Report by Abdur Rahman Siddiqui countersigned by Choudhry Khaliquzzaman on the Activities of the All-India Muslim League Palestine Delegation'. 28 June 1939, Quaid-e-Azam Papers, File No.49, pp. 117–132; reproduced in document 51 in Atique Zafar Sheikh and Mohammad Riaz Malik (eds),

Quaid-e-Azam and The Muslim World: Selected Documents 1937–1948 (Karachi: Royal Book Company, 1990), pp. 84–95.
103 *Ibid.*, p. 93.
104 See Article 26, Palestine mandate (emphasis added). The issue as to whether India could have actually brought a case before the Permanent Court would have been complicated due to the constitutional status of India in the League of Nations. See R. P. Anand, 'The Formation of International Organization and India: A Historical Study', *Leiden Journal of International Law* 23 (1) (2010), 5–21; T. Poulose, 'India as an Anomalous International Person (1919–1947)', *British Yearbook of International Law* 44 (1970), 201–212.
105 See Application Instituting Proceedings to the Submission 5 in the Memorial of Ethiopia in Pleadings, Oral Arguments, Documents, South West Africa Cases (Ethiopia v. South Africa; Liberia v. South Africa), Volume I, ICJ Reports 1966, p. 22.
106 See special note by Sir Abdur Rahman, representative of India, UN Special Committee on Palestine, Report to the General Assembly, Volume II, Annexes, Appendix and Maps, UN Doc. A/364, Add. 1, 9 September 1947, pp. 24–47. See also the issues raised in subcommittee 2 in Ad Hoc Committee on the Palestinian Question, Report of Sub-Committee 2, UN Doc. A/AC.14/32, 11 November 1947, especially pp. 5–24 and chapter IV, pp. 57–58.
107 Compare the questions raised by sub-committee 2, UN Doc. A/AC.14/32, 11 November 1947, pp. 57–58 to the questions raised by Egypt, Syria and Iraq, as reproduced in the 2 *Yearbook of the United Nations (1947–8)*, pp. 237–241.
108 For the debates at the UN partition see UN General Assembly, Official Records, 2, 1947, Plenary Meetings, II, Hundred and Twenty-Fifth Plenary Meeting, Held in the General Assembly Hall at Flushing Meadow, New York, on Wednesday, 26 November 1947, UN Doc. A/PV.125.
109 *Tehdise Nemat or Recollection of Divine Favours by Sir Muhammad Zafrulla Khan* (translated from Urdu by Kunwar Idris) (Qadian: Zafar & Sons, 2014), pp. 548–549.
110 Zafrulla Khan, *The Agony of Pakistan*, pp. 4–5. Islam was introduced to South Asia through mariners, merchants and Sufi missionaries. See Burjor Avari, *Islamic Civilization in South Asia* (London: Routledge, 2013), p. 8.
111 Devji, *Muslim Zion*, p. 137.
112 Muhammad Zafrulla Khan, *My Mother* (London: Gresham Press, 1981), p. 1.
113 *Ibid.*, p. 1.
114 See the report of subcommittee 2, UN Doc. A/AC.14/32 at p. 3, para 3.
115 *Ibid.*, pp. 39–41, paras 62–64.
116 *Ibid.*, pp. 49–52, paras 80–82.
117 *Ibid.*, p. 51, para 80, subparagraph (c).
118 *Ibid.*
119 See the arguments by the Muslim League (represented by Zafrulla Khan) in Sadullah et al., *The Partition of the Punjab 1947*, Vol. II, pp. 252–476. See also Chester, *Borders and Conflict in South Asia*, pp. 59–60.

120 Hundred and Twenty-Sixth Plenary Meeting, Held in the General Assembly Hall at Flushing Meadow, New York, on Friday, 28 November 1947, at 11am in UN General Assembly, Official Records, 2, 1947, Plenary Meetings, II, UN Doc. A/PV.126, 1369. See also the documentation in the report of subcommittee 2, UN Doc. A/AC.14/32, 11 November 1947, at p. 28, para 44, which lists all the countries that took in Jewish refugees between 1933 and 1946. The statistics demonstrate that the US only admitted 188,648 Jews, the UK 65,000, Canada 12,000, Australia 8,500 and South Africa 8,000. Palestine, by way of contrast, had admitted 118,378 Jews between 1920 and 1932. Yet the UN majority wanted Palestine to admit more Jewish refugees, despite its small size and even though it was in the midst of an armed insurrection with the Palestinian Arabs.

121 As mentioned above, the UNSCOP majority did not factor into the equation the additional 127,000 Bedouins living in the territory. The Bedouin community was excluded from the population statistics for Palestine because they were described as nomads and were not believed to count as a settled population. But as Zafrulla Khan made clear in his report for subcommittee 2, '[t]hese Bedouins have lived in Palestine for centuries and have as much right to be taken into account as any of the original inhabitants of the country. While they still maintain some of their special customs and usages, they are settled on the land and derive their livelihood from agriculture and grazing.' See the report of subcommittee 2, UN Doc. A/AC.14/32, 11 November 1947, at p. 40, para 62.

122 Sir Mohammed (Pakistan), UN General Assembly, Official Records, 28 November 1947, p. 1374.

123 *Ibid.*

124 *Ibid.*, p. 1375.

125 *Ibid.*, pp. 1376–1377.

126 Special note by Sir Abdur Rahman, representative of India, UNSCOP Report, Vol. II, p. 42.

127 Henry Cattan, 'Recollections on the United Nations Resolution to Partition Palestine', *Palestine Yearbook of International Law* 4 (1987–1988), 263.

128 See Official Records of the Second Session of the General Assembly, Ad Hoc Committee on the Palestinian Question, Summary Record of the Thirty-Second Meeting, Lake Success, New York, Monday, 24 November 1947, at 8.30pm. UN Doc. A/AC.14/SR.32, 25 November 1947 at paras. 67 and 68.

129 UN General Assembly 181 (II), 29 November 1947.

130 Rami Ginat, 'India and the Palestine Question: The Emergence of the Asio-Arab Bloc and India's Quest for Hegemony in the Post-Colonial Third World', *Middle Eastern Studies* 40 (6) (2004), 189–218, at 208.

131 See Moses, *The Problems of Genocide*, p. 367 quoting Savarkar.

132 P. R. Kumaraswamy, *India's Israel Policy* (New York: Columbia University Press, 2010), p. 94.

133 See Kumaraswany, 'India's dilemmas of pragmatism v. principles: Nehru's preference for a partitioned India but a federal Palestine' in this volume.

134 See the report of subcommittee 2, UN Doc. A/AC.14/32, 11 November 1947, at pp. 19–20, para 31.
135 *Ibid.*
136 Report of the United Nations Palestine Commission to the Second Special Session of the General Assembly, 10 April 1948, UN Doc. A/532, p. 39, para 7.
137 See Rosemarie M. Esber, *Under the Cover of War: The Zionist Expulsion of the Palestinians* (Alexandria: Arabicus Books, 2008); Ilan Pappé, *The Ethnic Cleansing of Palestine* (Oxford: Oneworld Publications, 2006); Benny Morris, *The Birth of the Palestinian Refugee Problem Revisited* (Cambridge: Cambridge University Press, 2004); Eugene L. Rogan and Avi Shlaim (eds), *The War for Palestine: Rewriting the History of 1948* (Cambridge: Cambridge University Press, 2001); Avi Shlaim, 'The Debate about 1948', *International Journal of Middle East Studies* 27 (3) (1995), 287–304; 'The Debate on the 1948 Exodus', *Journal of Palestine Studies* 21 (1991), 66–114; Benny Morris, *1948 and After: Israel and the Palestinians* (Oxford: Clarendon Press, 1990); Walid Khalidi, 'Plan Dalet: Master Plan for the Conquest of Palestine', *Journal of Palestine Studies* 18 (1) (1988), 4–33; Michael Palumbo, *The Palestinian Catastrophe: The 1948 Expulsion of a People from their Homeland* (London: Quartet Books, 1987); Benny Morris, *The Birth of the Palestinian Refugee Problem, 1947–1949* (Cambridge: Cambridge University Press, 1987). See also Moses, *The Problems of Genocide*, pp. 388–389.
138 On India's role in discrediting apartheid in South Africa see Mark Mazower, *No Enchanted Palace: The End of Empire and the Ideological Origins of the United Nations* (Princeton, NJ: Princeton University Press, 2009), pp. 149–189.
139 See UN Doc. A/2183, 12 September 1952, reprinted in *The United Nations and Apartheid 1948–1994* (New York: United Nations, 1994), pp. 223–224. The letter was signed by the Permanent Representatives of Afghanistan, Egypt, Indonesia, Iraq, Pakistan, Saudi Arabia, Syria, Burma, India, Iran, Lebanon, the Philippines and Yemen.
140 See General Assembly Resolution: Treatment of Indians in the Union of South Africa, UN Doc. A/RES/44 (I), 8 December 1946. General Assembly Resolution: Treatment of Indians in the Union of South Africa, UN Doc. A/RES/395, 2 December 1950.
141 See General Assembly Resolution: The Question of Race Conflict in South Africa Resulting from the Policies of Apartheid of the Government of the Union of South Africa, UN Doc. A/RES/616 A (VII), 5 December 1952.
142 General Assembly Resolution: The Question of Race Conflict in South Africa Resulting from the Policies of Apartheid of the Government of the Union of South Africa, UN Doc. A/RES/616 B (VII), 5 December 1952 (emphasis added).
143 In his speeches at the UN Security Council, Zafrulla Khan called for an impartial plebiscite to determine the fate of Kashmir. See his speech on 19 April 1948 reprinted in M. S. Deora and R. Grover (eds), *Documents on the Kashmir Problem*, Vol. 3 (New Delhi: Discovery Publishing House, 1991), p. 24. Zafrulla Khan also expressed his opposition to an Indian proposal to partition Kashmir

between India and Pakistan. See Josef Korbel, *Danger in Kashmir* (Princeton, NJ: Princeton University Press, 1966), p. 131.
144 Devji, *Muslim Zion*, p. 45.
145 See 'Separation Scheme' by Sir Zafrulla Khan, 6 March 1940. Zafrulla Khan's opposition to partition also features in his obituary. See 'Obituary. Sir Muhammad Zafrulla Khan: Distinguished Pakistani Statesman', *The Times*, 4 September 1985, col. F, p. 14. ('Zafrulla's instinct was to preserve the unity of India. He wanted a just settlement of Muslim demands, but he hoped that would be possible without partition.') See also Zafrulla's argument in *The Agony of Pakistan*, where he blamed Mountbatten for foisting a moth-eaten Pakistan on Jinnah in the hope of frightening him. Zafrulla Khan, *The Agony of Pakistan*, pp. 43–48.
146 This was the so-called 'hostage theory'. See Moses, *The Problems of Genocide*, pp. 372–379.
147 Zafrulla Khan, *The Agony of Pakistan*, p. 159.
148 *Ibid.*, p. 47.
149 Devji, *Muslim Zion*, p. 45.
150 See Victor Kattan, *From Coexistence to Conquest: International Law and the Origins of the Arab–Israeli Conflict 1891–1949* (London: Pluto Press, 2009), pp. 211–212.
151 *Ibid.* Most Jews remained in Egypt in the early 1950s, most Algerian Jews went to France, and most Lebanese Jews went to Europe, the US and Latin America during the Lebanese civil war (1975–90). As for the situation in Iraq and Yemen, see Moses, *The Problems of Genocide*, pp. 391–392.
152 For Zafrulla's recollections of Pakistan's role in these momentous events, see Zafrulla Khan, *Tehdise Namat*, pp. 586–614.
153 B. C. Rastogi, 'Alignment and Non-Alignment in Pakistan's Foreign Policy 1947–1960', *International Studies* 3 (2) (1961), 167.
154 *Ibid.*, citing Zafrulla Khan, Pakistan, Constituent Assembly Legislative Debates, I (1952), p. 621.
155 General Assembly Resolution 1514, 14 December 1960, paras 5 and 6.
156 Zafrulla Khan, *The Agony of Pakistan*, pp. 154–155.
157 *Ibid.*, p. 154.
158 *Ibid.*
159 Zafrulla Khan completed *The Agony of Pakistan* in November 1973. The book was published a year later.
160 Zafrulla Khan was born in Sialkot, which became part of Pakistan in 1947. However, the town of Qadian, the birthplace of Mirza Ghulam Ahmad, the founder of the Ahmadiyya movement, remained in India.
161 'Separation Scheme' by Sir Zafrulla Khan, p. 32.
162 Some readers may baulk at my inclusion of Israel in this list but remember that Israel's Arab population was subject to martial law from 1948 until 1967. Moreover, many of Israel's prime ministers have been generals. However, Israel, in contrast to most Arab countries, holds regular elections and has a freer press.
163 Sluglett and Kattan, *Violent Radical Movements in the Arab World*, p. 6.
164 Moses, *The Problems of Genocide*, p. 392.

8

'Unfinished' partition: territorial disputes, unequal citizens and the rise of majoritarian nationalism in India, Pakistan and Bangladesh

Amit Ranjan

The partition of British India in 1947 changed the geography of the Indian subcontinent and created a new religious, ethnic and demographic composition within India, Pakistan and Bangladesh (East Pakistan until 1971). Despite these changes, present interreligious relations have not overcome the colonial constructions and memories of violence related to the partition of India. For example, political debates over cow protection[1] is still not settled with some people being killed by cow vigilantes in India. The territorial claims and counterclaims by India and Pakistan over the status of the former princely state of Jammu and Kashmir (J&K) still causes tensions on the international border and the line of control (LoC) that separates them. India and Pakistan want to keep hold of J&K to prove their religious characters, in addition to acquiring its natural resources and its strategic location. For India, having a Muslim-majority area among the Hindu-dominated administrative regions displays its secular credentials as it demonstrates that India can accommodate a large Muslim population within its polity, while Pakistan claims J&K because this would conclude the 'unfinished' task of partition based on dividing the subcontinent on the basis of religion. Hence, the dispute over J&K is also ideological.[2] Another issue that remains unsettled after partition are the rights of the minorities of India, Pakistan and Bangladesh. As religion remains significant in the subcontinent, the political rights of citizens in Pakistan are different for people belonging to different religious groups. Like Pakistan, in Bangladesh Islam is the religion of the state. Unlike these two countries, there is no constitutional discrimination against minorities in India. However, social differences and discrimination remain.

In Pakistan and Bangladesh, majoritarian nationalism surged soon after the death of their founding leaderships in 1948 and 1975. In India, the political use of Hinduism by so-called secular political groups, such as the Indian National Congress, and the rise of the Hindu nationalist Bharatiya Janata Party (BJP), gradually strengthened majoritarian nationalism. In theory and practice, majoritarian nationalism is widely viewed as a dangerous form of nationalism for two reasons.[3] First, this form of nationalism asserts the superiority of the majority community and its dominance over minorities. Assertion of superiority and dominance of the majority alienates minorities. Second, majoritarian nationalists chiefly believe in the alignment of political, religious and linguistic borders, which is unrealistic in the present world.[4] Majoritarian nationalism is stirred up by populist leaders who are usually authoritarian in nature. Such populist authoritarian leaders claim to represent people who can only be from a single group; there is no room for pluralism.[5] In plural societies such as India, the rise of majoritarian nationalism deeply affects the functioning of democratic institutions that are largely regarded as secular. For example, the 1,045-page judgment on Ram Janmabhoomi (Hindu god Rama's birthplace) – Babri Masjid (a mosque built by Mughal Emperor Babur) land dispute case, delivered in November 2019 by the Indian Supreme Court, highly favoured the majority community's position in the dispute.[6] In the verdict, the Court ordered the Government of India to build a Hindu temple where a mosque once stood. To compensate the Muslim litigants in the case, the Supreme Court ordered the Government of India to provide five acres of land in another area of Ayodhya to build a mosque.[7] Significantly, four months after his retirement, Ranjan Gogoi, the former Chief Justice of India, who headed the bench that delivered the verdict on the Babri Masjid case, was nominated by the BJP-led union government to the upper house of the Indian Parliament.[8]

This chapter looks at the issues that have not yet been resolved bilaterally or domestically in contemporary India, Pakistan and Bangladesh, such as the territorial disputes and the communal tensions that arose following partition. The chapter argues that partition is not an event that ended in 1947, but rather a process that profoundly impacted the society and polity of India, Pakistan and Bangladesh. To begin, this chapter revisits the decision to partition British India in August 1947, when numerous territorial disputes arose.

Claims and counterclaims over territories

Under Sir Cyril Radcliffe, Boundary Commissions (BCs) were established in Bengal and Punjab to divide the provinces of British India. Radcliffe, a British barrister, had never visited India before taking up his assignment. The Bengal BC was additionally comprised of Justice Bijan Kumar Mukherjea, Justice C. G. Biswas, Justice Abu Saleh Mohamed Akram and Justice S. A. Rahman. The Punjab BC was additionally comprised of Justice Mehr Chand Mahajan, Justice Teja Singh, Justice Din Muhammad and Justice Muhammad

Munir.[9] To protect their special interests, the geographer Oskar Spate was hired by the Ahmadiyya group, who provided his services to the Punjab unit of the All-India Muslim League (AIML) that Muhammad Zafrulla Khan headed.[10]

The AIML primarily demanded the partition of India on the basis of religion. The Hindu-majority areas were to become part of India, while Muslim-dominated regions were to be allocated to Pakistan. However, the terms of reference of the BC stated: 'The Boundary Commission is instructed to demarcate the boundaries of the two parts of Bengal on the basis ascertaining the contiguous areas of Muslims and non-Muslims. In doing so, it will also take into account other factors.'[11] There was no concrete definition of what constituted 'other factors'; it was at the discretion of Radcliffe. At many places in his Award he considered railway lines, communication and canal systems as 'other factors'. In some cases, Radcliffe discussed the significance of these 'other factors' before turning to religious demography.[12]

On 17 August 1947, Radcliffe's Award was published, and the territories were divided between India and Pakistan. Among many, two of the decisions in Punjab that Pakistani scholars still contest are the allocation of Gurdaspur and Ferozepur to India. Ijaz Hussain argues that Radcliffe changed his earlier decision on Gurdaspur because of the Viceroy, Lord Mountbatten's, influence, and gave it to India even though it was a Muslim-majority district.[13] Demography wise, in the Gurdaspur district, the Muslim population was, according to 1941 census, a majority in all the *tehsıls*, except for the Pathankot.[14]

Ferozepur was claimed by both the Maharaja of Bikaner (India) and the Nawab of Bahawalpur (Pakistan). The princely state of Bikaner used to get water from the Ferozepur headwork through the Gang Canal, constructed in 1927.[15] According to Radcliffe's private secretary, Christopher Beaumont, 'Mountbatten persuaded Radcliffe of the importance of the adverse effects of Bikaner state if Ferozepur went to Pakistan, as well as the possibility of civil war.'[16] The Maharaja of Bikaner even threatened to accede to Pakistan if the BC awarded Ferozepur to Pakistan.[17] Eventually, Ferozepur was awarded to India.

In Bengal, the demarcation of the border in the middle of the river courses, such as the Muhuri and others, and the lack of proper consideration given to the *chars* (islands in the river formed by silts, a common feature of the many rivers in Bengal) created disputes between India and Pakistan (later Bangladesh). Some *chars* are so small that any flooding causes their disappearance, but some are very large where a village can be settled.[18]

In 1948, India and Pakistan agreed to set up the Indo-Pakistan Boundary Disputes Tribunal under Justice Algot Bagge, formerly a member of the Supreme Court of Sweden, to interpret Radcliffe's decision and to settle their territorial disputes. It had one member each from India and Pakistan. Justice (retired) N. Chandrasekhara Aiyer represented India while Justice Mohammed Shahabuddin represented Pakistan. Notably, of the four disputes that came before the Tribunal, three were either related to or about river waters. On 5 February 1950, the tribunal delivered its final award in which it interpreted Cyril Radcliffe's decision to confirm the boundary lines between India and Pakistan in the eastern sector. Despite the Tribunal's Award and the signing of the India–Pakistan Agreement in 1958,[19] many of the territorial disputes between India and Pakistan on their eastern border remain unsettled.

Besides Radcliffe's Award, the decisions taken by the princely states to join India and Pakistan also created disputes between the two countries. For instance, as discussed in detail below, the dispute over the former princely state of J&K remains unresolved. In addition to J&K, in 1947, some other princely states were also indecisive about whether to accede to India or Pakistan. For example, the ruler of Bahawalpur hoped to become independent of both dominions. After initial hesitation, in October 1947, Nawab Sir Sadiq Mohammad Khan Abbasi V of Bahawalpur signed the instrument of accession to join Pakistan. With regard to the princely state of Khairpur, which had celebrated its independence on 15 August 1947, there was no expectation that it would join Pakistan. However, on 3 October, the state signed the instrument of accession to join Pakistan.[20] There was also controversy over the state of Kalat which formed 80 per cent of the province of Baluchistan.[21] Initially, Kalat and Pakistan had signed a standstill agreement, but a few months after signing the agreement the Khan of Kalat, Mir Ahmed Yar Khan, declared the independence of Kalat and promulgated a constitution. Yar Khan considered the possibilities of joining India, Afghanistan, Iran, or even asking the United Kingdom for protectorate status. After exploring its options, Yar Khan decided to join Pakistan in March 1948, although he did not consult his council or Parliament over the decision. Prince Abdul Karim, the younger brother of Yar Khan, resisted the decision and led an insurgency. Many Pakistani historians believe that Karim's armed rebellion was a reaction to his sacking from the governorship of Makran. Karim tried to get help from Afghanistan and the Soviet Union, but was unsuccessful. He finally surrendered and was sentenced to ten years imprisonment.[22] Since then, Pakistan has faced an insurgency in Baluchistan.

Another controversy arose over the princely state of Junagadh, ruled by a Muslim prince called Muhammad Mahabat Khan III. He wanted to accede to Pakistan, even though Hindus were the vast majority in the state.[23] According to the 1941 census, the total population of the state was 816,344, out of which 534,321 were Hindus, 127,814 were Muslims and 8,073 were Jains. There was small number of Christians and a few Parsis, Sikhs and Jews.[24] On 13 August 1947, although assuring the prince of their loyalty, the Hindu subjects of Junagadh gave a memorandum to Mahabat Khan calling for accession to India. Shah Nawaz Bhutto, the dewan (prime minister) of Junagadh, reminded them that Kathiawar was once a part of the Sind and urged them to support the case to join Pakistan. But the heads of Mangrol and Babariwad, suzerains of Junagadh, declared their independence and joined the Indian dominion. Samaldas Gandhi then led a people's movement and set up the Arzi Hukumat (provisional government) in September in Bombay (now Mumbai).[25] Realising his weak position, the nawab fled to Pakistan after Indian troops reached the outskirts of Junagadh. Shah Nawaz Bhutto, who was authorised to take decisions, wrote a letter to the Indian Government seeking assistance in administering the state. Two days later, the Indian troops marched into Junagadh and took over the state.[26] In January 1948, Pakistan raised the issue of Junagadh in the United Nations Security Council (UNSC). Pakistan accused India of using force to 'annex and occupy' Junagadh. Under UN Security Council Resolution 39, the Commission set up for the 'peaceful resolution of Kashmir conflict' had the mandate to look at the 'other issues' raised by Pakistan, including Junagadh.[27] In February 1948, a referendum was held in Junagadh. Three months later, in April 1948, there were talks about holding a second referendum under the watch of the UN Security Council because the one in February was held under the presence of Indian forces.[28] However, the second referendum was not conducted, and India got to keep Junagadh due to an 'overwhelming victory in the first'.[29]

Unlike Bahawalpur, Junagadh and J&K, Hyderabad was not a border state. It was located in South India and covered present-day Marathwada in the Indian state of Maharashtra, Northern Karnataka and the Telangana region.[30] According to the 1941 census, the princely state of Hyderabad had a population of 16.34 million. Out of the total population of Hyderabad, over 85 per cent were Hindus, 12 per cent Muslims and 3 per cent Christians, Sikhs, Parsis, etc.[31] Mir Osman Ali Khan, the Nizam of Hyderabad, desired dominion status that Mountbatten rejected. V. P. Menon, Secretary to the Government of India in the Ministry of States, and Viceroy Mountbatten favoured the accession of Hyderabad to the Indian Union.[32] After rounds of talks between the representatives of the Indian dominion and the delegation of the Nizam, a standstill agreement was signed in November 1947. However, violating the spirit and letter of the agreement, in December 1947, the Nizam issued two ordinances. The first restricted the export of all precious metals from Hyderabad to India; the second declared Indian currency illegal tender in the state.[33] Negotiations were restarted between the Indian dominion and Hyderabad, but broke down again in June 1948. The Nizam ruled out accession to India, but was willing to enter into a Treaty 'for purposes of Defence, External Affairs and Communications'.[34] After Mountbatten left

India, tensions mounted between India and Hyderabad over border raids and breaches of the standstill agreement.[35] The Government of India then launched Operation Polo on 13 September 1948 against the Nizam, and forced his armed forces to surrender on 18 September 1948. After his militia surrendered, Hyderabad merged with India.[36]

In 1971, after a civil war and a third India–Pakistan war, East Pakistan was liberated from Pakistan and became known as Bangladesh. India and Bangladesh signed the Land Boundary Agreement (LBA) to resolve their territorial disputes in 1974. Bangladesh ratified the LBA in the same year, while India took four decades to ratify it. At that time, India delayed ratification, saying it would require a constitutional amendment to implement the agreement. The assassination of Sheikh Mujibur Rahman, the President of Bangladesh, on 15 August 1975, had created a trust deficit between the two countries that took its toll on resolving bilateral problems. After years of political uncertainties, in 2011 India and Bangladesh signed the protocol on the LBA. Subsequently, the LBA was ratified by the Indian Parliament and implemented in 2015.

Under the terms of the LBA, India received 2,777,038 acres of Adverse Possession[37] and transferred 2,267,682 acres of the same form of land to Bangladesh. Further, India received 51 of the 71 enclaves[38] (7,110,02 acres), while Bangladesh received 111 enclaves (17,160,63 acres).[39] In this arrangement, India lost 10,000 acres of land in enclaves but gained 500 acres of adversely possessed land.[40]

The unsettled territorial dispute over Jammu and Kashmir

The dispute over the status of J&K remains unfinished business between India and Pakistan. J&K was a Muslim-majority state ruled by a Hindu prince, Hari Singh. In 1947, many ex-service tribesmen from Poonch, under the leadership of Sardar Mohamed Ibrahim Khan, began to prepare themselves for armed rebellion against the Hindu ruler of J&K. The Pakistan Army's Colonel Akbar Khan prepared a plan to assist the rebels. The plan was to strengthen the Kashmiris themselves for revolt, and simultaneously take steps to prevent the arrival of any form of civilian or military assistance from India into Kashmir.[41] Akbar Khan had a meeting with the then Prime Minister of Pakistan, Liaqat Ali Khan, and Sardar Shaukat Hayat Khan, a minister in the Punjab Government.[42] On 23 October, around 2,000 tribesmen from North-West Frontier Province (now Khyber Pakhtunkhwa), aided by the Kashmir-born Chief Minister Khan Abdul and the Commissioner of Rawalpindi Division, Khawaja Rahim, crossed into Kashmir through the Jhelum Valley. Mashuds and Waziris were the main tribal groups, but many others joined them.[43] The invasion was resisted by the local population and the workers of the National Conference of Sheikh Abdullah. To address the situation, Hari Singh requested that Pandit Jawaharlal Nehru's government send Indian troops to J&K. On his request, Nehru's cabinet asked him first to sign an instrument of accession. On 26 October1947, Hari Singh signed the documents that provided for the accession of J&K to India. The next day, Indian Army troops were airlifted to Srinagar.

India hoped that Pakistan would cooperate in ousting the raiders. However, in a telegram Pakistan held India responsible for what was happening in Kashmir.[44] In December 1947, during the first Kashmir war (1947–48), Nehru brought the dispute over Kashmir before the UN Security Council.[45] India had referred the Kashmir issue under Article 35, which did not give the UN a mandate to impose a solution, but only to make recommendations.[46] In January 1948, under Resolution 39, the UN Security Council set up a United Nations Commission for India and Pakistan. Later, on 21 April 1948, after hearing the claims and counterclaims of both Indian and Pakistani representatives, the Security Council considered that 'the question of the accession of Jammu and Kashmir to India or Pakistan should be decided through the democratic method of a free and impartial plebiscite'.[47] However, the plebiscite never took place because, as a prerequisite, Pakistan was required to withdraw its forces from the territory that it captured through invasion, and India had to reduce its troops in the region to minimum strength. In August 1948, the UNSC proposed a two-way process to withdraw forces. In the first part, Pakistan had to withdraw its forces and nationals. In the second part, after notification by the UNSC, India would reduce its troops. India accepted the proposal, while Pakistan had reservations. In a nutshell, Pakistan did not agree to vacate the territory, which gave India a reason to renege its commitment to hold the plebiscite.[48] In December 1948, however, the two countries agreed to a ceasefire which became effective from one minute before 1 January 1949.[49]

After the ceasefire, two-thirds of J&K came under Indian control. Pakistan refers to the Indian side of J&K as Indian-held J&K and its side as Azad ('free') J&K and Gilgit-Baltistan (GB). India calls Azad J&K and GB 'occupied territories' or 'Pakistan-occupied J&K'. On 1 January 1949, India acquired 10,073 square miles in Jammu, 5,838 square miles in the Kashmir Valley, and 37, 754 square miles in Ladakh.[50] Pakistan acquired 4,494 square miles on its side of Kashmir, and 25,302 square miles in Gilgit-Baltistan.

Besides the UN, India and Pakistan also tried to find a solution to the J&K dispute bilaterally. In 1953, Prime Minister of Pakistan Mohammad Ali Bogra met Indian Prime Minister Nehru in London at the Commonwealth Prime Ministers' Conference. They met again in New Delhi, where they agreed to a joint communique that affirmed their desire to hold a plebiscite in J&K. The two leaders continued their talks, but they were postponed after the Governor-General of Pakistan Ghulam Mohammad fell ill.[51]

In 1958, General Mohammad Ayub Khan led a successful military coup in Pakistan and became head of the state. However, the change in regime did not affect the ongoing talks on water sharing from the Indus River System between India and Pakistan. In 1960, India and Pakistan signed the Indus Waters Treaty. In this agreement, India got the right to use the waters from the Ravi, Beas and Satluj rivers, while Pakistan got the rights to use the waters of the Indus, Jhelum and Chenab. Pakistan got rights to use the maximum quantity of waters from the allocated western rivers while India got limited rights over them. The conclusion of this water treaty did not, however, move the two countries closer on the J&K issue.

In 1962, after India's defeat in the war against China, India looked to the United States and the United Kingdom for military assistance. Both countries were ready to help India, but their assistance was conditional on reaching an agreement with Pakistan on the status of J&K that India found favourable to Pakistan. In 1963, a joint US–UK mission arrived in New Delhi with the Commonwealth Secretary, Duncan Sandy, and Averell Harriman, then US Secretary of State for Far Eastern Affairs. They wanted India and Pakistan to start talks and settle the J&K issue.[52] Sandy and Harriman succeeded in convincing Nehru to talk with Ayub Khan over the Kashmir and other related matters.[53] Five rounds of talks were held between the representatives of India and Pakistan. Sardar Swaran Singh represented India, while Zulfikar Ali Bhutto represented Pakistan. The first round of talks was held at Rawalpindi from 27 to 29 December 1962. The later rounds of talks moved to different Indian and Pakistani cities such as New Delhi (from 16 to 19 January 1963), Karachi (8 to 10 February 1963), Calcutta (now Kolkata) (12 to 14 March 1963), Karachi again (from 22 to 15 April 1963) and finally to New Delhi (from 15 to 18 May 1963).[54] After the second round of talks, to India's dismay, Pakistan and China agreed to a pact under which Pakistan ceded about 5,180 square kilometres of land on the Pakistan side of Kashmir to the Chinese.[55]

During the five rounds of talks, at one point the Pakistani side seriously considered solutions other than a plebiscite, and India offered to cede its claims over the territories under Pakistan's control. In addition, India also agreed to give a small tract of land to Pakistan in the Poonch to straighten out the border. Pakistan, however, refused to accept any such scheme that did not give it the entire Chenab Valley in Jammu (cutting the Pathankot–Srinagar road), although Pakistan was prepared to give India temporary transit rights through Jammu to be able to continue contesting Ladakh with China. India rejected the proposal because Pakistan was demanding too much.⁵⁶ The five rounds of talks proved in vain as the two sides could not agree on any formula. Ayub Khan and Nehru agreed to meet in New Delhi in June 1964. Before that, Sheikh Abdullah went to Pakistan, but his visit was cut short due to the death of Nehru in May 1964.⁵⁷

In 1965, the two countries engaged in a second war over J&K. The war ended with the defeat of Pakistan and the signing of a truce agreement at Tashkent. There they reaffirmed their obligations under the UN Charter not to resort to force and to settle their disputes through peaceful means. Both sides also agreed that all armed personnel would be withdrawn no later than 25 February 1966, and they would observe the ceasefire terms on the ceasefire line. From January 1948 to 1965, the UNSC discussed 'The India–Pakistan Question', which was about their disputes over J&K. After November 1965 it stopped discussing the item.⁵⁸ One of the primary reasons was that India's close ally, the Soviet Union, a permanent member of the UNSC, used its veto power to prevent any discussion of Kashmir in the UNSC. Also, the arbitration tribunal appointed by the United Nation's principal judicial organ – the International Court of Justice – in June 1965, to settle the India–Pakistan boundary issues in the Rann of Kutch region, did not satisfy India's demand.⁵⁹ The three-member tribunal, headed by Gunnar Lagergren, President of the Court of Appeal for Western Sweden, delivered the final verdict in 1968. In that verdict, 90 per cent of the Rann of Kutch region was given to India, and 10 per cent to Pakistan.⁶⁰

After the Bangladesh liberation war in 1971, in which India helped East Pakistan separate from West Pakistan, Indira Gandhi, then Prime Minister of India, and President Zulfikar Ali Bhutto of Pakistan, met at Simla in July 1972, and agreed to restore peace. Article 1(2) of the Simla Agreement declared that

> the two countries are resolved to settle their differences by peaceful means through bilateral negotiations or by any other peaceful means mutually agreed upon between them. Pending the final settlement of any of the problems between the two countries, neither side shall unilaterally alter the situation and both shall prevent the organization, assistance or encouragement of any acts detrimental to the maintenance of peaceful and harmonious relations.⁶¹

Additionally, Article 4(2) provided that:

> In Jammu and Kashmir, the line of control resulting from the cease-fire of December 17, 1971 shall be respected by both sides without prejudice to the recognised position of either side. Neither side shall seek to alter it unilaterally, irrespective of mutual differences and legal interpretations. Both sides further undertake to refrain from the threat or the use of force in violation of this Line.'⁶²

Under this Agreement the ceasefire line was transformed into the Line of Control.

Since the Simla Agreement, Indian leaders have reiterated the bilateral character of the dispute over J&K. In the late 1980s, J&K saw the rise of an armed insurgency. This development was partly the result of the alienation of the people of the Kashmir Valley and partly because of the support provided to such disgruntled and alienated sections of this community by the Pakistani security establishment. The Jammu Kashmir Liberation Front was the first militant group established in the valley, followed by Hizb-ul-Mujahideen, whose leader Syed Salauddin was defeated by rigging the 1987 elections in favour of a candidate from the National Conference, Ghulam Mohiuddin Shah, in the Indian side of J&K.[63] Salauddin later found shelter and support from the Pakistani agencies.

As a result of increasing attacks by the militants on the Indian side of J&K, the Parliament of India adopted a resolution on 22 February 1994, which emphasised that the whole of J&K is an integral part of India and that Pakistan had to vacate the territory that it had 'occupied through aggression'.[64] The resolution expressed deep concerns of Pakistan's role in providing training to the militants in the camps located on their side of Kashmir. It reiterated that such trained militants are 'indulging in murder, loot and other heinous crimes against the people, taking them hostage and creating an atmosphere of terror'.[65] The resolution also called on Pakistan to stop providing support to terrorism, which India considered a violation of the Simla Agreement, and adhere to the internationally accepted norms of interstate conduct that 'is the root cause of tension between the two countries'.[66]

However, in 1999 the Simla Agreement made a comeback in the Lahore Declaration adopted during Indian Prime Minister Atal Behari Vajpayee's visit to Lahore, after meeting his Pakistani counterpart, Muhammad Nawaz Sharif, when the two countries agreed to implement the agreement in letter and spirit. In the Memorandum of Understanding they agreed to 'intensify their efforts to resolve all issues, including the issue of Jammu and Kashmir'.[67]

Soon after the Lahore Declaration, militants operating from Pakistan, backed by the Pakistani Army, intruded and captured some of the military bases in the Kargil sector. The architect of this operation was General Parvez Musharraf, who was not happy with the peace talks or the Lahore Declaration. After a war in the Kargil sector in 1999, India reverted to its 1994 position.

In October 1999, Musharraf carried out a successful coup and became Head of State in Pakistan. In 2001, he met Vajpayee in the Indian city of Agra. The two leaders made efforts to reach agreement on J&K, but these ultimately failed. In 2004, Dr Manmohan Singh became the Prime Minister of India. His government continued with talks. In 2007, according to Khurshid Mohammad Kasuri, a former Foreign Minister of Pakistan, India and Pakistan almost reached an accepted solution to the status of J&K.⁶⁸ However, they could not move ahead because of many systemic and structural reasons.

In 2019, the BJP-led National Democratic Alliance Government revoked the Special Status granted to the Indian side of J&K under Article 370 of the Indian Constitution. The revocation of Article 370 has been a part of the BJP's political manifesto since the Bhartiya Jan Sangh days.⁶⁹ The government argued that, after the revocation of its Special Status, J&K would become democratic and experience economic growth. However, those who do not buy this argument believe that the revocation of Article 370 would further alienate the people of the Kashmir Valley. In Pakistan, radical Islamist groups and the Pakistani establishment have expressed their opposition to the revocation of the Special Status of J&K. They argue that the Indian Government's position vindicates Jinnah's words that Hindus will dominate the Muslims in a united independent India. Protests were held across Pakistan in solidarity with Kashmir against the scrapping of the Special Status under Article 370. Pakistan suspended trains to India. Pakistan's high commissioner to India-designate was delayed from assuming his position, and the Indian high commissioner was sent back to India. Trade with India stopped.

Protests against the revocation of Special Status under Article 370 were held in parts of the Kashmir Valley where a large number of gunslinging Indian security personnel were on the ground to silence protestors. Many people in the Kashmir Valley feel that they are slaves of the Indian establishment, with some Kashmiris even supporting a merger with China,⁷⁰ despite accusations that China is violating the human rights of its Uyghur Muslim minority. Disputes over territory also question the identity of the people living there. The next section discusses the identity of religious and ethnic minorities as citizens in India, Pakistan and Bangladesh.

Making of postcolonial citizens

Looking at the early days of India's partition, Zamindar argued that the two dominions imposed citizenship from above. The national identities were constructed.⁷¹ Joya Chatterjee also sees symmetry in the citizenship regimes of India and Pakistan that both produced a new figure – 'the minority citizen' – who was neither citizen nor alien, but a 'hybrid subject'.⁷² Minority citizenship was not only a product of 'bureaucratic rationality', or even of 'governmentality', but, on the contrary, 'produced by complex, often violent, interactions between government and a range of non-state actors, who forced their own ideas of nationality, justice, and entitlement onto the statute books'.⁷³

In terms of religious identity, although Pakistan was created as a separate state for Indian Muslims, both India's and Pakistan's leadership were not in favour of a population exchange, as it would create a severe economic burden.[74] After complete partition, India had 42 million Muslims, reduced to 35 million, while Pakistan had over 20 million non-Muslims. In the initial days of the partition, the citizenship of the new minorities was questioned as the majority communities from the two countries were looking for 'a pure and untainted national ethos'.[75] Partition not only affected Hindus and Muslims, but also Parsis, Buddhists, Chakmas, Khasis and other religious and tribal groups.

Although India helped in the liberation of Bangladesh, India–Bangladesh relations have remained tense over 'illegal' migrants and cross-border movements. Most of the trouble is in the Indian states of West Bengal, Assam, Tripura and Meghalaya. In 2015, after years of protests against the immigrants in Assam, the Government of India, under the supervision of the Supreme Court, began updating the National Register of Citizens (NRC) to detect and deport 'illegal' migrants from Assam. On 31 August 2019, the final list of NRCs for Assam was published. In that list, 1.9 million people were found non-eligible for Indian citizenship. After the list was published, the BJP rejected it. The party argued that several thousand Hindus and tribes had been excluded, while many 'illegal' Bangladeshi Muslims were included.

Migration from East Bengal into Assam dates to the late 1820s when tea plantations were established on a large scale.[76] This was an industry that required many workers who were mainly brought by the Assam Company from Bengal to Assam.[77] A few years after the tea plantation sector was developed in the late nineteenth century, oil was discovered in Assam, which attracted many other labourers from other parts of India, including from Bengal.[78] Most of the workers in the tea plantations were East Bengali Muslims. Later, with the emergence of modern professions, many Hindu Bengalis also moved to Assam. Another factor that encouraged immigration into the region in later years was the holding of elections where the number of voters mattered. In the late 1930s and 1940s, the Muhammed Saadulah government in Assam was accused of settling many Muslims, mainly from East Bengal, in Assam. Many of them were settled in wasteland areas.[79]

As migration was an important matter in Assam, the issue was raised in 1946 in the Constituent Assembly of India by Omeo Kumar Das, the representative from Assam.[80] Under Clause 6 B (ii) of the Indian Constitution, migrants who entered into Indian territory before 19 July 1948 from Pakistan were regarded as residents of India from the date of their entry, and they were accepted as Indian citizens from the day of commencement of the Constitution. Those who came on or after 19 July 1948 had to go through a legal process to obtain Indian citizenship.[81] In the case of Assam, where migration remained a cause of concern, the Immigrants (Expulsion from Assam) Act, 1950 was passed by the Central Government of India.[82] Assam witnessed another large-scale migration in 1971, following the Pakistani Army's unprecedented violence against the Bengali-speaking population, when between 7.5 and 8.5 million[83] people crossed into India. Many sought shelter in Assam. To settle the issue, after the liberation of Bangladesh, in 1971, a process of repatriating the refugees began.

Although the Government of Bangladesh maintains that the refugees returned to their country after liberation, many political groups in Assam say that a number of refugees remain in the state. Given the Government of India's reluctance to address the status of these refuges, the 'anti-foreigner' Assam Agitation (1979–85) led by the All-Assam Students Union (AASU) and the All-Assam Gana Sangram Parishad started. During the agitation, Assam witnessed violence against immigrants at Nellie near Gauhati, when some 2,000 workers were killed in 1983. Although the leadership of the agitation claimed that it was a secular agitation for the rights of the Assamese-speaking population, the agitation had a communal tone. After the Nellie massacre, a few of the Muslim student leaders parted with the AASU because of its growing anti-Muslim tone.[84] To address the demands of the agitators, the Parliament of India enacted the Illegal Migrant (Determination by Tribunal) Act, 1983. However, it could not satisfy the agitators and in 1985 the Assam Accord was signed between the agitators and the Government of India and Government of Assam. In that Accord, the agitators and the Government of India agreed to accept those people who entered Assam by midnight of 24 March 1971 as Indian citizens, subject to having valid legal documents. For those who entered Assam after that date, Clause 5.8 of the Assam Accord stipulated that: 'Foreigners who came to Assam on or after March 25, 1971 shall continue to be detected, deleted and practical steps shall be taken to expel such foreigners.'[85] Further, Clause 6 of the Accord further stated that 'Constitutional, legislative and administrative safeguards as may be appropriate, shall be provided to protect, preserve and promote the cultural, social, linguistic identity and heritage of the Assamese people.'[86] It is Clause 6 which the agitators want to implement in Assam by removing all non-Assamese, whether Hindus or Muslims, from the state.

As the Illegal Migrant (Determination by Tribunal) Act failed to prevent migration, or detect and deport foreigners, it was challenged in the Supreme Court of India, which struck it off the statute books in 2005. In 2012, during public interest litigation hearings filed by the Assam Public Works demanding direction to deport the migrants from Assam, the Indian Government clarified to the Supreme Court that it does not support cross-border immigration and will take steps to deport those living illegally in Indian territory. Later, in 2014, the Supreme Court of India issued directives to the state government to start updating the NRC.[87] The NRC process began in Assam in 2015 and concluded in 2019. Although the BJP government says it is committed to detecting and deporting foreigners from Assam, the bigger challenge is where to deport them to. Bangladesh has unequivocally stated many times that none of its citizens are living illegally in India.

Unlike the National Register of Citizens that entails withdrawing citizenship from those whose names are not found in the final NRC list, the BJP government in India introduced the Citizenship (Amendment) Bill to bestow Indian citizenship to Hindus, Jains, Sikhs, Parsees and Christians from Afghanistan, Pakistan and Bangladesh, who came to India before 31 December 2014.[88] Addressing a public rally at Silchar on 4 January 2019, Indian Prime Minister Narendra Modi described the Bill as a 'penance against the injustice and wrongdoings in the past'.[89] He also said that 'the citizenship bill is an atonement of the wrong that was done during India's Partition. I hope this bill is passed soon in Parliament. India will safeguard all who had been victims of partition.'[90] Notably, Silchar is home to many migrant Hindus from Bangladesh. Supporting the bill, Himanta Biswa Sarma, then Finance Minister, and now Chief Minister of Assam, said 'I strongly believe that if this bill is not passed, then Hindus in Assam will become a minority in just the next five years. That will be advantageous to those elements who want Assam to be another Kashmir and a part of the uncertain phase there.'[91] The fear expressed by Sarma exaggerates the demographic figures for Assam. The total population of Assam is about 31.69 million (2011 census), out of which Hindus comprise 61.47 per cent and are the majority in eighteen out of twenty-seven districts of the State. Muslims comprise 34.22 per cent of the total population and are the majority in nine districts. Others, such as Sikhs (0.07 per cent), Buddhists (0.18 per cent), Jains (0.08 per cent), and other religious minorities (0.09 per cent). Those who did not state their religion comprise 0.16 per cent of the total population.[92]

The Citizenship Amendment Act (CAA) was passed by the Indian Parliament in December 2019. It came into effect on 10 January 2020. Protests were held across India against the CAA. Critics of law and protestors believe that the CAA, combined with the NRC, discriminates against Muslims.[93] They claim that the CAA was passed to grant citizenship to those Hindus who could not find their names in the nationwide NRC list, while those Muslims who cannot find their names on the list would have to either leave India or prove their identity in the Indian courts. If they fail to do so, they could be thrown into one of India's many detention centres.[94]

From its early years, Pakistan created unequal citizens on the basis of religion. Articles 41(2) and 91(3) of Pakistan's Constitution, for example, reserve the offices of the President and the Prime Minister for Muslims only,[95] although there are no constitutional restrictions and prohibitions for members of non-Muslim communities to occupy other public offices. However, the Ahmadis, because of their religious belief, were politically excluded in Pakistan.[96] Under Article 260 (3b), the 'Quadiani group who call themselves Ahmadis or by any other name are "non-Muslim".'[97] Interpreting Article 260 (3b), in 2022, Justice Mansoor Ali Shah, along with Justice Amin-ud-Din Khan, in the 'Tahir Naqash case',[98] said that the provision neither disowns the Ahmadis as citizens of Pakistan nor deprives them 'of their entitlement to the fundamental rights guaranteed under the Constitution'.[99]

Like Pakistan, Bangladesh is an Islamic country. In 1947, many Urdu-speaking Muslims, popularly called 'Bihari Muslims' or 'stranded Pakistanis', moved to East Pakistan from the present Indian states of Bihar, Uttar Pradesh, Odisha etc. During the civil war of 1971 between the Bengali-speaking population and the Pakistan Army, many Urdu speakers from East Pakistan supported the Army. After the liberation of Bangladesh in 1971, some of them were accepted by Pakistan as its citizens, while several Urdu-speaking Muslims remained stateless in Bangladesh. The citizenship status of the camp-dwelling Urdu-speaking population was finally settled by the High Court's verdict in the 2008 case of 'Mohammad Sadaqat Khan (Fakku) and ten others v. Election Commission and others'. The court dismissed the state's claim that camp-dwelling Urdu-speaking people lost their citizenship by opting to go to Pakistan and for living in International Committee of Red Cross camps. The court noted: 'By keeping the question of citizenship unresolved on the wrong assumption over the decades, this nation (Bangladesh) has not gained anything, rather it was deprived of the contribution they could have made in nation-building.'[100] Despite such a judgment, the Bangladeshi state strongly holds a view that the Urdu-speaking population are not its citizens. This was demonstrated when, on 16 September 2021, the Director General of Bangladesh's Bureau of Statistics instructed the deputy commissioners of all districts to prepare a list of 'all stranded Pakistanis'. He explained that the move was a follow-up to a decision taken by the National Security Council under the Cabinet Division of the Government to update the list so that diplomatic efforts could be taken to prepare for their repatriation to Pakistan.[101]

In all three countries, citizenship is linked with the religion and ethnicity of the individual. Among the three, India is the only non-religious, secular country, but the increasing clout of Hindutva politics is creating deep communal fissures between Hindus and Muslims. The next section looks at the problems of religious minorities and their relations with the majority community.

Majoritarianism and the fate of religious minorities in India, Pakistan and Bangladesh

In India the state is secular, but society is not. This dichotomy between state and society has been ongoing since 1947. The Hindu right-wing groups that emerged in British India posed a challenge to state secularism and minorities early on. One such warning was in December 1947, soon after the partition of India, when M. S. Golwalkar, the leader of Rashtriya Swayamsevak Sangh (RSS), in his address to about 2,500 volunteers, was reputed to have said, according to a transcript written by the intelligence services:

> The Sangh will not rest content until it had finished Pakistan. If anyone stood in our way, we will have to finish him too, whether it was the Nehru Government or any other Government. The Sangh could not be won over. They should carry on their work. Referring to Muslims he said he had that no power on earth could keep them in Hindustan. They shall have to quit this country. Mahatma Gandhi wanted to keep the Muslims so that the Congress may profit by their votes at the time of election. But, by that time, not a single Muslim will be left in India. If they were made to stay here, the responsibility would be Government's, and the Hindu community would not be responsible. Mahatma Gandhi could not mislead them any longer. We have the means whereby such men can be immediately silenced, but it is our tradition not to be inimical to Hindus. If we are compelled, we will have to resort to that course too.[102]

Further, in 1947, after a large number of Hindus and Sikhs fled to north India, a substantial number of them, along with the Hindu right-wing groups' supporters, demanded that India – or some of its parts, such as East Punjab, Delhi and certain districts of western Uttar Pradesh – be cleared of their Muslim populations and have their lands handed over to them.[103] Despite these extreme views, the Indian state has succeeded in maintaining its secular character. Many Muslims have occupied important positions, and even the highest offices in the country. However, communal riots have occurred in which many Hindus, Sikhs and Muslims have been gruesomely killed by members of other communities. In 2014, the RSS-supported government under Narendra Modi was elected to office. Since then, India has witnessed a rise in muscular Hindu nationalism, and there has been an increase in the number of attacks on people holding dissenting political opinions or different social and religious beliefs, further eroding democratic institutions.

Even in present-day India, it is often asked whether a Muslim can really be an Indian.[104] This enduring legacy of partition has more to do with the failure of the Indian state to manage 'difference' since 1947. With the rise of majoritarianism and Hindutva politics the communal situation has further worsened. Expressing his views on the post-2014 communal situation in the country, former Vice-President of India, Hamid Ansari, on his last day in office, cautioned the people about the danger of exclusive and assertive nationalism in India.[105] In an interview with the *Indian Express*, Ansari said:

> India is secure. But the 'idea of India' is a matter of very considerable debate. To my mind, the idea of India which was crafted [is] one that is multi-layered, which accommodates a great deal of diversity. So, one can't say that there is this 'one idea of India', there are multiple 'ideas of India' and they all fit into each other. Sanguine? The 'idea' is being challenged with a certain frequency which makes me uncomfortable.[106]

In reaction, former Indian Vice-President Venkaiah Naidu said that: 'India is the most tolerant country ... Unfortunately, some people are trying to blow it out of proportion and trying to defame India, raising it to national forum.'[107] He added that India 'is the best model of secularism'.[108]

After its birth in 1947, it was thought that Pakistan would follow the direction of Turkey rather than Islamic models of the other Middle Eastern countries. Mohammad Ali Jinnah, in his only speech in the Constituent Assembly of Pakistan on 11 August 1947, proposed a secular vision for the country. Jinnah said: 'You may belong to any religion or caste or creed that has nothing to do with the business of the State ... in course of time Hindus would cease to be Hindus and Muslims would cease to be Muslims, not in the religious sense because that is personal faith of each individual, but in political sense as citizens of the State.'[109] At one point, it is believed that Jinnah even considered declaring the Muslim League a secular party and changing its name to the Pakistan National League.[110] As a symbolic reflection of secularism, Jinnah and the then Prime Minister of Pakistan, Liaquat Ali Khan, chose the flag, which is three-quarters green, signifying the Muslim majority, and one-quarter white, for the minorities.[111] Such visions bewildered many in the Muslim League and were criticised.[112] However, Jinnah's statements, visions and promises were marked with considerable ambiguities. On 25 January 1948, Jinnah publicly stated that Pakistan's Constitution would be based on Islamic law (*sharia*) 'to make Pakistan a truly great Islamic state'.[113] Also, Liaquat Ali Khan, while moving the Objectives Resolution to determine the principles of Pakistan's future Constituent Assembly, declared that the state will create conditions conducive to building a truly Islamic state.[114] All such ambiguities ended with the death of Jinnah on 11 September 1948, shortly after the formation of Pakistan, and the assassination of Liaquat Ali Khan three years later.[115] In 1956, Pakistan adopted a constitution that declared the republic an Islamic state.

In 1958, after a period of rule by successive civilian leaders, General Ayub Khan took power through a military coup. He allied with the Islamic groups to establish the legitimacy of the coup and gain political support. During this period, Sayyid Abul A'la Maududi (1903–79), the leader of Jammat-i-Islami, became very powerful. Maududi was against the partition of British India and called Jinnah a 'Kafir-i-Azam' instead of 'Quaid-i-Azam' because of his demand for Pakistan to be created. Maududi had support from the military, and wanted to replace Jinnah with a different nationalist icon that the Jammat could more easily claim affinity to.[116] Maududi settled on Muhammad Iqbal, though Iqbal's religious views were in glaring contrast with those of Maududi's.[117] Later, under General Zia-ul-Haq (1979–88), the Pakistani state adopted all signs and symbols of Islam and became a true Islamic state and society.

Since the early days of Pakistan, its minorities have faced discrimination and violence in different forms. During the partition of British India, the 'hostage population' or 'matching minority population' theory emerged.[118] The proponents of such a theory, mainly the Muslim League, believed that keeping minorities in Pakistan was essential to check the Hindu majority in India from committing any form of atrocity against their Muslim population.[119]

In present Pakistan, there have been many cases where girls from the Hindu minority community have been abducted by Muslim men, illegally married to the abductor, and then converted to Islam. This is especially so in upper and northern Sindh. In 2016, the Sindh Assembly passed the Criminal Law (Protection of Minorities) Act 2015 to protect the rights of minorities. Nevertheless, minorities remain under threat. For instance, in March 2022 a Hindu girl, Pooja Kumari, was shot dead in Rohri in the Sukkur district in Sindh for resisting abduction for conversion and forced marriage. Earlier, in July 2017, the Pakistan paper *Dawn* reported that, due to fear in the immediate neighbourhood, many members of the Hindu community from Sindh province in Pakistan had crossed to the Indian side of the border.[120] There is no data on how many Pakistani Hindus cross into India annually. However, in 2014, Ramesh Kumar Vankwani, then a member of Pakistan's National Assembly, revealed that every year around 5,000 Hindus from Pakistan, largely from Sindh province, migrate to India.[121] Many such migrations are legal, but several enter illegally. According to Government of India data, 25,447 Hindus from Pakistan, Bangladesh and Afghanistan have been given long-term visas since 2011, on the grounds of religious persecution.[122]

Sikhs, Christians and Parsees were also affected by partition. Like Hindus and Muslims, their communities also straddle the borders of the two states. Often members from these communities witnessed violence from the majority community. For example, in 1984, Sikhs were victims of communal violence.

The entire community was blamed for the assassination of Indira Gandhi, who was shot dead by her Sikh bodyguards. As news of the assassination spread, violence flared up in Delhi and then in other parts of India. In that pogrom, as per unofficial numbers, between 5,000 and 18,000 Sikhs were killed, thousands were attacked, several lost their properties, and many Sikh homes were burnt by Hindu mobs. During the pogrom the ten million Sikhs felt they were also a minority constituting just 2 per cent of the total population of India.[123] In Pakistan there are around 50,000 Sikhs. As they are also being attacked by radical Muslim groups, many of the community's members fled from the Khyber Pakhtunkhwa (KP) province (formerly known as North-West Frontier Province) where the majority of Sikhs in Pakistan live.[124] A recent case is of former Pakistan Tehreek-i-Insaf's party law maker from KP, Baldev Kumar, who sought political asylum in India.

After its liberation in 1971, Bangladesh adopted a secular constitution under Sheikh Mujibur Rahman, who became the first president of the country. However, soon after his assassination on 15 August 1975 politics changed in the country. In April 1977, General Ziaur Rahman (1977 to 1981) became the head of state. He enacted the Political Party Regulation Act to clear the way for Bangladesh Jamaat-e-Islami and other like-minded groups to participate in the political activities of the country. Subsequently, amendments were made to the Constitution to change the nature of the Bangladeshi state. In 1979, the word 'secularism' was deleted from the Preamble and Article 8 of the Constitution. A sentence declaring 'absolute trust and faith in the Almighty Allah', which should be 'the basis of all actions', was inserted through the Second Proclamation Order Number 1 in 1977. The words 'Bismillah-ar-Rahman-ar-Rahim' (In the name of Allah, the Beneficent, the Merciful) were also inserted above the Preamble to the Constitution.[125] General Rahman was assassinated during his visit to Chittagong in 1981. He was succeeded by another military man, General Hussain Mohammad Ershad (1982–1990). Like his predecessor, General Ershad also used Islam to consolidate his rule. In 1988, he declared Bangladesh an Islamic Republic.

In 2011, secularism was restored in Bangladesh through the 15th Amendment to the Bangladeshi Constitution. Islam, however, was retained as the state's religion. The amended Preamble pledges 'that the high ideals of nationalism, socialism, democracy and secularism, which inspired our heroic people to dedicate themselves to, and our brave martyrs to sacrifice their lives in, the national liberation struggle, shall be the fundamental principles of the Constitution'.[126] Article 8 of the Constitution now reads: 'The principles of nationalism, socialism, democracy and secularism, together with the principles derived from those as set out in this Part, shall constitute the fundamental principles of state policy.'[127] The substituted Article 12 of the Bangladesh Constitution states:

> The principle of secularism shall be realised by the elimination of – (a) communalism in all its forms; (b) the granting by the State of political status in favour of any religion; (c) the abuse of religion for political purposes; (d) any discrimination against, or persecution of, persons practicing a particular religion.[128]

Nevertheless, Islam remains the state's religion. Article 2A of the Bangladesh Constitution says: 'The state religion of the Republic is Islam, but the State shall ensure equal status and equal right in the practice of the Hindu, Buddhist, Christian and other religions.'[129] In 2016, the Bangladesh High Court rejected a 28-year-old petition to remove constitutional provision recognising Islam as the official religion of the country.[130]

Since the 1980s, Bangladesh has seen the spread of a radical version of Islam. A major reason for this development is the spread of Saudi Arabian sponsored *Wahhabism* across South Asia. The spread of radicalism, the emergence of militant groups, and increasing social tensions have intensified violence against Hindus and Buddhists in Bangladesh. According to a report by Ain o Salish Kendra, a well-known human rights group in Bangladesh, around 3,679 attacks on the Hindu community took place between January 2013 and September 2021. The attacks included vandalism of, and setting fire to, 559 houses, 442 shops and businesses, and about 1,678 attacks on Hindu temples, idols and places of worship.[131]

Conclusion

The state of J&K is regarded by the majority from both India and Pakistan as their own territory. Despite wars and formal talks between India and Pakistan, the political status of J&K remains unsettled. To secure the territory, Indian and Pakistani leaders have never hesitated to use force against the people living on their sides of J&K. Various reports prepared by independent scholars, and by the United Nations, highlight serious violations of human rights on both sides of J&K.[132] On 5 August 2019, the Government of India revoked the Special Status promised to J&K in the 1940s and demoted the state to the status of Union Territory.[133] Afterwards a curfew was imposed, all political leaders and activists were detained, and several youths were incarcerated in different parts of India. Some of them are still in prison.

As mentioned in this chapter, the citizenship issue is still being debated in India. To deal with the NRC issue, it is being suggested by some members of the Indian bureaucracy that many of those who may be declared 'foreigners' could be granted work permits[134] and allowed to live in the country. This will create several 'right-less'[135] and stateless people in the country. In Pakistan, the Hindus and other religious minorities remain unequal citizens. Denial of constitutional equality also make the minorities socially vulnerable, forcing them to live at the mercy of the majority community. In Bangladesh, as the chapter shows, the issue of Urdu-speaking Muslims remains unsettled. The Bangladeshi state still believes that Urdu speakers are 'stranded Pakistanis'.

With the rise of majoritarian nationalism, the relationships between the majority and minority communities in India, Pakistan and Bangladesh has deteriorated. Majoritarian nationalism has also harmed democracy and affected the democratic rights of the people in these countries. It has also provided a harbinger of what may turn into what Christophe Jaffrelot has called de facto ethnic democracy.[136] This is where the majority dominates minorities, even though both groups fully participate in the political processes of the country.

Notes

1. The cow is regarded as a sacred animal to the Hindus while Muslims consume cow meat. However, in ancient India people used to slaughter cows and oxen for food. See D. N. Jha, *The Myth of the Holy Cow* (London & New York: Verso, 2002). Largely, this practice stopped only after the emergence of Buddhism and Jainism in the sixth century BC.
2. See Lars Bilkenberg, *India–Pakistan: The History of Unsolved Conflicts*, vols I and II (Campusvej: Odnense University Press, 1998).
3. Anita Inder Singh, 'With the CAA, India is Hurtling Down the Path of Majoritarianism', *The Wire*, 2 January 2020, at https://thewire.in/politics/caa-majoritarian-nationalism (accessed 12 July 2022).
4. Ibid.
5. Angana P. Chatterji, Thomas Blom Hansen and Christophe Jaffrelot, 'Introduction', in Angana P. Chatterji, Thomas Blom Hansen and Christophe Jaffrelot (eds), *Majoritarian State: How Hindu Nationalism is Changing India* (New Delhi: Harper Collins, 2019), pp. 1–18, at p. 4.
6. Helen Regan, Swati Gupta and Manveena Suri, 'Hindus Allowed to Build on Disputed Holy Site, India's Supreme Court Rules', *CNN*, 9 November 2019, at https://edition.cnn.com/2019/11/08/asia/ayodhya-dispute-india-ruling-intl-hnk/index.html (accessed 15 March 2023).
7. In the Supreme Court of India: Civil Appellate Jurisdiction – Civil Appeal Nos. 10866–10867 of 2010 Supreme Court of India, Government of India, at https://main.sci.gov.in/supremecourt/2010/36350/36350_2010_1_1502_18205_Judgement_09-Nov-2019.pdf (accessed 25 November 2019).

8 The Indian Constitution calls for the separation of the judiciary and the executive. However, in the 1960s, Attorney General M. C. Setelvad complained that many members of the judiciary kept an eye on post-retirement political positions while they remained in service. In the past, (retired) Justice Ranganath Misra served as a member of the upper house between 1998 and 2004 from the Indian National Congress. Misra helped the Rajiv Gandhi government absolve the Congress during the 1984 anti-Sikh pogrom. See, generally, Rajeev Dhawan, 'The Revolving Door for Ranjan Gogoi does the Supreme Court and Parliament no Credit', *The Wire*, 25 March 2020, at https://thewire.in/law/the-revolving-door-for-ranjan-gogoi-does-the-supreme-court-and-parliament-no-credit (accessed 18 June 2021).
9 *Partition Commission Papers, Reports of the Members and Awards of the Chairman of the Boundary Commissions* (Alipore: Government Printing West Bengal Government Press, 1950).
10 Oskar Spate, *On the Margins of History: From the Punjab to Fiji* (Canberra: National Centre for Development Studies, Research School of Pacific Studies, Australian National University, 1991).
11 'The Gazette of India Extraordinary Part-I – Section 1', Ministry of External Affairs, Government of India, p. 51. *Reports of International Arbitral Awards: Boundary Disputes Between India and Pakistan Relating to the Interpretation of the Report of the Bengal Boundary Commission*, 26 January 1950 (United Nations, 2006), Volume XXI, pp. 1–51, at https://legal.un.org/riaa/cases/vol_XXI/1-51.pdf (accessed 24 March 2023).
12 Lucy P. Chester, *Borders and Conflicts in South Asia: The Radcliffe Boundary Committee and Partition of Punjab* (Manchester; New York: Manchester University Press, 2009), p. 80.
13 Ijaz Hussain, *Indus Waters Treaty: Political and Legal Dimensions* (Karachi: Oxford University Press, 2017).
14 *Partition Commission Papers*, p. 243.
15 Chester, *Borders and Conflicts in South Asia*.
16 *Ibid.*, p. 120.
17 *Ibid.*
18 'The Gazette of India Extraordinary Part-I – Section 1'.
19 For details, see *Agreement Between India and Pakistan on Border Disputes (East Pakistan)* (New Delhi, 1958), at https://peacemaker.un.org/sites/peacemaker.un.org/files/IN%20PK_580910_Agreement%20between%20India%20and%20Pakistan%20on%20Border%20Disputes%20%28East%20Pakistan%29.pdf (accessed 17 June 2021).
20 Yaqoob Khan Bangash, *A Princely Affair: The Accession and Integration of the Princely States of Pakistan, 1947–1965* (Karachi: Oxford University Press, 2015).
21 Yaqoob Khan Bangash, 'Modi, Balochistan and Gilgit', *Express Tribune*, 24 August 2016, at https://tribune.com.pk/story/1169354/modi-balochistan-gilgit (accessed 12 June 2021).
22 Rizwan Zeb, 'Roots of Resentment', *Friday Times*, 29 July 2016, at www.thefridaytimes.com/2016/07/29/roots-of-resentment/ (accessed 12 July 2022).

23 Srinath Raghavan, *War and Peace in Modern India* (Ranikhet: Permanent Black, 2010), p. 31.
24 Rakesh Ankit, 'Junagadh, India and the Logic of Occupation and Appropriation, 1947–1949', *Studies in History* 34 (2) (2018), 109–140, at 112.
25 *Ibid.*
26 Owen Bennet Jones, *The Bhutto Dynasty: The Struggle for Power in Pakistan* (Gurgaon: Penguin, 2020), pp. 31–32.
27 Amjed Jaaved, 'Junagadh Annexation (9 November 1947) and the Myth of the Indian Union', *Modern Diplomacy*, 7 November 2021, at https://moderndiplomacy.eu/2021/11/07/junagadh-annexation-november-9-1947-and-the-myth-of-the-indian-union/ (accessed 14 June 2022).
28 The question of Junagadh was raised by Pakistan before the United Nations Security Council on 15 April 1948. See Raghavan, *War and Peace in Modern India*, p. 63.
29 Ankit, 'Junagadh, India and the Logic of Occupation', p. 138.
30 Hyderabad is the capital of Telangana, which was carved out of Andhra Pradesh in 2014. Earlier, Hyderabad was the capital of Andhra Pradesh.
31 Mohan Guruswami, 'There Once was a Hyderabad', *Citizen*, 11 September 2019, at www.thecitizen.in/index.php/en/NewsDetail/index/9/17535/There-Once-Was-A-Hyderabad-#:~:text=The%201941%20census%20had%20estimated,Muslims%20accounting%20for%20about%2012%25 (accessed 18 July 2022).
32 *Ibid.*
33 *Ibid.*
34 A. G. Noorani, *The Destruction of Hyderabad* (New Delhi: Tulika Books, 2014), p. 142.
35 V. P. Menon, *The Story of the Integration of the Indian States* (New York: MacMillan, 1956), p. 333.
36 Noorani, *The Destruction of Hyderabad.*
37 Adverse Possession means those territories which were claimed by India or Bangladesh but lie on the other side of their border. See *India and Bangladesh: Land Boundary Agreement* (New Delhi: Ministry of External Affairs, Government of India, 2015), https://mea.gov.in/Uploads/PublicationDocs/24529_LBA_MEA_Booklet_final.pdf (accessed 17 April 2017).
38 There were about 225 small enclaves on the India–Bangladesh borders. Of these, there were about 119 Indian exchangeable enclaves in Bangladesh and the number of non-exchangeable enclaves was 11. Likewise, there were 72 Bangladeshi exchangeable enclaves in India and 23 non-exchangeable enclaves. See Avtar Singh Bhasin, *India–Bangladesh Relations: Documents 1971–2002*, Vol. 4 (New Delhi: Geetika Press, 2005).
39 *India and Bangladesh: Land Boundary Agreement*, pp. 4–5.
40 'Parl Approves Bill to Settle 41-year-old Border Issue with Bangladesh', *Deccan Herald*, 7 May 2015, at www.deccanherald.com/content/476213/parl-approves-bill-settle-41.html (accessed 10 June 2020).
41 Shuja Nawaz, *Crossed Swords: Pakistan, its Army, and the Wars Within* (Karachi: Oxford University Press, 2008), p. 45.

42 *Ibid.*
43 *Ibid.*, p. 49.
44 Sisir Gupta, *Kashmir: A Study in India–Pakistan Relations* (New Delhi: Indian Council of World Affairs, 1966), p. 127.
45 *Ibid.*, p. 135.
46 Victoria Schofield, *Kashmir in the Crossfire* (London; New York: I. B. Tauris), p. 162.
47 Resolution 47 (1948) / [adopted by the Security Council at its 286th meeting], of 21 April 1948, UN Security Council (3rd year: 1948), at https://digitallibrary.un.org/record/111955 (accessed 28 January 2020).
48 Joseph Korbel, 'The Kashmir Dispute after Six Years', *International Organization* 7 (4), 498–510, at 502.
49 Gupta, *Kashmir*, p. 189.
50 Christopher Snedden, *Understanding Kashmir and Kashmiris* (London: Hurst, 2015), p. 190.
51 Sumit Ganguly, *The Origins of War in South Asia: Indo-Pakistani Conflicts Since 1947* (London: Westview Press, 1986), p. 24.
52 *Ibid.* See also Major Satish Kumar Sinha, *Chasing a Mirage: The Question of Peace in Kashmir*, JCSP-37 (Toronto: Canadian Forces College, 2011), at www.cfc.forces.gc.ca/259/290/297/286/sinha.pdf (accessed 12 December 2020), p. 25.
53 Schofield, *Kashmir in the Crossfire*, p. 194.
54 Alastair Lamb, *Kashmir: A Disputed Legacy 1846–1990* (Karachi: Oxford University Press, 1993), pp. 239–240.
55 *Ibid.*
56 *Ibid.*
57 Schofield, *Kashmir in the Crossfire*, p. 199.
58 Snedden, *Understanding Kashmir*, p. 242.
59 *Ibid.*
60 See Alok Kumar Gupta, 'Other Territorial Disputes with Pakistan: Rann of Kutch and Sir Creek', in P. Sahadevan (ed.), *Conflict and Peacemaking in South Asia* (New Delhi: Lancer Books, 2001), pp. 272–295.
61 Simla Agreement, 2 July 1972, Ministry of External Affairs, Government of India, at https://www.mea.gov.in/Portal/LegalTreatiesDoc/PA72B1578.pdf (accessed 24 March 2023).
62 *Ibid.*
63 Sumantra Bose, *Kashmir: The Roots of Conflict* (Cambridge, MA: Harvard University Press, 2003), pp. 48–50.
64 Sixteenth Report of Committee on External Affairs (2016–2017) (Sixteenth Lok Sabha), *Ministry of External Affairs Indo-Pak Relations: Presented to Lok Sabha on 11 August, 2017, Laid in Rajya Sabha on 11 August, 2017* (New Delhi: Lok Sabha Secretariat, 2017), p. 128, at https://eparlib.nic.in/bitstream/123456789/65278/1/16_External_Affairs_16.pdf (accessed 24 March 2023).
65 *Ibid.*, p. 128.

66 *Ibid.*, p. 128.
67 Lahore Declaration, February 1999. Ministry of External Affairs, Government of India, at https://peacemaker.un.org/sites/peacemaker.un.org/files/IN%20PK_990221_The%20Lahore%20Declaration.pdf (accessed 24 March 2023).
68 'Kashmir Solution Just a Signature Away: Kasuri', *Times of India*, 24 April 2010, at http://amankiasha.com/tag/khursheed-mehmood-kasuri/ (accessed 16 June 2020).
69 Bhartiya Jana Sangh (BJS) was formed in 1951. Its most prominent leader Shyama Prasad Mukherjee opposed giving Special Status to J&K. He died in 1953 in jail in J&K. In 1977 the BJS merged with other political parties to form the Janta Party government under Morarji Desai. That government fell in 1979, and in 1980 the remaining members of the BJS joined forces and formed the BJP.
70 '"Kashmiris Dreams are Gone, They are Slaves", The Farooq Abdullah Interview', *The Wire*, 25 September 2020.
71 Vazira Fazila-Yacoobali Zamindar, *The Long Partition and the Making of Modern South Asia: Refugees, Boundaries, Histories* (New York: Columbia University Press, 2007), p. 12.
72 Joya Chatterjee, 'South Asian Histories of Citizenship, 1946–1970', *Historical Journal* 55 (4) (2012), 1049–1071, at 1051.
73 *Ibid.*, p. 1070.
74 Haimanti Roy, *Partitioned Lives: Migrants, Refugees, Citizens in India and Pakistan, 1947–1965* (New Delhi: Oxford University Press, 2012), p. 119.
75 Sekhar Bandyopadhyay, 'Partition and Community Relations in Bengal', in Anindita Ghoshal (ed.), *Revisiting Partition: Contestation, Narratives and Memories* (New Delhi: Primus, 2022), pp. 39–54, at p. 42.
76 Tea plantation in Assam was introduced by the Scot, Robert Bruce. See 'History of Indian Tea', Indian Tea Association, at www.indiatea.org/history_of_indian_tea (accessed 3 August 2018).
77 Edward Gait, *A History of Assam* (Calcutta; Simla: Thacker, Spink & Co., 1926), pp. 360–361.
78 Antara Datta, *Refugees and Borders in South Asia: The Great Exodus of 1971* (London: Routledge, 2013), p. 88.
79 Chandan Kumar Sharma, 'The Immigration Issue in Assam and Conflicts Around it', *Asian Ethnicity* 13 (3) (2012), 287–309 at 296.
80 Report of the Union Powers Committee, *Constituent Assembly Debate: Official Report*, Second Reprint, Volume V (New Delhi: Lok Sabha Secretariat, 1989), p. 95.
81 Part II – Citizenship, *The Constitution of India [As on May, 2022]*, pp. 4–5 at https://legislative.gov.in/sites/default/files/COI_English.pdf (accessed 24 March 2023).
82 The Immigrants (Expulsion From Assam) Act, 1950, at https://indiankanoon.org/doc/1523917/ (accessed 8 August 2018).
83 *A Story of Anguish and Action: The United Nations Focal Point for Assistance to Refugees from East Bengal to India* (UNHCR: Geneva, 1972).

84 Makiko Kimura, 'Memories of the Massacre: Violence and Collective Identity in the Narratives on the Nellie Incident', *Asian Ethnicity* 4 (2) (2003), 225–239, at 227.
85 Accord between AASU, AAGSP and the Central Government on the Foreign National Issue (Assam Accord), 15 August 1985, at https://peacemaker.un.org/sites/peacemaker.un.org/files/IN_850815_Assam%20Accord.pdf (accessed 14 March 2023).
86 *Ibid.*
87 Samudra Gupta Kashyap, 'Assam NRC: All Happy with First Part Draft, but What Happens Next?', Indian Express, 3 January 2018, at http://indianexpress.com/article/beyond-the-news/assam-national-register-of-citizens-nrc-all-happy-with-first-part-draft-but-what-happens-next-5009742/ (accessed 14 March 2023).
88 Press Information Bureau, Ministry of Home Affairs, Government of India, 8 January 2019, https://mha.gov.in/media/whats-new.
89 Sangeeta Barooah Pisharoty, 'Modi's Poll Speech in Assam Supporting Citizenship Bill Triggers a Maelstrom', *The Wire*, 7 January 2019, at https://thewire.in/politics/narendra-modi-poll-speech-silachar-assam-citizenship-bill-chaos (accessed 14 March 2023).
90 'In Assam, PM Modi Declares Will Get Controversial Citizenship Bill For Non-Muslims Passed to Atone for Partition', *News 18.com*, 4 January 2019, at www.news18.com/news/politics/in-assam-pm-modi-declares-citizenship-bill-for-non-muslim-refugees-soon-to-atone-for-partition-1991889.html (accessed 18 April 2020).
91 'After "Jinnah" Comment Himanta says Hindus will be Minority in Assam if Citizenship Bill not Passed', *The Hindu*, 7 January 2019, at www.thehindu.com/news/national/hindus-will-be-minority-in-assam-if-citizenship-bill-is-not-passed-says-himanta/article25932247.ece (accessed 14 March 2023).
92 Census Population Data, Assam Religion Census 2011, at www.census2011.co.in/data/religion/state/18-assam.html (accessed 23 December 2019).
93 'Massive Crowd, Multi-Faith Prayer at CAA Protest in Delhi's Shaheen Bagh', *NDTV*, 13 January 2020, at www.ndtv.com/india-news/multi-faith-prayer-in-delhi-as-shaheen-baghs-caa-protest-nears-week-5-2162911 (accessed 16 June 2021).
94 Author talked to the protestors against the CAA and NRC in Delhi and Mumbai.
95 The Constitution of the Islamic Republic of Pakistan, at http://na.gov.pk/uploads/documents/1333523681_951.pdf (accessed 18 July 2019).
96 See Ali Usman Qasmi, *The Ahmadis and the Politics of Religious Exclusion in Pakistan* (London; New York; Delhi: Anthem Press, 2015).
97 The Constitution of the Islamic Republic of Pakistan, pp. 155–156.
98 The Tahir Naqash case involved Ahmadis/Qadianis who were charged for offences under the Pakistan Penal Codes of section 298-B ('Misuse of epithets, descriptions and titles reserved for certain holy personages or places') and section 298-C ('Persons of Qadiani group calling themselves a Muslim or preaching or propagating his faith'). See Faisal Siddiqi, 'Minorities as Citizens', *Dawn*, 1

99 *Ibid.*
100 C. R. Abrar, 'The High Court said they were Bangladeshis', *Daily Star*, 18 January 2022, at www.thedailystar.net/views/opinion/news/the-high-court-said-they-were-bangladeshis-2941196 (accessed 14 March 2023).
101 *Ibid.*
102 Cited in Christophe Jaffrelot, 'A *De Facto* Ethnic Democracy? Obliterating and Targeting the Other, Hindu Vigilantes and the Ethno-State', in Angana P. Chatterji, Thomas Blom Hansen and Christophe Jaffrelot (eds), *Majoritarian State: How Hindu Nationalism is Changing India* (New Delhi: Harper Collins, 2019), pp. 41–68, at p. 55.
103 Gyanendra Pandey, 'Can a Muslim be an Indian?', *Comparative Studies in Society and History* 41 (4) (1999), 608–629, at 613–614.
104 Pandey, 'Can a Muslim Be an Indian?'
105 'Asserting your Nationalism Day In, Day Out is Unnecessary: Hamid Ansari', *The Wire*, 9 August 2017, at https://thewire.in/166419/asserting-nationalism-day-day-unnecessary-hamid-ansari/ (accessed 15 June 2019).
106 'Hamid Ansari Interview: "Idea" of India Being Challenged with a Certain Frequency which Makes me Uncomfortable', *Indian Express*, 10 August 2017, at http://indianexpress.com/article/india/pms-slogan-impeccable-sabka-saath-sabka-vikas-but-then-sabka-saath-means-sabka-saath-says-hamid-ansari-as-he-prepares-to-demit-the-office-of-the-vice-president-4789845/ (accessed 12 July 2019).
107 'Minority Issues Being Used for Political Purposes, says Venkaiah Naidu after Hamid Ansari Talks about Muslims 'Uneasiness'', *Indian Express*, 10 August 2017, at https://indianexpress.com/article/india/venkaiah-naidu-vice-president-minorities-muslim-democracy-tolerance-hamid-ansari-4790633/ (accessed 4 July 2019).
108 *Ibid.*
109 Mahomed Ali Jinnah, *Jinnah: Speeches and Statements 1947–1948* (Karachi: Oxford University Press, 2000), pp. 28–29.
110 Tariq Ali, *Can Pakistan Survive?: The Death of a State* (Harmondsworth: Penguin, 1983), p. 43.
111 H. Bolitho, *Jinnah: Creator of Pakistan* (Westport, CT: Greenwood Press, 1954), p. 198.
112 Pandey, 'Can a Muslim be an Indian?', pp. 612–613.
113 F. Shaikh, *Making Sense of Pakistan* (London: Hurst, 2009), p. 60.
114 *Ibid.*, p. 62.
115 Amit Ranjan, 'Public Interest and Private Gain in Pakistan: Managing the State despite the Predictions of Failure', *South Asia Research* 37 (3) (2017), 296–314.
116 Saadia Toor, *The State of Islam: Culture and Cold War Politics in Pakistan* (London: Pluto Press, 2008), pp. 107–108.
117 *Ibid.*

118 R. J. Moore, 'Jinnah and the Pakistan Demand', in Mushirul Hasan (ed.), *India's Partition: Process, Strategy and Mobilization* (Oxford: Oxford University Press, 2001), pp. 160–197.
119 *Ibid.*
120 '"Partition is Not Over": Pakistani Hindus Fleeing Persecution Find Little Refuge in India', *Dawn*, 31 July 2017, at www.dawn.com/news/1348748 (accessed 14 March 2023).
121 Irfan Haider, '5,000 Hindus Migrating to India Every Year', *Dawn*, 13 May 2014, at www.dawn.com/news/1105830 (accessed 14 March 2023).
122 Sai Manish, 'Citizenship Act: What will Attract Bangladesh and Pakistan Hindus to India?', *Business Standard*, 17 December 2019, at www.business-standard.com/article/current-affairs/citizenship-act-what-will-attract-bangladesh-and-pakistan-hindus-to-india-119121700951_1.html (accessed 12 May 2020).
123 Uma Chakravarti and Nandita Haksar, *The Delhi Riots: Three Days in the life of a Nation* (New Delhi: Lancer International, 1987), p. 23.
124 Mehreen Zahra Malik, 'With Killings on the Rise, Sikhs in Pakistan's Peshawar Weigh Exit', *TRT World*, 12 June 2018, at www.trtworld.com/magazine/with-killings-on-the-rise-sikhs-in-pakistan-s-peshawar-weigh-exit-18160 (accessed 19 July 2019).
125 Shantanu Majumder, 'Secularism and Anti-Secularism', in Ali Riaz and Mohammad Sajjadur Rahman (eds), *Routledge Handbook of Contemporary Bangladesh* (Oxford; New York: Routledge, 2016), pp. 40–51.
126 Government of the People's Republic of Bangladesh, 'The Constitution of the People's Republic of Bangladesh', at http://bdlaws.minlaw.gov.bd/act-details-367.html#:~:text=8.,fundamental%20principles%20of%20state%20policy.%5D (accessed 6 September 2022).
127 *Ibid.*
128 Government of the People's Republic of Bangladesh, 'The Constitution of the People's Republic of Bangladesh', Part II, at http://bdlaws.minlaw.gov.bd/act-367/section-24560.html (accessed 6 September 2022).
129 *Ibid.*
130 David Bergman, 'Bangladesh Court Upholds Islam as Religion of the State', *Al Jazeera*, 28 March 2016, at www.aljazeera.com/news/2016/3/28/bangladesh-court-upholds-islam-as-religion-of-the-state accessed 6 September 2022.
131 'With 3,679 Attacks in 9 Years, Bangladesh's Hindus at "Regular Threat" of Violence: ASK', *BDnews24.Com*, 18 October 2021, https://bdnews24.com/bangladesh/2021/10/18/with-3679-attacks-in-9-years-bangladeshs-hindus-at-regular-threat-of-violence-ask (accessed 28 January 2022).
132 Office of the United Nations High Commissioner for Human Rights, *Update of the Situation of Human Rights in Indian-Administered Kashmir and Pakistan-Administered Kashmir from May 2018 to April 2019* (Geneva: OHCHR, 2019), at www.ohchr.org/Documents/Countries/IN/KashmirUpdateReport_8July2019.pdf (accessed 14 March 2023).
133 Union Territories are administered directly by the Union government. There are six such territories in India: Delhi, Puducherry, Dadra and Nagar Haveli, Chandigarh, Lakshadweep, Daman and Diu. J&K will be the seventh.

134 Sanjib Baruah, 'The Missing 4,007,707', *Indian Express*, 2 August 2018, at https://indianexpress.com/article/opinion/columns/assam-nrc-draft-list-names-citizenship-5287213/ (accessed 5 August 2018).
135 *Ibid.*
136 Jaffrelot, 'A *De Facto* Ethnic Democracy?', p. 42.

9

Civil war, total war or a war of partition? Reassessing the 1948 War in Palestine from a global perspective

Arie M. Dubnov

'Scar tissue. Left by the Empire. Dangerous, scar tissue in the sun. Can flare up'.[1]

Decolonisation – a term used to describe an almost simultaneous replacement of intercontinental empires by postcolonial nation-states across the global South – features prominently in post-1945 global history accounts. Partition – the political division of geographical spaces into two states – was also *à la mode* at the same time, as we see in the case of the two Germanies, the two Koreas, the partition of the Indian subcontinent and the partition of Palestine. What, however, is the historical relation between decolonisation and partition, if at all? Was partition only a post-1945 phenomenon? Should we understand the mass-scale, often unprecedented violence, forced displacement and refugee crisis generated by partitions – about 700,000 displaced Palestinians is one case, between 15 to 20 million refugees and expellees in India in another – as part of the so-called 'dirty wars' of decolonisation and as inevitable results of what is often called 'the endgame of empire'? Were decolonisation and partition both products of a 'British world-system', to use the words of historian John Darwin,[2] that included informal modes of imperial influence that existed alongside formal and direct imperial control? Or perhaps part of that 'dialectic cycle of European calculations and colonized actions', as Cyrus Schayegh and Yoav Di-Capua put it recently,[3] in which local actors were not passive recipients of decisions imposed on them in a top-down manner from the imperial metropole? Should we continue using the two generic terms, decolonisation and partition, as if they refer to historical events or developments that can be clearly demarcated chronologically, as having a clear beginning and end? Or, rather, should we see them as open and ongoing processes, which continue to shape our politics today? Perhaps, besides being a scar from the past, partition is also an enduring political operation that was never completed and continues to breed pain and distress?

These are seemingly abstract, theoretical questions. But they have contemporary relevance, even urgency. The present chapter attempts to address some of these questions, without necessarily providing a comprehensive and authoritative answer. It suggests that we should trace back the idea of partition to the interwar years and locate it in a British imperial context. Paradoxically as it may seem from a contemporary vantage point, partition emerged as a colonial management tool for maintaining and controlling religious and ethnonational differences within empire, which, at the very same time, is compatible with the new, post-1914 language of self-determination. Next, this chapter argues that we should place the Palestine and India partitions of 1947–48 in a comparative framework or even, to be more precise, as parts of an entangled history that reaches the present.[4] Contemporary historiography has much to tell about the causes of the Palestinian *Nakba* – the term customarily used by Palestinians to mark 1948 as an *annus horribilis* that witnessed a military defeat and a mass eviction of Palestinians from their native lands.[5] Similarly, much has been written about the reckless adventurism and brutality of the Indian partition. And yet, until recently, we avoided connecting the dots that would rescue each of these histories from their horrific exceptionality.

Arguing for an entangled history of partitioned political spaces is not a common trope. National histories and area studies alike – the latter being a product of institutions built during the same postwar moment, as recent studies reminded us[6] – advanced our knowledge of the specifics of each case separately and helped us formulate many of the above questions but tended to treat 'regions' or 'arenas' distinctly, in separation and isolation, and thus have failed to capture these interconnected dynamics adequately. International and diplomatic history acknowledged the 'trans-local' aspects of these calamities. After 1945, struggles between Jews and Palestinian Arabs in mandatory Palestine 'had been sucked into the vortex of Big-Power rivalries', as J. C. Hurewitz put it in his then-ground-breaking, now somewhat forgotten study.[7] It is equally important to acknowledge the fact that the challenges and unprecedented scale of the refugee crises generated by partitions in India, as well as the Middle East, landed at the doorstep of the nascent United Nations. And yet the diplomatic history that examined these dynamics had its blind spots, primarily due to its fixation on the metropole. I would therefore prefer to shift our attention away from the decision-makers and political advisers in New York, Washington and London back to the political actors operating in Jerusalem, Lahore and New Delhi. There is still a long way to go for us to 'provincialise Europe', as Dipesh Chakrabarty called it,[8] but at least we would avoid the obvious trap of mistakenly equating *transnational history* with what is, in fact, a rather traditional account of British and American foreign policy in the early Cold War years.

Next to transnational framing, methodologically, I approach the questions mentioned above equipped with the intellectual historian's toolbox. What motivates me is an attempt to identify a conceptual genealogy and to recover the diverse ways and circumstances in which political keywords such as state, independence, sovereignty, self-government, autonomy and nation-state were coined, distributed and understood, and how partition politics is tied to these processes. Quentin Skinner, the founding father of the Cambridge School of intellectual history, reminds us constantly that these terms are never fixed or frozen. Once the conceptual genealogy unfolds, it reveals the contingent and contestable character of so many of these concepts, even 'the impossibility of showing that it has any essence or natural boundaries'.[9] Following Skinner's guidelines, I also consider teleological narratives to be a form of mythologisation rather than contextualisation, with the postcolonial linear narrative that reads the nation-state as a preconceived and inevitable outcome being a shining example of such coarse teleology. Yet, unlike Skinner, I want to examine how these concepts were translated – literally and figuratively – once they travelled outside the European world. Moreover, unlike some orthodox adherents of the Cambridge School, I see no inherent contradiction between the historicist effort to situate past political theories back in their 'contexts' and being simultaneously engaged in an active, conscious contribution to a 'presentist' conversation on the ways in which past forms of political thought, language and imagination inhabit our world today. It is time to discard the outdated, cliched image of historians as theory-averse empiricist antiquarians, and develop professional 'ethics', as historian Samuel Moyn called it, that provide room 'for speculation for the sake of relevance'.[10]

This is acutely relevant for any historian attempting to understand partition not only as a translational mode of doing politics but also as a political *episteme* that continued shaping political practices in Israel and India, and is still central to the politics of these post-partitioned states today. During the 1990s, the suggestion that a division of territories along ethnoreligious lines would provide a solution to communal animosity enjoyed a surprising, maybe even alarming, comeback. It was no coincidence that Radha Kumar, an Indian observer of international affairs, was among the first to notice that the 1995 Dayton Accords, which were designed to bring the exceptionally vicious ethnoreligious wars in the former Yugoslavia to an end, were to a large degree based on 'partition thinking' and symbolize its resurgence.[11] Whether accidentally or not, the Oslo Accords and 'the two-state solution' in Palestine/Israel resurfaced at the same historical moment.

More than a comeback, partition thinking remained continuously a subcurrent in India and Israel, sometimes also in tension with the attempt to instil democratic institutions in those states. Studying the emergence and evolution of political concepts and ideas should be sharply distinguished from the study of official state ideologies. As Israeli historian Gadi Algazi put it provocatively when discussing the meaning of Zionism today, studying partition primarily as an *ideology* can all too often become a convenient method of downplaying and concealing its current *practices*, which include settlement, unequal allocation of power, colonisation and dispossession.[12] The same applies to contemporary India: while it remains the world's biggest democracy, with a constitution that does not discriminate between people based on faith or ethnicity, one cannot avoid noticing the rise of an exclusionary Hindu nationalist sentiment and a weakening of its democratic institutions. 'If we look at what one might call the hardware of democracy', as Indian historian Ramachandra Guha put it more than a decade ago, Indians are entitled to self-congratulation, but 'if one examines the software of democracy, the picture is less cheering'.[13] During the months this chapter was written and revised, India modified its 1955 Citizenship Act and revoked the Special Status granted to Kashmir in 1947, as explored in the previous chapter by Amit Ranjan. Like India, Israel has also passed a highly controversial Basic Law defining it as a Jewish state and advanced, and later postponed, a plan for the annexation of the occupied territories in the West Bank, with the encouragement of the former US administration, under a pretence of a 'Peace to Prosperity' plan, better known as President Trump's 'Deal of the Century'. Let bygones be bygones? A belief that the demons of seven decades ago no longer haunt us, that they are locked in a tightly sealed Pandora's box, seems illusionary today.

With this present predicament in mind, this chapter suggests that in the process of its crystallisation, partition became a paradigm or a conglomerate of ideas that bundled together demography, territory and post-1919 conceptions of self-government and statehood (often short, surprising as it may sound, of full independence and sovereignty). Next, the chapter reassesses in this light the genesis of the Palestine partition plans (first in 1937, and reintroduced a decade later in 1947). The chapter's first main proposition is that, from this vantage point, the 1947–49 war in Palestine – a constitutive event in both Palestinian and Israeli national histories and collective memory – would be better understood as a *war of partition*. The chapter's second proposition is that neither in India/Pakistan nor in Israel/Palestine did partition prove to be a practical solution as its architects advertised it to be. The idea that two religious and ethnonational communities, which could not cohabit in the bosom of a single country, would miraculously transform into peace-loving neighbouring states rested on profoundly flawed logic, if not a phantasm. If anything, partition only intensified enmity and sedimented particularistic performances of exclusivist nationalism and incompatible religious differences, making these conflicts seem perpetual and intractable.

Its continuous appeal has more to do with the view of the nation-state as a standard, default unit of any political architecture and the limited legal and international imagination that rests on a homogenised mental map of the world based on such states, failing to absorb alternative forms of political organisation and power-sharing.

Minorities as a problem: from Wilsonian principles to ethnic cleansing

Partition is often thought of as a single, painful, maybe even traumatic act ('surgery', 'cut') that has a clear beginning and an end, or as a single, rather simple, political idea. Furthermore, from early on, critics of partition considered it as nothing more than a new formulation of the old imperial 'divide-and-rule' technique, which they contrasted with the benevolent, democratic spirit guiding the new internationalist institutions, whether it was the League of Nations or its successor organisation, the United Nations. In the case of Palestine, examples of this line of argument can be found in speeches given at the UN during the 1948 War: 'The United Kingdom had applied the principle of *divide et impera* in order to retain its position in the Middle East and so fanned the flames of conflict between the Arabs and the Jews', declared Dr Oskar Lange, Poland's delegate to the United Nations Security Council. During the same discussion, the Jerusalem-born Palestinian jurist Henry Cattan also blamed Britain for causing chaos, while emphasising the incompatibility of the very idea of partition with the progressive guiding principles inspiring the international system. Partition, Cattan argued, 'was thus the greatest injustice, the greatest treachery in the history of the world; a violation of the very principles proclaimed in the Covenant [of the League of Nations] and in the Mandate'. For Cattan, on the one end stood the 'sacred trust' that guided the architects of the mandate system, while on the other end was partition: a Machiavellian cunning reaction, causing the derailment of the train leading to self-determination.[14]

The appeal of such rhetorical gestures is obvious. It would be more accurate, however, to identify partition historically as a 'package deal' – i.e. a political design that incorporated at least three critical elements: border-making, state-making and population transfer. Adequately understood, partition is a multifaceted phenomenon that cannot be reduced to either one of the three. One cannot partition without drawing new international borders first, but the erection of geographical barriers alone does not constitute a partition. The newly created borders were made for a specific purpose – to generate new units called states, and states that rest on a clear logic of ethnic 'unmixing'.

Moreover, partition was not a product of a radical deviation from the spirit of the new internationalism as much as one of its products. The origins of this package deal lie firmly in interwar internationalist approaches to reconfiguring global order after the dissolution of some multinational empires – the Hapsburgs, the Romanovs, the Ottomans – and at the time to the remaining victorious Great Powers – Britain and France – could no longer ignore principled demands for 'home rule' and 'self-determination'. The name of the US President Woodrow Wilson is often evoked in these contexts due to his forceful wartime speeches and performances during the Peace Treaty in Versailles. Yet, as a growing number of historians showed in recent years, these left ample room for the continuation of empire.[15] In this new environment, the idea of clear demographic majority–minority relations, or what we may describe as political arithmetic based on a logic of 'counting heads', gained primacy and legitimacy on the international stage. This does not mean that interwar diplomats had no precedents in mind. One cannot deny the fact that the logic of 'counting heads', as David Ludden persuasively showed, was already apparent in Lord Curzon's 1905 division of Bengal – an imperial mass-scale redistricting aimed at separating the mostly Muslim (eastern) areas from the Hindu (western) ones – and that the shift to populations-focused politics, as Eric Weitz argued convincingly, has deep roots in pre-1914 European politics.[16] Indeed, Curzon did not have to wait for the Great War in Europe to end to state authoritatively to the audience at the University of Oxford that '[f]rontiers are indeed the razor's edge, on which hung suspended the modern issues of war or peace, of life or death to nations'.[17]

The First World War and its immediate aftermath do constitute, nevertheless, a watershed. Much more than 'pragmatic' tools for administrative divide and rule of successive empire builders and bureaucrats, such divisions morphed into organising principles that were brought to the forefront of world politics and regarded as compatible with the guiding principles of the League of Nations and the new internationalism. Moreover, the mass-scale forceful removal of populations did not accompany the frontier-making activities of earlier empire builders. After the collapse of a vast number of multinational empires, the new global order that had emerged was 'focused around a conception of discrete population groups, of majorities and minorities within states that represented one particular nationality, and, outside of Europe, of "civilizing" the natives toward self-rule'.[18] Minorities were not only born as a political construct but made their debut on the international stage as a problem to be solved, a challenge confronting the very idea of the nation-state. Empire was still seen by most as providing the best solution to this problem at the time. Lucien Wolf, who became one of the architects of the international minority protection schemes that guided the post-1919 planners, is an exemplar in that respect: an uncompromisingly anti-Zionist British Jew, Wolf was convinced that without protection that would come in the form of imperial citizenship, ethnonational and religious minorities are likely to fall between the cracks, abandoned to the caprice of new sovereign states who consider them a foreign element and potential threat.[19]

Partition was not divorced from this 'counting heads' logic. It emerged at a time when the very words 'majority' and 'minority' migrated into a new semantic field, no longer used exclusively to describe the parameters of parliamentary struggles in which each side in a deliberative assembly or an electoral body had to win a majority but applied after 1919 on communities.[20] The very idea that 'minorities', as the 2001 edition of the *International Encyclopedia of the Social & Behavioral Sciences* defines them, 'are people with distinct characteristics that distinguish them from the majority with whom they are associated' is premised on a relatively recent, century-old way of thinking about human groups.[21]

The proximity of partition politics to the semantic shift that gave new life to the term 'minority' allows us to situate it in more accurate ways temporally as well as geographically. Partition politics did not emerge as an inevitable consequence of the mode of thinking Rogers Brubaker defined as 'groupism' ('the tendency to represent the social and cultural world as a multichrome mosaic of monochrome ethnic, racial and cultural blocks'), but once minority became a word used to describe the relations between groups, and once minority became a challenge that had to be overcome, a problem to be solved.[22] It was even suggested that terms like minority (English) or *minorität* (German) seldom signified religious or ethnonational communities prior to 1918.[23]

Partition, of course, was not the only 'solution' proposed to the 'minority problems'. Until the late 1930s, imperial citizenship and protection were regarded by many as a better solution to the minorities problem, following Lucien Wolf's reasoning line. The series of international agreements known to us as the Minorities Treaties, drawn up between newly created or expanded states and the Principal Allied and Associated Powers, granting certain collective rights to citizens belonging to racial, religious or linguistic minorities, followed from that same idea. Notably, out of the fourteen states that signed such agreements, only two were located outside Europe (Iraq and Turkey).[24]

Counterintuitive as it may seem at first glance, partition proposals belong to the same family. They emerged in the context of an interwar minority protection regime as another technique to manage difference in societies that were described as divided along majority/minority lines, and in particular to appease national demands that were expressed in the idiom of minority protections. Crucially, they emerged in areas controlled by Britain, where there was little desire to allow for full national independence. The same assumptions were guided by the colonial bureaucrats, who could not ignore the language of self-determination and sought to make colonial self-rule a sufficient substitute, as well as by many local national elites.

As the Irish case shows, partition made its first effective appearance during the 1920s as a *tool of containment*: it created a partitioned state by name (Irish Free State) yet one that was incorporated into the Empire, with minimal devolution of power, allowing the continuation of British domination by other means. It neither appeased Irish nationalism nor decreased Protestant–Catholic rivalry. Its attainment hinged ultimately upon the shape and structure of the movement opposing the nationalism of the Irish Catholics: the unionists, who associated with Protestant Britain. As historian Alvin Jackson has shown, the Irish case underlines that, although some unionists toyed with an idea of separation of some sort, the origins of Ireland's partition lay fundamentally within the complexities of British metropolitan politics as both Liberal and (later) Tory politicians worked on the idea of cutting the island in a way that would protect the clear northeastern concentration of unionism, while hoping that attainment of nominal statehood (still formally attached to the Crown) would take the sting out of the anti-British sentiment of the republican Catholics. Ulsterisation was the result, yet it did not emerge, Jackson insists, in the context of any elaborate 'two nations' ideology as in India of the 1940s. Quite the opposite: naively, many 10 Downing Street men hoped that using the language of 'home rule' and 'self-government' would 'propagate imperial swans out of Anglophobic, nationalist ducklings'.[25] When partition was first proposed in the context of the Palestine mandate, in 1937, it was premised on similar assumptions about appeasement and containment of nationalist sentiments under an imperial umbrella. Far more radical, it already included an additional component: the redesign of political spaces also by population transfer.

Assuming that there was some rational thought guiding the British civil servants and the League's devotees in Geneva provides little assistance, however, to those wishing to understand the inconsistent, seemingly erratic behaviour of local elites who endorsed the idea of partition. The traditional accounts of Israeli historians rested on the suggestion that partition was the bitter pill Zionist activists were willing to swallow in order to gain their much-dreamed-of and promised nation-state. Recent historiography provides different explanations. Offering a trenchant critique of traditional teleological interpretations of the Zionist ideology, Israeli historian Dmitry Shumsky shows persuasively that key Zionist thinkers were seldom committed to the idea of the nation-state, and furthermore, many of them were abiding critics of the formula. Thinking as members of a minority national movement operating within multinational empires, Shumsky argues that, before the late 1930s and 1940s, most Zionists were well attuned to the voices of those who preferred the federative and hopefully also more egalitarian multinational state, not the nation-state, and put their energy into pushing towards that goal. They imagined their political future in an autonomous arrangement. If and when they used the term 'state' they were thinking of a state with a lowercase 's', not an independent and sovereign nation-state but as part of a larger federation or confederation.[26] Whether knowingly or unknowingly, Shumsky's book, which constitutes a bold paradigm shift within the context of Zionist history, reveals a dynamic not unfamiliar to scholars of decolonisation. Decolonising actors – colonial subjects who contemplated a better future for themselves – often found regional autonomies, continental (con)federations, commonwealths and leagues to be far more appealing political models than the nation-state.[27] However, Shumsky has little to say about partition, about forced deportations, and about how the Zionists played their cards vis-à-vis the British mandatory power.

In his recent PhD dissertation, aptly entitled 'People Who Count', Nimrod Lin traced and reconstructed this 'arithmetic' logic among Zionist demographers and politicians.[28] Lin put forward a thought-provoking proposition that revealed the extent to which 'state-thinking' was tied to the desire to transcend the status of 'minority' and fill in some of the gaps left open by Shumsky. Once partition was put on the table as a viable option, a potential path to reach statehood, Zionist leaders who in earlier phases envisioned some type of autonomy, shifted gears: precisely because they imagined the future Jewish state as a parliamentary democracy, they began arguing that this democratic regime could be created only *after* a solid Jewish demographic majority would be secured. Based on this reasoning, they did not want to rush to establish a sovereign state before massive Jewish immigration changed the demographic balance or, alternatively, to create a state that would not be democratic until such a majority would be achieved. It was in this context, and following the same logic, that Zionist plans to transfer Palestinian Arabs out of the Jewish state re-emerged. Further complicating the picture, and unsettling our account, was the annihilation of Jews in Nazi-occupied Europe and the imposition of Nuremberg Laws on Jews in parts of Vichy-controlled North Africa intensified the attraction of transfer ideas. Once the Jewish demographic reservoir had been destroyed, Zionist leaders had to search not only for new Jewish candidates for mass immigration but also for ways to engineer a space in which they would constitute a decisive majority.

The case of Vladimir (Ze'ev) Jabotinsky, the founding father of Revisionist Zionism, illustrates this logic and dynamic well. Jabotinsky was a divisive figure during his lifetime. He is remembered today primarily for the hawkish, militarist ethos he developed in essays such as 'The Iron Wall' (1923), which argued that the success of the Jewish colonisation project in Palestine depended on British help in defeating the Arabs militarily and denying them the chance for armed resistance. His early, pre-1914 political career – launched during the Helsingfors (Helsinki) Conference of Russian Zionists (1906), during which he championed the idea of *Gegenwartsarbeit* ('work in the present'), thereby calling to defend national minorities in the Russian Empire while simultaneously promoting Jewish colonisation in Ottoman Palestine – illustrates Shumsky's thesis particularly well. During the late 1920s, he became the first Zionist to enthusiastically endorse the proposal to terminate the mandate and turn Palestine into a dominion that would be added to the British Commonwealth of Nations, alongside Canada, New Zealand, South Africa and more. He solidified his political power, however, outside Palestine (British mandatory authorities regarded him a persona non grata and prevented him from re-entering the country), predominantly in Eastern Europe, in countries that witnessed the most rapid growth of the Betar youth movement. By 1935, the year in which Jabotinsky established the New Zionist Organisation to compete with the mainstream Zionists, Betar leadership could brag having about 70,000 members, attached to about 400 branches, half of whom were in Poland. This dimension of diaspora politics plays a significant role in explaining Jabotinsky's hostile reaction to the first Palestine partition proposal of 1937. Noteworthy in the context of our present discussion, he scrutinised the Peel Commission for toying with the idea of an involuntary removal of Arab communities from the future Jewish state. He wrote:

> The chatter regarding the 'transfer' of Arabs is even more irresponsible. From a Jewish point of view, it is nothing short of a crime. While the Royal Commission babbles on the 'instructive precedent' (that is, the expulsion of more than a million Greeks from Turkey), we witness one of the cases in which it toys with concepts that none of its members have any idea about.[29]

Jabotinsky's denunciation of the Peel Commission's proposal cannot be explained only as a result of an irredentist eagerness not to rip the territory of the 'greater land of Israel' (which included Transjordan in his mind) into tiny pieces alone. It was motivated, no less crucially, by deep-seated anxiety about the consequences such visionary plans might have if and when applied in east-central European states. The Jews of Poland, after all, were protected at the time by the shaky yet still existing minority treaties. As Gil Rubin showed, shortly after the Second World War outbreak, different views were aired. With the collapse of the minority treaties, once mass immigration of East European Jews into Palestine was rendered impossible, Jabotinsky began to advocate for the same transfer of the Arab population from Palestine, which he had objected to so fiercely a few years earlier. The shift in Jabotinsky's thinking, Rubin argues, should be seen as a product of the war. Suddenly and tragically, once earlier predictions about massive immigration were no longer relevant, shifting of the demographic balance had to be achieved through other means. Expulsion, the very same forced displacement he vehemently rejected only four years earlier, was now given a kosher stamp.[30]

These recent studies provide ample evidence that supports the argument that, by the late 1930s, one could not imagine or plan for partition without some form of transfer and ethnic cleansing. The reality on the ground in such pre-partitioned spaces rarely corresponded with the ethnonational phantasm of a nation-state that would emerge 'organically', a nation-state that would ideally be homogenous or, as a minimum, have a clear ethnic majority. Furthermore, democracy came to be seen as a viable or stable option only once it maintained an evident majority–minority equilibrium. Partition's attractiveness rose due to these, precisely because it offered a radical mode of political engineering and redesigning of demography with geography, a project of generating a new 'unmixed' space. In other words, partition came into fruition as a scheme at the moment it could tune into the desire to shift the demographic makeup radically, to meet the criteria of an algebraic logic of democracy. For that reason, it would be hard to find a case of partition which does not involve a considerable degree of ethnic cleansing, forced deportation, or 'transfer' of populations. Unlike older colonial divide-and-rule strategies, the rationale providing the subtext for partition was based on a new logic – the sinister logic of majoritarian democracy.

Because the terms we are evoking here have a provocative sound, and precisely because they arouse profound opposition and fierce scholarly and ideological debates, it is crucial to remind ourselves of what ethnic cleansing is: namely, the systematic forced removal of ethnic/religious groups from a given territory by a more powerful ethnic group, often with the intent of making it ethnically homogenous. The term 'ethnic cleansing' was coined in the early 1990s, in the context of the wars in the former Yugoslavia, following Serbian attacks on the Muslims of Bosnia-Herzegovina. It entered into circulation exactly because scholars were looking for a way to distinguish this mode of ethnic violence from genocidal, annihilationist violence. Ethnic cleansing is not an 'act of extermination' as Raphaël Lemkin defined it, directed against 'ethnic, religious or social collectivities'. Unlike genocide, which is focused on the desire to make the world 'clean' of a specific group of humans, 'ethnic cleansing' is a territory-centric term. It describes a policy of forcibly expelling an ethnic group – often by terror, less frequently by massacre – from a territory claimed by the state. Ethnic cleansing stops at the border. Genocide stops when the group is extinguished and when the genus becomes extinct.[31]

Global reframing: partition as a travelling theory

Understanding the logic of ethnic cleansing is essential if we wish to understand the stages of the war and the perception of the actors on the ground. Notably, the so-called 'Green Line' (1949 armistice borders) and the borders that appear on the maps accompanying the 1947 UN Resolution are not identical, and some battles did not stop at the border. But 'transgressing' these borders was conceived differently and justified in different ways. Zooming out from Palestine/Israel in 1948, the emergence of a logic of ethnic cleansing can also help us better understand the historical voyage of the idea of partition.

At least as far as British political thought goes, I would suggest seeing the 1923 Greco–Turkish exchange of populations as a crucial juncture and an important precedent. The Lausanne Treaty (July 1923) emerged against the backdrop of a long and bitter war, resulting in nearly 1.5 million people swapping homelands from one side of the Aegean Sea to the other. The young Arnold J. Toynbee, not yet a world historian as much as an intelligence expert and policy adviser, witnessed it first hand. For him, the realisation that the non-European Greece (embodying the 'Near East') and Turkey (the 'Middle East') were homogenising themselves, curiously enough, under the auspices and with the blessing of the new internationalist regime indicated that 'inoculation of the East with [Western] nationalism' and set the stage for a new type of clash of civilisations.[32] Though less melodramatic in their rhetoric, other British thinkers and policy advisers also looked at the reshaping of the Near East with great interest. It is neither a coincidence nor a historical accident that figures like Louis Mountbatten, who witnessed the atrocities of the Greco–Turkish War from a safe distance aboard the HMS *Revenge*, reappeared two decades later as India's last Viceroy, supervising Cyril Radcliffe's Boundary Award, which demarcated the boundary line dividing Punjab between India and Pakistan.[33] Not less crucial – these British observers had been encouraged by the fact that the Greco–Turk' exchange' was endorsed, even hailed, by the League of Nations in Geneva, as a liberal solution to the war. Fridtjof Nansen, the flamboyant Norwegian explorer, appointed in 1922 by the League of Nations as its first High Commissioner for Refugees, was also following the events in the Dardanelles closely. For him, peacebuilding required the unmixing of populations, and the separation of Greeks and Turks was justified in his view as preventing violence in the long term.[34] This 'pursuit of homogeneity' gave post-Ottoman Turkey its internationally recognised birth certificate as a sovereign state and was a pivotal moment in the history of interwar internationalism, but it had very little to do with decolonisation. It had more to do with the guiding principles of the League of Nations and its attempt to institutionalise minority protections (it proved impossible to completely cleanse minorities from the territories allocated to the new state, and the safety of the remaining minorities was to be guaranteed by the League).[35] These minority protection regimes collapsed very soon, but the idea of 'population exchanges' between states endured into the post-1945 world.

This Near Eastern or Mediterranean dimension adds a crucial factor that could help us answer the question: was partition an idea transplanted mechanically in different places, a template that was simply copy-pasted? Previous scholarship has already suggested the application of territorial partition in Ireland as a model of sorts for Palestine and, later on, for India. This is true to a large extent. Yet Ireland failed as a viable precedent in at least three senses. First, although the Anglo-Irish Treaty of 1921 granted dominion status for the twenty-six counties of the new Irish Free State, the colonial administrators in Palestine were reluctant to apply such a formula to the Yishuv or to the local Arab population. Talks about admitting Palestine into the Commonwealth like the Irish Free State (which was, despite its name, formally a dominion under the British Crown) never materialised. Second, constrained by the League of Nations in Geneva and by the mandate covenant in Palestine, the British had far less space in which to manoeuvre. Third, and more significantly, while the Irish partition was a pre-Lausanne plan, by the time the Palestine partition scheme was created, partition already included, alongside the idea of territorial division, the notion and vocabulary of population transfer. In this respect, the partitions of Palestine and India, unlike the Irish one, were fundamentally post-Lausanne partitions.

In other words, the fact that partition turned so astonishingly quickly into a 'travelling theory' (to borrow one of Edward Said's phrases[36]), one that connects Ireland, India and Palestine, does not mean that the theory was stable, resisting change. Moreover, the quintessentially British-imperial mindset in which these theories were developed does not mean that British thinkers were incapable of thinking beyond the pale, for they were, in fact, following quite closely other post-1919 political developments. Fast forward to the end of the Second World War, the redrawing of boundaries coupled with mass voluntary and involuntary migration reached new levels. As Israeli historian Yfaat Weiss suggested quite some time ago, we have good reasons to read the 1948 War in Palestine against the backdrop of the remaking of borders in Europe between 1944 and 1948 that resulted in the migration, expatriation and expulsion of millions of human beings. Nation-state formation, ethnic/national displacement and the construction of postwar property regimes after the Second World War in Poland, Czechoslovakia and Israel are all connected by their interrelation to collective memory. We should see 1948 as a watershed moment, according to Weiss: if before that year, ethnic cleansing was viewed on the international stage as basically positive, after this critical juncture it has been largely condemned. To use her words: 'The year 1948 is thus located in a kind of no-man's land between past legitimacy and present illegitimacy.'[37]

Methodologically, the parallelisms identified by Weiss when looking at Central Europe, like the similar patterns of partitions in the British imperial context I emphasise, are not based on comparative history as much as on commitment to a transnational perspective. The comparatists put the phenomena they study side by side, producing lists of similarities and dissimilarities. More crucially, a comparative approach assumes the units one compares – Israel and India, the Middle East and Central Europe – are entirely separate and distinct units of analysis. The transnational historian, on the other hand, treats these units as related to each other, as part of a whole. He or she is not composing lists of shared features, but searching for the shared context that makes these two cases part of a larger story. Much more than an academic fashion, such global or translational reframing is desperately needed to move us beyond entrenched nationalistic narratives, to bridge the artificial divide between Middle Eastern, Israeli and European histories, and gain a deeper understanding of the postwar moment.

Separation before partition

Understanding how partition became a travelling theory, and how it was imported (or transplanted) into new areas, does not mean that we should be divorced from the local circumstances. In other words, this imperial, transnational dimension is not divorced from local conditions, for the somewhat forgotten cantonisation and regional division plans of the mid-1930s that preceded it played a considerable role in preparing the ground, so to speak, to the internationalisation of the division.

References to the Swiss confederal model can already be found in the writings of the members of Brit Shalom in the late 1920s. They can also be found among the British administration: before Lord Peel's Commission of Inquiry arrived in Palestine in 1936, L. G. Archer Cust, the Assistant District Commissioner in Nazareth, played a central role in the story. The long memorandum on cantonisation he prepared for the Colonial Office on 18 January 1935 spoke explicitly of a 'delimitation of Arab and Jewish areas' that would create 'autonomous administrations [enjoying] as much legislative and executive authority as possible'. These, he explained, would 'replace the direct government by Mandatory [forces] by a supervision and inspectorial system'.[38] Not making a single reference to independent sovereign states, Cust's proposal fitted the federalist schema of colonial dominance perfectly. Importantly, in addition to the drawing of new demarcation lines, Cust also proposed the 'abolition of the unnatural and unnecessary Jordan frontier' to link up the Arab regions west and east of the Jordan River. The erasure of the borderline established between Palestine and Transjordan by the British had significant demographic implications: even if substantial Jewish immigration were to be permitted into Palestine, Jews would remain a minority in the new federal entity that would emerge.

The Zionists sent angry letters to the editor of the London *Times* in response, condemning Cust, debating whether the proposal violated the principle of the mandate. It was only a matter of time until the Zionists would come up with an alternative plan.[39] British colonial authorities not only expected such a counterproposal to land on their desks, but practically commissioned it: on 29 June 1936, Assistant Under-Secretary of State Sir (Arthur Charles) Cosmo Parkinson (1884–1967) wrote in a minute submitted to Colonial Secretary William Ormsby-Gore that although the cantonisation proposals 'may ultimately form a basis of a solution of our difficulties … it would be a big advantage if Dr Weizmann were to spontaneously and of his own accord make some suggestion [*sic*] on these lines, for I think the proposal would lose some of its force, and possibly effect if he were in a position to say that the original suggestion came from either the High Commissioner or the Colonial Office'.[40] Unsurprisingly, cantonisation plans surfaced time and again during the sittings of the Peel Commission.[41] When giving their testimonies, Josiah C. Wedgwood and Vladimir Jabotinsky voiced their objections to cantonisation, with Jabotinsky 'prepared to advise the Jews, who would eventually be in the majority in Palestine, to sit down at a round-table conference – a happy family of three, the Jews, the Arabs, and the English adviser'.[42] From these deliberations, we see that the idea of division of some sort was already in circulation when the Peel Commission arrived in Palestine. Moreover, they show the extent to which partition was thought of as a result of a complex pull–push dynamic, in which the 'outsider' colonial administrators and the 'insider' actors negotiated different proposals. Such dialogue was made possible by the hesitance of the very colonial rule that is often considered efficient, potent and confident. But the Commission's meetings also exposed the degree to which the Palestine triangle of Jews, Arabs and the British was not equilateral. The Arab representatives never enjoyed the degree of access to, and respect from, the British authorities enjoyed by the Jewish Agency, and the Arab decision to boycott the committee only increased the asymmetry. Equally clear was the fact that the idea to divide Palestine was not a simple 'colonialist invention' violently imposed on the inhabitants of the land in a top-down manner. The 1937 Palestine partition plan was a result of extended deliberations between outsiders and insiders, and the report's insistence that the two post-partition sovereign

Civil war, total war or a war of partition? 237

states would be linked to Great Britain by a treaty system discloses a very different sentiment than that which we find in India, and ultimately also in Palestine itself a decade later, in 1947.

Civil war? Total war?

We have thus far said very little about the partitions' bloody aftermaths. How should the conceptual genealogy of partition and its reframing in a global context affect how we study the violent conflicts triggered by it, if at all?

The historiography dedicated to examining the communal strife and horrendous atrocities prompted by partition in Ireland in the 1920s and the Indian subcontinent in the 1940s draws a direct line connecting the formal political act of signing a treaty or agreeing on a plan of division and the brutal struggles launched by them. In the Irish case, the term 'civil war' was immediately evoked by the historical actors themselves to describe the fights that broke out after signing the Anglo-Irish Treaty (1921) between the pro-treaty Provisional Government forces and the anti-treaty Irish Republican Army. The historiography endorsed this term, explaining the violent conflict of the 1920s as a fight of 'green against green', to echo the title of Michael Hopkins's popular account of the war, not only cutting the territory in two but also creating a divided society.[13] Though the term 'civil war' occasionally surfaced in British journalists' reportage about the violence in India,[44] it does not seem to be a category used by the local actors, nor does it function as a unified narrative or an umbrella concept in the vast body of secondary literature dealing with the breakup of the British Raj. Yet, it would be difficult to find a serious scholarly account of the violence that spiralled out of control from late 1946 onwards, which disconnects it from the negotiations and agreements made by local politicians and policy advisers, especially when the latter were deemed an extreme case of short-sighted reckless political adventurism.

A much more disjointed historiographical account characterises the literature dedicated to the war of 1948 in the Middle East. Can this conflict – called the War of Independence ('*Atzmaut* or *Komemiyut*) in the official Israeli national history, and *Nakba* (Disaster) in the Palestinian collective memory – be better understood as a war of partition? Naming is framing: the 1948 War was a war of partition, not only because it broke out in the context of United Nations Resolution 181 (II) of November 1947, namely the partition proposal; it was an ethnonational conflict that emerged out of the logic of partition that developed in the interwar period, a war that was about an attempt to reject partition for one side, and about transforming partition from a theory to practice for the other. When we reconstruct the path leading from the 1937 partition proposals to the dramatic events of 1947–49, the 1948 War becomes part of a larger, almost global, trend of reshaping political borders, no longer divorced from similar patterns of violence we see in Ireland and India/Pakistan, nor the 'dirty wars', as Benjamin Grob-Fitzgibbon called the violent decolonisation conflicts that were a permanent feature of the end of empire. Memory activism and struggles of commemoration and counter-commemoration are one of the defining characteristics of our present time.[45] NGOs and political activists' efforts to give visibility to a silenced Palestinian history emerged in response to present pessimism and the asymmetrical power balance between Israelis and Palestinians to come to terms with the conflict's origins and envision a new resolution for the future. They play a crucial role in civil society today, paving the way to a possible grassroots level truth and reconciliation between ordinary Israelis and Palestinians (or maybe, as Israeli sociologist Yifat Gurman suggests, show how reconciliation without truth during the Oslo years is slowly transformed into truth without reconciliation).[46] Nevertheless, an unfortunate side effect of these memory struggles is their tendency to rely on and strengthen the communal-to-atavistic approach to history. They enrich our understanding of the local, but steer us away from any global reframing. Academic historians are often caught in a conundrum, torn between an antiquarian 'positivistic' demand to steer away from presentism on the one hand, and a desire to contribute to this vibrant and charged civil discourse. Rewriting the history of the 1948 War as a war of partition, I suggest, offers a way of transcending this binarism. This is one of the next frontiers that future historiography should tend to.

At least two other alternative terms were evoked by historians who produced accounts of the 1948 War in Palestine: 'civil war' and 'total war'. Here again, naming is framing. Neither term, as far as I know, was used in real-time by the historical actors themselves. They were introduced subsequently by Israeli and Palestinian historians who sought to describe and explain the logic and patterns of violence. Neither term, I suggest, serves us well as a tool for analysis and conceptualisation.

The tag 'civil war' came to be handy as a way of distinguishing between different *phases* of the 1948 War. In particular, it helped historians who sought to differentiate between the violent clashes which took place before mid-May 1948 (that is, while British troops were still present in Palestine, between different Arab and Jewish militias), and the battles which took place after Israel's Declaration of Independence and the founding of the Israeli Defence Forces (IDF) up to the Armistice Agreements of 1949. 'Civil war' is a term used extensively, for example, in the works of Israeli historians such as Benny Morris and Yoav Gelber.[47] It makes an even earlier appearance in the studies of Netanel Lorch (1925–97), a veteran of the Jewish Brigade who fought alongside the Allied Forces in Europe, who also fought in 1948 and was the first Director of the Historical Section of the IDF.[48] For historians of the Israeli armed forces, the term offers an easy way of distinguishing between the actions of the Jewish paramilitary forces before the formal creation of the IDF (the very name was not coined before the end of May 1948, and only in early June did the members of the dissident paramilitary Irgun, headed by Menachem Begin, agree to join it). The term also found its way into the pioneering works of the Palestinian historian Walid Khalidi (b. 1925), one of the cofounders of the Institute for Palestine Studies (established in 1963) in Beirut.[49] Noteworthy is also the suggestion made by Israeli historian Motti Golani to further expand our use of the term beyond the 1948 War, which he considers to be the opening phase of one prolonged war between 1948 and 1973 ('the 25-year war'), during which a 'civil war [over Palestine] between the Jewish-Zionist settler society and Palestinian Arabs' turned into an 'interstate war'. Crucially, the next step in Golani's reframing/renaming argument is to suggest that, with the decline of conventional warfare between the Israeli military and the armies of neighbouring Arab states, 'civil war' made its sinister comeback and that, in fact, as all of Israel's armed conflicts from the 1970s onwards, 'whether inside or outside its own borders, were part of the renewed Palestinian civil war' that followed remarkably similar patterns of violence which one identifies during the British mandatory period.[50] Perhaps one of the term's attractions had to do with the desire of Israeli and Palestinian historians alike to avoid replicating British colonial terminology, which tended to categorise these forms of clashes as 'intercommunal violence'. Either way, today, the phrase 'civil war in [mandatory] Palestine' enjoys wide circulation, including, unsurprisingly, its own Wikipedia entry.[51]

In almost all of these cases, the term 'civil war' functions as a form of *periodisation* more than a comment on the *character of violence* or simply as a substitute for the term' intra-state conflict'. Paradoxical as it may sound, the term became a catchy phrase in part due to the fact that it insinuates that this was an expressly *uncivilised* war. Yet, although few of the most savage encounters which deeply scarred the two communities took place during this initial stage – including the massacres of Deir Yassin (April 9 1948) and the Hadassah medical convoy (13 April 1948) – it would be highly inaccurate to suggest that the 'gloves-off' brutality that characterises guerrilla warfare ended instantly at the minute David Ben-Gurion declared independence and was replaced by 'civilised' regular warfare between conventional armies, and the distinction between combatants and civilians was never transgressed. As far as international law is concerned, the transition into sovereignty did transform the national conflict into an international war, but this did not change the very fact that the territory under dispute was a partitioned space.

As far as Jewish history is concerned, it would be hard to find evidence that a term like civil war captures Jewish perceptions of the events. On the contrary, as Derek J. Penslar showed in his masterful analysis of centuries of Jewish preoccupation with war and the military, Jews seldom used figurative language to described violent events such as civil wars or *Bruderkrieg* (literally, 'brother war' or 'fraternal war', a term associated with the 1866 Austro–Prussian War) and did so only once Jews, who were recruited into rival armies, found themselves fighting their co-religionists. This was an acute dilemma during the First World War, but it had no relevance to the Second World War nor the 1948 War. On the contrary, testimonies of the Jewish overseas volunteers who joined the war effort disclose a strong sense of Jewish trans-local solidarity and a conviction that the war in Palestine continues the war for Jewish survival that was waged in Europe, alongside the 'traditional' motivations of foreign-war volunteers – a search for excitement, adventure and meaning in life, coupled with a strong passion and ideological conviction.[52] If anything, though the term 'civil war' captures the essence of the ethnonational conflict between Zionists and Palestinians, it was used more in intra-Jewish discussions as a warning that the disobedience of the paramilitary groups Etzel and Lehi could easily collapse into internal Jewish strife. After the *Altalena* incident – the shelling of a ship carrying weapons for the Irgun after it refused to surrender its cargo to the provisional Jewish Government (June 1948) – the suggestion that a 'civil war' might erupt and take the shape of a clash between Jews and Jews was no longer seen as an empty warning. Employment of the term 'civil war' (or its Hebrew and Yiddish equivalents – *milhemet ahim* and *broyder krig* – which literally mean 'war of brothers') for intra-Zionist debate can be traced to earlier years. Debates concerning the use of violence often stood at the backdrop: in a speech delivered in Yiddish in Warsaw in 1938, Jabotinsky did not hesitate to refer to a merciless '*broyder krig*' to describe the growing split between the heads of the Jewish Agency, who did not permit acts of revenge against the Arabs (the policy of 'Havlaga'), and the hawkish Revisionist Zionists, and even warned that 'if there will be a *broyder krig* – surely it will not be contained solely within the borders of the Land of Israel'.[53] By 1944, it was necessary for his self-appointed successor, Menachem Begin, to clarify: 'We will not go to civil war. Under no circumstances and despite all the provocations. Whatever happens, our soldiers will not use their arms against rival Jews.'[54] 'Civil war' here served as an intra-Jewish marker and reminder that the boundaries demarcating the close-knit ethnonational community are uncrossable.

Ultimately then, while the term 'civil war' illuminates the nature of the violent dispute in Palestine, it blurs it, for it implies that the war violated a pre-existing shared sense of brotherhood – that it was a war *within* a state that was fracturing due to a crisis of legitimacy and representation. As such, the term 'civil war' is a gross mischaracterisation of the political conditions in Palestine between November 1947 and May 1948, and is not really tied to the way the belligerents understood themselves either. The war was not the tearing of a single *civitas* (political community, a social body of the *cives* [citizens]), but an intercommunal conflict over the same country.[55] Nor am I familiar with contemporaneous primary sources in which Jews and Arabs compared themselves to Romulus and Remus or to Cain and Abel. Levels of hostility ran so high that even the biblical tropes of Jacob and Esau or Isaac and Ishmael were pushed sideways. In that sense, 'civil war' fails to function as a 'category of experience' which can be refracted through language and memory, the same way it does offer an unimpeachable theoretical model that captures some presumed essence of the event.

A second, less common, and probably also less convincing reframing effort involved introducing the term 'total war' to describe the 1948 War.[56] Unlike 'civil war', a concept with an exceptionally lengthy historical trajectory stretching back to antiquity, 'total war' is a quintessential twentieth-century term. It enjoys a notable intellectual pedigree nonetheless, echoing Erich Ludendorff's notorious proto-Nazi *Der totale Krieg* (1935, translated as *The Nation at War*) as well as Raymond Aron's alarmist Cold War liberal tome, *Les Guerres en Chaîne* (1951, translated as *The Century of Total War* 1954). Ludendorff's book was a hybrid treatise that mixed analysis of the German military's poor performance during the First World War with an authoritarian vision for the future. It envisioned total mobilisation of the state's workforce and economic resources for the purposes of warfare, ultimately resulting in cancelling out all distinctions between the military and civilian spheres and between times of war and peace, turning the nation-state into an efficient war machine led by a supreme military commander.[57] Aron, on his part, was motivated by a deep-seated Cold War anxiety concerning the ability of the fragile 'restored democracies' of Western Europe to withstand the destructive forces of modern warfare. Like Ludendorff, the apostle of 'total war', Aron also believed that the First World War unleashed an apocalyptic war of a new kind, while trusting that a European unity of some sort, accompanied by greater US involvement in the continent, would make European democracy safe from Soviet communism.[58]

The attempt to answer the question of whether a 'total war' of this kind ever existed in practice, as an empirical reality outside these intellectual treatises, is beyond the scope of this chapter. Nor will we able to evaluate here the degree to which historians like David A. Bell, who tried to extend the term's chronology and scope, added analytic precision to our understanding of modern warfare.[59] It would be worth pointing out, however, that there was a considerable gap separating the grandiose aspirations to reach a complete mobilisation of all of society's resources from the poor infrastructure and the actual limited military and economic resources available to any side in the 1948 War. As far as the Jewish side is concerned, there is no doubt that during the war – which immediately came to be seen as a struggle for existence in the wake of the Holocaust of European Jewry – political leaders like David Ben-Gurion and Eliezer Kaplan sought to centralise power, to utilise state authority and to mobilise the entire Jewish public in practically every sector of the economy. But were these actually successful? During the first months of the war, when the country was still ruled by the British, there was no adequate infrastructure to allow effective or full mobilisation. Recruitment calls requiring unmarried men born between these and other dates to report to recruitment bureaus were published in the Hebrew press or on bulletin boards in Jewish settlements, but they were not so much orders as advertisements encouraging recruitment. Success rates in recruiting large numbers of fighters were a function of morale, public pressure and ideological commitment. Although the recruitment percentages were high, they fell short of full mobilisation. Sanctions were used to push people to perform military service or perform essential labour services. Still, the sticks used by the Zionist authorities against those who did not conform did not include imprisonment but primarily involved public shaming, expulsion from labour organisations or calls to dismiss them from their jobs. Serious attempts were made to adjust the economy to serve the war effort, such as ensuring a supply of essential services, supplies and financing. Emergency regulations were introduced to improve control over the agriculture sector and town fortification, and a higher number of women entered the labour force. At the same time, the Yishuv leadership still relied heavily on diaspora support that came in the form of international volunteers and philanthropy.

Ultimately, the 1948 War in Palestine followed a familiar pattern of partition violence that one can also find in the cases of Ireland in the 1920s and South Asia in 1947, blurring the distinction between combatants and non-combatants, a hybrid of 'civil war' and 'conventional war', involving an amalgam of paramilitary forces and conventional armies, local forces and external support which came in the shape of foreign volunteers as well as funding.[60] Reframing our understanding of the 1948 War in Palestine, and seeing it as a war of partition, reveals the striking similarity this conflict had to the violence triggered by partition plans in Ireland and India/Pakistan in several ways. In particular, the similar dimensions pertain to the above-mentioned 're-engineering' of space: the political project of partition is either denied or continued and executed by other means, as military forces become the vehicle needed to turn religious and ethnically diverse regions into homogeneous 'homelands'. Additionally, the shared context of partition helps to highlight the fact that all three conflicts took place in similar circumstances, at the wake of global wars, that they were hybrid conflicts that included, alongside regular armies, paramilitaries ('irregulars'), civilians and out-of-the-country volunteers, and that in all cases veterans from the British imperial troops, who acquired the know-how of professional soldiering, brought their skill set into the war of partition.

Perpetuating partition after the war: legal mechanisms

Violence, indeed, played a central role in the 're-engineering' of space. Yet the partition as a project was not accomplished on the day armistice agreements were signed. Reframing 1948 as a war of partition can also help us better understand some of the fundamental institutional and legal mechanisms that were created during the war, or in its immediate aftermath, that were designed as tools of partition, as well as the odd 'division of labour' between these states' legal institutions and the international norms and organisations that were put in charge of aiding and protecting refugees.

Grey-state bureaucrats seldom attract scholarly attention. They were not necessarily the ones to draw the new international borders, but they did play a pivotal role in applying state authority and legal jurisdiction, which was vital for turning partition into a fact on the ground. Take, for example, Vazira Zamindar's book, *The Long Partition*, which provides numerous examples of the ways in which an emergent legal apparatus accompanied the creation of the new nation-states of India and Pakistan, further marginalising and pushing out north Indian Muslims into Pakistan.[61]

The dynamic in post-1948 Israel/Palestine – where the war did not create two nation-states in western Palestine that could enjoy 'reciprocity' but only one state and a looming refugee crisis – was radically different, for evident reasons. The legal mechanisms that were developed to respond to that new reality were not divorced from a broader, trans-local way of thinking. Take, for example, Israel's 1950 Absentee Property Law and Development Authority (Transfer of Property) Law, which is arguably the most efficient legal instrument created by Israel to turn 'abandoned' Palestinian properties into Israeli ones. As shown by the legal historian Alexandre (Sandy) Kedar, the dubious legal mechanism that allowed the appropriation of abandoned property was based on the logic of partition and was copied from South Asia precisely because its designers were operating under the assumption that similar conditions would emerge in Palestine/Israel.[62] Jurisprudence experts were not necessarily the first ones to identify the potential of borrowing ideas and practices from India and Pakistan: in the case of the Absentee Property Law, it was the cartographer Zalman Lifschitz (later Leef), appointed the Prime Minister's and Foreign Minister's Adviser on Lands and Borders, who closely followed the political developments in the Indian subcontinent and meticulously analysed the legislative processes involved. In a memo submitted to Israeli Prime Minister David Ben-Gurion in March 1949, Lifschitz asserted that India and Pakistan, which were dealing with similar dilemmas, had created the main legal precedents that should inform the Israeli legislator. As opposed to British law, which had limited the state's ability to seize enemy property to times of emergency and war, these precedents created civil mechanisms for the management and development of lands expropriated by the Government (i.e. settlement by Jews). During the stormy parliamentary discussions that ensued, the Jewish National Fund's legal adviser, Aharon Ben-Shemesh, backed Lifschitz's report, as did Treasury Minister Eliezer Kaplan.

The fact that Lifschitz turned his gaze to Pakistan rather than Britain should not surprise us. As demonstrated recently by Rephael Stern, in forging a new legal landscape for the new state separate from the legal norms set by the British, in 1948–49, Israeli legal thinkers would often cite examples from other new states that resisted the idea that they should be seen, from a legal point of view, as successor states following the colonial power. Hence Israeli lawmakers cited the Irish Free State, another fruit of partition, that had proclaimed that obligations arising from their predecessor's treaties were not inherently binding, or Tanganyika's refusal to consider British treaties as automatically applying to itself, and Pakistan, that declined to enforce British arbitration treaties.[63]

No less striking is the fact that the forgotten drafts of Israel's Constitution were also based on the logic of partition, as I argued recently, in the context of the tempestuous debates surrounding Israel's controversial Basic Law defining Israel and the Jewish Nation-State.[64] Debates concerning Israel's short-lived failed attempt to create a constitution tend to overlook the fact that this constitution was first mentioned in UN Resolution 181 (II) of November 1947, which anticipated that a constitution would be accepted for each of the states that would be created in post-partition Palestine. Next, it made it into Israel's Proclamation of Independence (14 May 1948), which declared that a constitution 'shall be adopted by the Elected Constituent Assembly not later than the 1st October 1948'.[65]

Several preliminary versions of that future constitution were prepared during those dramatic months, with one in particular, drafted in late 1947 or early 1948 by Dr Leo (Yehuda Pinchas) Kohn, the Secretary of the Jewish

Agency's Political Department, and modelled after the Constitution of the Irish Free State. Kohn's initial sketch was anchored in the circumstances of the time: it stated that the seat of government would be on Mount Carmel and not in Jerusalem, which was to become a corpus separatum (separated body) belonging to neither of the two partitioned states, and suggested names such as Yehuda, Zion, The Land of Israel or The Western Land of Israel for the future state. And although it defined the state as 'the national home of the Jewish people', it purposely refrained from delegating the job of determining who is a Jew to an Orthodox Chief Rabbi – an attempt to prevent the rabbinate from playing a role equivalent to the Catholic Church in Ireland – and envisioned instead that there would be no state endowment of any religion.[66]

Kohn's proposals were taken seriously, going through several cycles or revisions and rewriting. Thus, when the members of the People's Council declared Israel an independent state, following the wording of Resolution 181 and stating that an elected Constituent Assembly (*H'assefa Hamechonenet*) would prepare a constitution for the new state by 1 October 1948, they had already an initial sketch in mind. The constitutional committee was formed on 8 July 1948. On 25 January 1949, the first general election was held for the Constituent Assembly, whose function was to establish a constitution and then disseminate and declare new elections to the legislature. And yet, the members of this Assembly and First Knesset not only missed the deadline they imposed on themselves, but also failed to propose an agreed-upon constitution. Over time, several constitutional proposals were submitted to a constitutional committee, but all were rejected because of objections and disagreements. More than extreme wartime conditions, what explains the failure to come up with a constitution has more to do with the pushback coming from the representatives of the Orthodox community, who found Kohn's proposal too liberal and secular. It was predominantly an intra-Jewish debate between those who sought to replicate a liberal or republican constitution, and those worried that a modern constitution would come into conflict with Jewish law. It revealed the large gaps between the democratic and Jewish elements in the new polity, and the decision to avoid deciding – not to ratify the Constitution – may have been yet another attempt to prevent catalysing an even more immense gulf between the two camps.[67]

Palestinian Arabs who remained within the territory of the new Israeli state became a minority in their own land, comprising about 15 per cent of the general population, and were put under strict military rule (established on 21 October 1948, and nullified only in 1966).[68] Metaphorically as well as literally, these and other non-Jewish citizens of the new state were not invited to participate in the debate over Israel's Constitution, nor played a role in torpedoing the initial effort to create one. Poignantly, the legal instrument used by Israel's provisional government to impose military rule over its Arab citizens was the Defence (Emergency) Regulations enacted by the British mandatory government in 1945 to combat Jewish anticolonial insurgency. This seemingly inconsistent dynamic, whereby the new post-partitioned state could at once distinguish itself from the colonial *ancien régime* when that fitted its needs, while using other devices it inherited from its predecessors, should not surprise us. It problematises simplistic accounts about a complete rupture from the colonial age, as it scrutinises the suggestion that the postcolonial state is nothing but an offshoot busy copying and imitating its colonial ancestor.[69] These were the colonial and the immediate postcolonial roots of what Israeli historian Nitzan Lebovic aptly described as 'a strange constitutional hybrid between a liberal [Hans] Kelsenian understanding of universal law and an authoritative, Jewish, and etatist approach to politics'.[70]

Preventing Palestinian refugees from returning to their original homes and claiming Israeli citizenship on the one hand, and the passing of Israel's Law of Return (*ḥok hashvūt*, in July 1950) signified the culmination of a process by which the new post-partition state defined itself as a receptacle for Jewish refugees while handing over to the UN Relief and Works Agency for Palestine Refugees in the Near East (established in 1949) the task of tending to the stateless Palestinian refugees.[71] This was a post-partition 'division of labour' which Israelis and Palestinians live with to this day, in which the new nation-state is understood as a vehicle meant to protect and empower one ethnic element at the expense of other ethnic minorities while delegating the task of refugee rehabilitation and resettlement to international organisations.

Conclusion: 'unfinished business', not a 'closed event'

Let us return to the question that opened this chapter: what, if at all, is the historical relation between decolonisation and partition? Decolonisation is the umbrella term historians use to describe the withdrawal of European powers from former colonies, traditionally subdivided into three 'waves' or 'phases', stretching from the mid-1940s to the end of the 1970s. The first phase, happening in the immediate aftermath of the Second World War and resulting in the independence of India, Pakistan, Ceylon/Sri Lanka and Burma/Myanmar, is particularly important in the context of our present discussion. And yet, to equate partition with decolonisation involves a categorical confusion between a historical *phenomenon* and the historical *context* in which the phenomenon evolved and manifested itself. A transnational recontextualisation of the first three British partitions – Ireland,

Palestine and India – provides the most precise possible view of the difference between the origins of this idea in the interwar years and its execution in the radically different circumstances of post-1945 world politics. As Penny Sinanoglou shows in her recent, empirically rich, authoritative account of British colonial policy in Palestine, during its short but dramatic career, partition 'shifted from a tool of imperial control to one of internationally managed decolonization'.[72] Quite so. Once we zoom out from Palestine, we can identify even more clearly that partition was actually born as a strategy of British imperial rule across different territories, emerging in the interwar years in the context of intra-imperial reform and restructuring. Partition was not the good old *divide et impera* method of imperial conquest and expansion. For colonial domination, like nationalism, also comes in a variety of forms and colours. Partition was a twentieth-century imperial control technology born out of an attempt to 'contain' nationalism and uphold the Empire's integrity, not the desire to grant independence and quit the stage.

The gap between the original intentions and the outcome could never be more striking: partition emerged as an idea anchored in imperial federalist thought, an attempt to divide territories based on ethnonational demographic logic without abandoning the Empire, ended up in post-1945 conditions as a quick and dirty strategy for an empire that was breaking down rapidly. Ironically, when it emerged, it was anchored in the language of 'diversity within unity', not the logic of sovereign nation-states standing by themselves, divorced from empire, and lacking any trace of even the loosest federal tie. Post-1945, in order to become 'visible' and 'recognisable' in the international arena, former colonial subjects were prompted to organise themselves in nation-states, demolishing traces of former cohabiting and accentuating protean ethnic, linguistic and religious differences.[73] Decolonisation is, for that reason, a term that should be distinguished from partition. At the same time, it is a term that can help us better understand the specific political circumstances, modes of thought, and the diplomatic context in which partition moved from theory to practice. As decolonisation unfolded and the nation-state became the default mode of political organisation, partition became fashionable, but this was also when the term changed its original meaning.

Conveniently ignoring partition's disastrously violent history and its imperial roots is no longer an option. What is not less striking about the conventional understanding (nay, justifications) of partition was the way it fitted with the master-narratives offered by older postcolonial national histories. Whether state-sponsored or not, post-independence histories tend to be both teleological, localised and apologetic. They were *teleological* due to the reductive way they approached the messiness of the past, seeking to distil the one linear road ('nation-building'), leading inevitably to the pathos-filled moment of national independence. Once we assume that all roads lead to Rome, all alternative political paths are considered dead ends; once the nation-state ('Rome') is viewed as the end of the long journey, it is hard to recognise the fact that formal national sovereignty seldom marked the end of informal dependence on greater powers. Second, there is an inherent paradox of *localism* in these teleologies: the national histories are produced by the experts who interpret the idioms and customs of a particular locality, by authors who are invested in identifying the 'uniqueness' and 'unprecedented' nature of the specific test case they study. They do not merely steer away from broader transnational or global patterns or contexts. They are incapable of recognizing the very fact that narrating past events in such a manner is not unique but is the standard template of historical tales produced in postcolonial states. In numerous cases, the moment of independence is presented as the culmination point of a long, inevitable historical process of national liberation and never as a historical contingency. This is not unique but a trademark of postcolonial states' self-narration. Lastly, these master-narratives are *apologetic* because they are invested in minimising – and, when possible, erasing – all traces of criminal levels of violence that accompanied these mythical moments of independence. Partition and its bloody aftermath are rendered the 'pangs of birth' of the nation, narrated as an epic account of the nation's migration from servitude to freedom. Nationalist historians would seldom volunteer to ruin this triumphant tale by obsessing over the 'dark side' of independence and sovereignty.

Tracing back the idea of partition to the interwar years and locating it in a British imperial context allows us to scrutinise some conventional teleological narratives about the road to national sovereignty. Above all, the pre-1947/48 history of partition politics shows that it emerged first and foremost as one piece of an imperially sponsored restructuring of the global order along ethnonational lines, corresponding to the new language of self-determination of the so-called 'Wilsonian Moment', as historian Erez Manela called it, but not as a means to promote decolonisation *avant la lettre*.[74] On the contrary, partition was part of a new sophisticated arsenal of political tools of indirect and informal imperial rule. And yet, the way in which the theory turned into practice in 1947–48, in the context of imperial breakdown, changed its meaning. Ultimately, partition turned into a quick and dirty 'exit strategy' of an empire in retreat, the opposite of the original intentions. Read from that angle the story of partition – and the road to 1948 – turns about to be a story of unintended consequences.

Are partitions done deals, traumatic events that belong to the past alone? Metaphors often shape our imagination as well as our historical understanding.

Too many of the accounts of partition available to us are predicated on a misreading of partitions as short but traumatic 'closed events', rather than seeing them as initiations of a re-engineering project of political spaces and an ongoing process. That is, we tend to understand partition as a painful, maybe even traumatic, act ('surgery', 'cut') with a clear beginning and an end. This reading is misleading whether we are discussing Israel/Palestine or the South Asian context. As anthropologist Cabeiri Robinson writes in her study of Jammu and Kashmir, the in-between and in-betwixt regions that serve as reminders of partition's 'unfinished' nature: 'Partition is still too often approached as a historical event that produced an immediate and clear rupture between Pakistan and India. It is better understood as a long process of creating a new categorical and classificatory system that established political and cultural (rather than simply territorial) separations between the new nation-states.'[75]

Partitions created what could best be described as *partitioned* (and not necessarily postcolonial) *political spaces* in which ethnonational separations are conceived as an ongoing project. Put otherwise, 'sufficient' or 'complete' partition was never a reality that was fully achieved on the ground, but a distant horizon. In partitioned spaces, nationalised actors are participating in a process, striving towards a future 'stable' state, which would have a clear ethnonational or religious-national majority. Such a design could be accomplished through constant engineering of space to fit demography, state discrimination against minorities, and, when needed, forced deportation. Read this way, the history of partition is far from triumphant. Instead, it serves as a reminder of post-Wilsonian democratic thought's built-in weakness, which finds it difficult to imagine a stable and well-organised state not based on a clear ethnonational and religious majority.

British playwright Howard Brenton captured this idea well in his 2013 play, *Drawing the Line*, retelling the story of Cyril Radcliffe's Boundary Commission, which provides the motto for this chapter: partitions are like scar tissue left by the Empire, – dangerous, for they can easily flare up. Although the cataclysmic events of 1947–48 are gone, partition is still with us. In Israel today, as in India and Pakistan, the triumph of partition politics keeps on shaping the politics of both regions. Indeed, rather than being a 'done', finished historical event, partition was and remains a syndrome still in the making. We are interested in partitions because they are still with us, and they continue to cast a long shadow on our present. It is not only that they failed to provide a magic solution to communal, religious or ethnonational conflicts. These partitions were not painful, but short surgeries that came to an end and succeeded. Partition jumps back out of dusty history books precisely because it is an ongoing process and 'unfinished business', continuing to shape the domestic and the foreign politics in all these countries. We need to understand it in order for us to understand own our own history and to evaluate the way it continues to govern us. We need to capture how partition functions, ultimately, as a specific form of engagement with a heterogeneous social and political world, as a mode of understanding and reshaping it, as a political episteme: it shapes not only collective memories of past traumas and events, but also present fears, anxieties and conceptions of the geopolitical space and, consequently, political visions for the future.

If history is here to provide us with a perspective, understanding how the local conflict was connected to larger, global processes, and recognising how strikingly similar the patterns of violence in Israel/Palestine and the ones we find elsewhere in the post-1945 world, are part of the project. Arguments about the uniqueness and exceptionality of the Israeli–Palestinian conflict are, in that respect, utterly unhelpful. Unsurprisingly, they would often come from those entrenched in a nationalistic reading of history. It was George Orwell, prophetic as always, who recognised the risks of selective nationalist memory as early as May 1945, when he wrote:

> All nationalists have the power of not seeing resemblances between similar sets of facts. ... The nationalist not only does not disapprove of atrocities committed by his own side, but he has a remarkable capacity for not even hearing about them. ... A known fact may be so unbearable that it is habitually pushed aside and not allowed to enter into logical processes, or on the other hand it may enter into every calculation and yet never be admitted as a fact, even in one's own mind.[76]

Too many young Israelis today are subject to a project of state-sponsored denial and historical amnesia. Growing up in Israel, I consumed and later taught textbooks that do not recognise the Palestinian Other. Recent years' attempts to outlaw the use of the term *Nakba* prolong the ban on declassification of archival documents that are now more than seven decades old because they might appear embarrassing or disquieting, and prohibit the publication of hundreds of photos from 1947–49, a visual record of Palestine's ethnic cleansing, are alarming symptoms of this aggressive amnesia. Paradoxically, the immense energy dedicated to attempts to hide our past only remind us how much partition is still here with us. Increasing separation and segregation, the hallmarks of contemporary Israeli politics, have a long past to draw upon, predating the post-Oslo moments. Increase in separation measures through fences – physical, legal and administrative barriers – the myriad ways in which contemporary Jewish-Israel frames itself speaks to a sad truth: contemporary desires to separate are the transfigured products of these earlier forbears.

Notes

1 Howard Brenton, *Drawing the Line* (London: Nick Hern Books, 2013), p. 70.
2 John Darwin, *The Empire Project: The Rise and Fall of the British World-System, 1830–1970* (Cambridge: Cambridge University Press, 2009).
3 Cyrus Schayegh and Yoav Di-Capua, 'Roundtable: Why Decolonization?', *International Journal of Middle East Studies* 52 (1) (2020), 37–45, at 139.
4 Arie M. Dubnov, 'Jewish Nationalism in the Wake of World War I: A "State-in-the-Making" or the Empire Strikes Back? [in Hebrew]', *Israel: Studies in Zionism, and the State of Israel* 23 (2016), 5–35; Arie M. Dubnov, 'Notes on the Zionist Passage to India, Or: The Analogical Imagination and its Boundaries', *Journal of Israeli History* 35 (2) (2016), 77–214; Arie M. Dubnov, 'On Vertical Alliances, "Perfidious Albion" and the Security Paradigm', *European Judaism* 52 (1) (2019), 67–110; Arie M. Dubnov and Laura Robson (eds), *Partitions: A Transnational History of Twentieth-Century Territorial Separatism* (Stanford, CA: Stanford University Press, 2019).
5 The word *Nakba* (نكبة), literally meaning 'the catastrophe', made its first appearances during the war itself. It was introduced into scholarly writing as early as 1948 by Constantin Zurayk, a Damascus-born Christian historian, in his book *Ma'nā an-nakba*, which appeared in English translation eight years later: Constantine K. Zurayk, *The Meaning of the Disaster*, translated by Richard Bayly Winder (Beirut: Khayat's College Book Cooperative, 1956). As an avid supporter of a broad-based Arab nationalism, Zurayk considered Palestine an integral part of the 'Arab nation' and thus used *Nakba* to signal a double collapse, both of Arab nationalism and a broader anti-colonialist struggle in the region. For additional early uses of the term, see Shay Hazkani, *Dear Palestine: A Social History of the 1948 War* (Stanford, CA: Stanford University Press, 2021), chapter 1, esp. pp. 63–65. Research, documentation and efforts at preservation of Palestinian heritage developed considerably with the establishment of the Institute of Palestine Studies (1963) and the Palestine Liberation Organisation Research Center (1965), both in Beirut, though access to documents held by Israeli state authorities remains a challenge to this day. Notably, the meaning of the term did not remain frozen in time. Given the continuation of the Palestinian refugee crisis, and particularly after the Occupation of Gaza and the West Bank during the 1967 war on the one hand and with the rise of settler colonial studies in academic circles on the other hand, *Nakba* is no longer a term referring to a single historical event as much as an ongoing process that combines military occupation, discriminatory policies, persecution and forcible displacement. For further discussion see Anaheed Al-Hardan, 'Al-Nakbah in Arab Thought: The Transformation of a Concept', *Comparative Studies of South Asia, Africa, and the Middle East* 35 (3) (2015), 622–638; Honaida Ghanim, 'From *Kubaniya* to Outpost: A Genealogy of the Palestinian Conceptualization of Jewish Settlement in a Shifting National Context', in Marco Allegra, Ariel Handel and Erez Maggor (eds), *Normalizing Occupation: The Politics of Everyday Life in the West Bank Settlements* (Bloomington: Indiana University Press, 2017), pp. 151–171; Areej

Sabbagh-Khoury, 'Tracing Settler Colonialism: A Genealogy of a Paradigm in the Sociology of Knowledge Production in Israel', *Politics & Society* 50 (1) (2021), 44–83.

6   Ali Mirsepassi, Amrita Basu and Frederick Stirton Weaver (eds), *Localizing Knowledge in a Globalizing World: Recasting the Area Studies Debate* (Syracuse, NY: Syracuse University Press, 2003); Zachary Lockman, *Field Notes: The Making of Middle East Studies in the United States* (Stanford, CA: Stanford University Press, 2016).

7   J. C. [Jacob Coleman] Hurewitz, *The Struggle for Palestine* (New York: Norton, 1950), p. 309. The book originates in Hurewitz's wartime work at the Near East Desk of the Office of Strategic Services, an important breeding ground for area studies expertise. See Osamah F. Khalil, *America's Dream Palace: Middle East Expertise and the Rise of the National Security State* (Cambridge, MA: Harvard University Press, 2017), pp. 43–44.

8   Dipesh Chakrabarty, *Provincializing Europe: Postcolonial Thought and Historical Difference* (Princeton, NJ: Princeton University Press, 2000).

9   Quentin Skinner, 'A Genealogy of the Modern State: British Academy Lecture', *Proceedings of the British Academy* 162 (2009), 325–370, at 326.

10 Samuel Moyn, 'History and Political Theory: A Difficult Reunion', *Theory & Event* 19 (1) (2016), muse.jhu.edu/article/607285.

11 Radha Kumar, 'The Troubled History of Partition', *Foreign Affairs* 76 (1) (1997), 22–34. A similar observation was made by the LSE-based political scientist Sumantra Bose (great-grandson of the controversial anti-British radical leader Subhas Chandra Bose) and developed in his book: Sumantra Bose, *Contested Lands: Israel–Palestine, Kashmir, Bosnia, Cyprus, and Sri Lanka* (Cambridge, MA: Harvard University Press, 2007).

12 Gadi Algazi, 'Zionism in the Present Tense', in Michaela Birk and Sfeffen Hagemann (eds), *The Only Democracy?: Zustand Und Zukunft Der Israelischen Demokratie* (Berlin: Aphorism A, 2013), pp. 47–62.

13 Ramachandra Guha, *India after Gandhi: The History of the World's Largest Democracy* (New York: Ecco, 2007), p. 738.

14 Comments on the Progress Report Nations Mediator (a/648): 217th Meeting, Held at the Palais De Chaillot, Paris, on Monday 22 November 1948, A/C.1/SR.217. United Nations Digital Library, at https://digitallibrary.un.org/record/774025?ln=en (accessed 14 March 2023). I would like to thank Victor Kattan for bringing this document to my attention.

15 Erez Manela, *The Wilsonian Moment: Self-Determination and the International Origins of Anticolonial Nationalism* (Oxford: Oxford University Press, 2007); Mark Mazower, *Governing the World: The History of an Idea* (New York: Penguin, 2012); Glenda Sluga, *Internationalism in the Age of Nationalism* (Philadelphia: University of Pennsylvania Press, 2013); Susan Pedersen, *The Guardians: The League of Nations and the Crisis of Empire* (Oxford: Oxford University Press, 2015); Mira L. Siegelberg, *Statelessness: A Modern History* (Cambridge, MA: Harvard University Press, 2020).

16 David Ludden, 'Spatial Inequity and National Territory: Remapping 1905 in Bengal and Assam', *Modern Asian Studies* 46 (3) (2012), 483–525; Eric D. Weitz,

'From the Vienna to the Paris System: International Politics and the Entangled Histories of Human Rights, Forced Deportations, and Civilizing Missions', *American Historical Review* 113 (5) (2008), 313–343.
17 George Nathaniel Curzon, *Frontiers*, Romanes Lecture, 1907 (Oxford: Clarendon Press, 1908), p. 7.
18 Weitz, 'From the Vienna to the Paris System', p. 1326.
19 Mark Levene, *War, Jews, and the New Europe: The Diplomacy of Lucien Wolf, 1914–1919* (Oxford: Oxford University Press, 1992).
20 On this point I rely on Till van Rahden, *Vielheit: Jüdische Geschichte Und Die Ambivalenzen Des Universalismus* [*Plurality: Jewish History and the Ambivalence of Universalism*] (Hamburg: HIS Hamburger Edition, 2022).
21 Zig Layton-Henry, 'Minorities', in Neil J. Smelser and Paul B. Baltes (eds), *International Encyclopaedia of the Social and Behavioral Sciences*, 1st edn (Oxford: Pergamon, 2001), pp. 9894–9898.
22 Rogers Brubaker, *Ethnicity without Groups* (Cambridge, MA: Harvard University Press, 2004).
23 Van Rahden, *Vielheit*.
24 The other twelve were (in alphabetical order) Albania, Austria, Bulgaria, Czechoslovakia, Estonia, Greece, Hungary, Latvia, Lithuania, Poland, Romania and Yugoslavia. Turkey was one of the last states to sit down at the negotiation table with the Allied Powers, but in the Turkish case it was the Lausanne Treaty (1923) that became the defining document which set out a series of rights and freedoms for the non-Muslim minorities. See Yeşim Bayar, 'In Pursuit of Homogeneity: The Lausanne Conference, Minorities and the Turkish Nation', *Nationalities Papers* 42 (1) (2014), 108–125; Lerna Ekmekcioglu, 'Republic of Paradox: The League of Nations Minority Protection Regime and the New Turkey's Step-Citizens', *International Journal of Middle East Studies* 46 (4) (2014), 657–679.
25 Alvin Jackson, 'Irish Unionists and the Empire, 1880–1920: Classes and Masses', in Keith Jeffery (ed.), *An Irish Empire?: Aspects of Ireland and the British Empire* (Manchester: Manchester University Press, 1996), pp. 123–148, at p. 124. See also Alvin Jackson, *Home Rule: An Irish History, 1800–2000* (New York: Oxford University Press, 2003).
26 Dmitry Shumsky, *Beyond the Nation-State: The Zionist Political Imagination from Pinsker to Ben-Gurion* (New Haven, CT: Yale University Press, 2018).
27 Michael Collins, 'Decolonisation and the "Federal Moment"', *Diplomacy & Statecraft* 24 (1) (2013), 21–40; Frederick Cooper, *Citizenship between Empire and Nation: Remaking France and French Africa, 1945–1960* (Princeton, NJ: Princeton University Press, 2014); Gary Wilder, *Freedom Time: Negritude, Decolonization, and the Future of the World* (Durham, NC: Duke University Press, 2014).
28 Nimrod Lin, 'People Who Count: Zionism, Demography and Democracy in Mandate Palestine' (Unpublished PhD dissertation, University of Toronto, 2018). See also Lin's Hebrew article, "Al Ma Anhnu Medaprim Ksheanu Medabrim 'Al Medina? Mahshevet Hamidan Hatziyonit Bitkufat Hamadat Beheksherha Haglobali'im [What are we Talking About when we Talk About State? The

Global Context of Interwar Zionist Political Thought]', *Israel: Studies in Zionism and the State of Israel* 27–28 (2021), 187–212.

29 Vladimir (Ze'ev) Jabotinsky, '*al ha-khaluka* [*On Partition*] (Tel Aviv: Berit ha-tsahar, 1937) [translation mine, AD].

30 Gil S. Rubin, 'Vladimir Jabotinsky and Population Transfers between Eastern Europe and Palestine', *Historical Journal* 62 (2) (2018), 1–23.

31 For additional discussion see A. Dirk Moses, 'Raphael Lemkin, Culture, and the Concept of Genocide', in Donald Bloxham and A. Dirk Moses (eds), *Oxford Handbook of Genocide Studies* (Oxford: Oxford University Press, 2010), pp. 19–41; A. Dirk Moses, *The Problems of Genocide: Permanent Security and the Language of Transgression* (Cambridge: Cambridge University Press, 2021), chapter 3; James Loeffler, 'The First Genocide: Antisemitism and Universalism in Raphael Lemkin's Thought', *Jewish Quarterly Review* 112 (2) (2022), 139–163. Notably, Moses and Loeffler differ in their interpretations of Lemkin's thought and have different views of Lemkin's early attraction to Zionism.

32 Arnold J. Toynbee, *The Western Question in Greece and Turkey: A Study in the Contact of Civilizations* (New York: Howard Fertig, 1970 [orig. 1923]), p. 18.

33 Ashely Jackson, *The British Empire and the Second World War* (London: Hambledon Continuum, 2006), p. 311.

34 Alexander Betts and Gil Loescher, *Refugees in International Relations* (Oxford: Oxford University Press, 2011), p. 40.

35 For recent studies on the Conference of Lausanne see Bayar, 'In Pursuit of Homogeneity'; Ekmekcioglu, 'Republic of Paradox'; Umut Özsu, *Formalizing Displacement: International Law and Population Transfers* (Oxford: Oxford University Press, 2015).

36 Edward W. Said, 'Traveling Theory', in *The World, the Text, and the Critic* (Cambridge, MA: Harvard University Press, 1983), pp. 226–247.

37 Yfaat Weiss, 'Ethnic Cleansing, Memory and Property – Europe, Israel/Palestine, 1944–1948', in Dan Diner, Raphael Gross and Yfaat Weiss (eds), *Jüdische Geschichte Als Allgemeine Geschichte: Festschrift Für Dan Diner Zum 60. Geburtstag* (Göttingen: Vandenhoeck & Ruprecht, 2006), pp. 158–185. For a valuable account of the connection between transfer politics, refugee crises and the making of the European post-1945 order, see Jessica Reinisch and Elizabeth White (eds), *The Disentanglement of Populations: Migration, Expulsion and Displacement in Post-War Europe, 1944–9* (New York: Palgrave Macmillan, 2011).

38 Cust's memorandum is included in a folder containing a list of cantonisation proposals prepared between February and November 1936: National Archives, Kew; Colonial Office: 'Cantonisation of Palestine: Proposals', CO 733/302/9 (formerly CO 733/302/75288), at http://discovery.nationalarchives.gov.uk/details/r/C823557 (accessed 14 March 2023).

39 See [Lord] Melchett [aka Alfred Moritz Mond], 'Palestine', *The Times*, 1 March 1935, p. 10; followed by a reply by Archer Cust, 'Palestine', *The Times*, 5 March 1935, p. 12, and Norman Bentwich, 'The Palestine Mandate', *The Times*, 7

October 1935, p. 8; followed by yet another reply by Archer Cust, 'The Palestine Mandate', *The Times*, 17 September 1935, p. 10.
40 Minutes dated 29 June 1936, included in 'Cantonisation of Palestine: Proposals', The National Archives, CO 733/302/9. For discussion see also Lauren Banko, *The Invention of Palestinian Citizenship, 1918–1947* (Edinburgh: Edinburgh University Press, 2016), chapter 3, esp. pp. 186–188.
41 Penny Sinanoglou, 'British Plans for the Partition of Palestine, 1929–1938', *Historical Journal* 52 (1) (2009), 31–52; Laila Parsons, 'The Secret Testimony of the Peel Commission (Part II)', *Journal of Palestine Studies* 49 (2) (2020), 8–25.
42 'The Palestine Inquiry: Jewish Demands', *The Times*, 12 February 1937, p. 16. For transcripts and notes of Jabotinsky's testimony, see Jabotinsky Papers, Aleph-1/36–4, Jabotinsky Institute, Tel Aviv.
43 Michael Hopkinson, *Green Against Green: The Irish Civil War* (Dublin: Gill and Macmillan, 1988).
44 See for example the newsreel 'India's Civil War: 1,000,000 Indians on the Move', *British Pathé* (19 September 1947), at www.britishpathe.com/video/1-000-000-indians-on-the-move/query/india+partition (accessed 14 March 2023). I would like to thank Jayita Sarkar for bringing this video clip to my attention.
45 Yifat Gutman, *Memory Activism: Reimagining the Past for the Future in Israel–Palestine* (Nashville, TN: Vanderbilt University Press, 2017); Basma Fahoum and Arie M. Dubnov, 'Agnotology in Palestine/Israel: Tantura and the Teddy Katz Affair Twenty Years On', *The American Historical Review* 128 (1) (2023), 371–383. https://doi.org/10.1093/ahr/rhad050.
46 Benjamin John Grob-Fitzgibbon, *Imperial Endgame: Britain's Dirty Wars and the End of Empire* (London; New York: Palgrave Macmillan, 2011).
47 Yoav Gelber, *Palestine, 1948: War, Escape and the Emergence of the Palestinian Refugee Problem* (Brighton: Sussex Academic Press, 2006); Benny Morris, *1948: A History of the First Arab–Israeli War* (New Haven, CT: Yale University Press, 2008). The term is also used in passing in Hurewitz, *The Struggle for Palestine*, pp. 311, 315 and *passim*, though without a systematic or clear definition.
48 Netanel Lorch, *Israel's War of Independence, 1947–1949*, 2nd rev. edn (Hartford: Hartmore House, 1968). The book was first published in Hebrew in 1958 under the title *Ḳorot milḥemet ha-'atsma'ut*. I would like to thank Shay Hazkani for pointing this out to me.
49 See, for example, Khalidi's statement that we should actually talk of how '[t]he two wars of 1948 ensued: the Civil War from November 1947 to May 15, 1948, during which the Palestinian community was pulverized; and the Regular War from May 15, 1948 to the Armistice Agreements in 1949'. Walid Khalidi, 'A Palestinian Perspective on the Arab–Israeli Conflict', *Journal of Palestine Studies* 14 (4) (1985), 35–48 at 40. It was not picked up by Rashid Khalidi (b. 1948), who preferred to use the term 'the first Arab–Israeli war'. See Rashid Khalidi, *Palestinian Identity: The Construction of Modern National Consciousness* (New York: Columbia University Press, 1997), chapter 8 and *passim*.
50 Motti Golani, 'From Civil War to Interstate War and Back Again. The War over Israel/ Palestine, 1945–2000', *Zeithistorische Forschungen/Studies in Contemporary History* 2 (2005), 54–70.

51 '1947–1948 Civil War in Mandatory Palestine', *Wikipedia* (entry last updated 14 March 2023, at 13:44 (UTC)), at https://en.wikipedia.org/wiki/1947%E2%80%931948_civil_war_in_Mandatory_Palestine (accessed 15 March 2023).
52 Derek J. Penslar, *Jews and the Military: A History* (Princeton, NJ: Princeton University Press, 2013), esp. chapters 4 and 6. In fact, Penslar suggests that a clear Zionist ideology was seldom the prime motivator. An interesting attempt to place these volunteers in a comparative perspective can be found in Nir Arielli, *From Byron to Bin Laden: A History of Foreign War Volunteers* (Boston, MA: Harvard University Press, 2018).
53 Vladimir Jabotinsky, 'Far Der Havlagh Vet Men Nidrertrekhtike Farreter Fun Nishta Keyn Brik Tsvishn Aunz Aun Di Alt [For the Restraint will be Degraded Traitors; There is No Bridge between Us and the Old [Zionists]]', *Unzer Welt* [Warsaw], 12 August 1938, pp. 4–6 at p. 6.
54 Menachem Begin, 'Lo Tihiye Milhemet Ahim [There Will be No War between Brothers]', *Herut*, 3 December 1944, p. 1. *Herut* was the underground newspaper of the Etzel, published between 1942 and 1948.
55 Notably, as David Armitage reminds us, a working definition of the obscure category 'civil war' as an 'armed conflict not of an international character' emerged at the very same time in the deliberations leading to the Fourth Geneva Convention (August 1949). Adding such a clause went against earlier objections that such a nebulous definition would cover too wide a range of acts within the frontier of a single state. David Armitage, *Civil Wars: A History in Ideas* (New York: Alfred A. Knopf, 2017), chapter 6, esp. pp. 200–203. For a critical engagement see Mary Dudziak, 'On the Civil-Ness of Civil War: A Comment on David Armitage's Civil War Time', *American Society of International Law: Proceedings of the Annual Meeting* 111 (2017), 14–19, https://doi.org/10.1017/amp.2017.153.
56 Moshe Naor, 'Israel's 1948 War of Independence as a Total War', *Journal of Contemporary History* 43 (2) (2008), 241–257.
57 Erich Ludendorff, *The Nation at War*, translated by A. S. [Angelo Solomon] Rappoport (London: Hutchinson and Company, 1936).
58 Raymond Aron, *The Century of Total War*, translated by E. W. Dickes and O. S. Griffiths (Garden City, NY: Doubleday, 1954).
59 David Avrom Bell, *The First Total War: Napoleon's Europe and the Birth of Modern Warfare* (London: Bloomsbury, 2007). Bell drew some fire from critics for using the term 'total war' not only in reference to the Napoleonic wars against foreign countries but also when discussing the brutal 1793 crushing of the Royalist and Catholic counter-revolution in Vendée – a region in France – thereby blurring the lines distinguishing 'total wars' from 'civil wars'.
60 In the India–Pakistan case, this point was demonstrated by Ian Talbot and Gurharpal Singh, who insist that partition violence, beginning in August 1946 and ending only in March 1950, was qualitatively different from earlier forms of communal violence, as the violence emerged as a political resource and was organised with the singular objective of clearing out minority populations: Ian

Talbot and Gurharpal Singh, *The Partition of India* (Cambridge: Cambridge University Press, 2009), chapter 3. Yasmin Khan also shows how political leaders in British India hired criminals to unleash ethnic violence for political ends in the new electoral democracies: Yasmin Khan, *The Great Partition: The Making of India and Pakistan* (New Haven, CT: Yale University Press, 2007).

61 Vazira Fazila-Yacoobali Zamindar, *The Long Partition and the Making of Modern South Asia: Refugees, Boundaries, Histories* (New York: Columbia University Press, 2007).

62 Alexandre ('Sandy') Kedar, 'Expanding Legal Geographies: A Call for a Critical Comparative Approach', in Irus Braverman, Nicholas K. Blomley, David Delaney and Alexandre Kedar (eds), *The Expanding Spaces of Law: A Timely Legal Geography* (Stanford, CA: Stanford University Press, 2014), pp. 95–119.

63 Rephael G. Stern, 'Legal Liminalities: Conflicting Jurisdictional Claims in the Transition from British Mandate Palestine to the State of Israel', *Comparative Studies in Society and History* 62 (2) (2020), 359–388, esp. 375–376.

64 Arie M. Dubnov, 'Israel's Jewish and Democratic Balance: A Historian Reflects on the Nation-State Law', *Fathom* 21 (2018), 2–13.

65 For the full text of the Declaration of Israel's Independence, see https://avalon.law.yale.edu/20th_century/israel.asp (accessed 14 March 2023).

66 Leo [Yehuda Pinchas] Kohn, 'hatza'at hukah [Proposal for a Constitution]', translated by Moshe Zilberg, no date, Ben-Gurion Archives, Aleph 13/2393/507759. It is worth mentioning that before Jerusalem, the term 'Corpus separatum' was used to describe the unique legal status of the city of Fiume (today's Rijeka, Croatia) which enjoyed a semi-autonomous status within the Habsburg Empire from 1776 until its collapse in 1918.

67 Nir Kedar, 'Ben-Gurion's Opposition to a Written Constitution', *Journal of Modern Jewish Studies* 12 (1) (2013), 1–16; Amihai Radzyner, 'A Constitution for Israel: The Design of the Leo Kohn Proposal, 1948', *Israel Studies* 15 (1) (2010), 1–24.

68 The pioneering study on the subject was Sabri Jurays, *The Arabs in Israel*, translated by Inea Bushnaq (New York: Monthly Review Press, 1976; originally published in Hebrew, 1966). For more recent studies see Shira Robinson, *Citizen Strangers: Palestinians and the Birth of Israel's Liberal Settler State* (Stanford, CA: Stanford University Press, 2013); Leena Dallasheh, 'Nazarenes in the Turbulent Tide of Citizenships: Nazareth from 1940 to 1966' (unpublished PhD dissertation, New York University, 2012); Adel Manna, *Nakba and Survival* (Oakland, CA: University of California Press, 2022).

69 For a fuller, empirically rich and theoretically sophisticated elaboration of this point, see Stern, 'Legal Liminalities'.

70 Nitzan Lebovic, 'Neutral Angles: *Mamlachtiut* (Etatism) and Law in the Israeli Court, 1947–1961', *New German Critique* 42 (3) (2015), 41–67, at 41.

71 It is beyond the scope of the present chapter to provide an analysis of the various areas of international law (including refugee law, human rights law, the law relating to stateless persons, and more) the treatment of Palestinian refugees fell under. For an updated, comprehensive analysis see Lex Takkenberg and

Francesca P. Albanese, *The Status of Palestinian Refugees in International Law* (Oxford: Oxford University Press, 2020).
72 Penny Sinanoglou, *Partitioning Palestine: British Policymaking at the End of Empire* (Chicago; London: University of Chicago Press, 2019).
73 An argument put forward recently by Maria Birnbaum, 'Recognizing Diversity: Establishing Religious Difference in Pakistan and Israel', in Andrew Phillips and Christian Reus-Smit (eds) *Culture and Order in World Politics: Diversity and its Discontents* (Cambridge: Cambridge University Press, 2020), pp. 250–270.
74 Manela, *The Wilsonian Moment*.
75 Cabeiri de Bergh Robinson, *Body of Victim, Body of Warrior: Refugee Families and the Making of Kashmiri Jihadists* (Berkeley, CA: University of California Press, 2013).
76 George Orwell, 'Notes on Nationalism' [orig. May 1945], in *England Your England and Other Essays* (London: Secker and Warburg, 1953), pp. 41–67.

10

Partitioned identities? Regional, caste and national identity in Pakistan

Iqbal Singh Sevea

Since its emergence in 1947, the state of Pakistan has grappled with the challenge of constructing a national identity that either supersedes or incorporates various markers of linguistic, regional and ethnic identity. Following the partition of British India, Pakistan had to construct a shared sense of belonging for the various groups that fell within its borders and the millions of displaced individuals who flooded into the new state. It literally had to create a new Pakistani identity among individuals who, on the one hand, lacked a sense of 'sameness' with others inhabiting the territorial boundaries of the state, and, on the other hand, continued to share linguistic, regional, ethnic and religious identities with people across the border. The prominent Pashtun leader, Khan Abdul Wali Khan (1917–2006), pithily reflected both the complex identities inhabited by individuals in Pakistan and the challenge confronting the state when he asserted that he had 'been a Pashtun for four thousand years, a Muslim for 1300 years and a Pakistani for just over forty'.[1]

Like nation-states, national identities are not natural. Benedict Anderson's work has drawn attention to the fact that while members of a nation will never know or meet most of their fellow members, they may develop a mental image of their affinity to each other. Hence, the nation is a socially constructed or imagined community. Furthermore, despite actual inequality and exploitation, the nation is imagined as a deep and horizontal comradeship.[2] Developing Anderson's foundational work, scholars have studied the various mechanisms through which the nation is socially constructed, continuously narrated and drawn attention to the use of symbols like flags and anthems.[3] Similarly, national identities are produced, perpetuated and challenged discursively. There is, thus, a need to analyse the discursive strategies and linguistic devices employed by the state to construct 'national sameness' and the various forms of official patronage and censorship employed to construct a national identity.[4]

The realms of education, media and national celebrations are particularly important means through which the state seeks to develop a notion of a common past, a vision of a shared future and the image of the ideal citizen. Specific aspects of the past are highlighted (and interpreted in particular ways) in the national curriculum and media while others are neglected.[5] On their part, national celebrations and commemorations are opportunities for the state to promote specific heroes as well as to demonstrate and assert the power of the state. For instance, in India, Mahatma Gandhi's funeral shortly after the partition of the Indian subcontinent was organised with a view towards enabling the ruling Indian National Congress Party to assert the power of the new state and also stake the party's right to sovereignty.[6] The state, however, is not the only actor involved in constructing the boundaries of identity. Various discourse actors, such as intellectuals, artists and religious leaders, seek to challenge and define notions of community. These various actors draw upon, reify and recast notions of ethnic markers, homeland and cultural artefacts.

This chapter examines how regional, caste and linguistic identities, which have a transnational dimension, relate to, are reshaped by, and resist, the Pakistani state's attempts to shape a national identity and notion of a shared past. It focuses specifically on the province of Punjab, which was partitioned between India and Pakistan. The first section will examine diverging attempts in Pakistan to shape an official past and identity. It will be shown that the history of Pakistan was linked to the trajectory of Islam in South Asia, and the ideal citizen was projected as being modern, urbane and one who spoke Urdu. The chapter will then turn to analyse contrasting representations and celebrations of identity in Punjabi popular culture. The aim is to analyse how alternative imaginations of the self and community in films, songs and ballads respond to and challenge the state constructions of nationhood. Particular focus will be paid to the popular portrayal of two rebellious figures – Maula Jatt and Dullah Bhatti. Maula Jatt is an extremely popular cinematic rebel who has featured in numerous Pakistani Punjabi films. Films featuring Maula Jatt are largely centred around caste and regional pride, and often demonstrate a rejection of state and religious institutions. Dullah Bhatti is a sixteenth-century rebel celebrated for his resistance to the Mughal Emperor, Akbar.

Regional, caste and linguistic identities in Punjab are not, however, approached in this chapter as primordial and unchanging. Indeed, the act of 'partitioning' and the subsequent displacement of people gave rise to conceptions of loss, displacement and separation which in turn shaped notions of identity. For instance, the Sikh *ardas* or supplication to God that is recited after prayers or religious ceremonies, and prior to undertaking a significant task, demonstrates the impact that the partition of India has had on social identities. A key stanza of the *ardas* reads:

Hei akal purakh aapne paanth te sada ahai darar jio
Sri Nankana Sahib te hor gurdwara-a gurdham-a to
Jinha to-on paanth nu vichoria gia hai,
Khulhe darshan didar te seva sambhal da dan
Khalsa-ji nu baksho

> O' Immortal One, eternal and benevolent guardian of the panth [religious community]
> Bestow upon the Khalsa [the pure] the beneficence of unobstructed visit to and management of
> Sri Nankana Sahib and other shrines and places of the Guru
> From which the panth has been separated.[7]

Sri Nankana Sahib is one of the most important Sikh religious sites. It is built at the site at which the first guru, or teacher of the Sikhs, Nanak, was born. With the partition of the province of Punjab in 1947, Sri Nankana Sahib came to be in Pakistan while most Sikhs fell in or moved to India.[8] The reference to the lack of access to Nankana Sahib demonstrates how dislocation from areas in Pakistan has been canonised as a pivotal and defining moment in the development of Sikh identity and religious experience. It is important to note here that the *ardas* was formulated to encapsulate and emphasise key aspects of Sikh history as well as core doctrines of Orthodox Sikhism. Moreover, the *ardas* is recited daily across the globe by Sikhs, many of whom are as separated from Sri Nankana Sahib in Pakistan as they are from religious sites in India.

Partition and the shaping of a distinct identity

In Pakistan, efforts at constructing a distinct national identity have largely focused on stressing the bonds of religion and language. Being Muslim has been promoted as a factor that supersedes ethnic and regional identities. Official history, education and textbooks emerged as important terrain through which to construct such an identity. In fact, in official historiography, Pakistan is historically and geographically linked to the trajectory of Islam in South Asia. In addition to this trajectory, the state's language policy was guided by the aim of developing a distinct identity.

There are more than seventy living languages spoken across Pakistan. It was in the backdrop of this linguistic diversity that Urdu was declared to be the national language in 1948. Urdu was promoted as a means of developing social cohesion. The arguments presented by figures like Mohammad Ali Jinnah (1876–1948), the founder of Pakistan, in support of Urdu reveal important dimensions of the new state's language policy and the assumptions underlining conceptions of a distinct Pakistani identity. Addressing a gathering at Dacca University on 24 March 1948, Jinnah stated:

> We have broken the shackles of slavery, we are now a free people. ... Thwarted in their desire to prevent the establishment of Pakistan, our enemies turned their attention to finding ways and means to weaken and destroy us...
>
> Our enemies, among whom I regret to say, there are still some Muslims, have set about actively encouraging provincialism in the hope of weakening Pakistan and thereby facilitating the reabsorption of this Province into the Indian Dominion. ... Let me restate my views on the question of a State language for Pakistan. For official use in this Province, the people of the Province can choose any language they wish. ... There can, however, be only one *lingua franca*, that is, the language for intercommunication between the various provinces of the State, and that language should be Urdu and cannot be any other. The *State language, therefore, must obviously be Urdu, a language that has been nurtured by a hundred million Muslims of this subcontinent, a language understood throughout the length and breadth of Pakistan and above all, a language which, more than any other provincial language, embodies the best that is in Islamic culture and Muslim tradition* and is nearest to the language used in other Islamic countries.[9] (emphasis added)

This speech was delivered in response to protests in East Pakistan against what was seen by the Bengali-speaking population of the region as the imposition of Urdu upon them. These comments by Jinnah demonstrate two interesting dimensions that underscore the selection of Urdu as the national language. First, Urdu was seen as a language that would lessen the threat of provincialism in the new state. Languages like Bengali and Punjabi, which were spoken by large segments of the population but associated firmly with specific regions, were seen as posing a threat to the cohesion of the newly formed state. It is worth noting here that Pakistan inherited provinces that were broadly organised along linguistic lines. The colonial state had sought to locate and define the vernacular languages of provinces and prioritise these vernaculars in provincial administration and education. In a number of cases, this resulted – rather controversially – in the standardisation of languages and scripts into defined vernaculars like Sindhi, Punjabi and Urdu, and their association with specific provinces as a whole.[10] It is further worth noting that, given that subsequent constitutions in Pakistan determined that resources would be divided between provinces on the basis of the size of their population, competition among provinces for resources carries the potential of taking on ethnic and linguistic overtones. Unlike languages like

Sindhi and Punjabi, Urdu was not associated with any region or province. In fact, Urdu was the native language of a small minority of Pakistan's population. According to the census report of 1951, only 3.4 per cent of Pakistan's population spoke Urdu as their native language.[11]

Second, Urdu was associated with the Muslims of the Indian subcontinent and presented as being intrinsically linked to 'Islamic culture'. The genealogy of such an assertion can be traced to the communalisation of languages that occurred from the late nineteenth century. In the late nineteenth and early twentieth centuries, Hindi and Urdu came to be defined as distinct languages and codified along the lines of their respective scripts. While Hindi was firmly linked with the Devanagari script, Urdu was differentiated on the basis of its Persian-Arabic script. These now firmly defined languages were mobilised as means of social mobilisation. Hindi and the Devanagari script were associated with Hindus.[12] Urdu came to be associated with Muslims and was championed by Muslim social reformers and leaders as the language of the community. Those who had led the campaign for the demand for the creation of Pakistan and the subsequent state authorities adopted such a discourse about languages being linked to religious identities. This was clearly reflected in a statement by Liaquat Ali Khan (1895–1951), the first prime minister of Pakistan, at the Second Session of the Constituent Assembly of Pakistan, held on 25 February 1948:

> Pakistan has been created because of the demand of a hundred million Muslims in this sub-continent and the language of a hundred million Muslims is Urdu ... Pakistan is a Muslim state and it must have as its lingua franca the language of the Muslim nation.[13]

In addition to this, Urdu was also seen as a language that was well placed to facilitate an interaction with Muslim modernity. Regional languages were often described as unsophisticated, unstructured and unable to express modern sociopolitical ideas.

As alluded to above, the promotion of Urdu as the national language was opposed by groups in various regions. East Pakistan was at the forefront of resisting the imposition of Urdu. The Bengali-speaking population of East Pakistan actually constituted the majority of Pakistan's population. This was a point stressed by Dhirendra Nath Dutta, a representative from East Pakistan, at the Second Session of the Constituent Assembly of Pakistan, when he argued that Bengali should not be viewed merely as a provincial language. On 25 February 1948, he moved an amendment on the rules of procedures of the Assembly to give Bengali equal status along with Urdu as a state language of Pakistan.[14] Anger over the neglect of Bengali and the imposition of Urdu led to mass protests in East Pakistan in 1948 and 1952, and was the catalyst to the uprisings of 1971 that led to the eventual emergence of Bangladesh. An analysis of the mass protests that erupted over the issue of language in East Pakistan is beyond the scope of this chapter. Suffice it to note here that the Bengali language was intrinsically linked to the identity of the people of the region and that their opposition to what they saw as 'linguistic and cultural imperialism' led to a mass uprising which in turn culminated in the secession of East Pakistan and the emergence of the new state of Bangladesh in 1971.[15] Similarly, as will be discussed in greater detail below, a group of Punjabi intellectuals asserted that Pakistan's language policy was an attack on their cultural identity and position within the new state.

Education was the other major medium through which the state attempted to cultivate a national identity. There was a concerted effort to shape a historical narrative that reified a distinct Pakistani identity by selectively representing aspects of the past and highlighting specific events and heroes. National imagination is, after all, as dependent upon memory as it is on forgetting.[16] Scholars have pointed out that the domination of the state over civil society in the construction and dissemination of knowledge in general, and the writing of history in particular, has ensured that the educational system has been intrinsically linked to the need to construct a national ideology.[17]

An analysis of Pakistani textbooks demonstrates the concerted efforts to nationalise the past and through this shape a Pakistani identity founded on religious affiliation. In a recent study of the crafting of official history in Pakistan, Ali Usman Qasmi has described the dominant historical narrative as a 'master narrative' which presents accounts of the past that define the historical identity of a community.[18] Censorship and patronage to specific textbooks and authors has allowed the state to shape this master narrative. Ayesha Jalal has noted that the unequal division of labour between state and civil society in Pakistan, particularly the state's role in the production of textbooks, has enabled it to set the boundaries for the writing of Pakistani history.[19] Overall, the state's control over public education, development of a national education curriculum to be taught across all Pakistani state schools and its ability to extend patronage and enforce censorship provided it with the ability to shape official narratives and histories.

In 1962, the military ruler Ayub Khan (1907–74) centralised the production of textbooks in Pakistan. The newly established West Pakistan Text-book Board was vested with the authority to implement 'educational policies of Government in respect of the production and publication of text-books' and 'the laying down of specifications of textbooks, for their preparation and publication'.[20] This effectively meant that textbooks were no longer selected from pre-existing works but rather sanctioned by the Board, with the parameters and topics of the textbooks being determined by the Board.

In the coming decades, the state would play a more active role in shaping a national education. In 1972, Pakistan Studies was introduced as a compulsory subject at secondary and higher levels.

Central to the nationalist historiography of Pakistan is the attempt to stress the distinctiveness and pervasiveness of Muslim identity. There are three important facets to this strand of nationalist historiography. First, textbooks in Pakistan generally trace the emergence of Pakistan not to 1947 but to 711. This was the year that the forces of the Umayyad Caliphate, led by Mohammad bin Qasim, first conquered parts of the Indian subcontinent. This is taken as the point at which Islam entered the subcontinent. For instance, in his *A Textbook of Pakistan Studies*, M. D. Zafar states that 'Pakistan came to be established for the first time when the Arabs under Mohammad-bin-Qasim occupied Sindh and Multan in the early years of the eight century, and established Muslim rule in this part of the South-Asian [sic] subcontinent', and that Pakistan then spread to include the whole of north India, Bengal, and even parts of southern India.[21] Zafar goes on to state that '[a]lthough Pakistan was created in August 1947, yet except for its name, the present-day Pakistan has existed, as more or less a single entity, for centuries'.[22] Second, Islam is presented as a unified system of belief and a culture that provides its adherents with a well-defined identity that superseded linguistic and regional identities. This organic unity of Islam is contrasted against Hinduism, which is described as caste-ridden and hierarchical.[23] Last, the Muslims of the subcontinent are described as having been involved in a constant struggle with the majority Hindu community to retain their identity and rights.[24] Thus, the emergence of Pakistan is presented as an inevitability and Islam is inherently linked with the ideology of Pakistan.

Representations of caste and regional identity in popular culture

If we turn away from official representations towards the realm of popular culture, we find the celebration of diverse sets of identities that seemingly challenge the national ideology. This section will focus in particular on the representation of transnational caste-based rural identities in Punjabi cinema. Such representations have not been static and have not been immune from official censorship and patronage. They have responded both to the official national narratives discussed above and to shifts in political power in the state.

The representation of caste identities in Pakistani cinema is particularly interesting given the widely held view that Muslims do not ascribe to caste practices. The prevalence of such a view has resulted in the neglect of caste-based sociopolitical dynamics in Pakistan. Scholars working on Pakistan have generally adopted the term *biradari* (loosely defined as brotherhood) to refer to various social groupings that can be the basis for sociopolitical mobilisation. David Gilmartin has drawn attention to the salience of *biradari* in the form of ethnic divisions based on an ideology of descent among Kashmiris who have settled in urban Punjab.[25] *Biradari* links also play a key role during elections as candidates are often chosen on the basis of their links with *biradaris* in specific districts.[26] Despite the importance of the category, there has been scant scholarly attention paid to delineating what the term connotes. Like the social category *qawm*, *biradari* can signify a lineage, caste, ethnic and linguistic group.[27] It has been employed by both Muslims and non-Muslims in various parts of South Asia to describe a myriad of social and political groupings. The looseness and ambiguity of the term and its multiple uses indicate that *biradari* is a form of community consciousness that was not limited to the confines of the community as an actual social group.[28] The *biradari* as a grouping and rallying point was thus able to reconstitute itself and shift its boundaries. Needless to say, community consciousness shifted with changes in circumstances, situations and the context.

It is suggested here that *biradari* is also employed in Pakistan to refer to caste-based identities. In the realm of popular culture, caste-based affiliations are clearly evident from the multitude of regional language films and songs that celebrate caste groups like *jatt* and *gujjar*. This is reflected in the numerous Pakistani Punjabi films whose titles openly refer to, if not celebrate, caste identities. These range from *Jatt te Dogar*[29] and *Jatt, Gujjar te Natt*,[30] both of which were released in the early 1980s, to *Buddha Gujjar*,[31] released in 2012, to the *The Legend of Maula Jatt* (2022).[32] Each of these films stratify society in accordance with *biradari* or, here, caste-based identities, and depict the protagonist – who represents the specific caste group mentioned in the title – as the embodiment of masculinity and valour.

The phenomenon of caste-based cinema was ushered in by the 1979 film *Maula Jatt*.[33] Despite officially being banned by the Zia-ul-Haq regime, ostensibly on the grounds of the extreme violence depicted, this film proved to be one of the biggest commercial successes in the history of Pakistani cinema. The film was loosely based on an Urdu short story by Ahmad Nadeem Qasmi (1916–2006) entitled 'Gandhasa'.[34] Qasmi's story revolves around the figure of the menacing ruffian, Maula, who is out to enact revenge upon those involved in the murder of his father. Qasmi's story was the basis for the film *Weshi Jatt*[35] in which the legendary Pakistani actor Sultan Rahi (1938–96) played the role of Maula. Such was the popularity of the character that Sultan Rahi was to go on to play Maula in a host of films, including *Maula Jatt* (1979), *Jatt in London* (1981), *Maula Bukhsh* (1988), *Gandhasa* (1991) and *Maula te Mukho* (1991).[36]

The popularity of the character of Maula and the success of films like *Maula Jatt* established a new highly popular genre of films and signalled the emergence of a new type of hero: a revenge-seeking, hypermasculine, rural and proudly violent figure. Sultan Rahi, who appeared in more than 700 Punjabi and Urdu films, embodied this new type of hero. Moreover, the commercial success of films like *Maula Jatt* firmly established the ascendancy of a new genre of rural revenge sagas. Indeed, the film *Maula Jatt* was to go on to determine the aesthetic, linguistic and narrative content of much of Punjabi cinema (both in Pakistan and India).[37]

It is important to note here that the character of Maula Jatt and the emergence of Sultan Rahi as the superstar of Pakistani cinema symbolised an important shift in Pakistani society and popular culture. Prior to this, the quintessential hero in Pakistani films had been depicted as being educated, Urdu-speaking, morally upright, well-groomed and soft-spoken. These were qualities that represented manliness in the initial decades of Pakistani cinema; a manliness that encapsulated the ideals and visions of nation-building, and idealism in the young state of Pakistan.

The popularity of Maula Jatt and Sultan Rahi marked the emergence of a new type of a hero, one who was rural, loud, hypermasculine, unabashedly violent, fluent in colloquial Punjabi, and had very little to do with the nation or state. In terms of dress, conduct, speech and values, Maula was at odds with previous presentations of heroes and ideals of nation-building. In many ways, he posed a challenge to nationalist visions. He was firmly grounded in a regional identity (Punjabi), celebrated communal alliances (including caste) over a national identity, and displayed total disregard towards the everyday institutions of the state – primarily the police and the judiciary. A detailed discussion of shifting notions of masculinity and depictions of the hero in Pakistani popular culture is beyond the scope of this chapter.[38] It is however important to note that the valorisation of caste-based identities in Pakistani popular culture was itself a response to a specific sociopolitical context and attempts to shape a particular official Pakistani narrative.

In the 1970s, the rural masses and the urban poor were increasingly feeling marginalised and disconnected from the state's visions of national development. Sensing this alienation, Zulfiqar Ali Bhutto (1928–79), the founder and chairman of the Pakistan People's Party (PPP), crafted a populist political agenda that would particularly appeal to this section of the population. In his speeches, Bhutto emphasised that the *awam* (public or people) had been the bedrock of Pakistan, but had been repeatedly neglected by previous leaders.[39] He sought to differentiate himself from those leaders by consciously modelling himself as a champion of the masses. This is poignantly reflected in the political slogan of his party: *Roti, Kapra aur Makan* (Food, Clothing and Shelter). As Bhutto and the PPP attempted to stitch together a coalition of the peasantry, feudal leaders and working classes, sections of the traditional elite of Pakistan were alienated by the new political culture.[40]

The PPP, however, failed to usher in the systemic political and economic reforms it promised. While Bhutto himself remained popular with the urban and rural poor, the failure to build the PPP's organisational structure and neglect of state institutions resulted in the party relying on large landlords for political support.[41] Blatant rigging of both the national and state elections of 1977 by the PPP resulted in large-scale street protests in a number of cities. The mass protests were followed by a military coup that signalled the end of the Bhutto era and ushered in a dictatorship that sought both to win legitimacy and provide a new basis for national unity by pursuing a policy of Islamisation. Zia-ul-Haq (1924–88), the general who headed the coup, would in effect launch the longest period of military rule in Pakistan. For the purposes of this chapter, it is important to note that Zia's period, much more so than that of Ayub Khan, asserted the importance of having one strong male leader who would be able to use coercion and force to administer justice.

In this context of sociopolitical disruption, one witnessed increasing disillusionment among the rural masses and urban poor with the state and its institutions. At the same time, urban centres in Punjab, especially Lahore, witnessed the decline of the traditional middle-class, which had embraced the state-sponsored vision of modernity. This traditional middle-class had arisen in the 1950s and 1960s through modern educational institutions, and gained state employment. They were, thus, linked with urbane nationalist visions discussed above. They were increasingly replaced in the 1980s by a new middle-class that consisted of second-generation migrants from smaller towns and rural areas who were not as 'Westernised' as the previous group.[42] Zia had been scathing about what he described as the 'Westernisation' of Pakistani society, and called for the Islamisation of society and politics. Zia's regime focused on bringing the legal and educational spheres in line with what he promoted as Islamic norms. The regime also employed the media extensively to legitimise itself and bring society in line with its conservative representation of Islam. Women were at the centre of these reforms, and key aspects of the Islamisation programme were framed in terms of protecting their modesty.[43] As the space of women in the public sphere came to be restricted, a strand of hypermasculinity came to the forefront.

The new hero, as characterised by Maula Jatt, reflected developments in the sociopolitical milieu. Shedding Western attire and *sherwanis*, which had been associated with the urban elite, clad in *kurta* and *chaadra* (long cloth tied from the waist down), Maula Jatt symbolised a celebration of the 'real' and manly rural folk, as opposed to the urban sections of Pakistan. In fact, in the film *Maula Jatt*, the only individuals depicted in 'Western' attire and speaking in Urdu were the police, judges and medical staff. These instruments of the state were in turn depicted as being disconnected from the people and not understanding the language and social norms of the rural masses. This is reflected, for instance, in a scene in *Maula Jatt* where Maula's love interest, Mukho, visits him in the hospital and finds that she is unable to interact with the nurses and doctors who do not understand the rural Punjabi she speaks.[44]

While echoing Zia's critique of the Westernised and urbane elite, popular culture from the period, particularly Punjabi cinema, did not celebrate his Islamisation policies. Instead, rural and caste-based identities came to the forefront. The films being discussed here depict a rural society ordered in terms of caste affiliations rather than religious identity. In essence, the Maula Jatt films present a rural social order centred around the Jatts. Members of other caste groups are depicted as wanting to be friends with Maula. In fact, in *Maula Jatt* friends from 'subordinate' caste groups are even shown to be jostling to be his friends and having internal rivalries as a result of the desire to be as close to him as possible. However, in becoming his friends, they assume a subservient position to him. Echoing colonial assumptions of martial and non-martial caste groups, the Jatt is depicted in these films as the protector and representation of masculinity.[45] Moreover, these roles replicate/reify traditional functions associated with various caste groups in rural social organisation. In the Maula Jatt films, for instance, an individual whose caste is traditionally seen as a group that carries out various services for higher castes is depicted as the caretaker of Maula's *manji*. The *manji* is a traditional stringed bedstead which has associations with norms of authority. In this instance, as Maula was the central source of authority, only he could sit on his *manji*.

Dullah Bhatti, collective representation and counter histories

The realm of popular culture not only provides an insight into officially neglected registers of identity, but also reflects attempts at collective representation and, more controversially, versions of local history that challenge official historiography and national ideologies. This section explores the wide circulation and appropriations of the tales of Dullah Bhatti, the heroic rebel celebrated for rising against the Mughal Emperor, Akbar. Instead of searching for the authentic version of the life of Dullah Bhatti, this section focuses on the various narrations of the tale in Pakistan. It should be noted from the onset that in these narrations, Dullah's rebellion portrays Punjab as a unified and distinct rebel province resisting the centralising and 'foreign' state.

Ballads celebrating Dullah's life and adventures have been popular for more than a century, and in the early twentieth century a number of chapbooks on his life were published in Punjab. While these ballads and chapbooks differ in many details on the life and times of Dullah, there are some key facets that the various narrations of his life share.[46] Abdullah Rai Bhatti was born in Pindhi Bhattian a few months after his father and grandfather, Farid and Sandal respectively, had been executed on the orders of Akbar. Farid's and Sandal's bodies were subsequently hung on display at the gates of the fort of Lahore as a warning to anybody who dared to rebel against the Mughals. In some versions, Akbar's son, Salim, was also born on the same day as Dullah. Akbar was advised by his *najumis* (astrologers) that Salim needed to be suckled on the milk of a Rajput wet nurse who was the wife of a brave warrior. Thus, it came to pass that both Dullah and Salim spent their childhood under the care of Dullah's mother. Both learned manly sports such as archery, wrestling and horse riding. While physically strong, Dullah seems to have spent much of his time with a gang of youths who went about breaking water pots carried by women. On one such occasion, someone taunted Dullah that while he was displaying his manliness by disturbing the women of the village, the death of his father and grandfather remained unavenged.

Shocked, Dullah prevails upon his mother to tell him who his forefathers were and why they had been executed. He now learns that Farid and Sandal had resisted Mughal demands for higher land revenues and had taken to banditry. Dullah now forms an army of his own and embarks on banditry with the aim of disrupting the Mughal Empire's hold over Punjab. In response, Akbar sends out a large expedition to arrest Dullah and destroy his forces. Unable to find Dullah, the Mughal forces capture his wife, mother, daughters and son and take them to Lahore. Realising what has happened, Dullah rides to engage the Mughal forces. On catching up with the troops he writes to the general, Nizamuddin, condemning him for his unmanly conduct of taking the women of the family captive. In return, Dullah and his entourage are challenged to a duel in which Dullah's men will individually fight four Mughal soldiers. On the first day, Dullah easily defeats four Mughal soldiers. On the second day his uncle is defeated by the Mughal's through the use of deceit. In a fit of rage, Dullah wreaks terror on the Mughal soldiers. Nizamuddin then employs deceit to trap Dullah. Pretending to have been won over by Dullah's valour, he promises to shape a resolution between Dullah and Akbar, prevailing on the former to travel with him to Lahore. Once in Lahore, Nizamuddin laces Dullah's alcohol with poison. Dullah is subsequently put in chains and thrown into a dungeon. He dies while in custody – a victim of deceit on the part of the Mughals.[47]

As noted above, the veracity of the tale of Dullah Bhatti is not the focus of this chapter. Instead, I am interested in the moral stances in contemporary recitations of the life of Dullah and how visions of the past make such narrations powerful sources of collective representation. Life histories, such as that of Dullah Bhatti, owe more to ongoing social processes and to popular reinterpretations and cultural accretions of generations than to an actual life as lived or defined in a single work.[48] The repeated stress on deceit on the part of the Mughals, and their having 'taken' women, speaks to the portrayal of the Mughal Empire and the Mughals as dishonourable, unmanly and illegitimate. In contemporary narrations, it is common to find the Mughal's being described as lacking in *izzat* (honour) and having killed their own family members in their quest for power.[49] The life of the hero is an attempt to depict the truth about how Punjab was conquered – through deceit. In a recent discussion of the *qissa* of Dullah Bhatti on the popular television programme *Hasb-e-Hal*, a commentator stated that the life of Dullah reveals that Akbar was a 'usurper', and it was sad that while the Mughals were celebrated in Pakistan, Dullah Bhatti was not given any official recognition.[50] Akbar, in various contemporary iterations of the *qissa*, comes to symbolise varying 'evils' inflicted upon Punjab – ranging from cultural imperialism to brutally high taxation.

Such moral stances on the part of the narrators provide insights into the articulation of ethnic and collective identities. Punjabi and Rajput identities are being contrasted with the deceitful and unmanly nature of the Mughals. Dullah's refusal to accept Mughal sovereignty is frequently presented as a natural disdain on the part of a Punjabi-Rajput to bow to someone from a Mughal family. In the telling of Dullah's life, the refrain '*Rajputan de shaan de khilaaf hain ke oh kise Mughali khandaan de age sher jhookai*' ('It is against the honour of the Rajputs to bow in front of someone from the Mughal lineage') is often used.[51]

Masculinity and valour are qualities that come to be associated with Rajputs and Punjab. Punjab is repeatedly described as the land of '*surmey*' (warriors) and '*sher*' (lion) who can only be defeated by deceit. Here the fact that Salim was suckled by a Rajput lady who was the wife of a warrior is particularly illustrative of the hierarchy of masculinities being presented. In fact, in some narratives the entire clash between Dullah and Akbar is presented as one of competing masculinities and the *surmey* of Punjab striving to restore the honour of the family and region.[52] In such narrations, the socioeconomic conditions of the period are not presented – issues of honour, insults and masculinity being the central tropes.

Through Dullah Bhatti, the region of Punjab comes to be presented as one that is masculine and in open rebellion against the usurping centralising and culturally imperialist power. Such a description of Punjab as a province of the brave that resists a centralising and illegitimate centralising state allows this story to be appropriated by various figures – including supporters of Zulfiqar Ali Bhutto. In the early 1980s, the eminent film producer Agha G. A. Gul announced that he planned to remake his 1956 blockbuster film, *Dullah Bhatti*. Apparently, the inauguration of the film gave rise to concerns about how Dullah Bhatti would be represented and discussions over his place in the history of Pakistan. Such concerns, it is said, led the Pakistan People's Party to organise a public seminar on Dullah Bhatti which was attended by a number of leading political and intellectual figures, including Ahmed Bashir and Mohammad Hanif Ramay – who was to be the Governor and Chief Minister of Punjab. This heavily publicised seminar is said to have caught the attention of the Zia-ul-Haq military regime as it was reported that, in the course of the seminar, attempts were being made to equate Zulfiqar Ali Bhutto with Dullah Bhatti and Zia with the centralising 'usurper', Akbar. Consequently, action was taken against a number of those who participated in the seminar. Notably, Ahmed Bashir was removed from his post at the National Film Development Corporation.[53] Clearly both the PPP and the Zia regime were aware of the potential of popular histories and folk traditions to challenge state ideologies and legitimise rebellion. It is interesting to note here that it was emphasised by some that, like Dullah Bhatti, Bhutto was also from a Rajput family.

Crucially, Dullah Bhatti featured heavily in the work of proponents of Punjabiyat who sought to pose a challenge to the state-imposed dominance of Urdu. Important intellectuals and writers such as Najm Hosain Syed (b. 1936) and Mohammad Hanif Ramey (1930–2006) employed Dullah Bhatti as a metaphor and symbol to demonstrate the heroic spirit of Punjab and, perhaps more importantly, its tradition of resisting political and cultural domination. The Punjabiyat movement was a cultural and intellectual response by urban intellectuals to what they perceived to be the country's overemphasis on Urdu and Islam as integrative symbols and the consequent neglect of the Punjabi language.[54] Figures associated with the movement argued that the language and unique history of Punjab had been oppressed by the centralising tendencies of the Pakistani state. In 1985, Hanif Ramey published his controversial book, *Punjab ka Muqadma* (*The Case of Punjab*), in which he described Urdu as a 'foreign language' imposed on Punjab and lamented that Punjabis themselves had failed to display the respect and devotion to their mother tongue, Punjabi, that it merited.[55] Two aspects of the writings of members of this movement are particularly pertinent to note. Firstly, they represented Punjab as the victim of state oppression. They lamented that the Pakistani state's attempts at developing a national identity had resulted in the cultural and political marginalisation of the Punjabi language and heritage. As Alyssa Ayres has noted, there is paradox here as Punjab, which is the wealthiest and most populated province in Pakistan, has long functioned as an ethnic and political hegemon and the centre against which other regions struggle in a search for power.[56] Secondly, they stressed the need to write about, highlight and celebrate Punjabi heroes from the past.

During the Zia-ul-Haq regime, opportunities to openly write about regional identity were curtailed. As a result, a number of works by the proponents of Punjabiyat were banned or censored. It is precisely in such contexts of censorship and control over the realms of education that the importance of oral traditions as counter-histories needs to be noted. Popular narrations of the *qissa* of Dullah Bhatti continued to celebrate a regional Punjabi identity, which itself was developed on the basis of resistance against an illegitimate centralising tyrant. Najm Husain Syed, notably, composed a *var* (epic poem or narrative ballad of war), *Dullae-da-Var* (1972), which was subsequently staged as *Takhat-i-Lahor*. In the *var* and the play, the clash between Dullah and Akbar (and by extension the clash between Punjab and the centre) is compared to the battle of Karbala. Tellingly, Akbar's description of it as a battle between *qanoon* (law) and *jurm* (crime) is rejected; instead it is described as one between a *zalim* (tyrant) and the *mazlum* (oppressed).[57] The use of the life history of Dullah to inspire pride among contemporary Punjabis is perhaps best indicated by Dullah's statement after he has been tortured to death by Akbar: 'be warned Badshah, until the water of the five rivers flows like blood in the veins of the people of Punjab, Dullah Bhatti will continue to live'.[58]

Conclusion

This chapter has employed popular culture as a means of exploring the representation of caste, linguistic and regional identities in Pakistan. At a broader level it has sought to demonstrate how films, ballads, chapbooks and plays reveal complex imaginations of the self and community, which respond to and challenge official constructions of nationhood. In the case of Pakistan, caste, linguistic and regional identities have a transnational dimension. Yet, these markers of identities are neither static nor unchanging. Cinematic representations of rural, vernacular and caste-based societies, and the celebration of Dullah Bhatti by proponents of the Punjabiyat movement, were in themselves responses to state-sponsored attempts to shape a national language, ideology and past. Given the state's control over the realm of education in particular, popular culture also emerged as a terrain through which to construct counter-histories. For instance, members of the Punjabiyat movement lamented what they perceived to be the official neglect of aspects of Punjab's past and strove through their writings to inculcate a pride in the 'distinct' history of the region and its heroes.

Notes

1 Quoted in Ian Talbot, *Pakistan: A Modern History* (New Delhi: Foundation Books, 2009), p. 1.
2 Benedict Anderson, *Imagined Communities: Reflections on the Origin and Spread of Nationalism*, revised edition (London: Verso, 2006).
3 See, for instance, Partha Chatterjee, *The Nation and its Fragments: Colonial and Postcolonial Histories* (Princeton, NJ: Princeton University Press, 1993); Michael Biling, *Banal Nationalism* (London: Sage Publications, 2010).
4 I draw here from Ruth Wodak, Rudolf de Cillia, Martin Reisigl and Karin Liebhart, *The Discursive Construction of National Identity*, translated by Angelika Hirsch, Richard Mitten and J. W. Unger (Edinburgh: Edinburgh University Press, 2009). This study provides an important analysis of the ways in which states attempt to construct sameness.
5 Anderson, *Imagined Communities*, pp. 187–206.
6 Yasmin Khan, 'Performing Peace: Gandhi's Assassination as a Critical Moment in the Consolidation of the Nehruvian State', *Modern Asian Studies* 45 (1) (2011), 57–80.
7 See www.sikhnet.com/files/ereader/Ardas%20%5BGurmukhi%5D.pdf (accessed 9 October 2019). The original is in Gurmukhi. Transliteration and translation are my own.
8 For an in-depth discussion of the position of Sikhs during the negotiations leading up to partition, and the challenges that confronted the Sikhs following partition, see Tan Tai Yong and Gyanesh Kudaisya, *The Aftermath of Partition in South Asia* (London: Routledge, 2000), pp. 101–124.
9 Mahomed Ali Jinnah, *Jinnah: Speeches and Statements, 1947–1948* (Karachi: Oxford University Press, 2000), pp. 155–158.
10 For the case of Sindhi see Matthew Cook, *Annexation and the Unhappy Valley: The Historical Anthropology of Sindh's Colonization* (Leiden: Brill, 2015), and for the case of Urdu and Punjabi see Farina Mir, *The Social Space of Language: Vernacular Culture in British Colonial Punjab* (Berkeley, CA: University of California Press, 2010).
11 Rounaq Jahan, *Pakistan: Failure in National Integration* (New York: Columbia University Press, 1972), p. 12.
12 For communalisation of these languages and sociopolitical mobilization, see Christopher King, 'The Hindi-Urdu Controversy of the North-Western Provinces and Oudh and Communal Consciousness', *Journal of South Asian Literature* 13 (1/4), 111–120; Francis Robinson, *Separatism Among Indian Muslims* (Cambridge: Cambridge University Press, 1974), pp. 69–80.

13 Quoted in Tariq Rahman, *Language and Politics in Pakistan* (Karachi: Oxford University Press, 1996), p. 86.
14 See Rafiqul Islam, 'The Bengali Language Movement and the Emergence of Bangladesh', *Contributions to Asian Studies* 11 (1978), 142–152, at 143.
15 For a detailed discussion on this see Philip Oldenburg, '"A Place Insufficiently Imagined": Language, Belief, and the Pakistan Crisis of 1971', *Journal of Asian Studies*, 44 (4) (1985), 711–733.
16 Anderson, *Imagined Communities*, pp. 187–206.
17 Ayesha Jalal, 'Conjuring Pakistan: History as Official Imagining', *International Journal of Middle East Studies* 27 (1) (1995), 73–89.
18 Ali Usman Qasmi, 'A Master Narrative for the History of Pakistan: Tracing the Origins of an Ideological Agenda', *Modern Asian Studies* 53 (4) (2019), 1066–1105.
19 Jalal, 'Conjuring Pakistan', p. 77.
20 'The West Pakistan Text-book Board Ordinance, 1962 Ordinance XLI of 1962', at https://joshandmakinternational.com/resources/laws-of-pakistan/information-media-and-pemra-laws-of-pakistan/the-west-pakistan-text-book-board-ordinance-1962-ordinance-xli-of-1962/ (accessed 1 October 2019).
21 M. D. Zafar, *A Textbook of Pakistan Studies* (Lahore: Aziz Publishers, 1982), p. 4.
22 *Ibid.*, p. 23.
23 See, for instance, Ishtiaq Hussain Qureshi, *The Muslim Community of the Indo-Pakistan Subcontinent (610–1947): A Brief Historical Analysis*, 2nd edn (Delhi: Renaissance, 1977), pp. 89–137.
24 *Ibid.*
25 David Gilmartin, *Empire and Islam: Punjab and the Making of Pakistan* (London: I. B. Tauris, 1988), pp. 82–88.
26 'Electable, Biradari, Party Politics in Punjab', *Dawn*, 2 July 2018, at www.dawn.com/news/1417351 (accessed 3 July 2018).
27 For a detailed engagement with the term *qawm* see Iqbal Singh Sevea, *The Political Philosophy of Muhammad Iqbal* (New York: Cambridge University Press, 2012), pp. 151–163.
28 I draw here from the view that in any discussion on the political action of community it is pertinent to view community as a form of consciousness, not just as an 'actual' social group. See Raymond Williams, *Keywords: A Vocabulary of Culture and Society* (New York: Oxford University Press, 1983), p. 75.
29 *Jatt te Dogar* [motion picture], directed by Imtiaz Qureshi, Pakistan (country): Punjabi (language), 1983.
30 *Jatt, Gujjar te Natt* [motion picture], directed by Arshad Mirza, Pakistan (country): Punjabi (language), 1983.
31 *Buddha Gujjar* [motion picture], directed by Syed Noor, Pakistan (country): Punjabi (language), 2002.
32 *The Legend of Maula Jatt Buddha Gujjar* [motion picture], directed by Bilal Lashari, Pakistan (country): Punjabi (language), 2022.
33 *Maula Jatt* [motion picture], directed by Younis Malik, Pakistan (country): Punjabi (language), 1979.

34 Ahmad Nadeem Qasmi, *Ahmad Nadeem Qasmi ke Numa'indah Afsane* (New Delhi: Modern Publishing House, 2007).
35 *Weshi Jatt* [motion picture], directed by Hasan Askari, Pakistan (country): Punjabi (language), 1975.
36 For a more detailed analysis of the film *Maula Jatt* and Qasmi's short story, *Gandhasa*, see Iqbal Singh Sevea '"Kharaak Kita Oi!": Masculinity, Caste, and Gender in Punjabi Films', *BioScope: South Asian Screen Studies* 5 (2) (2014), 129–140.
37 See, Alyssa Ayres, *Speaking Like a State: Language and Nationalism in Pakistan* (Cambridge: Cambridge University Press, 2009), pp 93–99; Sevea, '"Kharaak Kita Oi!"'.
38 For a fuller discussion on shifting notions of masculinity in Pakistani popular culture see Sevea, '"Kharaak Kita Oi!"'.
39 See Ayesha Jalal, *The Struggle for Pakistan: A Muslim Homeland and Global Politics* (Cambridge, MA: Harvard University Press, 2014), pp. 177–215.
40 For a fuller discussion on this see Arif Hasan, 'The Roots of Elite Alienation', *Economic and Political Weekly* 37 (44/45) (2002), 4550–4553.
41 Talbot, *Pakistan*, pp. 218–220 and 243–244.
42 See Ammara Maqsood, *The New Pakistani Middle Class* (Cambridge, MA: Harvard University Press, 2017).
43 See Rajat Imran, 'Legal Injustices: The Zina Hudood Ordinance of Pakistan and its Implications for Women', *Journal of International Women's Studies* 7 (2) (2005), 78–100.
44 *Maula Jatt* [motion picture].
45 For a fuller discussion on masculinity and caste see Sevea, '"Kharaak Kita Oi!"'.
46 The most popular *qissa* (tale) of Dullah Bhatti was written by Kishan Singh Arif (1836–1904). His *qissa* was regularly republished in the early twentieth century, both in Shahmukhi and Gurmukhi.
47 I have drawn these from various print and oral narrations of Dullah Bhatti's life. See, for instance, Kishan Singh, *Qissa Dullah Bhatti Ka* (Lahore: Sant Singh and Sons Booksellers, 1921); Kishan Singh, *Dullah Bhatti Kalan* (Amritsar: Chattar Singh Jeevan Singh Publishers, 1917(?)); Kishan Singh, *Qissa Dullah Bhatti* (Amritsar: Hardit Singh Kitab Farosh, 1914); 'Shareef Ragi Qissa Dulla Bhatti cd1', at www.youtube.com/watch?v=PqmP4wNYLZo&t=3s (accessed 30 October 2019); 'Dulla Bhatti by Nau Lakhhi Group of Shahkot', at www.youtube.com/watch?v=_KCRD01enlU (accessed 30 October 2019); 'Dullah Bhatti Braveheart of Punjab', at www.youtube.com/watch?v=pIqcZk4ukUg (accessed 30 October 2019).
48 David Arnold and Stuart Blackburn, 'Life Histories in India', in David Arnold and Stuart Blackburn (eds), *Telling Lives in India: Biography, Autobiography, and Life History* (Bloomington, IN: Indiana University Press, 2004), p. 12.
49 See 'Story of Akbar and Dullah Bhatti', *Hasb-e-Hal*, Dunya TV, at www.youtube.com/watch?v=MJJskhwluNw (accessed 13 August 2018).
50 *Ibid.*
51 *Ibid.*

52 'Shareef Ragi Qissa Dulla Bhatti cd1'.
53 'Story of Akbar and Dullah Bhatti'.
54 See Tariq Rahman, 'The Punjabi Movement in Pakistan', *International Journal of the Sociology of Language* 1996 (122) (1996), 73–88.
55 See Muhammad Hanif Ramey, *Punjab ka Muqadama* (Lahore: Sang-e-Meel, 2010).
56 Alyssa Ayres, 'Language, the Nation, and Symbolic Capital', in Anshu Malhotra and Farina Mir (eds), *Punjab Reconsidered: History, Culture, and Practice* (New Delhi: Oxford University Press, 2012), pp. 35–57.
57 Najm Husain Syed, *Takhat-i-Lahor* (Amritsar: Rawi Sahita Prakashana, 2005).
58 *Ibid.*

Afterword
Partition as imperial inheritance

Penny Sinanoglou

The partitions of India and Palestine, like many partitions, contained at their core dual processes of severing and building. Both partitions occasioned immense physical and ideological violence and rupture, and they also engendered intense creation – of new names, new dwellings, new borders, new nations. In different ways, both partitions were and are incomplete and are ongoing. The work of the authors of this volume has been in some measure to reverse those processes – that is, to connect across geographic, temporal and historiographic distance and to dismantle the always already quality of the nation.[1] Pulling scholars of the partitions of India and Palestine into conversation with each other allows us to unpack the particularities of each partition and to recognise the common myths of nation-state formation accompanying them. Both partitions were of a type that became so persistent in the twentieth century that the very meaning of the word 'partition' has been shaped by it. What distinguishes this kind of partition is less the division itself than its protagonist and its aftermath. This kind of partition is one in which a territory previously understood primarily as a whole is divided by an outside power into two or more successor states, at least one of which defines itself as the inheritor of a continuous legacy from the pre-partitioned whole. That legacy might be expressed in the new state's name, its political systems, its international relations, or some combination of these. In this category we might, for instance, include Ireland, Germany, Korea and Vietnam, in addition to the two cases examined in this volume.

With this type of partition of territory comes the partition of history, too, as the successor states rewrite histories of the pre-partitioned whole and of the partition itself to tell stories of nascent, sometimes thwarted, other times victorious nations that were always there waiting to be revealed. Those proto-national histories tend to obscure both the immense range of possible outcomes – in which the nation-state with its eventual borders was only one among many possibilities, and often a fairly unlikely one at that

– and patterns of transnational or broader historical connection. One of the advantages of a volume such as this one is that it recovers commonalities between Palestine and India, even as it highlights local specificities. For historians of India, Pakistan, Bangladesh, Palestine and Israel, these links serve as a useful reminder of the transnational features of national histories, and for historians of other partitioned states they provide starting points for other fruitful comparisons.

Finally, bringing the partitions of India and Palestine into a common frame is particularly instructive for those of us who are historians of the British Empire, and it is within this context that this afterword takes up its examination. Utilising two very different temporal and geographic frames, I approach the partitions of India and Palestine as features of late British imperialism. First, I focus on the period immediately surrounding the partition announcements in 1947 to uncover a common narrative of 'haste' that shaped contemporary and later historiographic understandings of partition as an imperial scuttle. Here, we see that the discourse of a hasty partition served to largely obscure British agency and culpability, and to at least somewhat successfully erase what was in fact a long history of British planning for, and engagement with, the concept of partition. In both India and Palestine, British officials had experimented for decades with plans and practices of territorial separation that were inextricably linked to questions of representative government and sovereignty. The intense and at times chaotic partitions of 1947–48 were neither *sui generis* nor exclusively decolonising moves; they had their roots in practices of imperial control.

Having established the longer histories of British partitionist thinking in India and Palestine, I next aim to expand the temporal and geographic frame in which we consider partition more generally, reminding us of earlier and other episodes of partition, and recalling the multiple valences of the word 'partition' in order to identify the conceptual elements that shaped the kind of partition that came to dominate by the mid-twentieth century. My argument is that partition's deep roots in the colonial conquest and acquisition of land and the international management of European imperial competition are critically important for our understanding of its re-emergence at the end of empire. Far from representing a moment of straightforward decolonisation and national birth that was then marred by violence on the ground, partition in fact already contained a legacy of the violence of colonial domination and the cloaking of that violence in diplomatic international discourse. Similarly, while the forced migrations that accompanied both the Indian and Palestinian partitions had intensely local proximate causes, their roots also lay in other, earlier moments of territorial division and controlled or forced mobility. Recovering partition's history outside of the confines of

1947–48 reminds us that, even as partition was a method and sign of decolonisation, it was simultaneously British imperial praxis.

Narratives of speed in the partitions of India and Palestine

Though there are striking differences between politics as they developed over two centuries of Company and Crown rule in India, and as they began to emerge over a quarter century in Britain's League of Nations mandate in Palestine, there are a number of compelling empirical and interpretive reasons to place the attempted or effected partitions of India and Palestine within a common analytical frame. This volume has advanced such a project by bringing case-specific chapters into conversation with each other and by offering several chapters that explicitly link the two partitions. This linkage is not new; in discussions about possibilities of territorial separation over the years preceding 1947/48, British politicians, local leaders, imperial bureaucrats and international operatives had constantly drawn analogies between the two territories, and in the months surrounding the partitions these references became more frequent and more public.[2] And indeed, despite the particular circumstances and unique politics surrounding each partition there are a number of factual threads that connect India and Palestine. Both territories were under British control at the moment of (attempted) partition and those moments were remarkably close together, and the partitions of India and Palestine were given formal articulation within months of each other between the summer and early winter of 1947. The armed conflict and intercommunal violence that both precipitated and resulted from partition or its attempt created millions of refugees in the Indian subcontinent and the Middle East. Each partition was unfinished and is ongoing in its own way, but what they have in common is that they caused immense dislocation and bloodshed in the short term, and continue to resonate politically, economically, socially and culturally through to the present.[3]

One revealing connection between the two partitions was the way in which the speed of British withdrawal and partition planning was discussed, both at the time and in later historiography. On 20 February 1947, the British Government issued a statement asserting that it would hand over power in India, either to a central government or, in certain areas, to provincial governments, no later than June 1948. Speaking for the opposition in a parliamentary debate two weeks later, Winston Churchill railed against such a plan on both practical and moral grounds, drawing particular attention to the undue speed with which he claimed the current government was undertaking a transfer of power in India. 'It is with deep grief', he said, 'that I watch the clattering down of the British Empire, with all its glories and all the services it has rendered to mankind ... But let us not add – by shameful flight, by a premature, hurried scuttle – at least, let us not add, to the pangs of sorrow so many of us feel, the taint and smear of shame.'[4] Instead, Churchill argued, Britain should hand over the problem of India to the United Nations, just as it had done with the problem of Palestine. Impressing on Parliament what he saw as a horrifying contrast between the short timeframe and immensity of the population and land in question, Churchill drew an explicit parallel between India and Palestine, saying:

> We are told that we cannot walk out of Palestine because we should leave behind us a war between 600,000 Jews and 200,000 [sic] Arabs. How, then, can we walk out of India in 14 months and leave behind us a war between 90 million Muslims and 200 million caste Hindus, and all the other tribulations which will fall upon the helpless population of 400 million? Will it not be a terrible disgrace to our name and record if, after our 14 months' time limit, we allow one fifth of the population of the globe, occupying a region nearly as large as Europe, to fall into chaos and into carnage?[5]

From the other end of the political spectrum some twenty years later, W. H. Auden's damning poetic evaluation of Radcliffe's determination of the partition boundary in India similarly drew attention to the ostensibly compressed timeline of partition:

> 'Time', they had briefed him in London, 'is short. It's too late / For mutual reconciliation or rational debate' / The maps at his disposal were out of date / And the Census Returns almost certainly incorrect, / But there was no time to check them, no time to inspect / Contested areas. The weather was frightfully hot, / And a bout of dysentery kept him constantly on the trot, / But in seven weeks it was done, the frontiers decided, / A continent for better or worse divided.[6]

The temporal constraints Britain faces in Auden's poem are numerous: not just the seven weeks in which to draw the line of partition, but the longer failure to keep maps current and the daily rush experienced by Radcliffe. Critics of Britain and the United Nations' 1947 Partition Plan for Palestine similarly attacked the speed of events. For instance, Sami Hadawi, who had worked for the British mandate government in Palestine and later headed the Institute for Palestine Studies in Beirut, contrasted the fact that 'the rights and patrimony of the Arabs of Palestine had the been subject of no fewer than eighteen investigations within 25 years', with the United Nations' 'hasty, frivolous, and arrogant treatment of the Palestine question'.[7] Spanning decades and ideological persuasions, the idea that Britain rushed out of the Empire is repeated, and this notion has likewise become a commonplace in scholarly literature, with references to Britain's 'shameful flight' and to decolonisation spreading across the British imperial world 'like a brushfire'.[8]

The forces of decolonisation-through-partition are seen as unfolding so quickly and violently that they are likened to natural disasters (though whether the disaster is interpreted as being inflicted on British power and prestige or local peoples depends on the position of the analyst).

The rise in decolonisation history over the past fifteen years, however, has started to complicate narratives of haste at the end of empire, in part by revising a longstanding assumption of inevitability that underlay much of the earlier work on partition and decolonisation. In the cases of India and Palestine in particular, scholars have set out to identify and articulate the ambiguities and uncertainties, the many might-have-beens and roads not taken on the way to partition. As Yasmin Khan has reminded us, '[t]here was nothing "inevitable" about Partition and nobody could have predicted, at the end of the Second World War, that half a million people or more were going to die'.[9] It is certainly possible to identify differences between Palestine, where partition had been considered in various forms by officials for decades, and India, where formal planning was compressed into a few months.[10] But it is also worth noting that British officials had already engaged in various forms of territorial separatism in South Asia – for example, in the partition of Bengal from 1905–11, the separation of Sindh from Bombay in 1936, and the separation of Burma in 1936, which Sana Aiyar has termed 'India's first partition'.[11] In both India and Palestine, then, we must recognise that partition was both carefully considered and deployed over a much longer period than 1947–48. It was neither inevitable nor unprecedented, but instead a familiar tactic for establishing and negotiating imperial power.

Partition and the international negotiation of empire

Indeed, we should recall that for most of modern history, the word 'partition' had nothing to do with the creation of a newly independent state; on the contrary, at the international level it variably signalled conquest, elimination of a state and absorption into an empire. The partition of Africa by European powers in the late nineteenth century is a key example, and one that is instructive. We might also think of the events a century earlier during the partition of Poland (1772–95), which likewise saw the gradual dismemberment and absorption of Polish lands into the neighbouring Russian and Hapsburg empires and the Kingdom of Prussia.[12] Partition, in the African context, eliminated extant states, drew new borders, and formalised colonial conquest, establishing parameters for European economic domination of space that were as much about keeping rival powers out as they were about facilitating the continued extraction of material resources and development of markets that European states had been engaging in well before the partition.[13] Britain had both a strong presence in Africa before formal partition and was a key participant in the partition itself.

Certain features of this partition look quite different from the partitions of the 1940s on which this volume has focused: most obviously, this was a partition leading to formal European rule rather than formal European departure. But there are plenty of elements that will be familiar: the partition was implemented through treaties between European powers and local African leaders and was given effect through international agreements concluded between the European powers themselves, for instance at the Congress of Berlin in 1884–85. The partition of Africa rested on a complex matrix of political claims-making, both on the ground and in the international arena, and was designed to avert intra-European conflict and facilitate European economic expansion. Though it was not yet the superpower it would be by the 1940s partitions, the United States played a key role in recognising and legitimising particular European holdings in Africa during the Congress of Berlin (though it did not ratify the 1885 treaty), and set out to protect its own potential interests there as well.[14] The nineteenth-century partition of Africa established two threads that remain evident in the twentieth-century partitions of India and Palestine: first, it laid the groundwork for the internationalisation of imperial territorial questions, and second, it linked Euro-American interests to the practice of dividing territory and assigning sovereignty. As several chapters in this volume have shown, the partitions of India and Palestine were highly internationalised in different ways, and though on their surface they effected the ejection of a European state, underneath they were designed very much around European (and American) interests.

Those interests were, of course, at the forefront of the post-First World War settlement, during which Britain negotiated with many of the same European powers that had partitioned Africa to cartographically parcel out the territories of the defeated Ottoman and Austro-Hungarian empires. These early twentieth century partitions created both new sovereign states and, in much of the former Ottoman Empire, a set of states (among them, Palestine) that had little of the sovereignty associated with the term, and which were categorised as League of Nations mandates. Disputes over new international borders engaged European diplomats, representatives of various ethnic minorities and non-European communities, journalists, and eventually members of the public. Many inhabitants of the former Ottoman Empire protested the creation of new states under European oversight and the legal categorisation of these new territories as League of Nations mandates. The redrawing of the Ottoman Middle East went ahead regardless, in many cases expressly ignoring these stated wishes, and this has established as axiomatic for historians the deeply imperial character of the partitions that took place in 1919, and in which Britain played such an essential role.

The creation of Palestine as a League of Nations mandate was perhaps the most contentious example of imperial power made manifest on the new map of the Middle East. As is well known, the terms of the British mandate for Palestine incorporated the text of the 1917 Balfour Declaration, and thereby stipulated the establishment of a Jewish National Home in Palestine, to be supported through the institution of immigration and land policies favourable to Jewish settlement. The Jewish National Home had no cartographic form, yet its conceptual existence was critical to Palestine's place on the map, and it was dependent on long-standing practices of settler colonialism. Both of these facts underscored for opponents at the time, and for scholars in the present, the intertwining of European imperial power and the post-First World War partition of the Ottoman Empire. British (and of course, French) imperial objectives continued to shape the former Ottoman Levant for decades – and some might even argue now, a century – after.[15]

Those longer histories challenge the narrative, standard at the time and repeated in plenty of histories thereafter, that the period after the end of the Second World War was one in which the British suddenly rushed out of the Empire, beating a sloppily executed rapid retreat while either they or the United Nations attempted – successfully in the case of India, unsuccessfully in Palestine – to impose a partition plan. They also raise the question of why or to what end narratives of haste and slap-dash last-minute partitions developed.

First, we must recognise that the presentation of definite and short timelines for withdrawal from both India and Palestine was a tactical move on Britain's part, meant to force the hands of various actors – the Muslim League, the Congress, Palestinian Arab and Zionist leaders, to say nothing of the United States and the new United Nations. The use of short deadlines was part of Britain's withdrawal toolkit, and indeed in a Cabinet meeting in autumn 1947 discussing the situation in Palestine, Prime Minister Clement Attlee drew an explicit parallel to the case of India, where, he felt, the announcement of a definite date of withdrawal had hastened a concrete solution to the struggle over political sovereignty.[16] Second, playing up the speed of the planned withdrawal was designed to placate both the British public and Britain's American allies, both of which were aware in different ways of the vast resources of both money and manpower being devoured by the endgame of empire. Finally, there was no compelling tactical or rhetorical reason to emphasise the continuities in planning for partition across the decades; if anything, such recollections would have reminded all interested parties that partition had been variably undertaken, vetted, attempted, reversed and rejected in both Palestine and India. Crucially, all earlier partitions and partition plans had existed in an imperial framework – that is, under British auspices and envisioning a British imperial future. The failure of empire and the failure of partition were inextricably linked.

In 1947 India, then, the advantage of presenting partition as something fresh, new and hastily cobbled together, was that it obscured partition's long imperial roots and made it more plausibly an exclusively decolonising tool. In the case of Palestine, Foreign Secretary Ernest Bevin was strenuously opposed to partition, championing instead the creation of a binational Palestine in order not to alienate neighbouring Arab states. Drawing attention to the long British history of advocating partition would hardly have served his purposes. Instead, a quick and decisive move to withdraw and to turn the entire question over to the United Nations allowed Britain to at least attempt to put distance between it and partition, even as reams of British paperwork on partition were handed over to United Nations officials.[17] All these factors together go some way towards explaining the popularity of the notion that both the partitions of India and Palestine were new, rushed, poorly planned and chaotically executed. Yet it is precisely the myth of shambolic departure that concealed the strategies of imperial control inherent in partition.

Partition as imperial inheritance

In making connections between India and Palestine, we are returning to the perspectives of some our subjects, a number of whom, from British politicians and administrators to anticolonial nationalists, sought to draw exactly these kinds of analogies. There are dangers to this analogy making, of course, inasmuch as we risk flattening differences between the partitions of India and Palestine or buying wholesale an unproblematic view of partition as a hastily and sloppily executed decolonising manoeuvre. The benefit, however, is that we are reminded of the intensely imperial quality of partition. We are left to question how new, and indeed how decolonising, partition really was, and to highlight the connections and discontinuities between the lived experience of partition and decolonisation and the rhetoric surrounding it.

What we may well conclude is that two seemingly opposed strands in fact existed at the same time. Partition was both long-contemplated and hastily attempted, a process by which new states were made and one through which the British Empire created client states and washed its hands of responsibility for imperial violence. It is important for us to recognise that there were very real elements of speed and chaos in both the Indian and Palestinian partitions and decolonisations, particularly on the ground and from the perspective of ordinary people. At the same time, by 1947/48, thinking about, attempting, enacting and planning for partition had been taking place in India since the very early twentieth century, and in Palestine since the inception of the mandate some twenty-five years earlier. Seeming – and perhaps being – unprepared, unwilling and at times overwhelmed might, in fact, have helped to protect Britain's global image in the long term with regard to the partitions of India and Palestine. For some, the memory of these two partitions is of forces overtaking the decolonising power, of irrational hatreds unleashed, and of the mass displacement and death wrought not by the British, but by the very people gaining independence.

But the scale, horror and lasting personal, political and geopolitical effects of the violence, death and displacement in India and Palestine distract from the British role in precipitating them. In other words, one might say that imperial prestige survived the horrors of partition better than perhaps it should have, and that this is linked to the narrative of partition undertaken supposedly at the last minute and in a haphazard manner, as if the British actors were unwilling. The scale of apparent disorder that precipitated and followed the mass dislocation and death of both partitions seems to have effectively prevented many historians from considering the degree to which planning had been taking place for decolonisation and/or partition for decades. It has also prevented us from interrogating the political utility for Britain of fostering a perception of haste, and of recognising the logistical, political and moral work that this perception did for Britain. Hasty deadlines and slipshod management may have damaged Britain's reputation in the short term, but in the longer term partition allowed Britain to distance itself from the violence of empire, and to develop strong relationships with some of the successor states.

In part, Britain's post-Second World War and post-independence relationships with these new states depended on how effectively the rhetoric of haste came to shape narratives of decolonisation. The speed of these two (attempted) partitions and decolonisations lies at the core of debates over the legacy of empire and who is to blame for post-imperial trauma. In the Churchillian camp are those who say that the British Empire was glorious and ended badly because the British cut and run, while the Audenites see ineptitude and shame all around. Alternatively, as I have argued, partition – with its violence, dislocation, forced migration and ethnic cleansing – was neither an aberration nor an error. It was a long-standing imperial practice and a manifestation of imperial logic at the end of empire.

Notes

1 This work builds, of course, on other comparative and connective studies about India and Palestine specifically, as well as about partitions more generally. See,

among many others, Arie M. Dubnov and Laura Robson (eds), *Partitions: A Transnational History of Twentieth-Century Territorial Separatism* (Stanford, CA: Stanford University Press, 2019); John Docker, 'The Two-State Solution and Partition: World History Perspectives on Palestine and India', *Holy Land Studies* 9 (2) (2010), 147–168; Rami Ginat, 'India and the Palestine Question: The Emergence of the Asio-Arab Bloc and India's Quest for Hegemony in the Post-Colonial Third World', *Middle Eastern Studies* 40 (6) (2004), 189–218; T. G. Fraser, *Partition in Ireland, India and Palestine: Theory and Practice* (London: Macmillan, 1984).

2 Lucy Chester, '"Close Parallels"? Interrelated Discussions of Partition in South Asia and the Palestine Mandate (1936–1948)', in Dubnov and Robson, *Partitions*, pp. 128–153; Kate O'Malley, '"Indian Ulsterisation?" – Ireland, India, and Partition: The Infection of Example?', in Dubnov and Robson, *Partitions* pp. 111–127; Penny Sinanoglou, 'Analogical Thinking and Partition in British Mandate Palestine', in Dubnov and Robson, *Partitions*, pp. 154–172.

3 For more on contemporary connections, see Jonathan D. Greenberg, 'Generations of Memory: Remembering Partition in India/Pakistan and Israel/Palestine', *Comparative Studies of South Asia, Africa and the Middle East* 25 (1) (2005), 89–110; S. S. Tabraz and D. Sambandhan, 'A Tale of Two Partitions', *Economic and Political Weekly* 42 (44) (2007), 33–35.

4 HC Deb, 6 March 1947, vol. 434, col. 678.

5 *Ibid.*, cols 676–677.

6 W. H. Auden, 'Partition' (1966).

7 Sami Hadawi, *Bitter Harvest: A Modern History of Palestine* (New York: New World Press, 1967), pp. 68, 74, quoting Alfred Lilienthal.

8 Two examples out of many are Stanley Wolpert, *Shameful Flight: The Last Years of the British Empire in India* (New York: Oxford University Press, 2006); Moti Golani, *End of the British Mandate for Palestine, 1948: The Diary of Sir Henry Gurney* (New York: Palgrave Macmillan, 2009), p. 8.

9 Yasmin Khan, *The Great Partition: The Making of India and Pakistan* (New Haven, CT: Yale University Press, 2007), p. 22.

10 For a detailed examination of the partition process in India, see Lucy P. Chester, *Borders and Conflict in South Asia: The Radcliffe Boundary Commission and the Partition of Punjab* (Manchester: Manchester University Press, 2013). On the long history of partition planning in Palestine, see Penny Sinanoglou, *Partitioning Palestine: British Policymaking at the End of Empire* (Chicago: University of Chicago Press, 2019).

11 Sana Aiyar in Christoph Emmrich, Joseph McQuade, Sana Aiyar and Thibaut d'Hubert, 'Towards a Burma-Inclusive South Asian Studies: A Roundtable', *Modern Asian Studies* 57 (1) (2023), 283–320, at 288; Gordon Johnson, 'Partition, Agitation and Congress: Bengal, 1904 to 1908', *Modern Asian Studies* 7 (3) (1973), 533–588; Richard P. Cronin, *British Policy and Administration in Bengal, 1905–1912: Partition and the New Province of Eastern Bengal and Assam*, 1st edn (Calcutta: Firma KLM, 1977).

12 Sharon Korman, *The Right of Conquest: The Acquisition of Territory by Force in International Law and Practice* (Oxford: Clarendon Press, 1996); Victor Kattan,

'To Consent or Revolt? European Public Law, the Three Partitions of Poland (1772, 1793, and 1795) and the Birth of National Self-Determination, *Journal of the History of International Law/Revue d'histoire du droit International* 17 (2) (2015), 247–281.
13 Stig Forster, Wolfgang J. Mommsen and Ronald Robinson (eds), *Bismarck, Europe, and Africa: The Berlin Africa Conference 1884–1885 and the Onset of Partition* (Oxford: Oxford University Press, 1989).
14 Andrew Priest, *Designs on Empire: America's Rise to Power in the Age of European Imperialism* (New York: Columbia University Press, 2021), chapter 5. In a sign of the United States becoming entrenched in partitionist politics, it was party to the 1899 Tripartite Convention which partitioned Samoa between Germany, the United Kingdom and the United States.
15 Leonard V. Smith, 'Drawing Borders in the Middle East after the Great War: Political Geography and "Subject Peoples"', *First World War Studies* 7 (1) (2016), 5–21; Karen Culcasi, 'Disordered Ordering: Mapping the Divisions of the Ottoman Empire', *Cartographica: The International Journal for Geographic Information and Geovisualization* 49 (1) (2014), 2–17. On the interwar and postwar implications, see Sinanoglou, *Partitioning Palestine*; Aiyaz Husain, *Mapping the End of Empire: American and British Strategic Visions in the Postwar World* (Cambridge, MA: Harvard University Press, 2014). For a recent argument about the significance of 1919 in contemporary refugee policy, see Karen Culcasi, Emily Skop and Cynthia Gorman, 'Contemporary Refugee-Border Dynamics and the Legacies of the 1919 Paris Peace Conference', *Geographical Review* 109 (4) (2019), 469–486.
16 Cabinet Minutes (47) 76, 20 September 1947. The National Archives (UK) [TNA]: CAB 128/10.
17 See, for instance, the memorandum prepared by Douglas Harris, 'Palestine: Study of Partition', April 1947. TNA: FO 371/61858.

Index

Ahmed, A. 39
Ahmad, S. 119
AIML *see* All-India Muslim League
Al-Aqsa 146
Al-Azmeh, F. 94
Al-Banna, H. 93
Algazi, G. 225
Al-Husseini, H. A. 140
Ali, A. 142–143
Al-Khoury, F. 81
All-India Muslim League (AIML) 61–62, 124–125, 195
All-Palestine Government (APG) 147
Anglo-Irish Treaty (1921) 234
Anti-foreigner Assam Agitation (1979–85) 205
APG *see* All-Palestine Government
Auchinleck, (General) C. 45

Balfour Declaration 76, 117, 139, 169, 284
Bangladesh 198
    Article 2A 212
BCs *see* Boundary Commissions
Ben-Gurion, D. 80
Bhatti, A. R. 270
Bhatti, D. 269–273
Bhutto, S. N. 197
Bhutto, Z. A. 200, 201, 267–268, 272
Bihari Muslims 207
Bismillah-ar-Rahmanar-Rahim 21
Boundary Commissions (BCs) 194
Britain and partition India 41–46
British decolonisation
    Asia and Africa 37

British India and mandate Palestine, partition in 114
    Arab–Jewish conflict, solution to 171
    governance, communal colonial sociology of 116–117
    law, colonial sociology of 117–121
    mandate regime, Palestine 118–121
    national religious communities, population division 115
    personal linkages between 126–129
    plans 124–126
    representation strategies 121–124
    Roman law thinking, India 118
    Zionist project 117
British India partition
    Congress and Nehru 163
    Indian National Congress 163
    Muslim League and Jinnah 163
    road to partition, Congress 167–169

Cabinet Mission Plan 15, 19, 41, 122, 168–169
Cattan, H. 79, 177, 226
Chadha, G.
    Viceroy's House, film 36
Citizenship Amendment Act (CAA) 206
Congress Working Committee (CWC) 142
Coupland, R. 78, 114, 126–128
Criminal Law (Protection of Minorities) Act (2015) 210

Cust, L. G. A. 235
Cyril Radcliffe's Boundary Award 194, 233

Damascus Committee 94
  appeal 95–97
  'Muhammad's Youth' (*Shabab Muhammad*) 96
Dayton Accords (1995) 224
deadlock 114
decolonisation 222
  dirty wars 222
  self-determination, language 2
decolonising actors 230
Dubnov, A. 21, 127
Dutta, D. N. 263

Emerson, R. W. 57

Farsakh, L. 84
Fraser, T. G. 1, 126

Gandhi, M. 141
Gandhi, S. 197
Government of India (GOI) Act 1(935)
  statutory safeguards failure 163–164
'Green Line' 233
Guha, G. 225

Harris, D. G. 126
Hasan, M. 141
Haycraft Commission 116
Hitchens, C.
  contemporaneous partition policy 35
holy words
Bismillah-ar-Rahman-ar-Rahim 21, 211
Harshan Kumarasingham 11
Hurewitz, J. C. 223
Husayn-McMahon Correspondence (1915–16) 146
Husain, A.
  American and British strategic visions 36, 195

ICJ *see* International Court of Justice
Illegal Migrant (Determination by Tribunal) Act (1983) 205
Indian National Congress
  British India, partition of 163

International Court of Justice (ICJ) 20, 160
Iqbal, M. 65
Irish Free State 234
Israeli–Palestinian dispute 91
  anti-US riots in Damascus 99–100
  catastrophe (*al-Nakba*), contemporary understandings of 97–99
  Damascus Committee appeal 95–97
  great strike in support 94–95
  Jihad declaration, 17 December (1947) 100–102
  Muslim Brotherhood, role 91–93
  defence 102–105
  Syrian 93–4
  Syrian Muslim Brotherhood, role 93–94
  Zionist Jews' intervention 92

Jabotinsky, V. (Ze'ev) 230
Jalal, A. 15
Jammu Kashmir Liberation Front 202
Jenkins, (Sir) E. 42
Jinnah, Q-i-A. M. A. 15, 57
  appearance, as described by Beverley Nichols 62
  Congress and Muslim League, crucial link between 62
  and Dadabhai Naoroji 59
  death 63
  historical background of 58–59
  hunger strike, defence of 59
  Islamic law (*sharia*) 209
  as a lawyer 58, 59
  mass politician, appearance as 60
  'patient cool-headed man', description of self as 60
  political journey 60–61
  role model 59
  Rowlatt Act (1919) 59
  named Kafir-i-Azam 210
  partition opposition 69
  politician 58
Johnson, A. C. 47, 48
Joint Defence Council 45

Karmi, G. 83, 85
Kashmir war 199–201

Kasuri, K. M. 202
Khan, A. 264
Khan, K. A. W. 259
Khan, L. A. 263
Khan, M. A. Y. 196
Khan, M. O. A. 197
Khan, M. Z. 81, 230, 150, 164, 166, 168, 174–177
Khilafat Movement 138
Kumar, R. 224
Kumaraswamy, P. R. 18

Lahore Declaration 202
Land Boundary Agreement (LBA) 198
Lausanne Treaty 233
LBA *see* Land Boundary Agreement
League of Nations 76, 77
Lehi, Revisionist Zionist organisation 80
Likhovski, A. 117, 120
Lin, N. 230
London Round Table Conference 140

Majoritarian nationalism 193, 194
Manto, S. H. 64–65
Menon, V. P. 197
Moonje, (Dr) B. S. 166
Morley, J. 58
Mountbatten, (Viceroy) Lord
  bad press in Pakistan 40
  British and Congress interest, convergence of 39, 40
  British Government's strategy, implementing 49
  British prestige and stage-managing independence 46–48
  closing months 44
  controversial Viceroyalty 48–49
  critics 38–39
  fascination with film and self-publicity 49
  Indian agreement to partition 38–41
  Indian Army, partition impact on 36
  India-Pakistan, Commonwealth membership 44
  Jinnah, contrasting personality 40
  Kashmir dispute, pro-India attitude 41
  re-examination 50
  role as Viceroy 38
  sixth staff meeting 41
  wartime Burma campaign, role in 47
Moyn, S. 224
Muslim Brotherhood
  Cairo-based Arab Higher Committee 94
  Damascus Committee strikes and protests 94
  Palestine defence 102–105
  parliamentary members 96
  Syrian 96
Muslims, political importance
  India and UNSCOP 142–145
  Nehru's duality 150–152
  Palestine and India's partition, federal plan for 142–150
  in Palestine and India 139–142
    al-Husseini, H. A. 140
    Gandhi, views 141–142
    London Round Table Conference 140
    Turkey, O. 140

Naoroji, D. 59
National Democratic Alliance Government 203
Nehru, J.
  preference for partitioned India but federal Palestine 138

O'Leary, B.
  views on partition 35
Ormsby-Gore, W. 170
Ottoman Empire 139
Ottoman legal system 119
Ovendale, R.
  British policy towards Palestine (1945–46) 35

Pakistan Constitution
  Articles 41(2) and 91(3) 206
  identities, regional, caste and linguistic 260, 265–269
  stranded Pakistanis 207
Pakistan Scheme
  Muslim League, rejection 164–166
  Hindu-majority rule, Jinnah's fear 164

Palestinian Liberation Organisation
    (PLO) 86
Palestinian *Nakba* 223
Palin Commission report 116
Pandit, V. 177
Paris Peace Conference (1919) 2
partition
    caste and regional identity
        representations 265–269
    civil war 237–243
    colonial policy 6–9
    contrasting 12–15
    etymology 4–6
    Gandhi's funeral 260
    global reframing 233–235
    holy lands involvement 9–10
    identity issue 3
    institutions' role 10–11
    League of Nations, United Nations,
        ideology difference 2
    legal mechanisms after war
        243–246
    mechanics of 11–12
    national identities, Pakistan 259
    ongoing event 246–250
    political spaces, division 21
    separation before 235–237
    similarity 9
    shaping identity 261–265
    Wilsonian principles, minorities
        226–232
partition India *see also* British India
        and mandate Palestine,
        partition in
    birth of Pakistan 159
    Britain and decision to partition
        41–46
        All-India settlement 42
        civil war, avoiding 41
        Commonwealth politics 44–45
        India Office's long-standing
            resistance 43
        Mountbatten's acceleration 42
        Nehru complained 42
        oriental barracks 45
        Pakistan's birth 42
        Second World War, ending 44
        unfinished business 45
    Britain's post-independence influence
        37
    British Government, approved by 163
        GOI Act (1935) 163–164
        Muslim League and Zionist
            claims 166–167
        Pakistan Scheme 164–166
    cabinet debates 36
    communal conflict 39
    comparing and contrasting with
        Palestine 161–162
    geography changed 193
    majoritarian nationalism 193
    nationalists and communal
        opponents' role 50–51
    pro-India stance 36
    pro-Pakistan lobby 37
    unfinished disputes 193
        Jammu and Kashmir 198–203
        postcolonial citizens, making
            203–207
        religion, majoritarianism and
            minorities 208–212
        territories, claims and
            counterclaims 194–198
Partition Plan, June 1947
    Indian politicians' acceptance 36
partition Palestine *see also* British India
        and mandate Palestine,
        partition in
    birth of Israel 159
    Britain's administration 169–170
        majority rule, parliament opposes
            170–172
    British Government, approved by
        Muslim League and Zionist
            claims 166–167
    comparing and contrasting with
        India 161–162
    federal proposal *versus* 82–85
    India and Pakistan vote against
        177–179
    mandate regime 118–119
    multiple legal jurisdictions, early
        administration of 119–121
    Permanent Court of International
        Justice, attempt to refer
        172–174
    related events 76–79
        Arab Higher Committee 78–79
        disappointed Zionist leadership
            78

High Commissioner 77
post-Ottoman political remaking 77
UN, debate at 174–177
UN decision 79–81 (*see also* United Nations Special Commission on Palestine (UNSCOP))
United Nations Special Commission, split on 75
UNSCOP's consideration, local conditions 85
Zionist immigration 76
PCIJ *see* Permanent Court of International Justice
Peel Commission (1937) 80, 171
Peel, R. 78
Permanent Court of International Justice (PCIJ) 19, 160
Pethick-Lawrence, F. 43

Qasmi, A. U. 264

Rabita al-'Ulama 100
Rahi, S. 267
Rahman, (Sir) A. 143–144
Rahman, A. 83
Roberts, A. 38
Robson, L. 16, 18, 128
Rothschild, W. 76
Round Table Conference 172–173
Rowlatt Act (1919) 59

Sarila, N. S.
  India's partition as conspiracy 35–36
  Pakistan's strategic value, contrary to 37
Seikaly, S. 117
Sevea, I. S. 21, 22
Simla Agreement 202
Singh, H. 198, 199

Skinner, Q. 224
Supreme Muslim Council and the Zionist Organisation 18

Tagore, R. 65
Turkey, O. 140
Turner, J. 47, 48

United Arab Republic (1950s) 85
United Nations Special Commission on Palestine (UNSCOP) 79–80
  Ben-Gurion, D. 80
  India and 142–145
  Lehi, Revisionist Zionist organisation 80
  majority report's partition plan 81
  Peel Commission (1937) 80–81
  split on Palestine 75
UNSCOP *see* United Nations Special Commission on Palestine

Vaad Leumi 77

Wauchope, (Sir) A. 170

Zia-ul-Haq, M. 20, 210, 266, 268, 273
Zionists 77
  commission 122, 123
  editor of London *Times*, letters to 236
  ideology 229
  intervention in decolonisation of Palestine 92
  leadership 78
  movement 77
  Muslim League, difference between claims 162, 166–167
  Palestine, in 124, 161
  partition at UN 79
  Western Wall demonstrations 77–78

EU authorised representative for GPSR:
Easy Access System Europe, Mustamäe tee 50,
10621 Tallinn, Estonia
gpsr.requests@easproject.com

www.ingramcontent.com/pod-product-compliance
Lightning Source LLC
Chambersburg PA
CBHW051602230426
43668CB00013B/1949